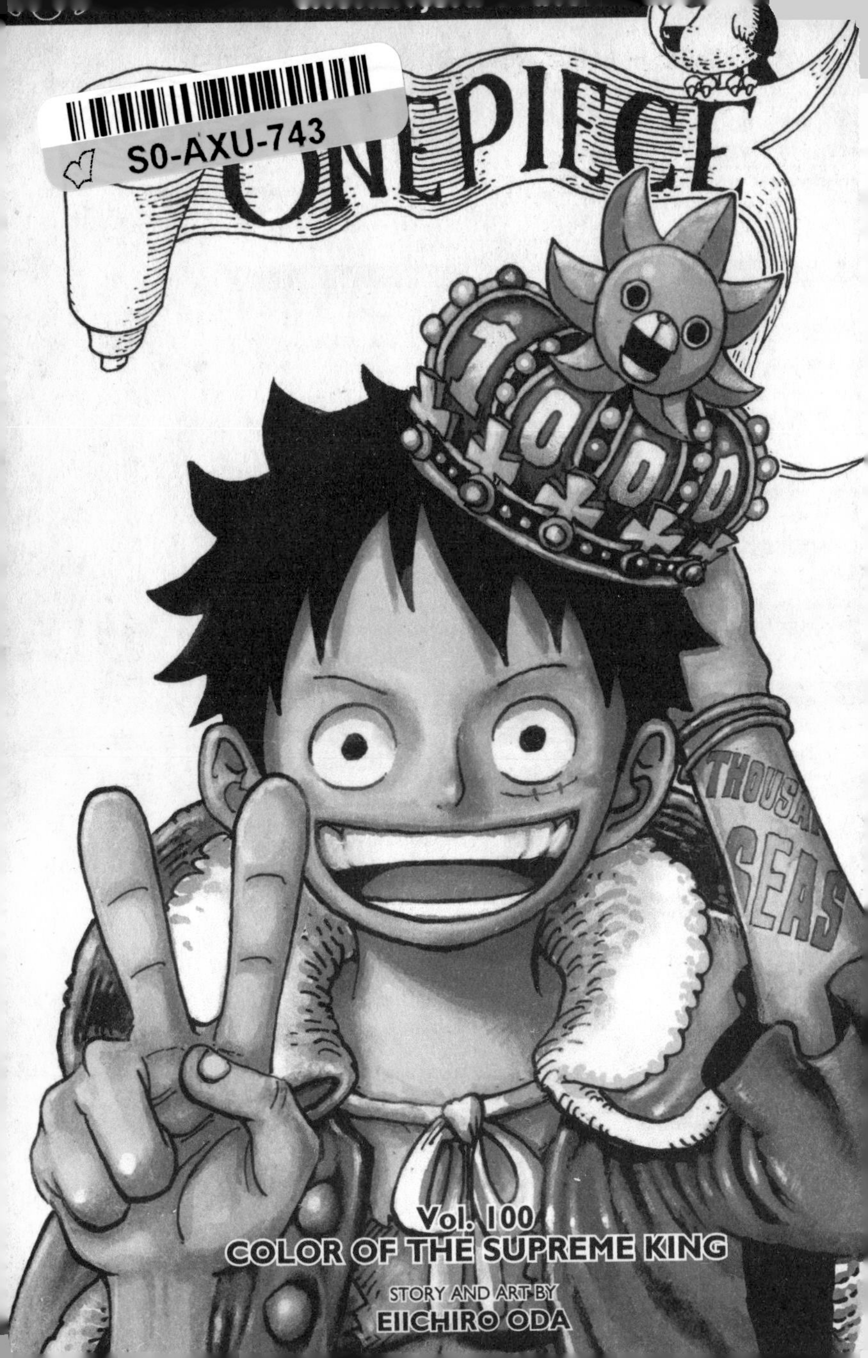
1000
SEAS

ONE PIECE

Vol. 100

COLOR OF THE SUPREME KING

STORY AND ART BY
EIICHIRO ODA

The Straw Hat Crew

Chopperemon [Ninja]
Tony Tony Chopper

Studied powerful medicines in the Birdie Kingdom as he waited to rejoin the crew.

Ship's Doctor, Bounty: 100 berries

Luffytaro [Ronin]
Monkey D. Luffy

A young man dreaming of being the Pirate King. After two years of training he rejoins his friends in search of the New World!

Captain, Bounty: 1.5 billion berries

Orobi [Geisha]
Nico Robin

Spent time on the island of Baltigo with Dragon, Luffy's father and leader of the Revolutionary Army.

Archeologist, Bounty: 130 million berries

Zolojuro [Ronin]
Roronoa Zolo

Swallowed his pride on Gloom Island and trained under Mihawk before rejoining Luffy.

Fighter, Bounty: 320 million berries

Franosuke [Carpenter]
Franky

Upgraded himself into "Armored Franky" in the Future Land, Baldimore.

Shipwright, Bounty: 94 million berries

Onami [Kunoichi]
Nami

Learned about the climates of the New World on Weatheria, a Sky Island that studies the atmosphere.

Navigator, Bounty: 66 million berries

Bonekichi [Ghost]
Brook

Originally captured by Long-Arm bandits for a freak show, he is now the mega-star "Soul King" Brook.

Musician, Bounty: 83 million berries

Usohachi [Toad Oil Salesman]
Usopp

Received Heraclesun's lessons on the Bowin Islands in his quest to be the "king of the snipers."

Sniper, Bounty: 200 million berries

Jimbei, First Son of the Sea [Former Warlord]

A man loyal to the code. Acted as rear guard against Big Mom to help Luffy escape, then rejoined before the raid.

Helmsman, Bounty: 438 million berries

Sangoro [Soba Cook]
Sanji

Honed his skills fighting with the masters of Newcomer Kenpo in the Kamabakka Kingdom.

Cook, Bounty: 330 million berries

Shanks

One of the Four Emperors. Waits for Luffy in the "New World," the second half of the Grand Line.

Captain of the Red-Haired Pirates

Land of Wano (Kozuki Clan)

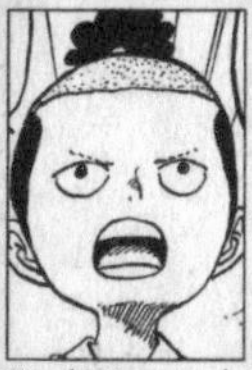
Kozuki Momonosuke
Daimyo (Heir) to Kuri in Wano

Akazaya Nine

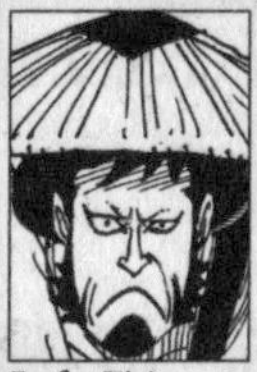
Foxfire Kin'emon
Samurai of Wano

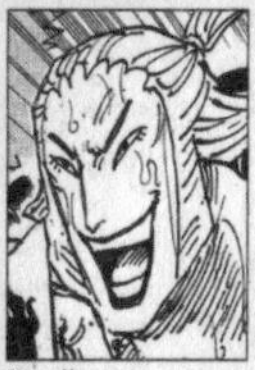
Denjiro
Formerly Kyoshiro

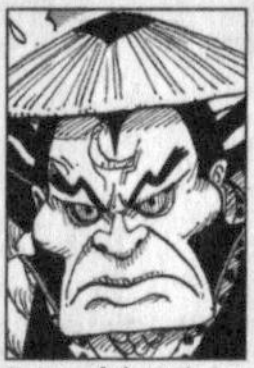
Raizo of the Mist
Ninja of Wano

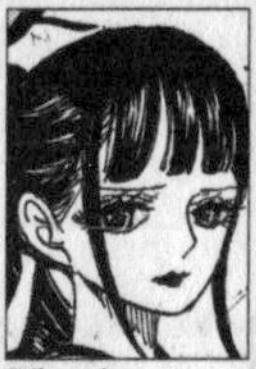
Kikunojo
Samurai of Wano

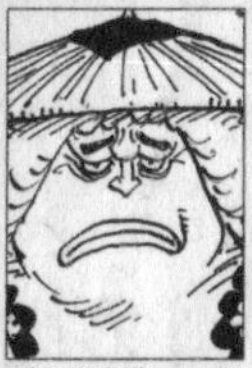
Ashura Doji (Shutenmaru)
Chief, Atamayama Thieves Brigade

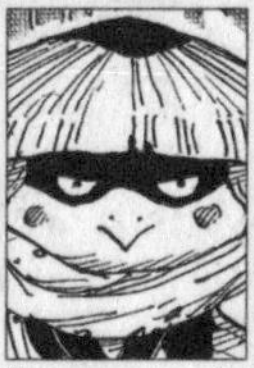
Kawamatsu
Samurai of Wano

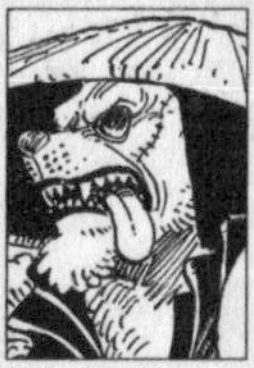
Duke Dogstorm
King of the Day, Mokomo

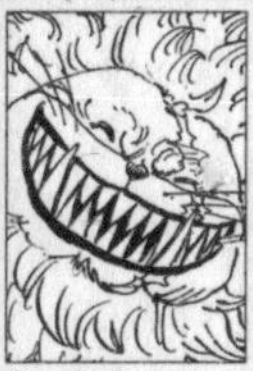
Cat Viper
King of the Night, Mokomo

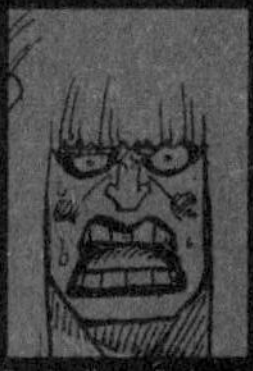
Evening Shower Kanjuro
Samurai of Wano

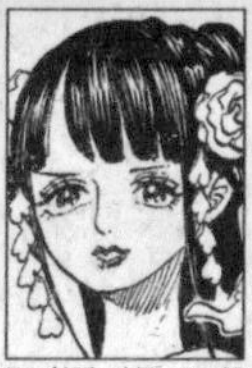
Kozuki Hiyori (Komurasaki)
Momonosuke's Little Sister

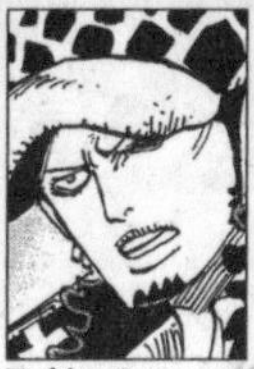
Trafalgar Law
Captain, Heart Pirates

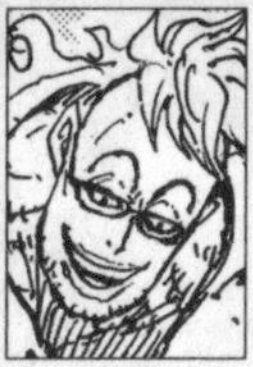
Marco the Phoenix
Former 1st Div. Leader, Whitebeard Pirates

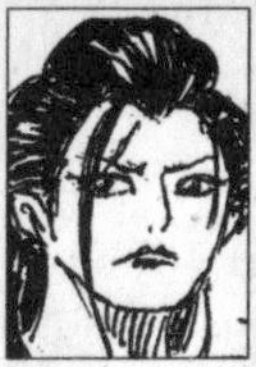
Izo
Former 16th Div. Leader, Whitebeard Pirates

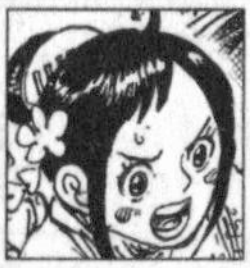
Otama

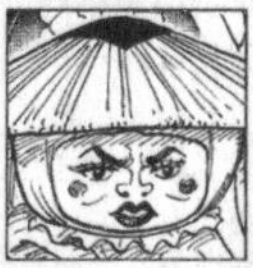
Shinobu

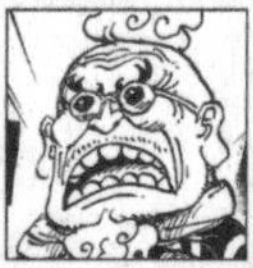
Hyogoro the Flower

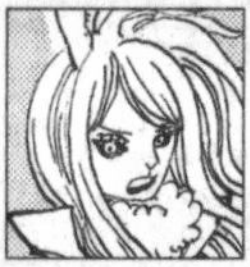
Carrot

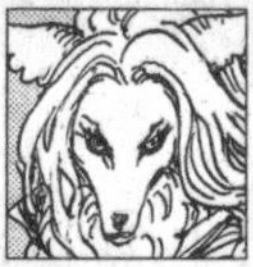
Wanda

Kid Pirates

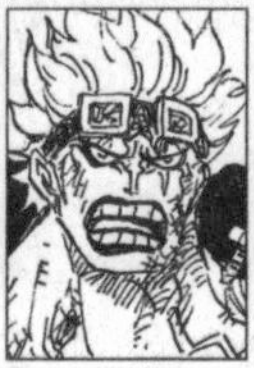
Eustass Kid
Captain, Kid Pirates

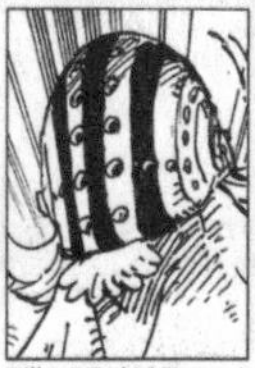
Killer (Hitokiri Kamazo)
Fighter, Kid Pirates

Animal Kingdom Pirates

Lead Performers

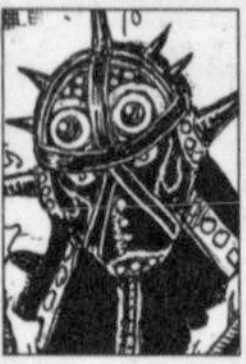

King the Wildfire

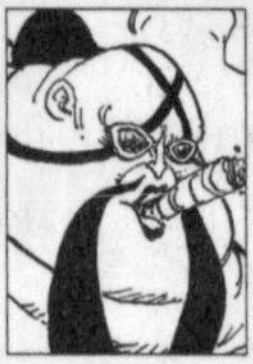

Queen the Plague

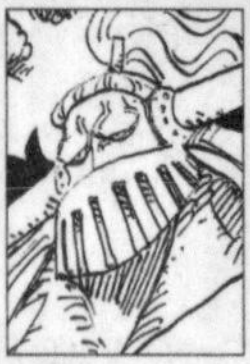

Jack the Drought

Kaido, King of the Beasts (Emperor of the Sea)

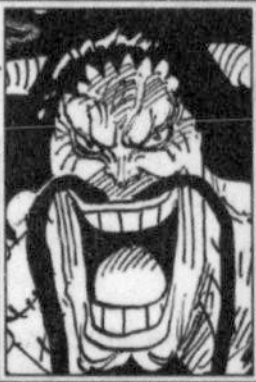

A pirate known as the "strongest creature alive." Despite numerous tortures and death sentences, none have been able to kill him.

Captain, Animal Kingdom Pirates

Tobi Roppo

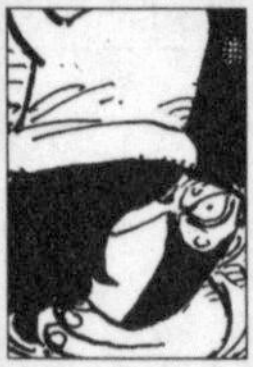

Page One

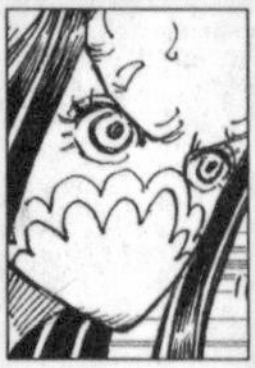

Ulti

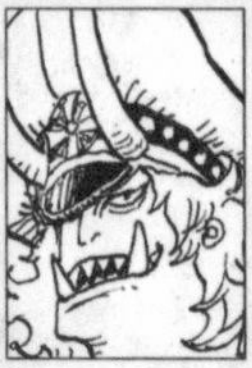

Sasaki

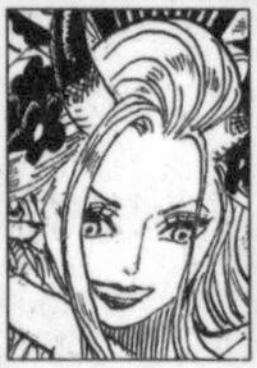

Black Maria

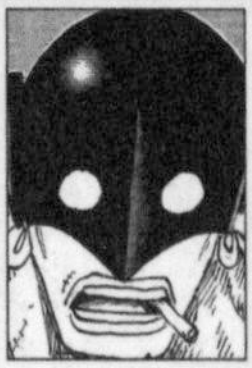

Who's-Who

Headliners

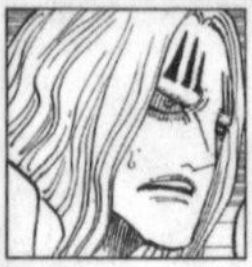

Basil Hawkins

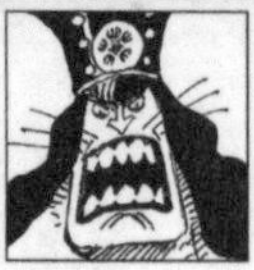

Holdem

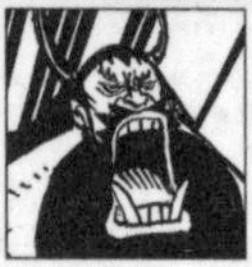

Babanuki

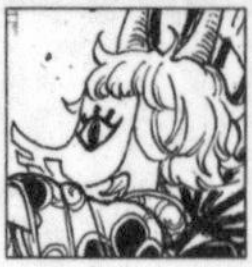

Bao Huang

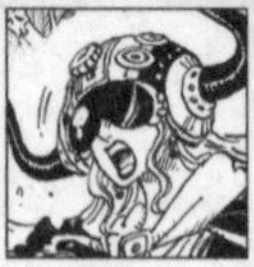

Solitaire

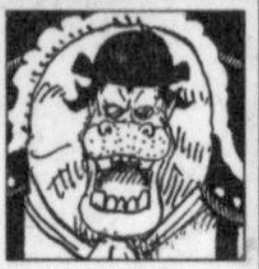

Dobon

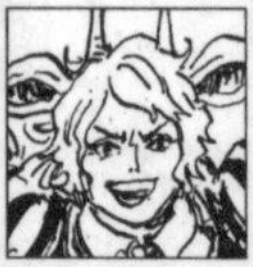

Hamlet

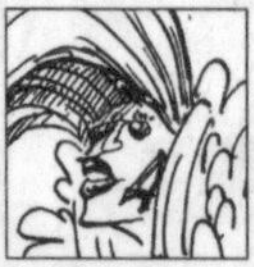

Fourtricks

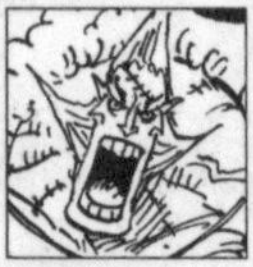

Briscola

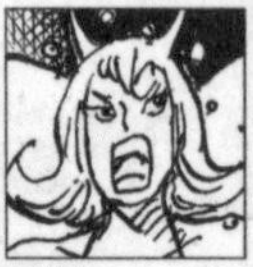

Mizerka

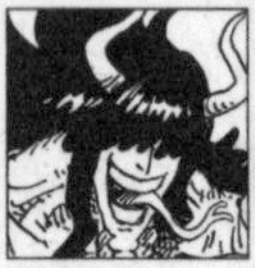

Poker

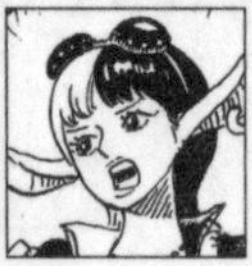

Speed

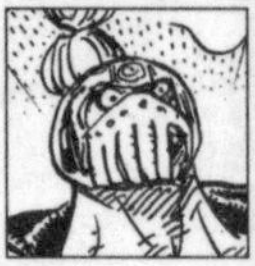

Daifugo

Betray the Animal Kingdom Pirates thanks to Otama's ability.

on Luffy's side. The Akazaya samurai face off against Kaido on the roof of the castle but are broken by his overwhelming power... Big Mom joins with Kaido, and then Luffy's group reaches the roof, setting the stage. Luffy helps the Akazaya escape, then challenges Kaido and Big Mom! The good guys unleash combination attacks that seem to do damage, but the two emperors are enjoying the fight... Is it even possible to beat this ultimate alliance of pirates?!

The story of ONE PIECE 1»100

Big Mom Pirates

Big Mom
(Emperor of the Sea)

One of the Four Emperors. Uses the Soul-Soul Fruit that extracts life span from others.

Captain, Big Mom Pirates

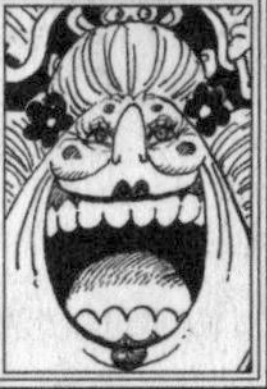

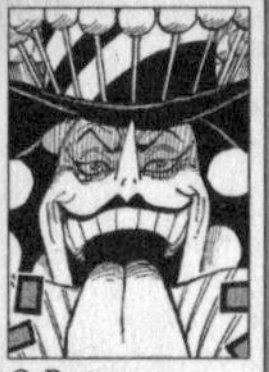

C. Perospero

1st Son of Charlotte

Informant

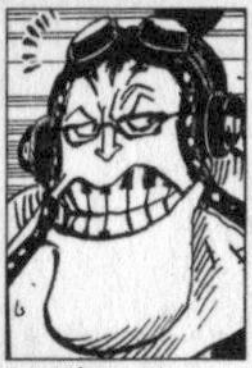

Scratchmen Apoo

Captain, On-Air Pirates

Land of Wano (Kurozumi Clan)

Kurozumi Orochi

The ruler of Wano, using Kaido's help. He cunningly schemed to overthrow his archenemy, the Kozuki Clan.

Shogun of Wano

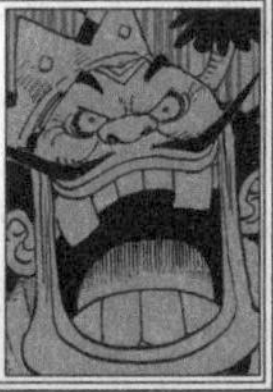

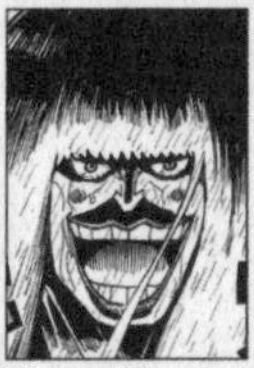

Kurozumi Kanjuro

Orochi's Spy

Left Kaido's Pirates to fight on Luffy's side!

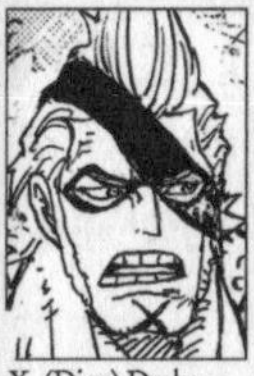

X. (Diez) Drake

Former Tobi Roppo

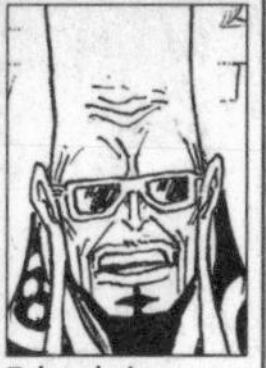

Fukurokuju

Former Leader, Orochi Oniwabanshu

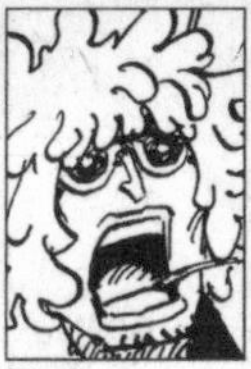

Hotei

Former Leader, Mimawari-gumi

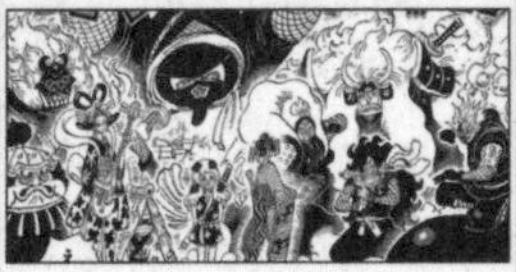

Orochi Oniwabanshu

Former Private Ninja Squad of the Shogun

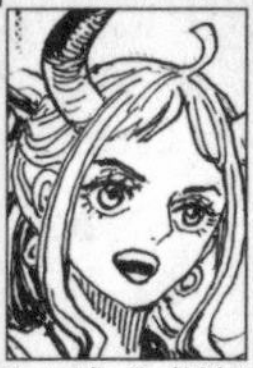

Yamato (Alias: Kozuki Oden)

Kaido's Daughter

Numbers

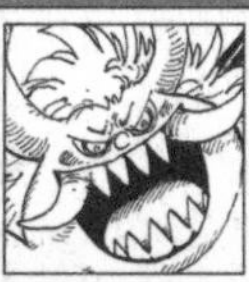

Jaki (No. 4)

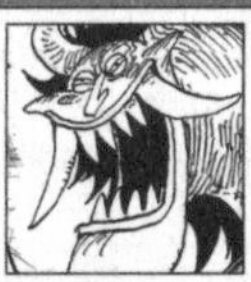

Goki (No. 5)

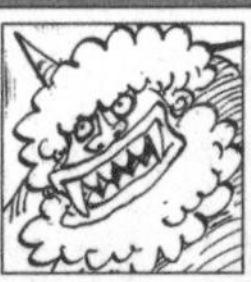

Nangi (No. 7)

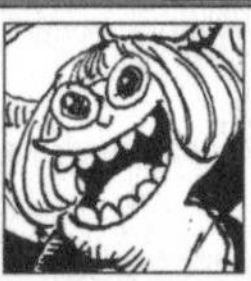

Haccha (No. 8)

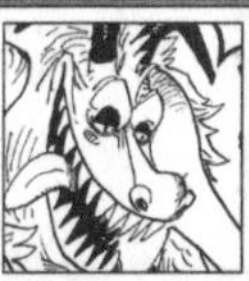

Juki (No. 10)

Story

After two years of hard training, the Straw Hat pirates are back together, first at the Sabaody Archipelago and then through Fish-Man Island to their next stage: the New World!!

Luffy and crew join with Momonosuke's faction in order to defeat Kaido, one of the Four Emperors. With all the allies in place, the raid on Onigashima begins!! As battles break out across the island, Kaido's daughter Yamato shows up and swears to fight

Vol. 100
COLOR OF THE SUPREME KING

CONTENTS

Chapter 1005:
DEMON CHILD

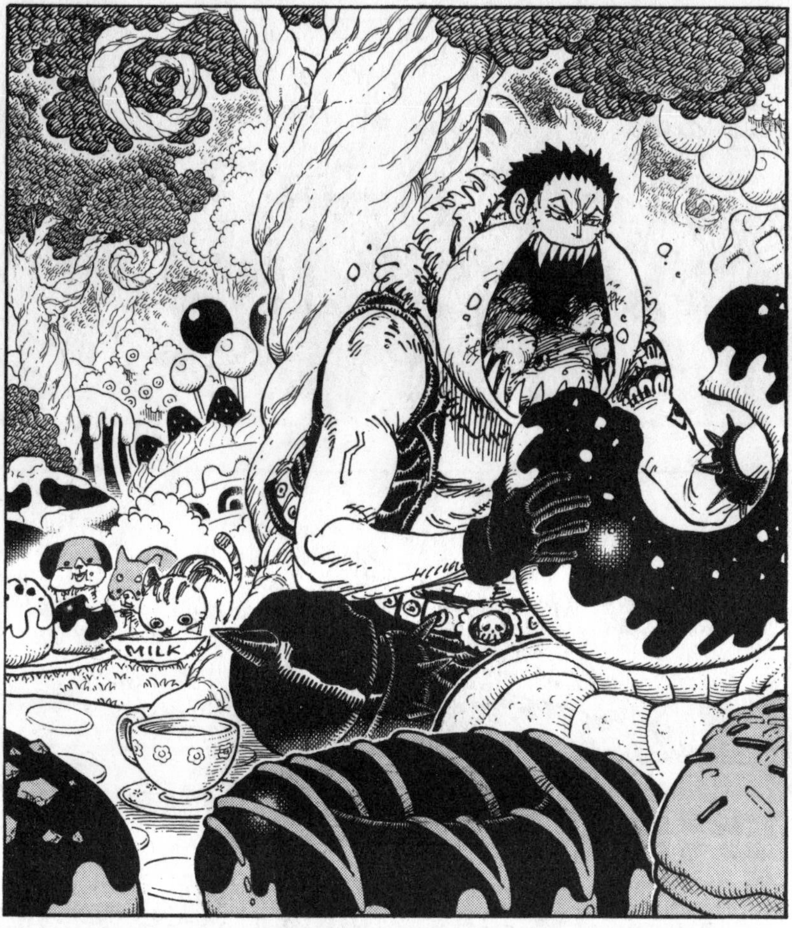
MILK

READER REQUEST: "KATAKURI GIVING HUNGRY KITTENS AND PUPPIES MILK AND DONUTS" BY GUM-FLAME FRUIT

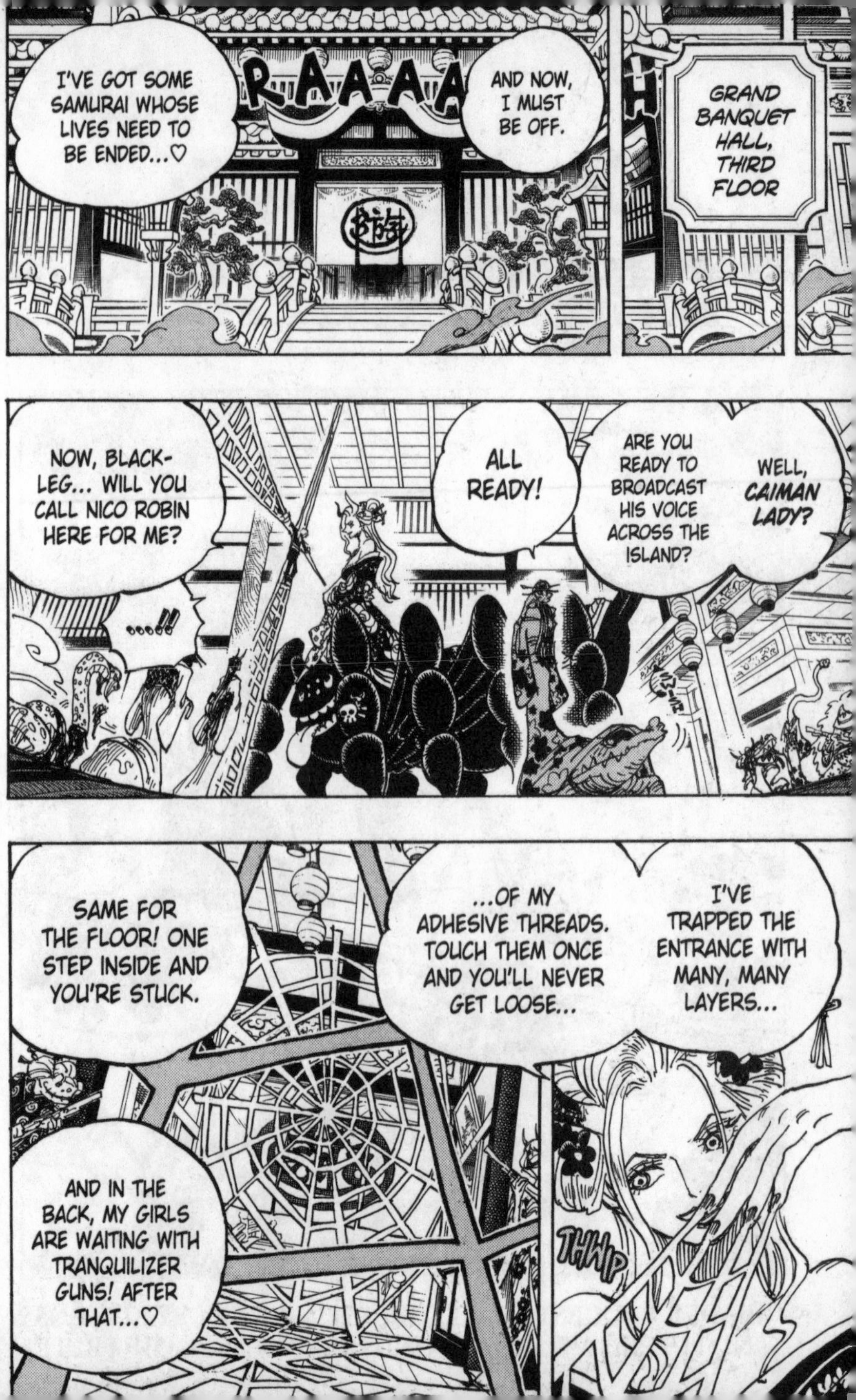
GRAND BANQUET HALL, THIRD FLOOR
AND NOW, I MUST BE OFF.
RAAAAH
I'VE GOT SOME SAMURAI WHOSE LIVES NEED TO BE ENDED...♡
WELL, CAIMAN LADY?
ARE YOU READY TO BROADCAST HIS VOICE ACROSS THE ISLAND?
ALL READY!
NOW, BLACK-LEG... WILL YOU CALL NICO ROBIN HERE FOR ME?
.....!!
I'VE TRAPPED THE ENTRANCE WITH MANY, MANY LAYERS...
...OF MY ADHESIVE THREADS. TOUCH THEM ONCE AND YOU'LL NEVER GET LOOSE...
THWIP
SAME FOR THE FLOOR! ONE STEP INSIDE AND YOU'RE STUCK.
AND IN THE BACK, MY GIRLS ARE WAITING WITH TRANQUILIZER GUNS! AFTER THAT...♡

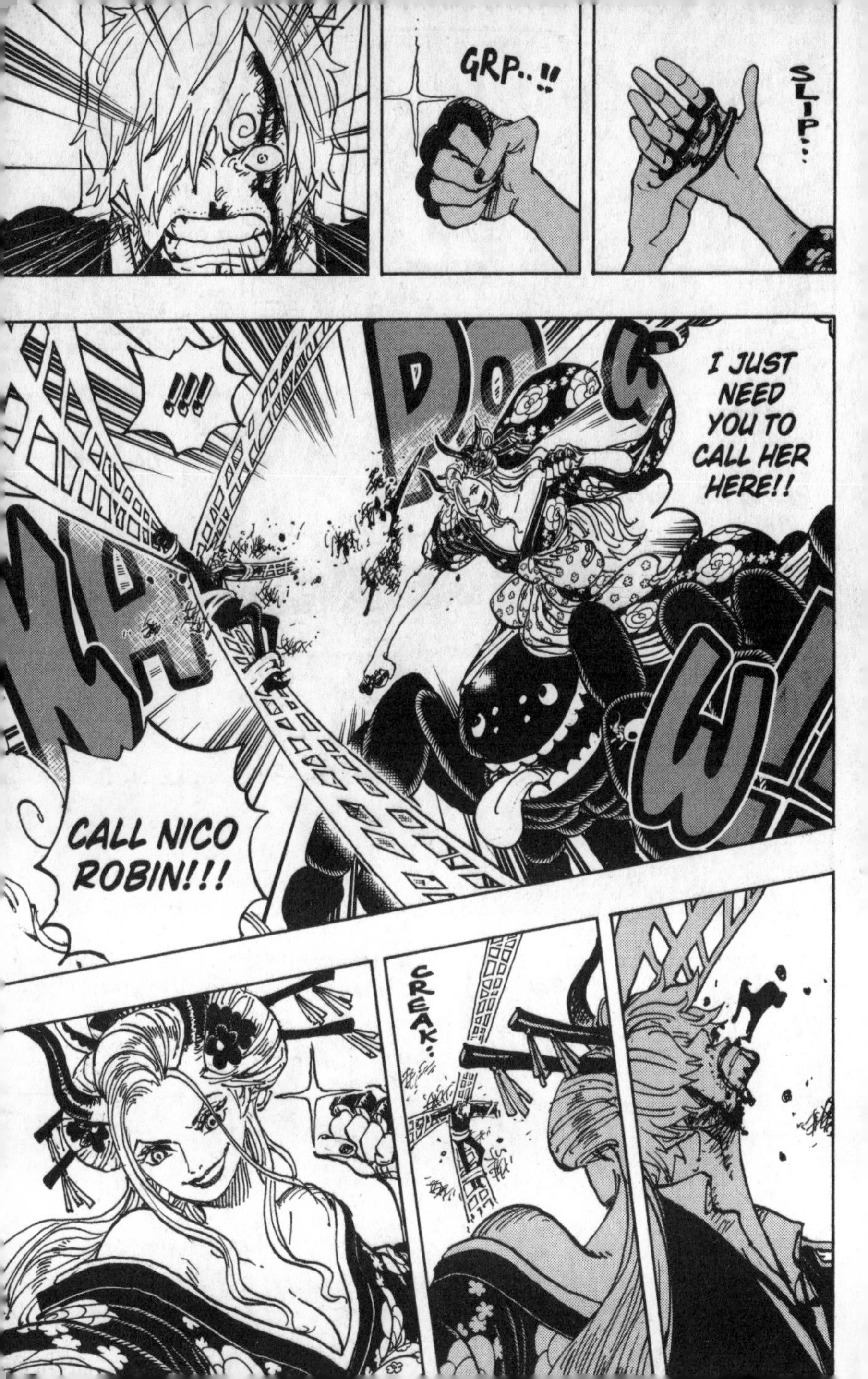
SLIP..
GRP..!!
I JUST NEED YOU TO CALL HER HERE!!
!!!
CALL NICO ROBIN!!!
CREAK..

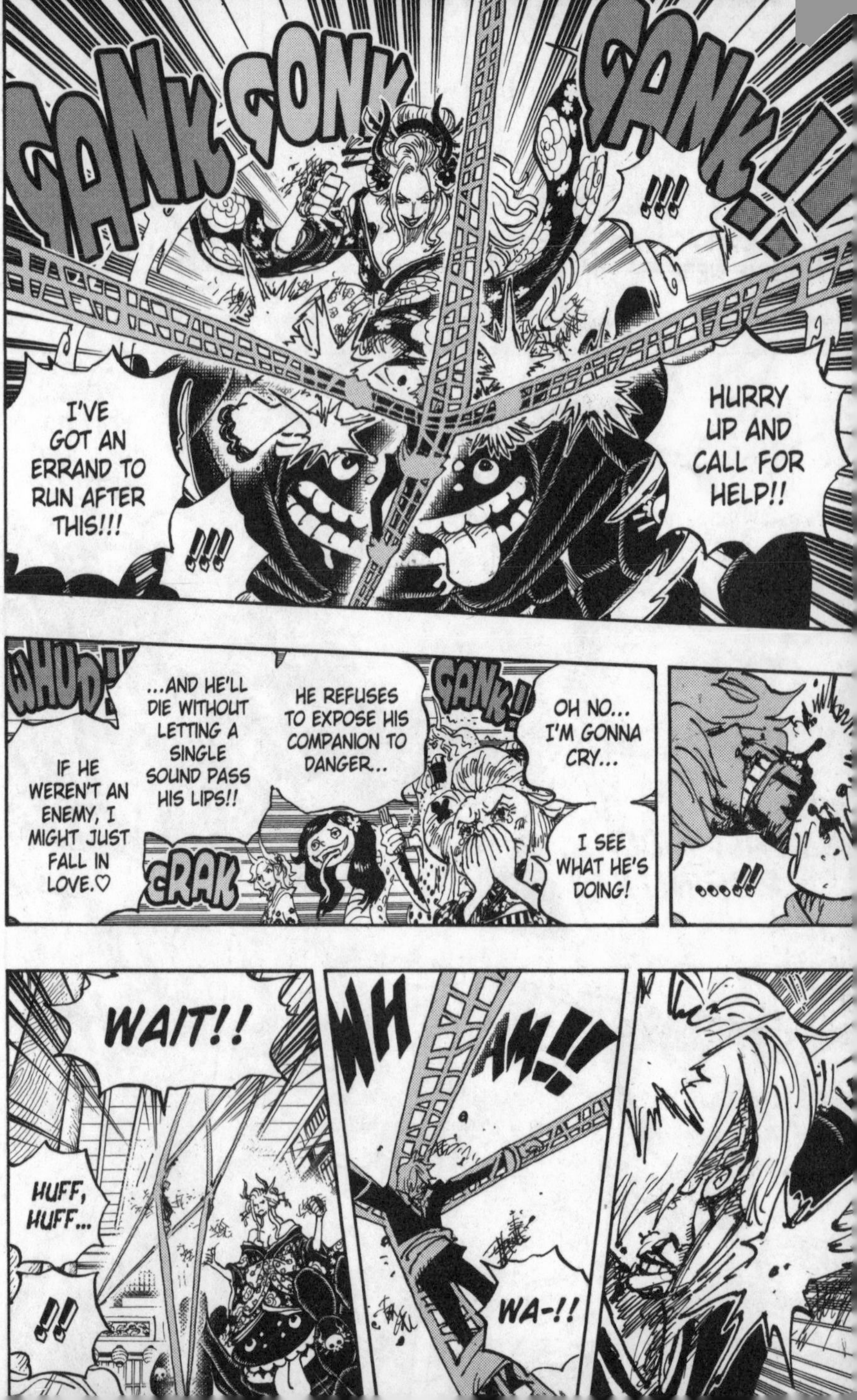
GANK!!
GONK
GANK
!!!
HURRY UP AND CALL FOR HELP!!
I'VE GOT AN ERRAND TO RUN AFTER THIS!!!
!!!
....!!
OH NO... I'M GONNA CRY...
I SEE WHAT HE'S DOING!
GANK!!
HE REFUSES TO EXPOSE HIS COMPANION TO DANGER...
...AND HE'LL DIE WITHOUT LETTING A SINGLE SOUND PASS HIS LIPS!!
WHUD!!
IF HE WEREN'T AN ENEMY, I MIGHT JUST FALL IN LOVE.♡
CRAK
WHAM!!
WA-!!
WAIT!!
HUFF, HUFF...
!!

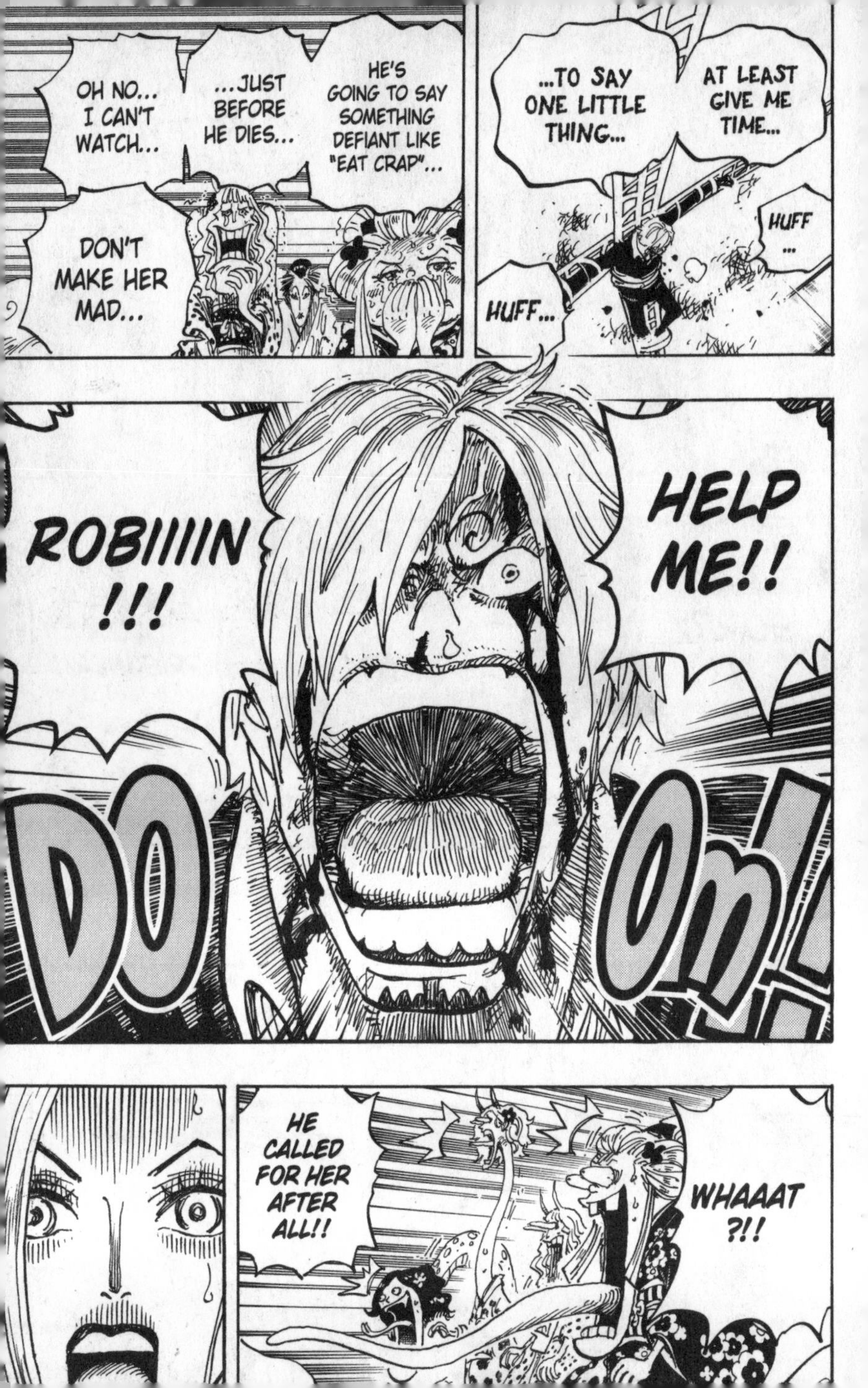
AT LEAST GIVE ME TIME...
...TO SAY ONE LITTLE THING...
HUFF ...
HUFF...
HE'S GOING TO SAY SOMETHING DEFIANT LIKE "EAT CRAP"...
...JUST BEFORE HE DIES...
OH NO... I CAN'T WATCH...
DON'T MAKE HER MAD...
HELP ME!!
ROBIIIIN!!!
DOOM!
WHAAAT?!!
HE CALLED FOR HER AFTER ALL!!

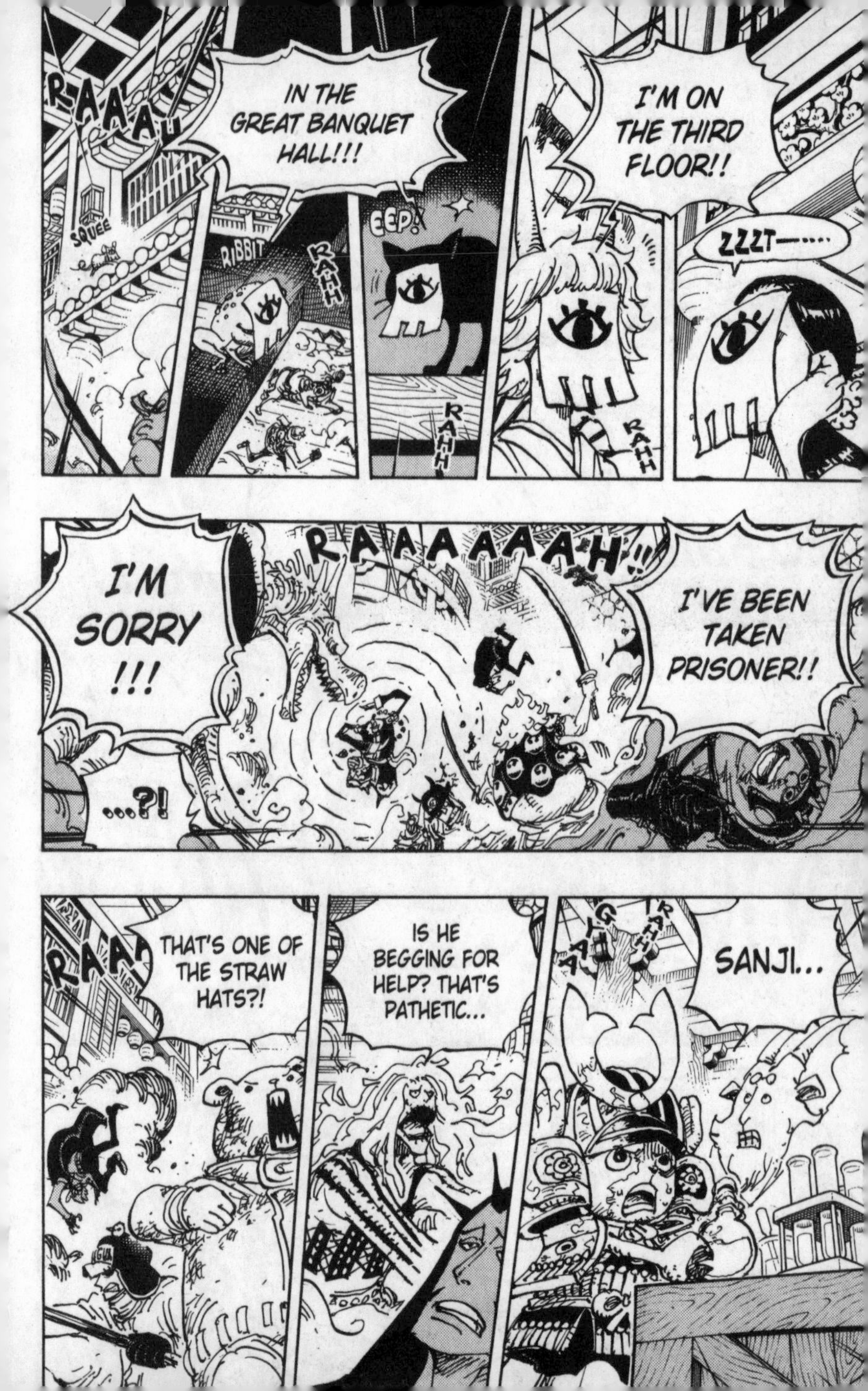
I'M ON THE THIRD FLOOR!!
ZZZT—.....
RAHH
IN THE GREAT BANQUET HALL!!!
EEP!
RAHH
RAHH
RIBBIT
R-A-A-A-H
SQUEE
I'VE BEEN TAKEN PRISONER!!
RAAAAAAAH!!
I'M SORRY!!!
...?!
SANJI...
RAHH
GYAA
IS HE BEGGING FOR HELP? THAT'S PATHETIC...
THAT'S ONE OF THE STRAW HATS?!
RAA

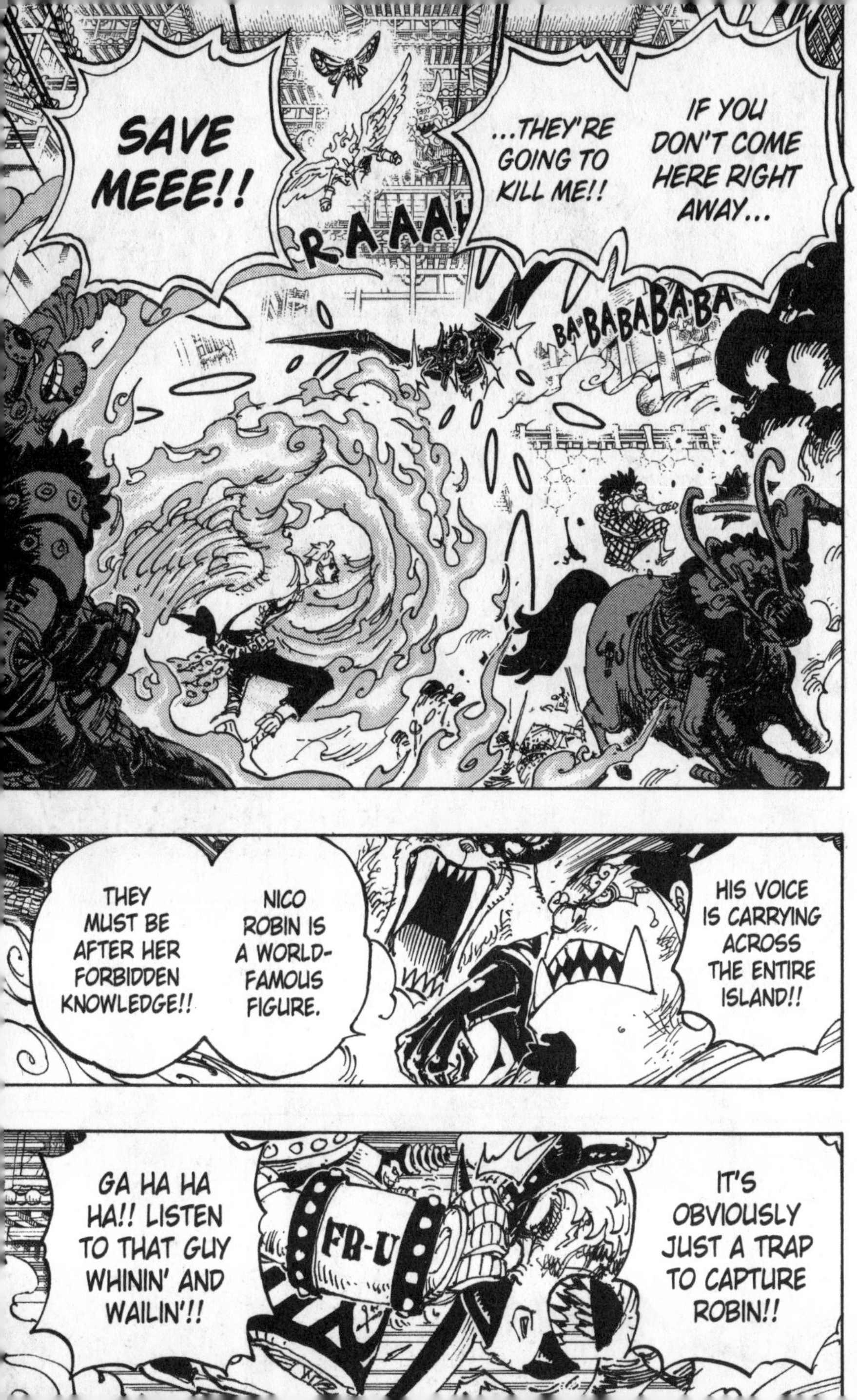
IF YOU DON'T COME HERE RIGHT AWAY...
...THEY'RE GOING TO KILL ME!!
SAVE MEEE!!
RAAAH
BA BA BA BA BA BA
HIS VOICE IS CARRYING ACROSS THE ENTIRE ISLAND!!
NICO ROBIN IS A WORLD-FAMOUS FIGURE.
THEY MUST BE AFTER HER FORBIDDEN KNOWLEDGE!!
IT'S OBVIOUSLY JUST A TRAP TO CAPTURE ROBIN!!
FB-U
GA HA HA HA!! LISTEN TO THAT GUY WHININ' AND WAILIN'!!

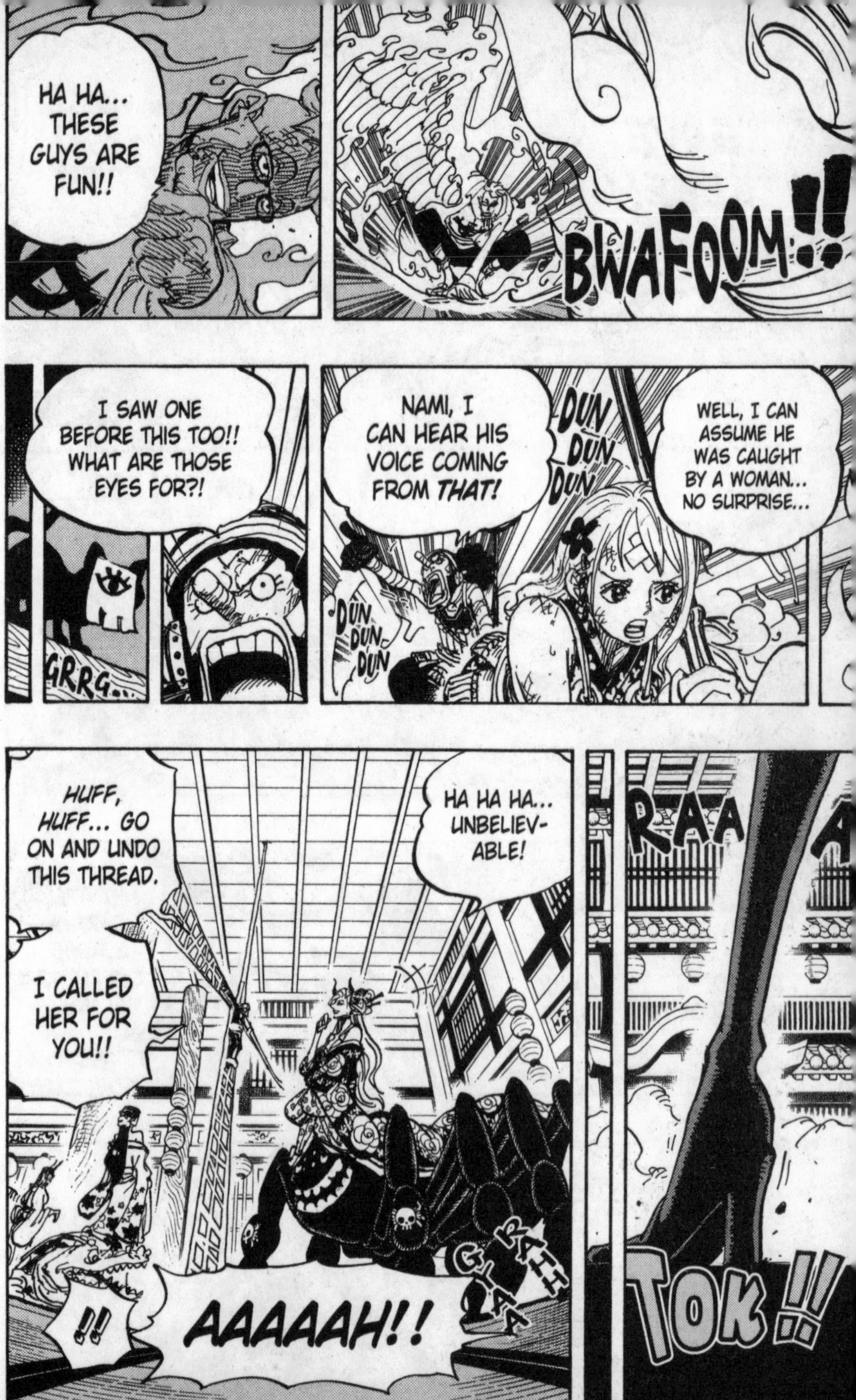
BWAFOOM!!
HA HA... THESE GUYS ARE FUN!!
WELL, I CAN ASSUME HE WAS CAUGHT BY A WOMAN... NO SURPRISE...
DUN DUN DUN
NAMI, I CAN HEAR HIS VOICE COMING FROM THAT!
DUN DUN DUN
I SAW ONE BEFORE THIS TOO!! WHAT ARE THOSE EYES FOR?!
GRRG...
RAA
A
TOK!!
HA HA HA... UNBELIEV-ABLE!
HUFF, HUFF... GO ON AND UNDO THIS THREAD.
I CALLED HER FOR YOU!!
GRATH
GYAA
AAAAAH!!
!!

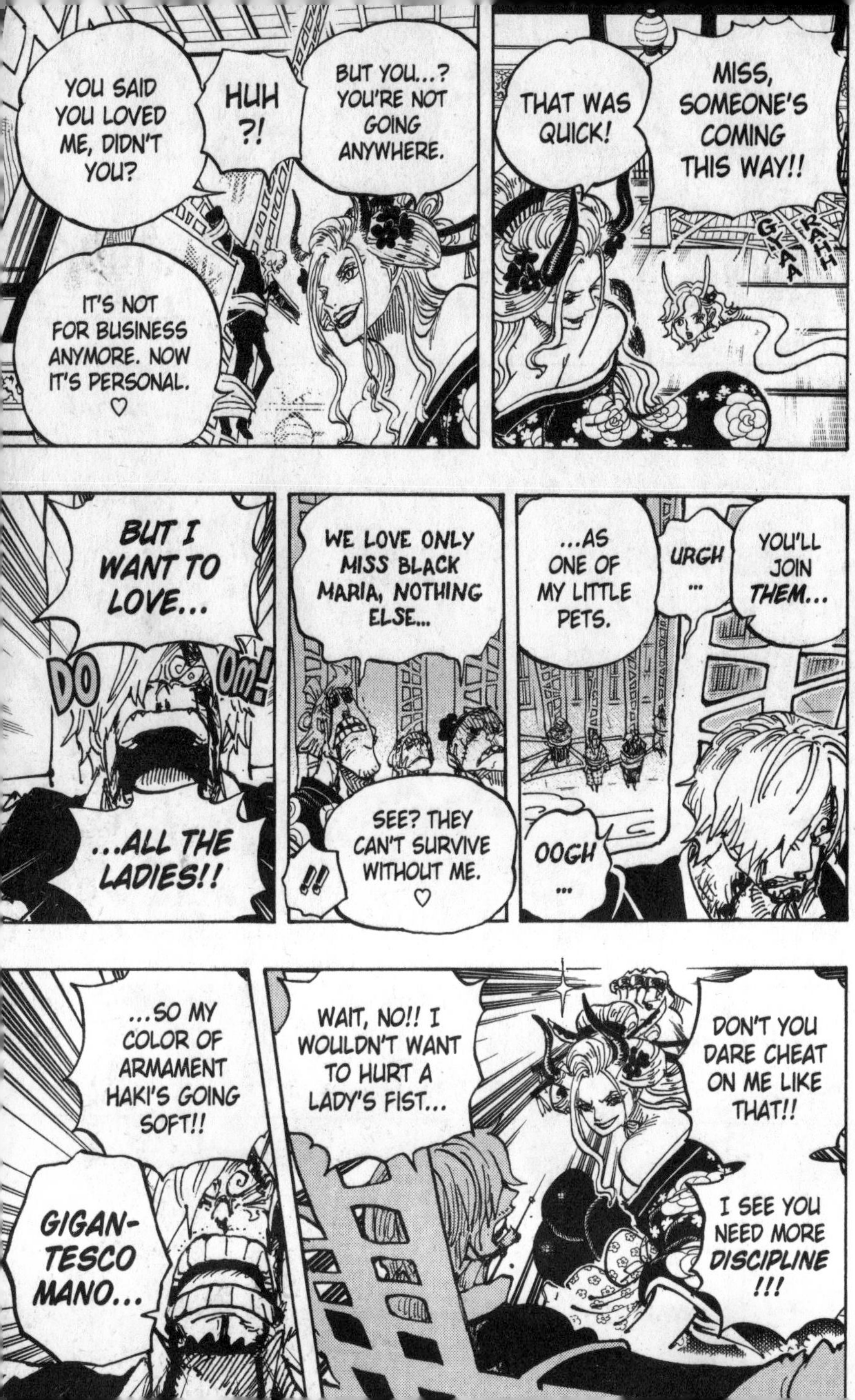
MISS, SOMEONE'S COMING THIS WAY!!
THAT WAS QUICK!
GYAA
RAHH
BUT YOU...? YOU'RE NOT GOING ANYWHERE.
HUH ?!
YOU SAID YOU LOVED ME, DIDN'T YOU?
IT'S NOT FOR BUSINESS ANYMORE. NOW IT'S PERSONAL. ♡
YOU'LL JOIN THEM...
URGH ...
...AS ONE OF MY LITTLE PETS.
OOGH ...
WE LOVE ONLY MISS BLACK MARIA, NOTHING ELSE...
!!
SEE? THEY CAN'T SURVIVE WITHOUT ME. ♡
BUT I WANT TO LOVE...
DOOM!
...ALL THE LADIES!!
DON'T YOU DARE CHEAT ON ME LIKE THAT!!
I SEE YOU NEED MORE DISCIPLINE !!!
WAIT, NO!! I WOULDN'T WANT TO HURT A LADY'S FIST...
...SO MY COLOR OF ARMAMENT HAKI'S GOING SOFT!!
GIGAN-TESCO MANO...

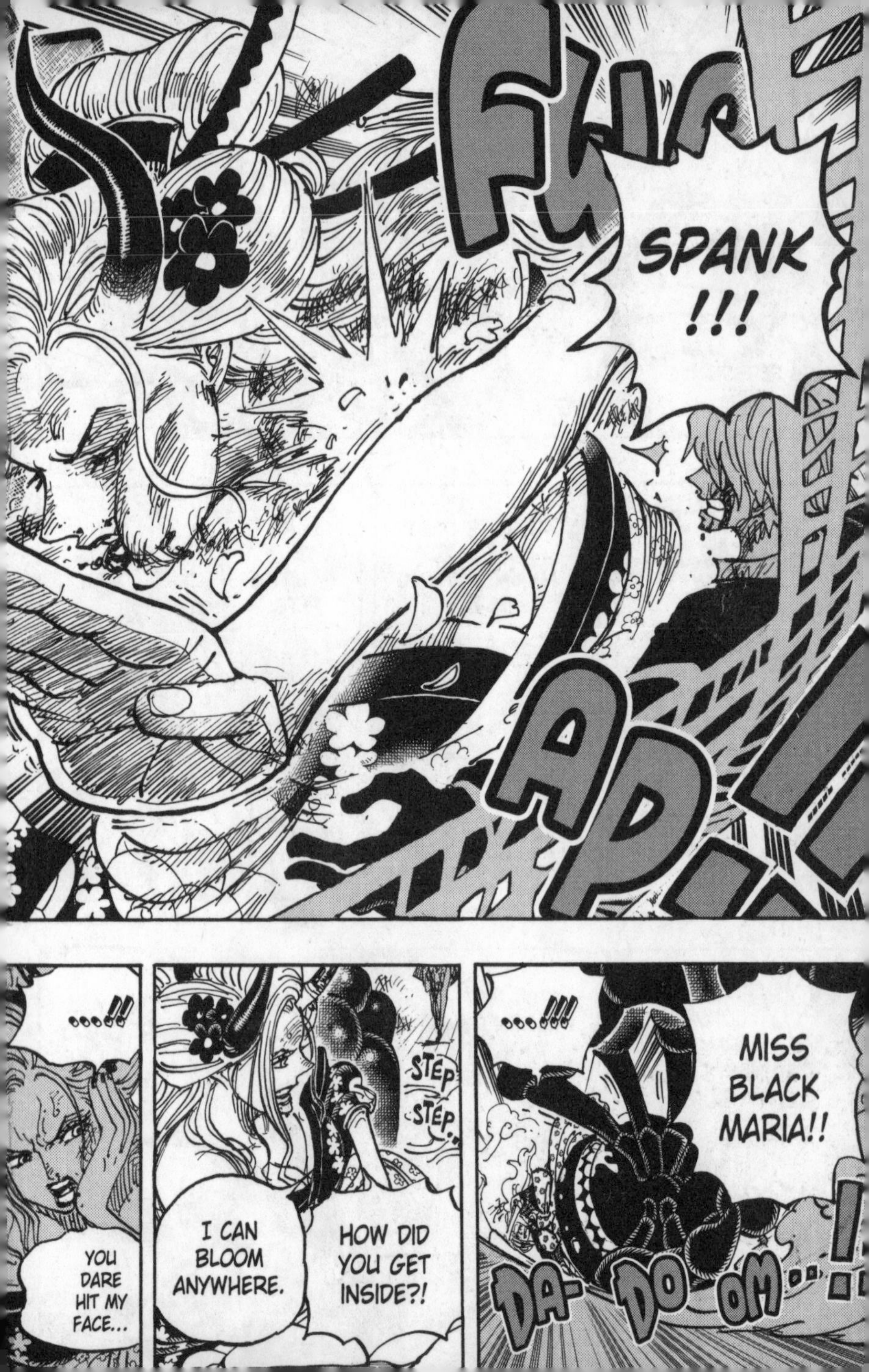
SPANK !!!
MISS BLACK MARIA!!
...!!!
DA-DO-OM..!!
STEP STEP..
HOW DID YOU GET INSIDE?!
I CAN BLOOM ANYWHERE.
...!!
YOU DARE HIT MY FACE...

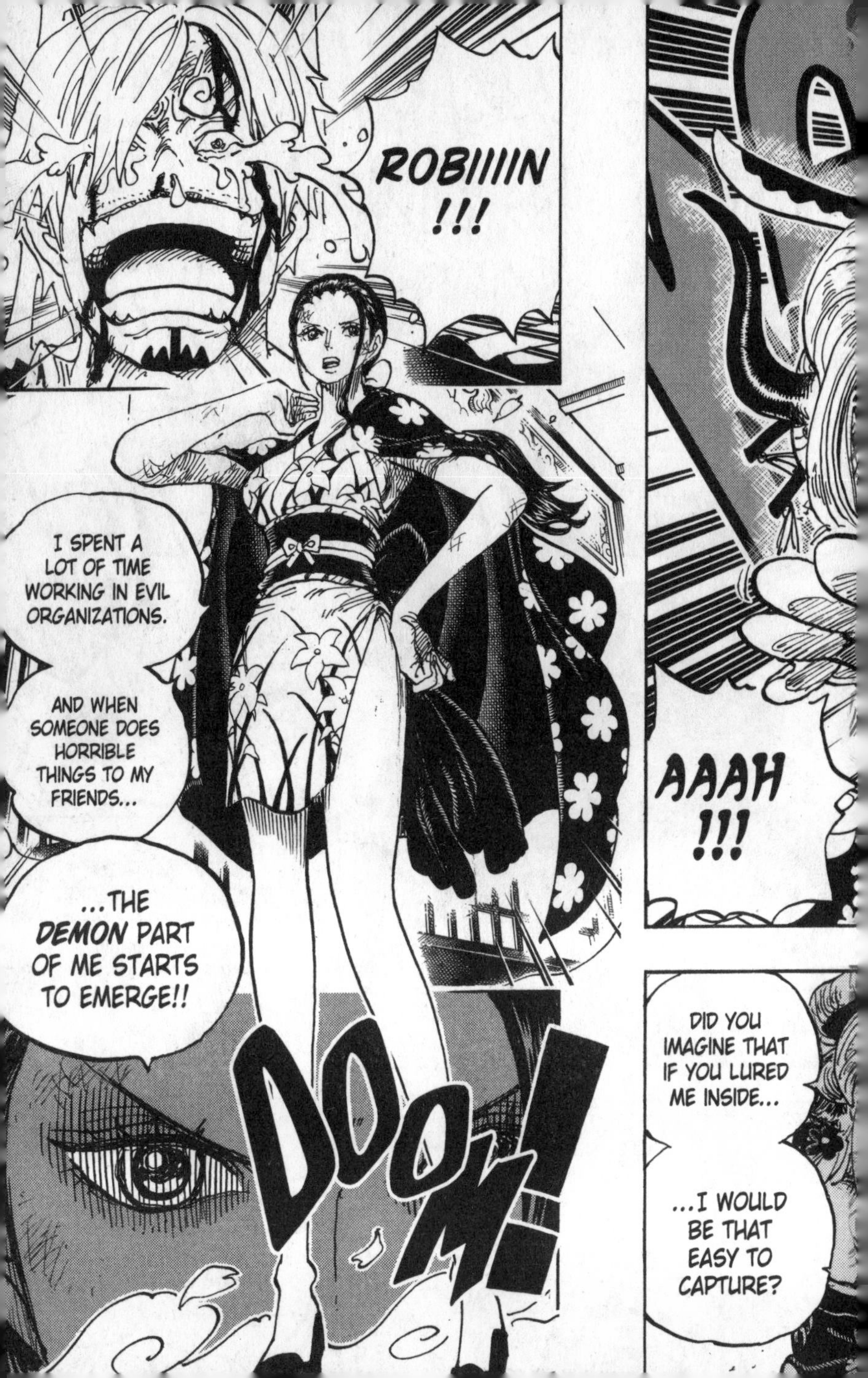
AAAH !!!
ROBIIIIN !!!
I SPENT A LOT OF TIME WORKING IN EVIL ORGANIZATIONS.
AND WHEN SOMEONE DOES HORRIBLE THINGS TO MY FRIENDS...
...THE DEMON PART OF ME STARTS TO EMERGE!!
DOOM!
DID YOU IMAGINE THAT IF YOU LURED ME INSIDE...
...I WOULD BE THAT EASY TO CAPTURE?

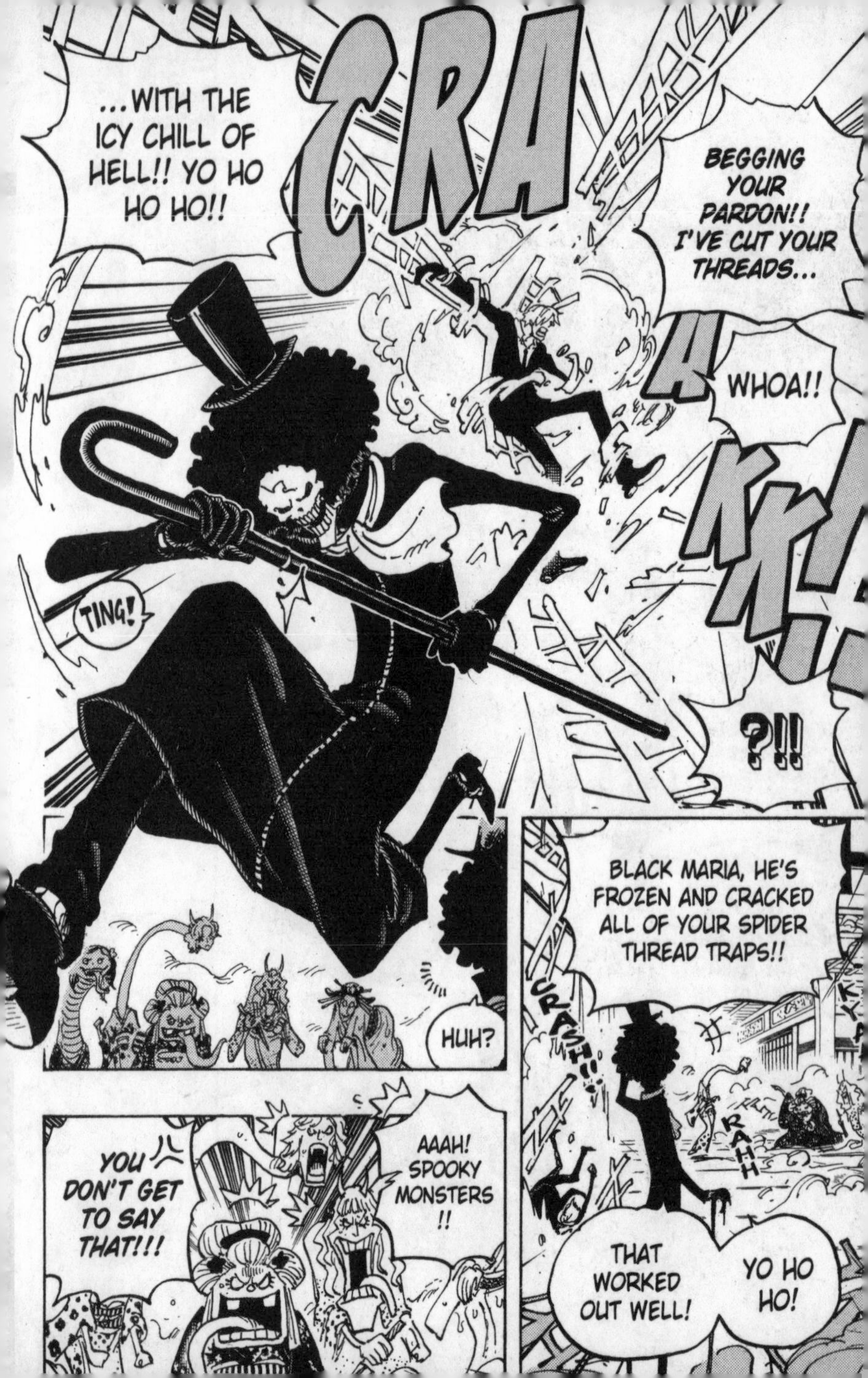
BEGGING YOUR PARDON!! I'VE CUT YOUR THREADS...
CRA
...WITH THE ICY CHILL OF HELL!! YO HO HO HO!!
A
WHOA!!
KK
TING!
?!!
BLACK MARIA, HE'S FROZEN AND CRACKED ALL OF YOUR SPIDER THREAD TRAPS!!
CRASH!!
RAHH
YO HO HO!
THAT WORKED OUT WELL!
HUH?
AAAH! SPOOKY MONSTERS!!
YOU DON'T GET TO SAY THAT!!!

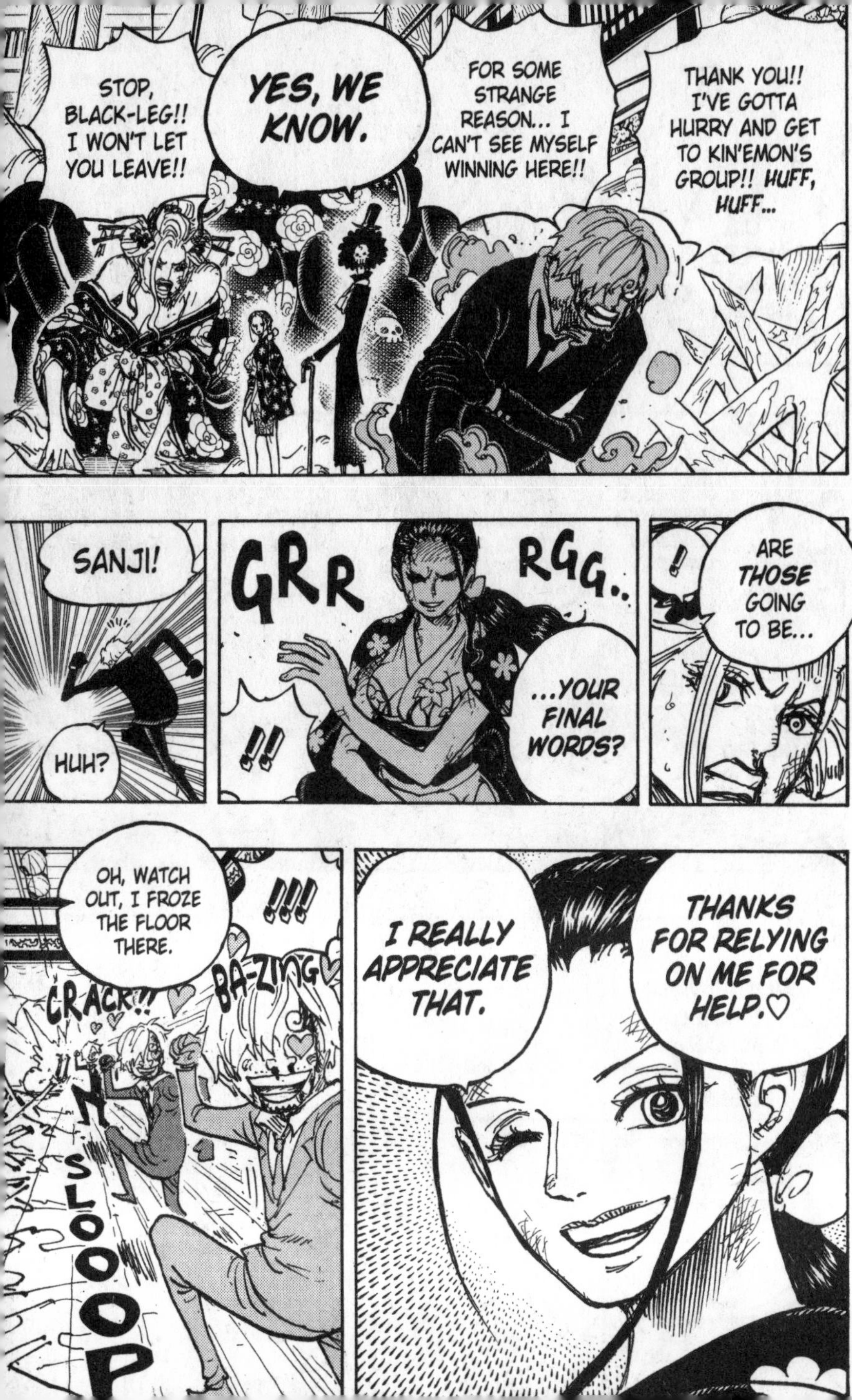
THANK YOU!! I'VE GOTTA HURRY AND GET TO KIN'EMON'S GROUP!! HUFF, HUFF...
FOR SOME STRANGE REASON... I CAN'T SEE MYSELF WINNING HERE!!
YES, WE KNOW.
STOP, BLACK-LEG!! I WON'T LET YOU LEAVE!!
!
ARE THOSE GOING TO BE...
GRR
RGG..
...YOUR FINAL WORDS?
!!
SANJI!
HUH?
THANKS FOR RELYING ON ME FOR HELP.♡
I REALLY APPRECIATE THAT.
OH, WATCH OUT, I FROZE THE FLOOR THERE.
!!!
BA-ZING♡
CRACK!!
SLOOOP

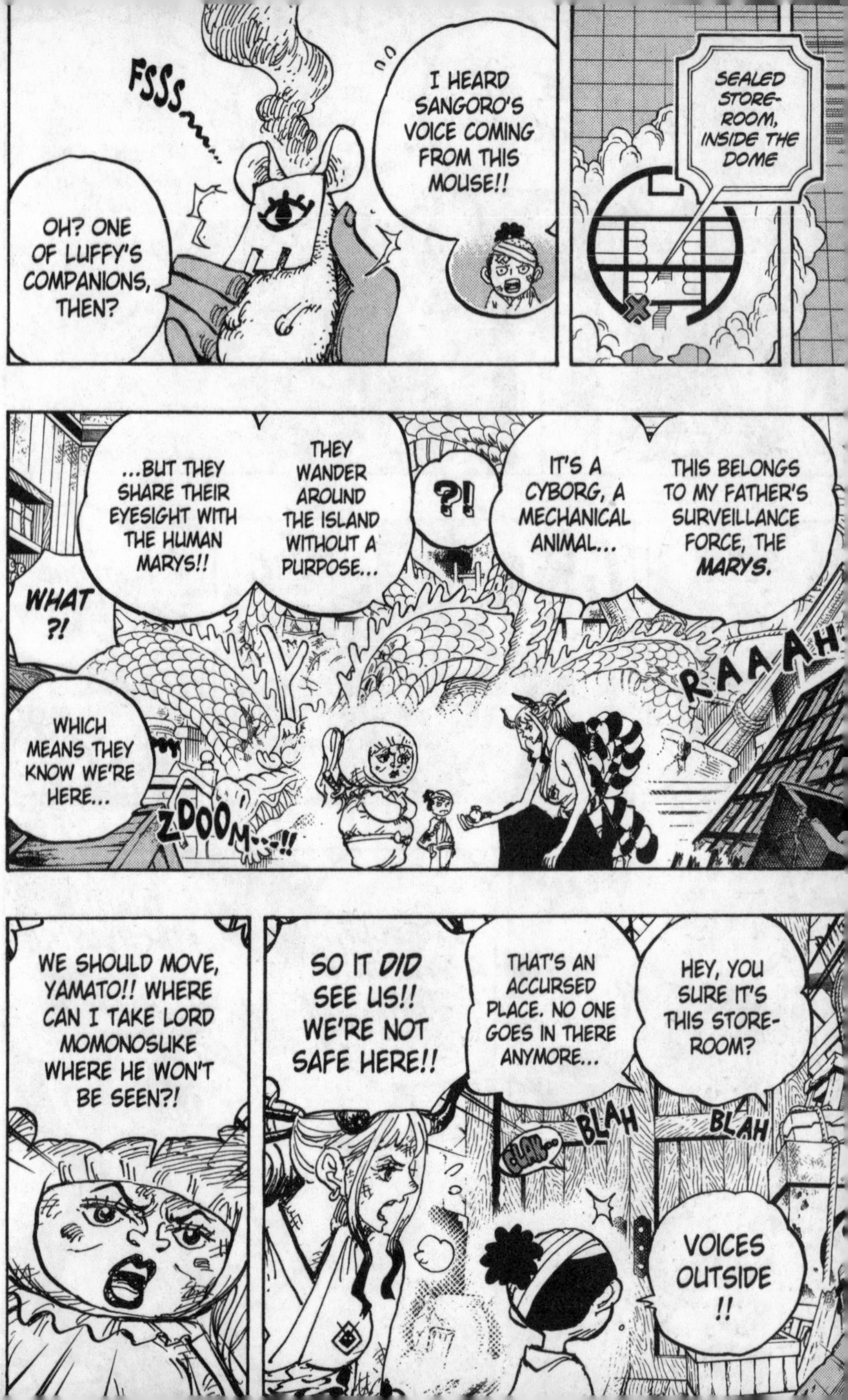
SEALED STORE-ROOM, INSIDE THE DOME
I HEARD SANGORO'S VOICE COMING FROM THIS MOUSE!!
FSSS
OH? ONE OF LUFFY'S COMPANIONS, THEN?
RAAAAH
THIS BELONGS TO MY FATHER'S SURVEILLANCE FORCE, THE MARYS.
IT'S A CYBORG, A MECHANICAL ANIMAL...
?!
THEY WANDER AROUND THE ISLAND WITHOUT A PURPOSE...
...BUT THEY SHARE THEIR EYESIGHT WITH THE HUMAN MARYS!!
WHAT ?!
WHICH MEANS THEY KNOW WE'RE HERE...
ZDOOM!!
HEY, YOU SURE IT'S THIS STORE-ROOM?
THAT'S AN ACCURSED PLACE. NO ONE GOES IN THERE ANYMORE...
BLAH
BLAH
CLAK
VOICES OUTSIDE !!
SO IT DID SEE US!! WE'RE NOT SAFE HERE!!
WE SHOULD MOVE, YAMATO!! WHERE CAN I TAKE LORD MOMONOSUKE WHERE HE WON'T BE SEEN?!

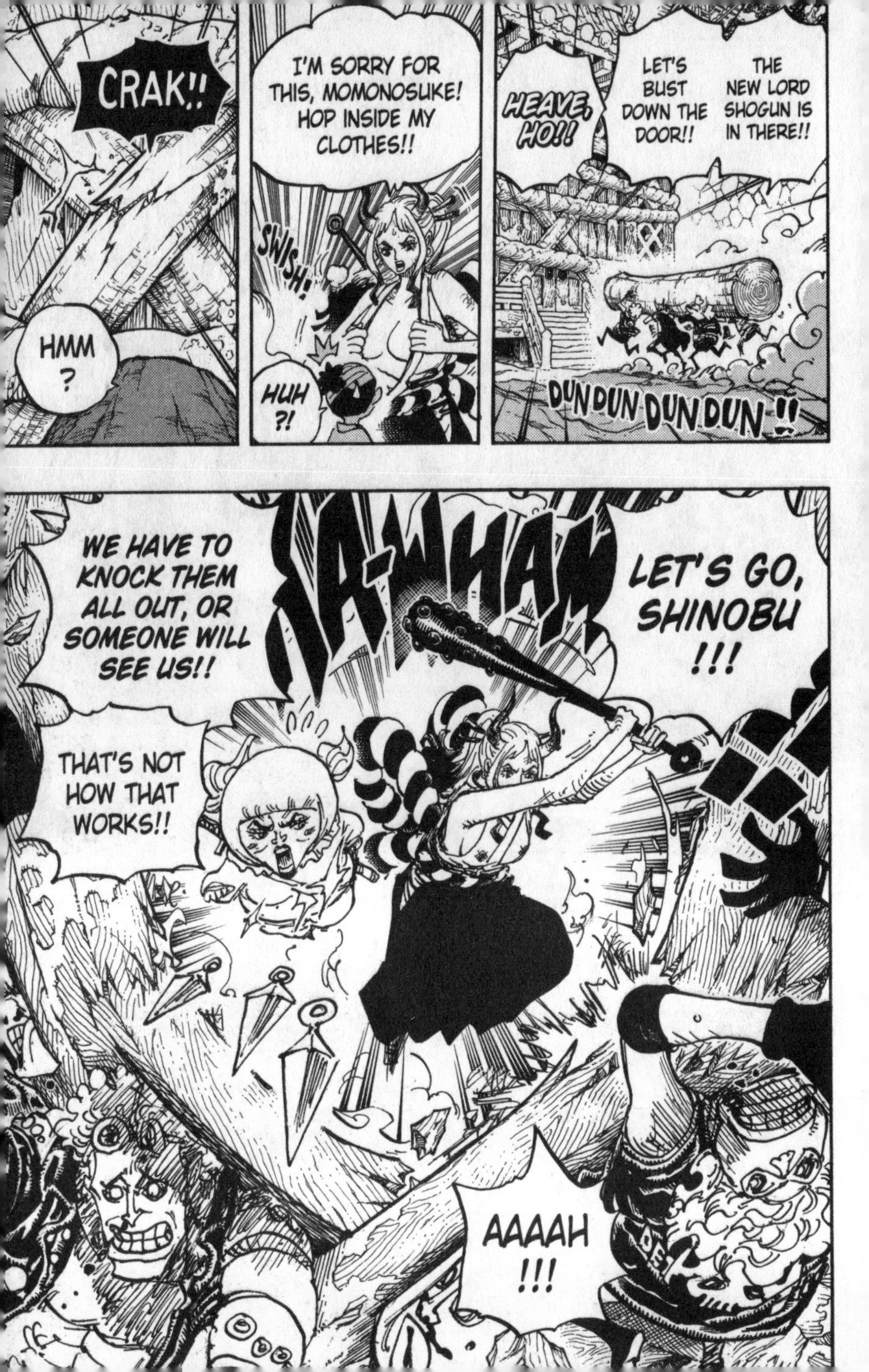
THE NEW LORD SHOGUN IS IN THERE!!
LET'S BUST DOWN THE DOOR!!
HEAVE, HO!!
DUN DUN DUN DUN!!
I'M SORRY FOR THIS, MOMONOSUKE! HOP INSIDE MY CLOTHES!!
SWISH!
HUH ?!
CRAK!!
HMM ?
LET'S GO, SHINOBU !!!
KA-WHAM
WE HAVE TO KNOCK THEM ALL OUT, OR SOMEONE WILL SEE US!!
THAT'S NOT HOW THAT WORKS!!
AAAAH !!!

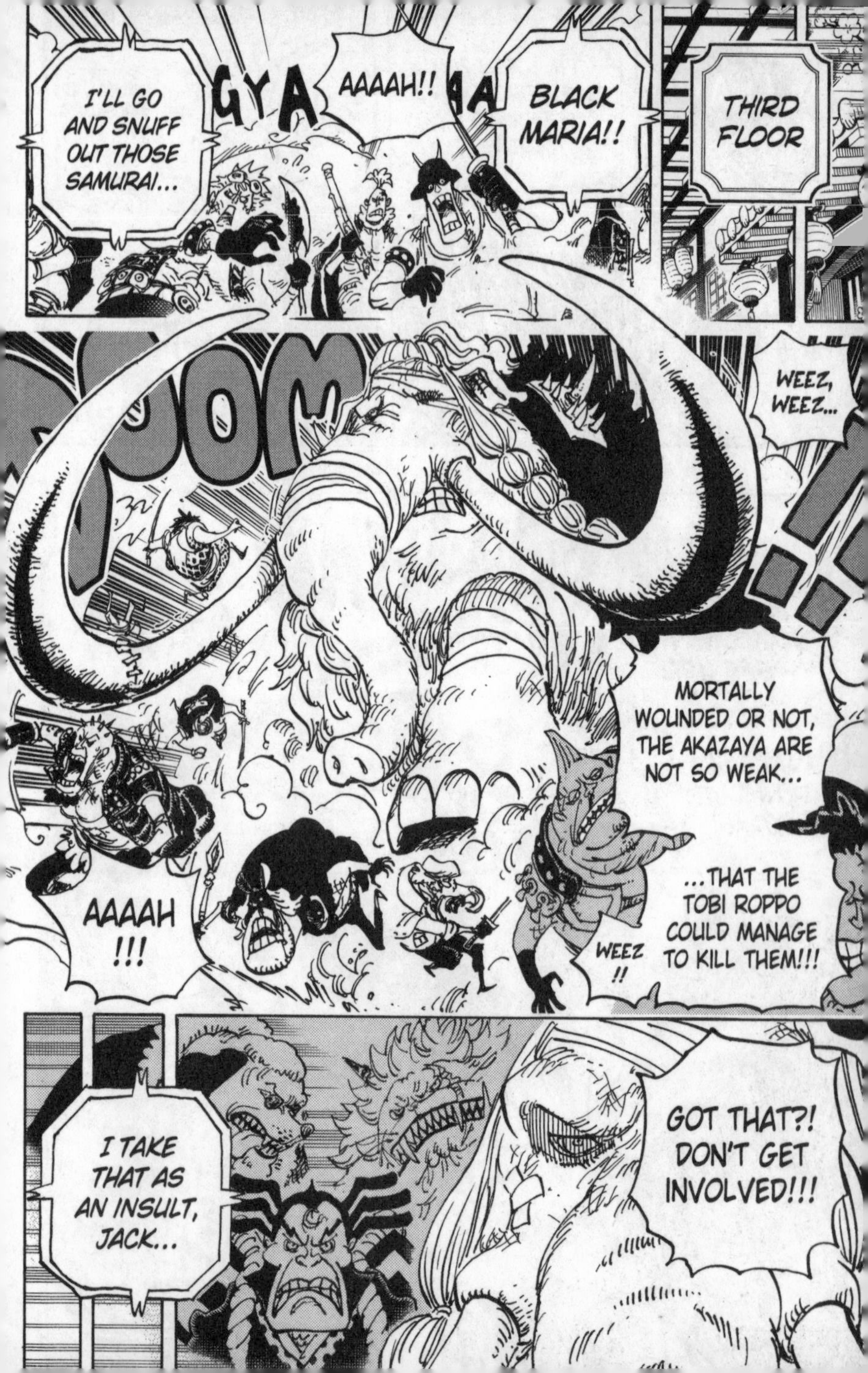
THIRD FLOOR
BLACK MARIA!!
AAAAH!!
I'LL GO AND SNUFF OUT THOSE SAMURAI...
WEEZ, WEEZ...
MORTALLY WOUNDED OR NOT, THE AKAZAYA ARE NOT SO WEAK...
...THAT THE TOBI ROPPO COULD MANAGE TO KILL THEM!!!
WEEZ !!
AAAAH !!!
GOT THAT?! DON'T GET INVOLVED!!!
I TAKE THAT AS AN INSULT, JACK...

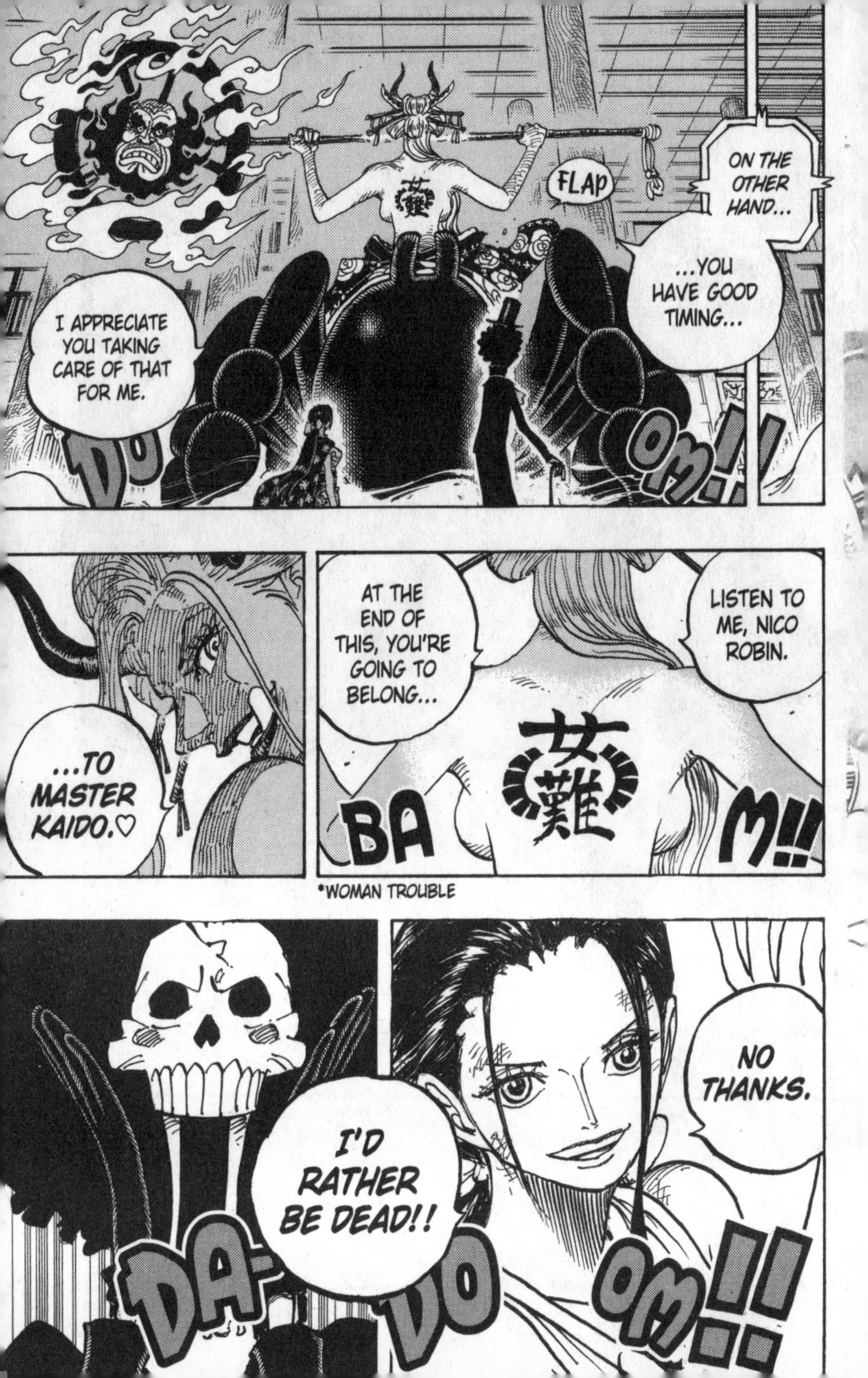
ON THE OTHER HAND...
...YOU HAVE GOOD TIMING...
FLAP
I APPRECIATE YOU TAKING CARE OF THAT FOR ME.
DOOM!!
LISTEN TO ME, NICO ROBIN.
AT THE END OF THIS, YOU'RE GOING TO BELONG...
BAM!!
...TO MASTER KAIDO.♡
*WOMAN TROUBLE
NO THANKS.
I'D RATHER BE DEAD!!
DA-DOOM!!

HYOGORO THE FLOWER

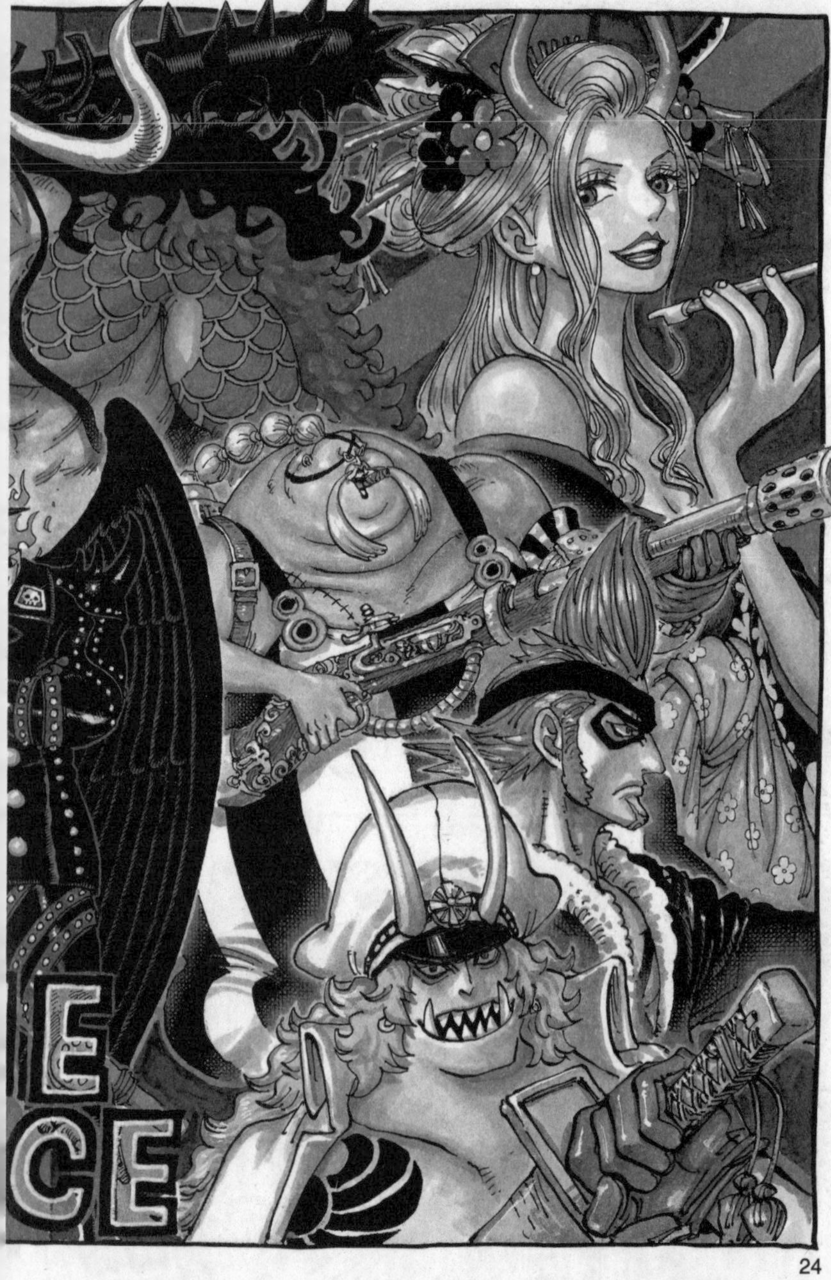
E
CE

Chapter 1006: THE HONORABLE

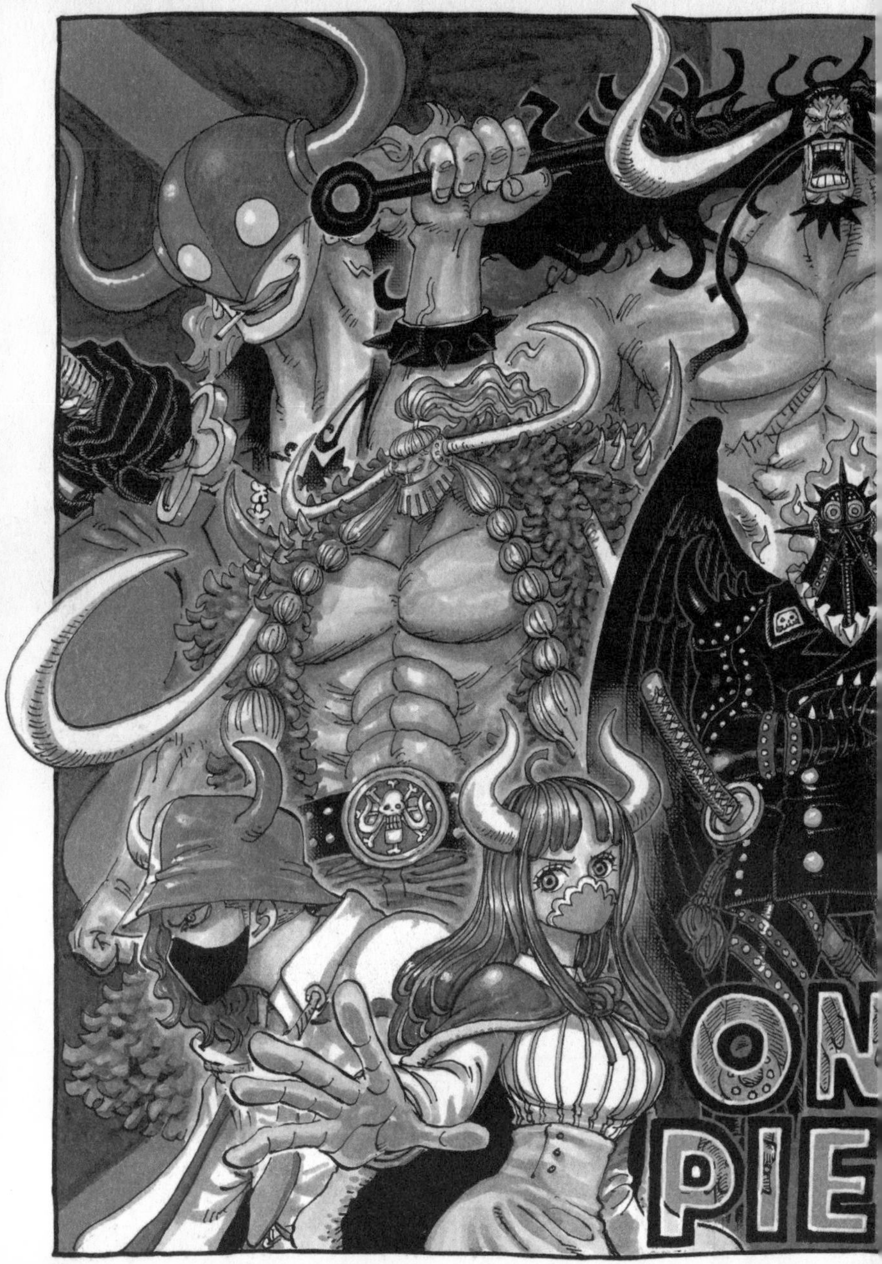
ONE PIECE

vol.**100**

ONE PIECE

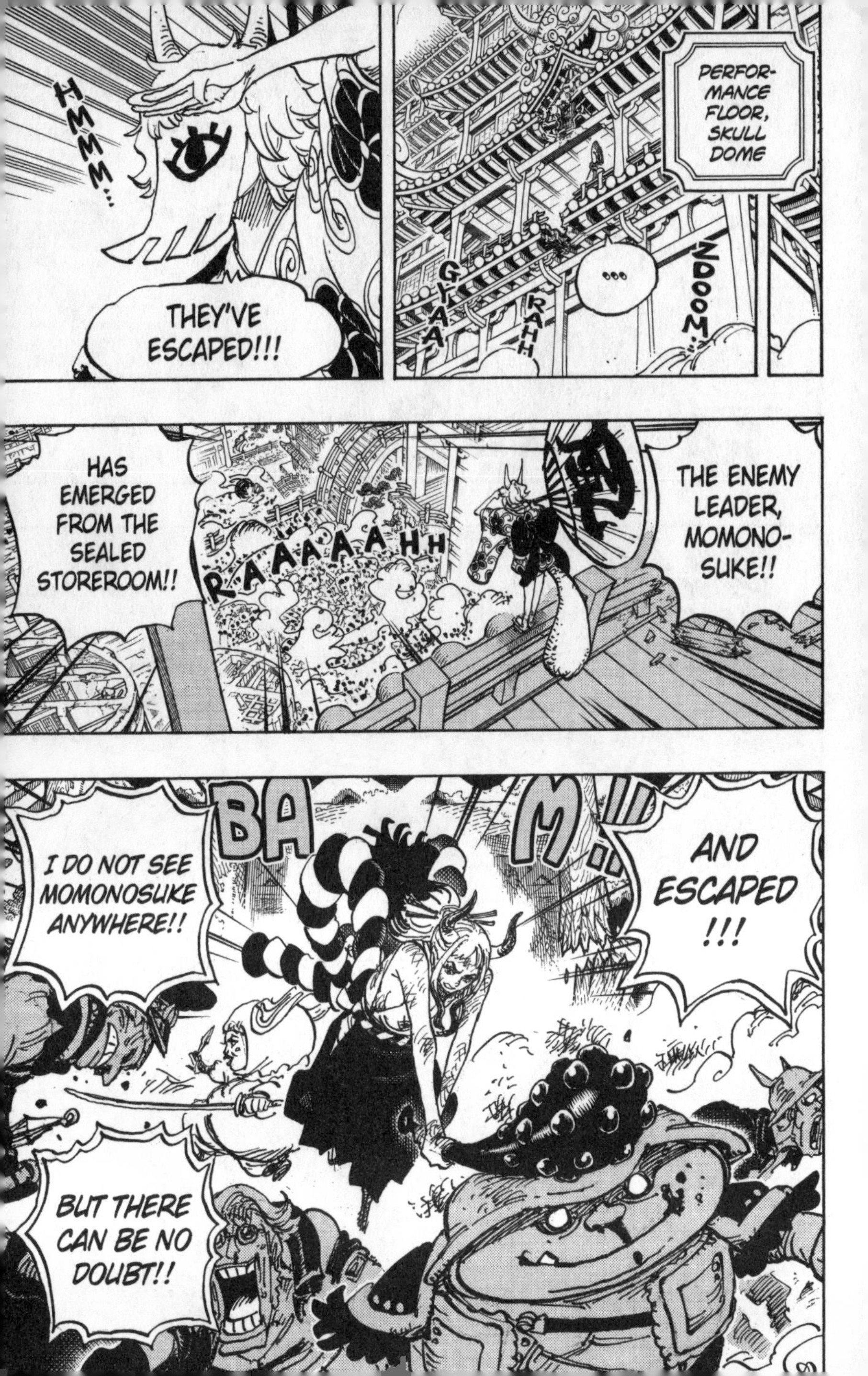
PERFORMANCE FLOOR, SKULL DOME
GYAAA
RAHH
...
ZDOOM!!
HMMM...
THEY'VE ESCAPED!!!
THE ENEMY LEADER, MOMONOSUKE!!
RAAAAAHH
HAS EMERGED FROM THE SEALED STOREROOM!!
AND ESCAPED!!!
BAM
I DO NOT SEE MOMONOSUKE ANYWHERE!!
BUT THERE CAN BE NO DOUBT!!

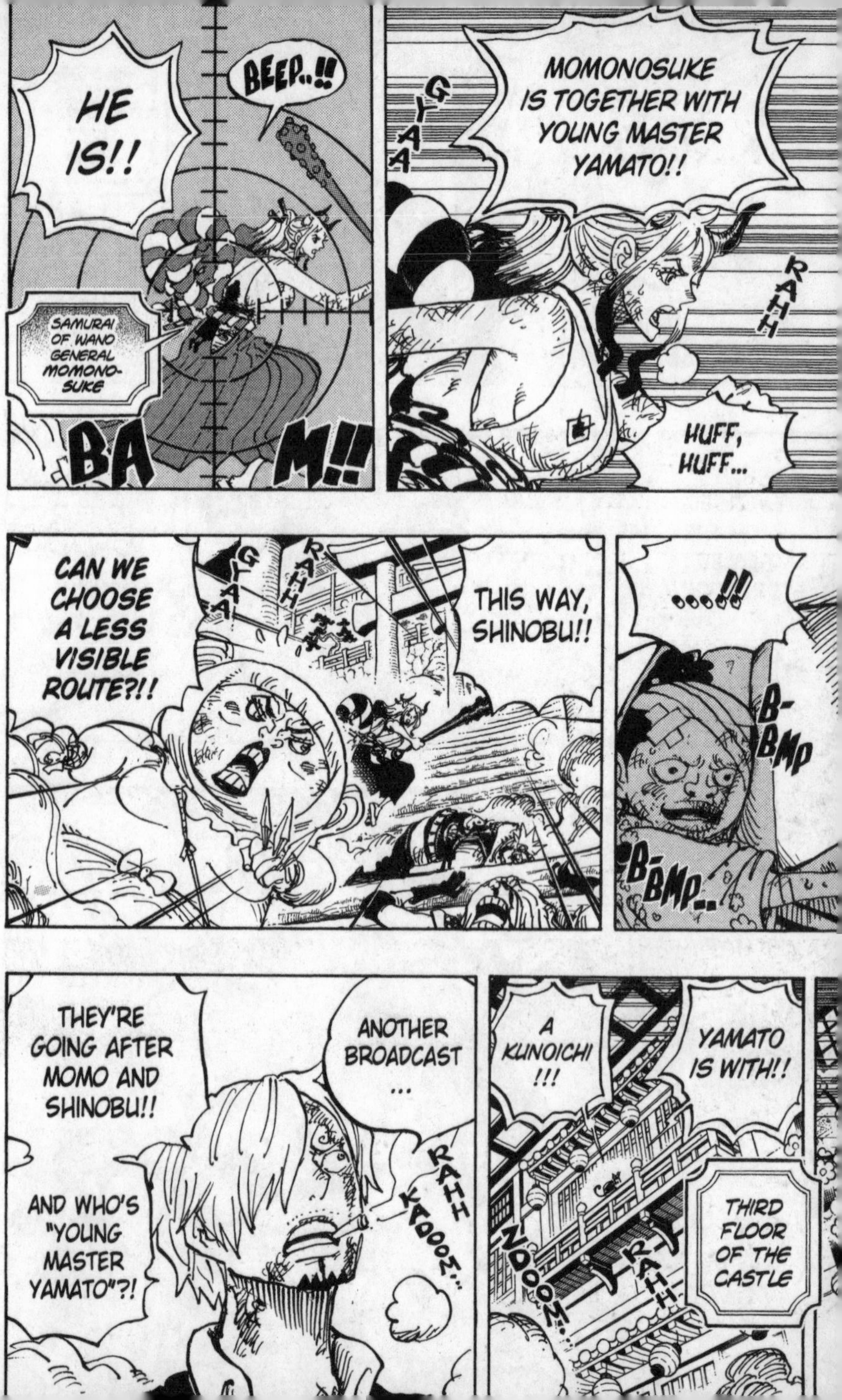
MOMONOSUKE IS TOGETHER WITH YOUNG MASTER YAMATO!!
GYAAA
RAHH
HUFF, HUFF...
BEEP..!!
HE IS!!
SAMURAI OF WANO GENERAL MOMONOSUKE
BAM!!
....!!
B-BMP
B-BMP..
THIS WAY, SHINOBU!!
GYAA
RAHH
CAN WE CHOOSE A LESS VISIBLE ROUTE?!!
YAMATO IS WITH!!
A KUNOICHI!!!
THIRD FLOOR OF THE CASTLE
RAHH
ZDOOOM...
ANOTHER BROADCAST ...
THEY'RE GOING AFTER MOMO AND SHINOBU!!
RAHH
KADOOOM...
AND WHO'S "YOUNG MASTER YAMATO"?!

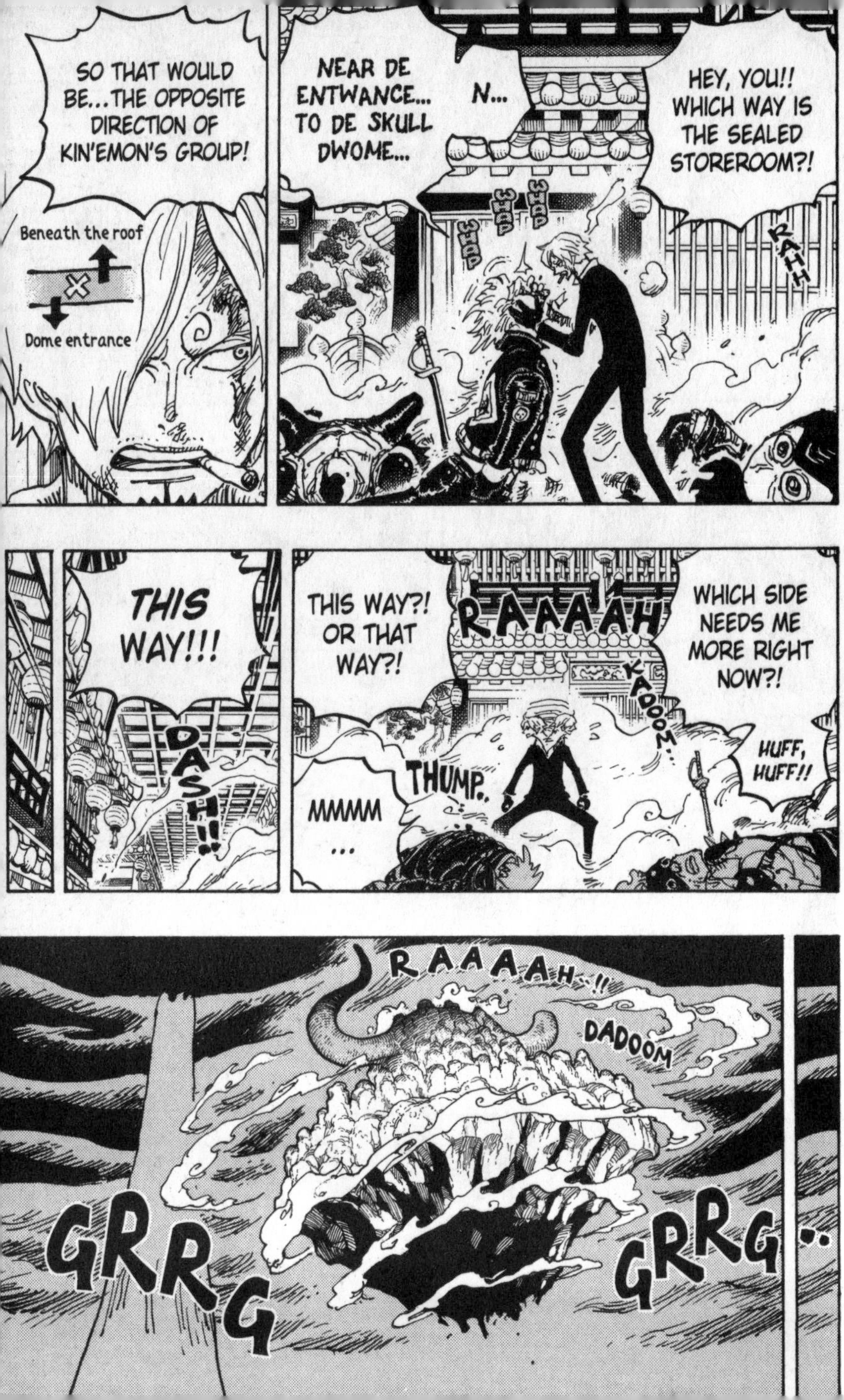
HEY, YOU!! WHICH WAY IS THE SEALED STOREROOM?!
RAHH
WHAP
WHAP
WHAP
N...
NEAR DE ENTWANCE... TO DE SKULL DWOME...
SO THAT WOULD BE...THE OPPOSITE DIRECTION OF KIN'EMON'S GROUP!
Beneath the roof
Dome entrance
WHICH SIDE NEEDS ME MORE RIGHT NOW?!
RAAAAH
KADOOM...
HUFF, HUFF!!
THIS WAY?! OR THAT WAY?!
THUMP..
MMMM ...
THIS WAY!!!
DASH!!
RAAAAH..!!
DADOOM
GRRG
GRRG..

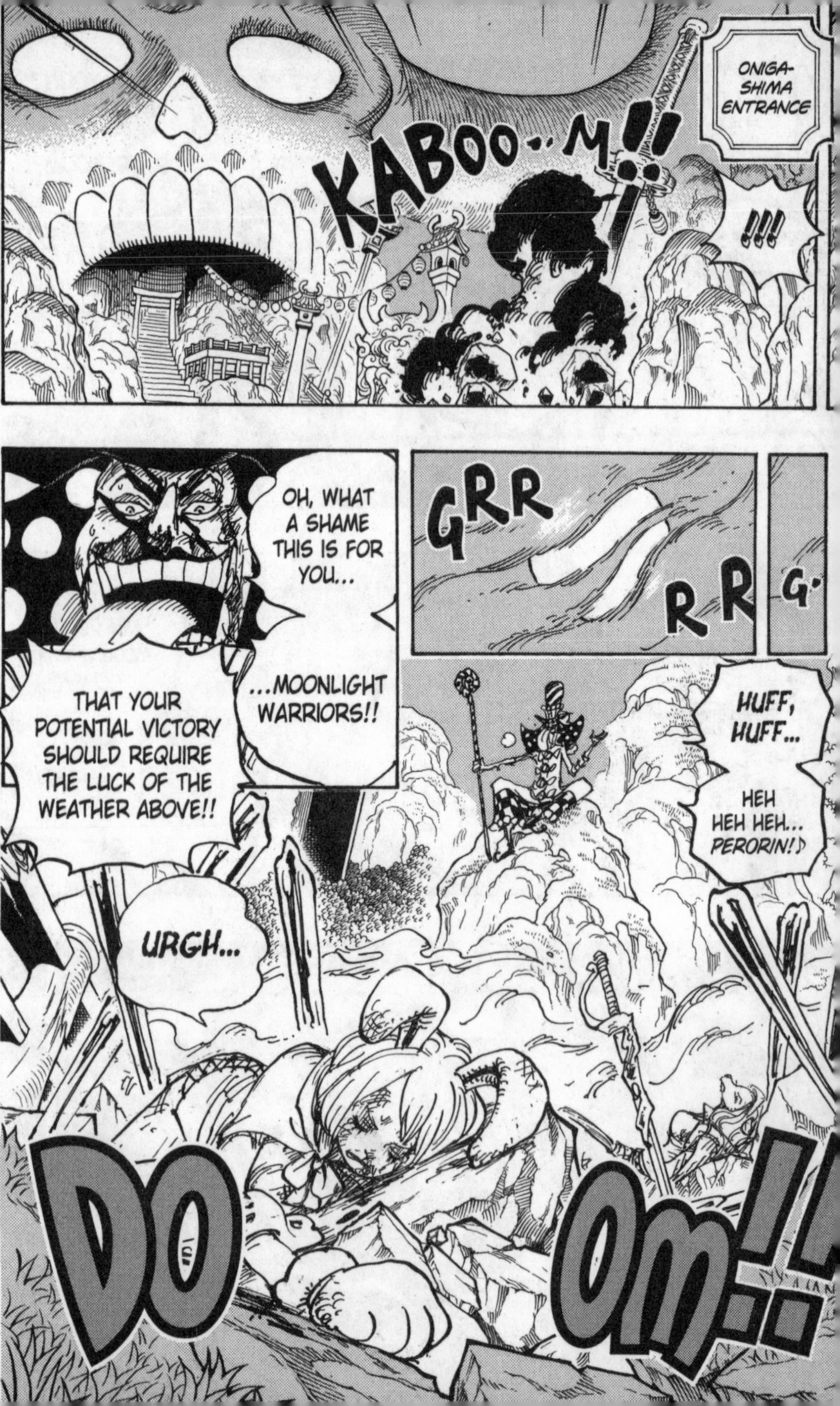
ONIGA-SHIMA ENTRANCE
KABOO--M!!
!!!
G'
GRR
RR
OH, WHAT A SHAME THIS IS FOR YOU...
...MOONLIGHT WARRIORS!!
THAT YOUR POTENTIAL VICTORY SHOULD REQUIRE THE LUCK OF THE WEATHER ABOVE!!
HUFF, HUFF...
HEH HEH HEH... PERORIN!♪
URGH...
DO
om!!

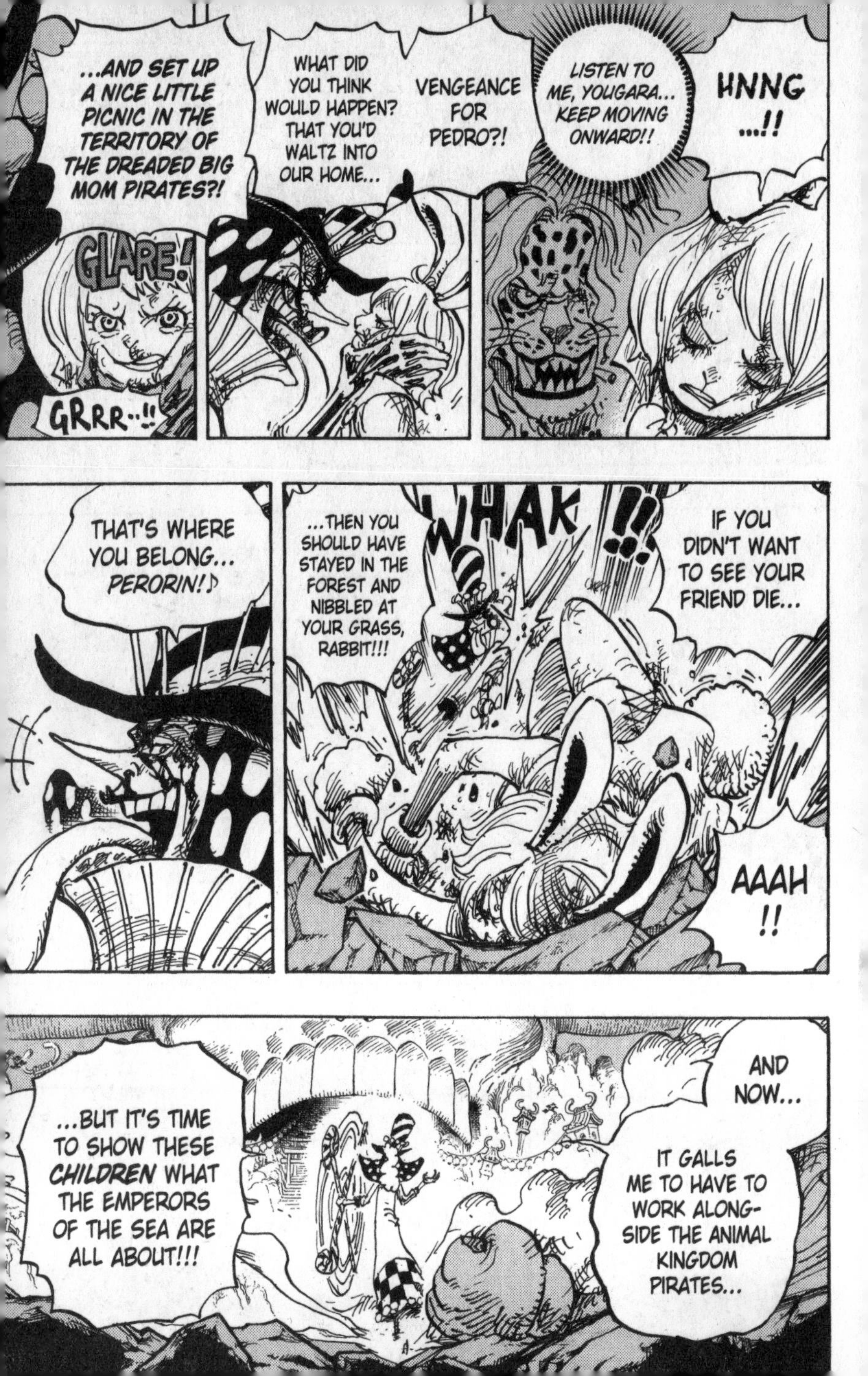
HNNG ...!!
LISTEN TO ME, YOUGARA... KEEP MOVING ONWARD!!
VENGEANCE FOR PEDRO?!
WHAT DID YOU THINK WOULD HAPPEN? THAT YOU'D WALTZ INTO OUR HOME...
...AND SET UP A NICE LITTLE PICNIC IN THE TERRITORY OF THE DREADED BIG MOM PIRATES?!
GLARE!
GRRR..!!
IF YOU DIDN'T WANT TO SEE YOUR FRIEND DIE...
WHAK!!
...THEN YOU SHOULD HAVE STAYED IN THE FOREST AND NIBBLED AT YOUR GRASS, RABBIT!!!
AAAH!!
THAT'S WHERE YOU BELONG... *PERORIN!*♪
AND NOW...
IT GALLS ME TO HAVE TO WORK ALONG-SIDE THE ANIMAL KINGDOM PIRATES...
...BUT IT'S TIME TO SHOW THESE *CHILDREN* WHAT THE EMPERORS OF THE SEA ARE ALL ABOUT!!!

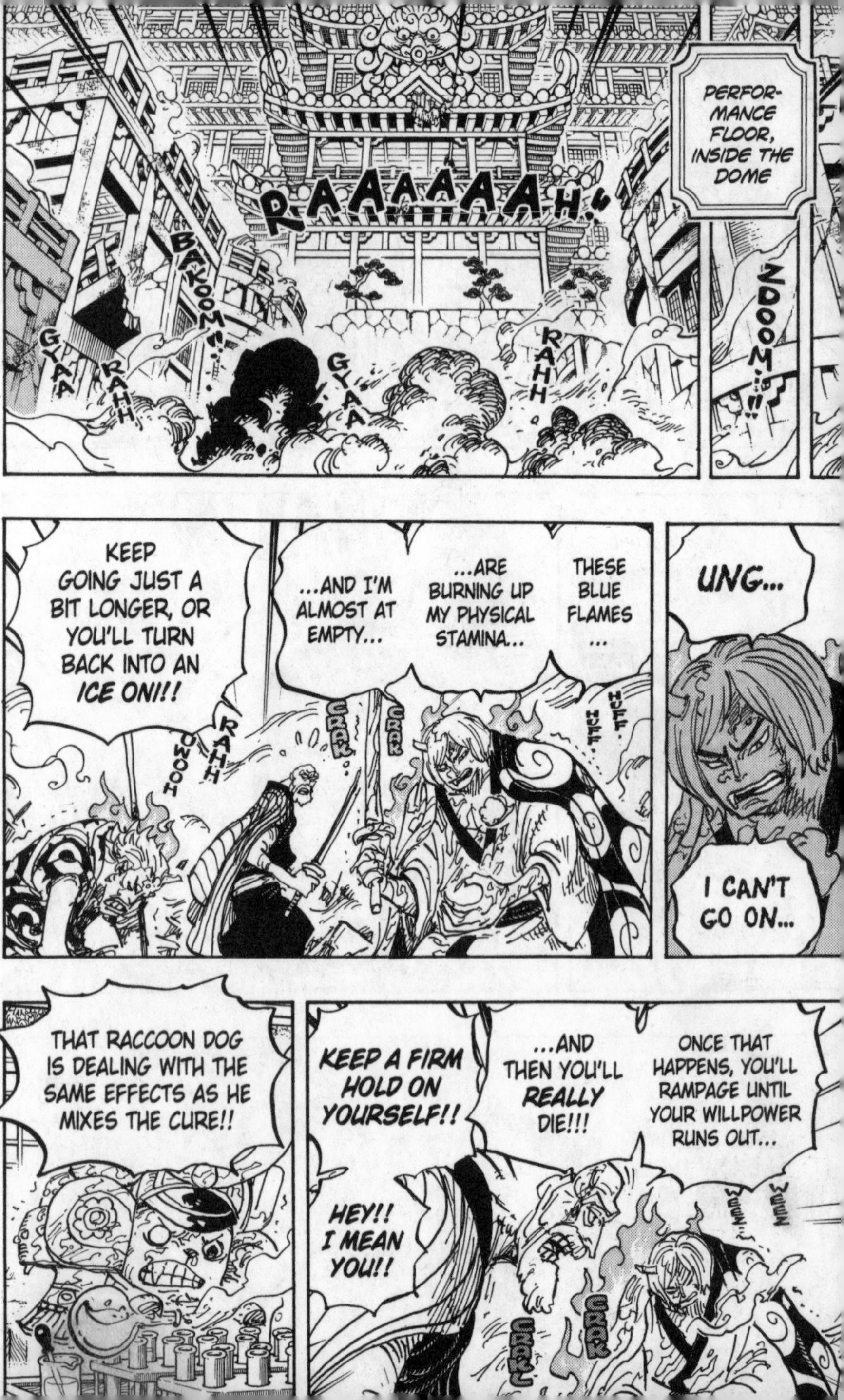
PERFORMANCE FLOOR, INSIDE THE DOME
ZDOOOM!!
RAAAAAAH!!
RAHH
BAKOOM!!
GYAA
RAHH
GYAA
UNG...
I CAN'T GO ON...
THESE BLUE FLAMES...
...ARE BURNING UP MY PHYSICAL STAMINA...
...AND I'M ALMOST AT EMPTY...
HUFF HUFF
CRAK
CRAK
KEEP GOING JUST A BIT LONGER, OR YOU'LL TURN BACK INTO AN ICE ONI!!
RAHH
UWOOH
ONCE THAT HAPPENS, YOU'LL RAMPAGE UNTIL YOUR WILLPOWER RUNS OUT...
...AND THEN YOU'LL REALLY DIE!!!
KEEP A FIRM HOLD ON YOURSELF!!
WEEN
WEEN
HEY!! I MEAN YOU!!
CRAK
CRAK
THAT RACCOON DOG IS DEALING WITH THE SAME EFFECTS AS HE MIXES THE CURE!!

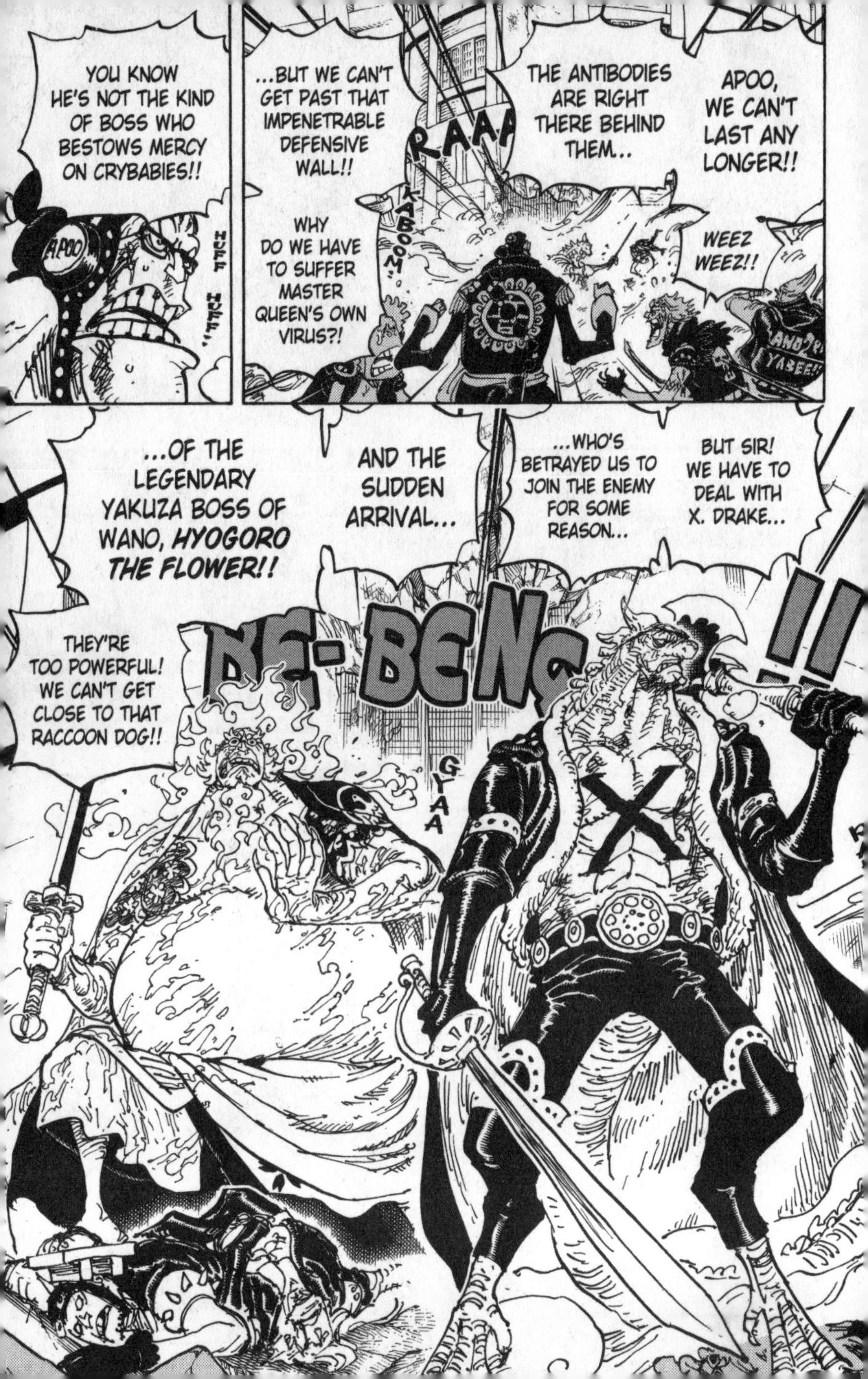
APOO, WE CAN'T LAST ANY LONGER!!
THE ANTIBODIES ARE RIGHT THERE BEHIND THEM...
...BUT WE CAN'T GET PAST THAT IMPENETRABLE DEFENSIVE WALL!!
RAAA
KABOOM
WEEZ WEEZ!!
YABEE!!
WHY DO WE HAVE TO SUFFER MASTER QUEEN'S OWN VIRUS?!
YOU KNOW HE'S NOT THE KIND OF BOSS WHO BESTOWS MERCY ON CRYBABIES!!
APOO
HUFF HUFF
BUT SIR! WE HAVE TO DEAL WITH X. DRAKE...
...WHO'S BETRAYED US TO JOIN THE ENEMY FOR SOME REASON...
AND THE SUDDEN ARRIVAL...
...OF THE LEGENDARY YAKUZA BOSS OF WANO, *HYOGORO THE FLOWER!!*
BE-BENG!!
THEY'RE TOO POWERFUL! WE CAN'T GET CLOSE TO THAT RACCOON DOG!!
GYAA

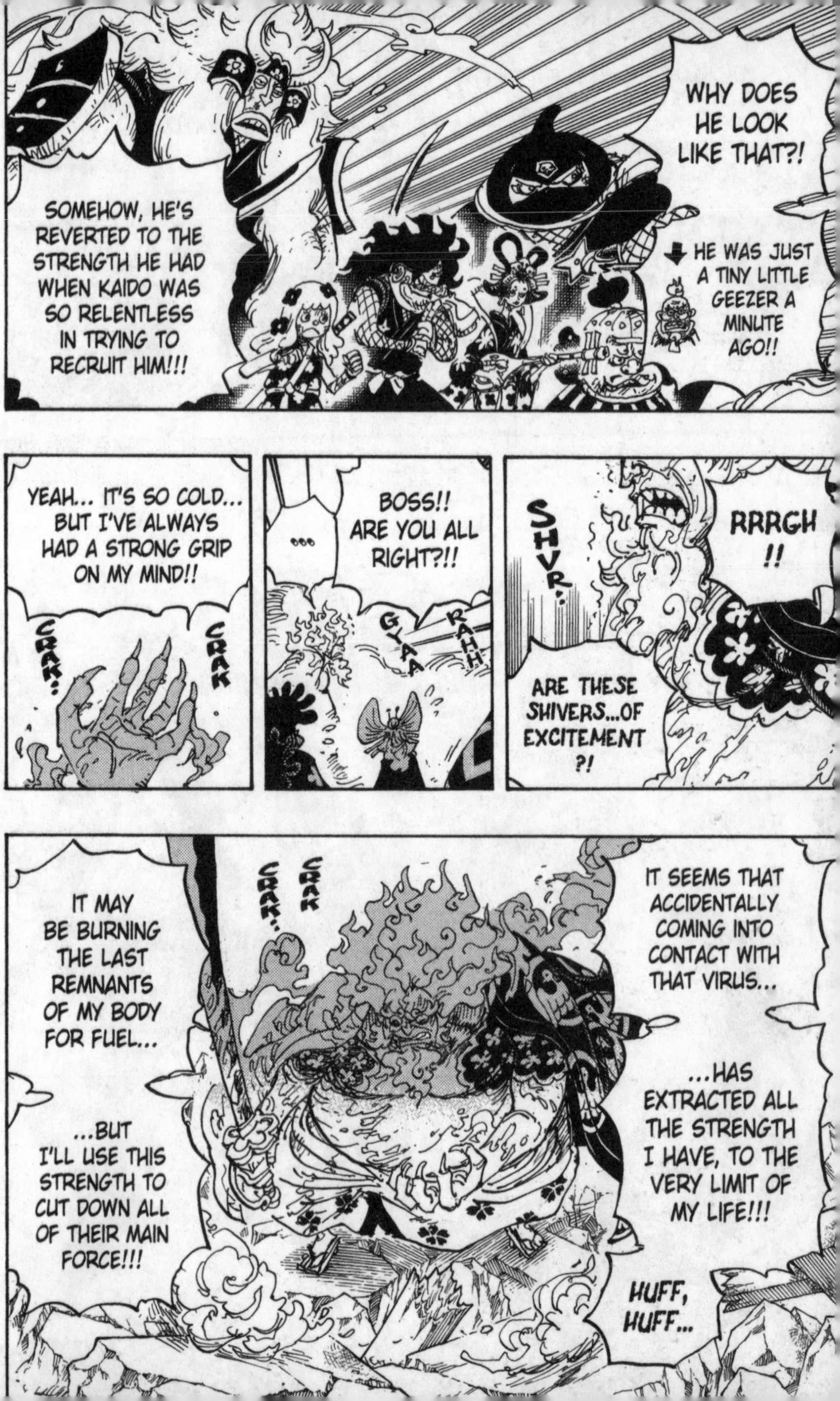
WHY DOES HE LOOK LIKE THAT?!
HE WAS JUST A TINY LITTLE GEEZER A MINUTE AGO!!
SOMEHOW, HE'S REVERTED TO THE STRENGTH HE HAD WHEN KAIDO WAS SO RELENTLESS IN TRYING TO RECRUIT HIM!!!
RRRGH !!
SHVR..
ARE THESE SHIVERS...OF EXCITEMENT ?!
BOSS!! ARE YOU ALL RIGHT?!!
...
RAHH
GYAA
YEAH... IT'S SO COLD... BUT I'VE ALWAYS HAD A STRONG GRIP ON MY MIND!!
CRAK
CRAK..
IT SEEMS THAT ACCIDENTALLY COMING INTO CONTACT WITH THAT VIRUS...
...HAS EXTRACTED ALL THE STRENGTH I HAVE, TO THE VERY LIMIT OF MY LIFE!!!
HUFF, HUFF...
CRAK
CRAK..
IT MAY BE BURNING THE LAST REMNANTS OF MY BODY FOR FUEL...
...BUT I'LL USE THIS STRENGTH TO CUT DOWN ALL OF THEIR MAIN FORCE!!!

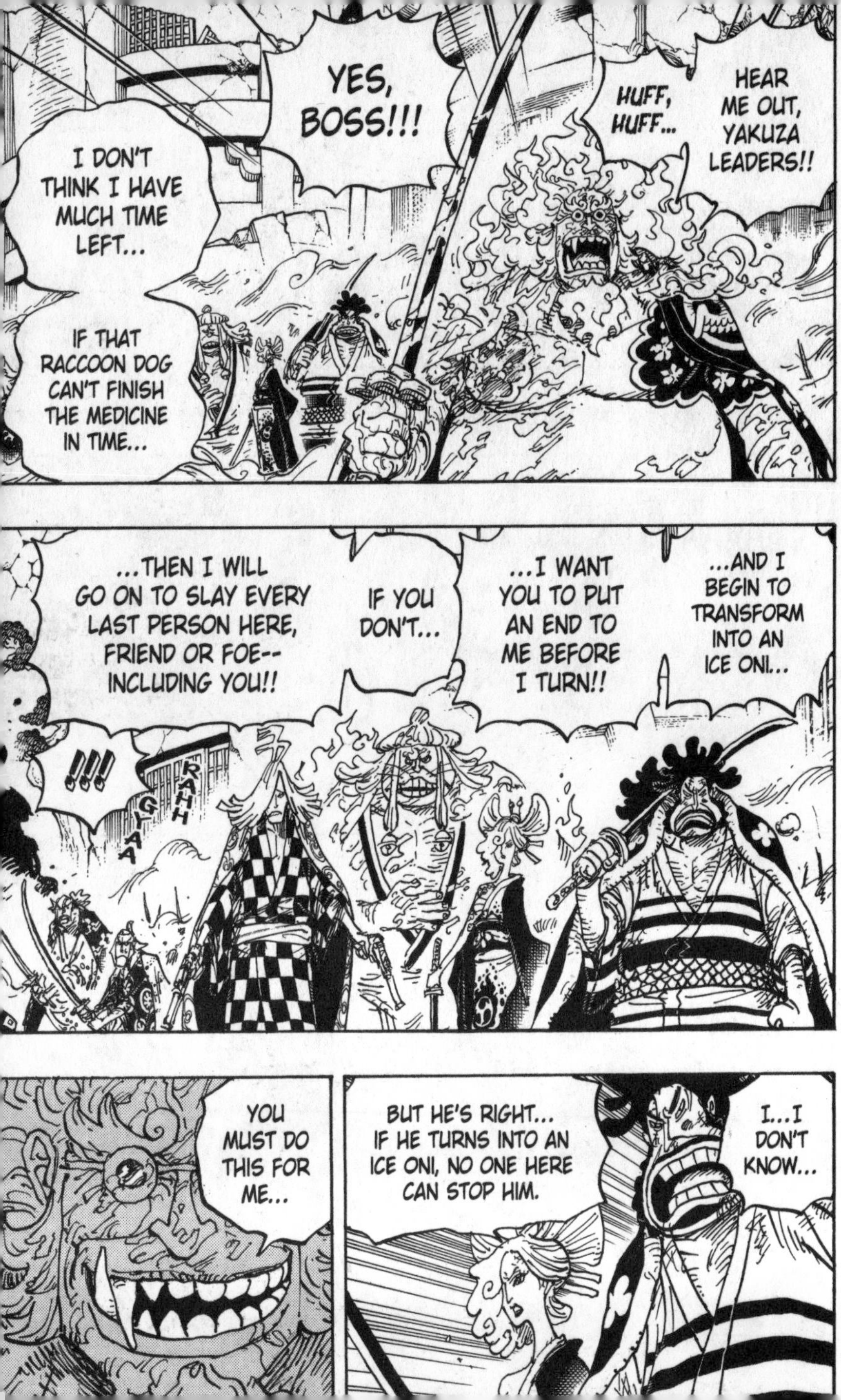
HEAR ME OUT, YAKUZA LEADERS!!
HUFF, HUFF...
YES, BOSS!!!
I DON'T THINK I HAVE MUCH TIME LEFT...
IF THAT RACCOON DOG CAN'T FINISH THE MEDICINE IN TIME...
...AND I BEGIN TO TRANSFORM INTO AN ICE ONI...
...I WANT YOU TO PUT AN END TO ME BEFORE I TURN!!
IF YOU DON'T...
...THEN I WILL GO ON TO SLAY EVERY LAST PERSON HERE, FRIEND OR FOE--INCLUDING YOU!!
RAHH
GYAA
!!!
I...I DON'T KNOW...
BUT HE'S RIGHT... IF HE TURNS INTO AN ICE ONI, NO ONE HERE CAN STOP HIM.
YOU MUST DO THIS FOR ME...

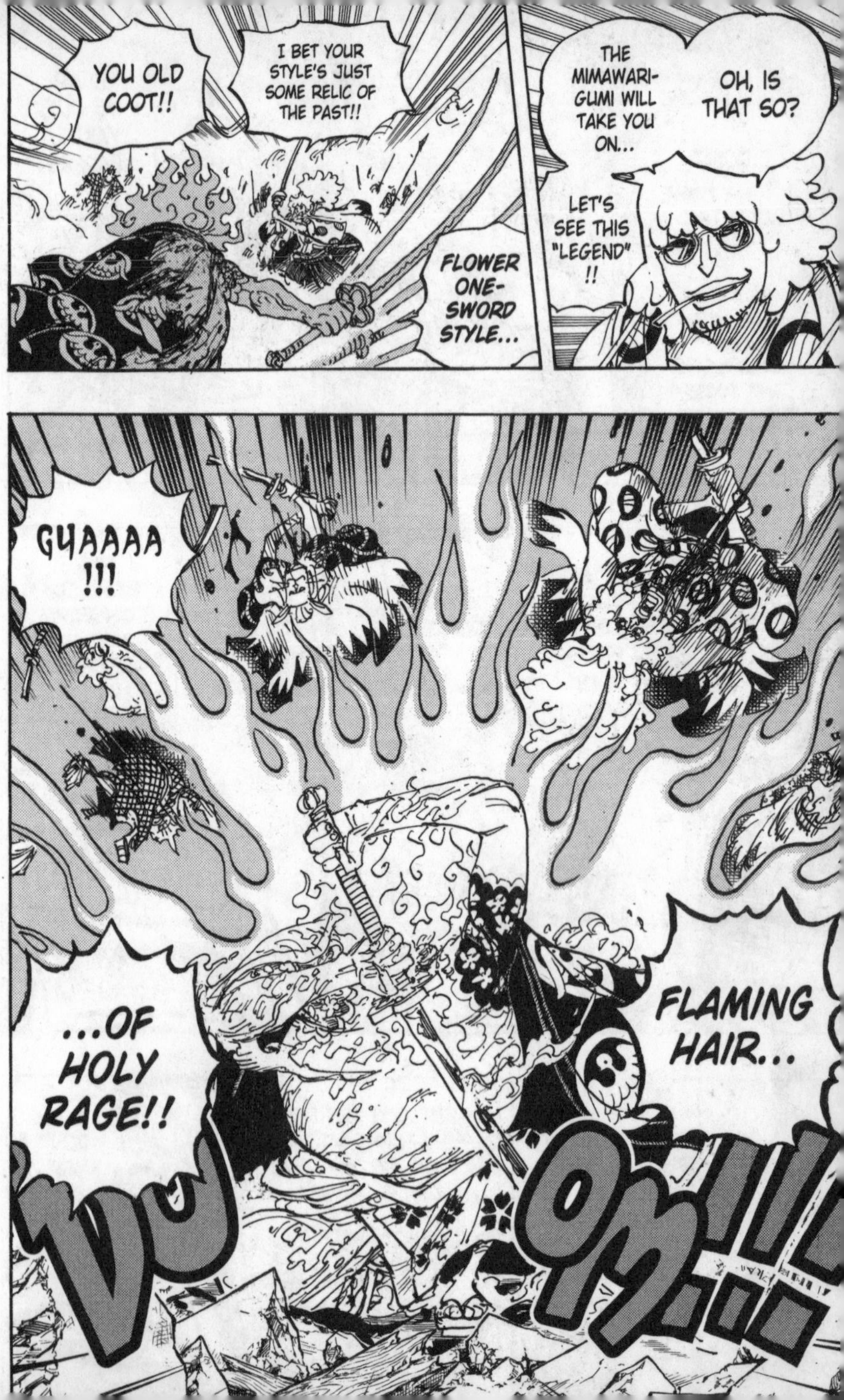
OH, IS THAT SO?
THE MIMAWARI-GUMI WILL TAKE YOU ON...
LET'S SEE THIS "LEGEND" !!
I BET YOUR STYLE'S JUST SOME RELIC OF THE PAST!!
YOU OLD COOT!!
FLOWER ONE-SWORD STYLE...
GUAAAA !!!
FLAMING HAIR...
...OF HOLY RAGE!!

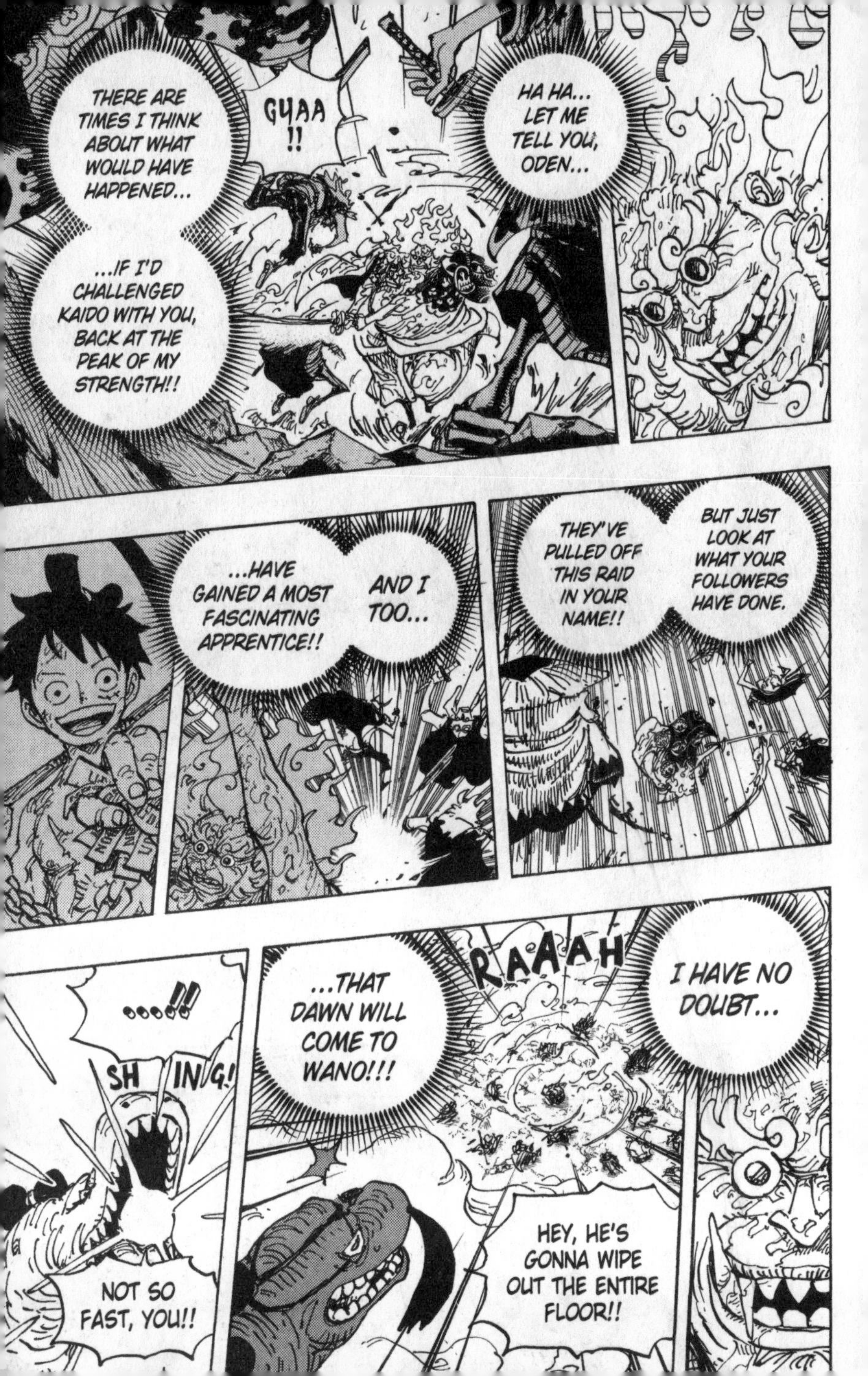
HA HA... LET ME TELL YOU, ODEN...
GUAA!!
THERE ARE TIMES I THINK ABOUT WHAT WOULD HAVE HAPPENED...
...IF I'D CHALLENGED KAIDO WITH YOU, BACK AT THE PEAK OF MY STRENGTH!!
BUT JUST LOOK AT WHAT YOUR FOLLOWERS HAVE DONE.
THEY'VE PULLED OFF THIS RAID IN YOUR NAME!!
AND I TOO...
...HAVE GAINED A MOST FASCINATING APPRENTICE!!
I HAVE NO DOUBT...
RAAAH
...THAT DAWN WILL COME TO WANO!!!
HEY, HE'S GONNA WIPE OUT THE ENTIRE FLOOR!!
....!!
SHING!
NOT SO FAST, YOU!!

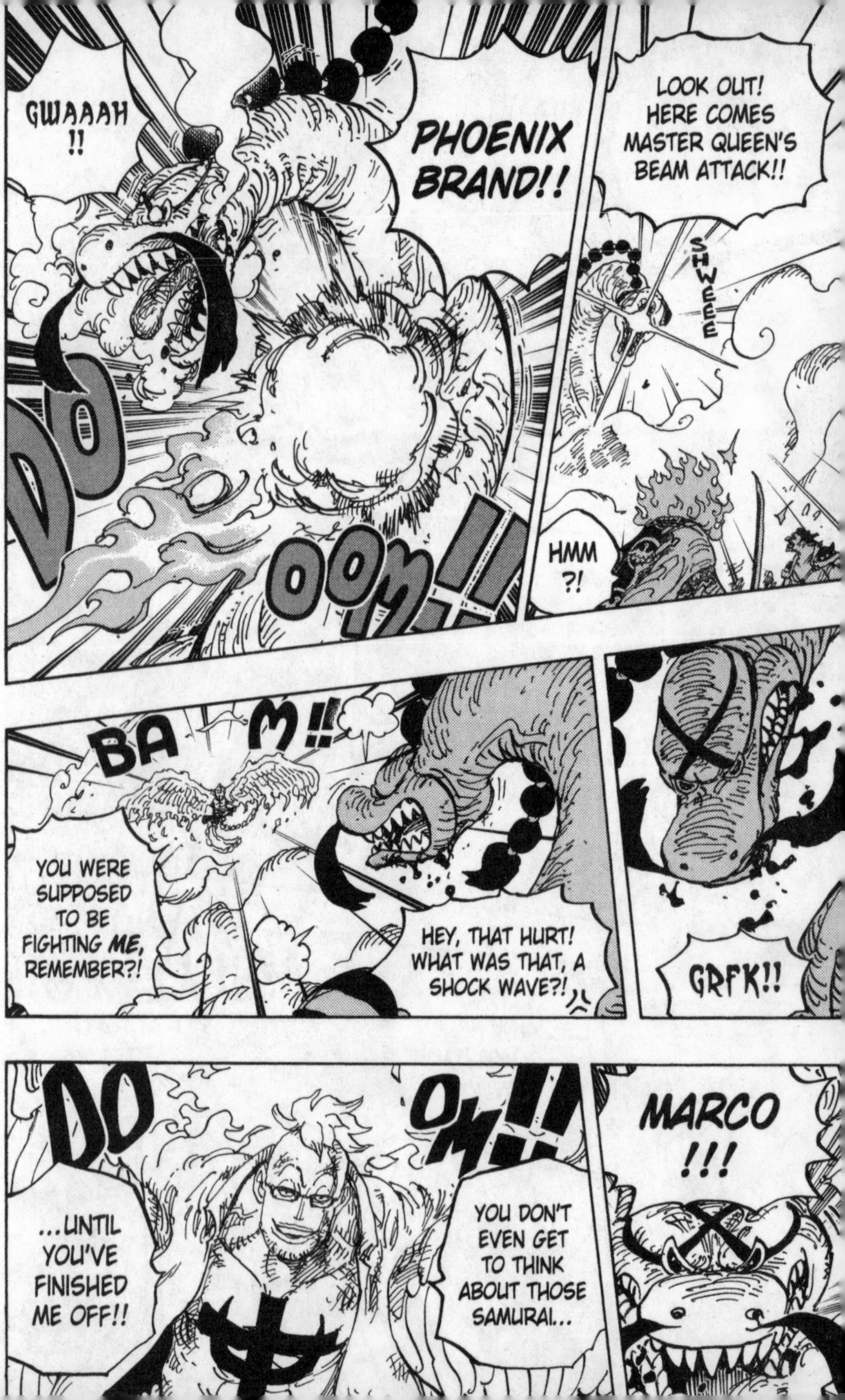
LOOK OUT! HERE COMES MASTER QUEEN'S BEAM ATTACK!!
SHWEEE
HMM ?!
PHOENIX BRAND!!
GWAAAH !!
DOOOM!!
GRFK!!
BAM!!
HEY, THAT HURT! WHAT WAS THAT, A SHOCK WAVE?!
YOU WERE SUPPOSED TO BE FIGHTING *ME*, REMEMBER?!
MARCO !!!
DOOM!!
YOU DON'T EVEN GET TO THINK ABOUT THOSE SAMURAI...
...UNTIL YOU'VE FINISHED ME OFF!!

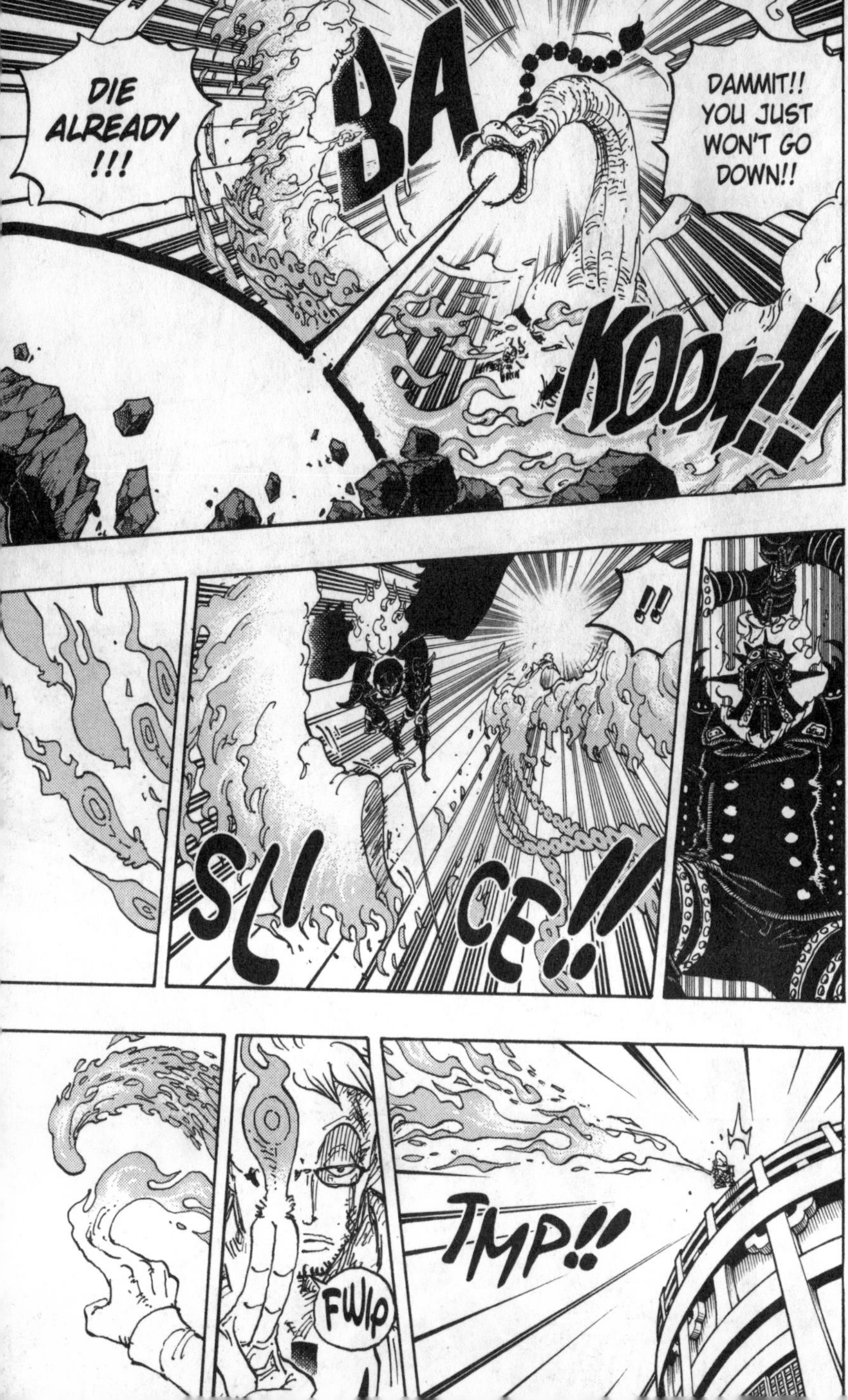
DAMMIT!! YOU JUST WON'T GO DOWN!!
DIE ALREADY!!!
BA
KOOM!!
!!
SLICE!!
TMP!!
FWIP

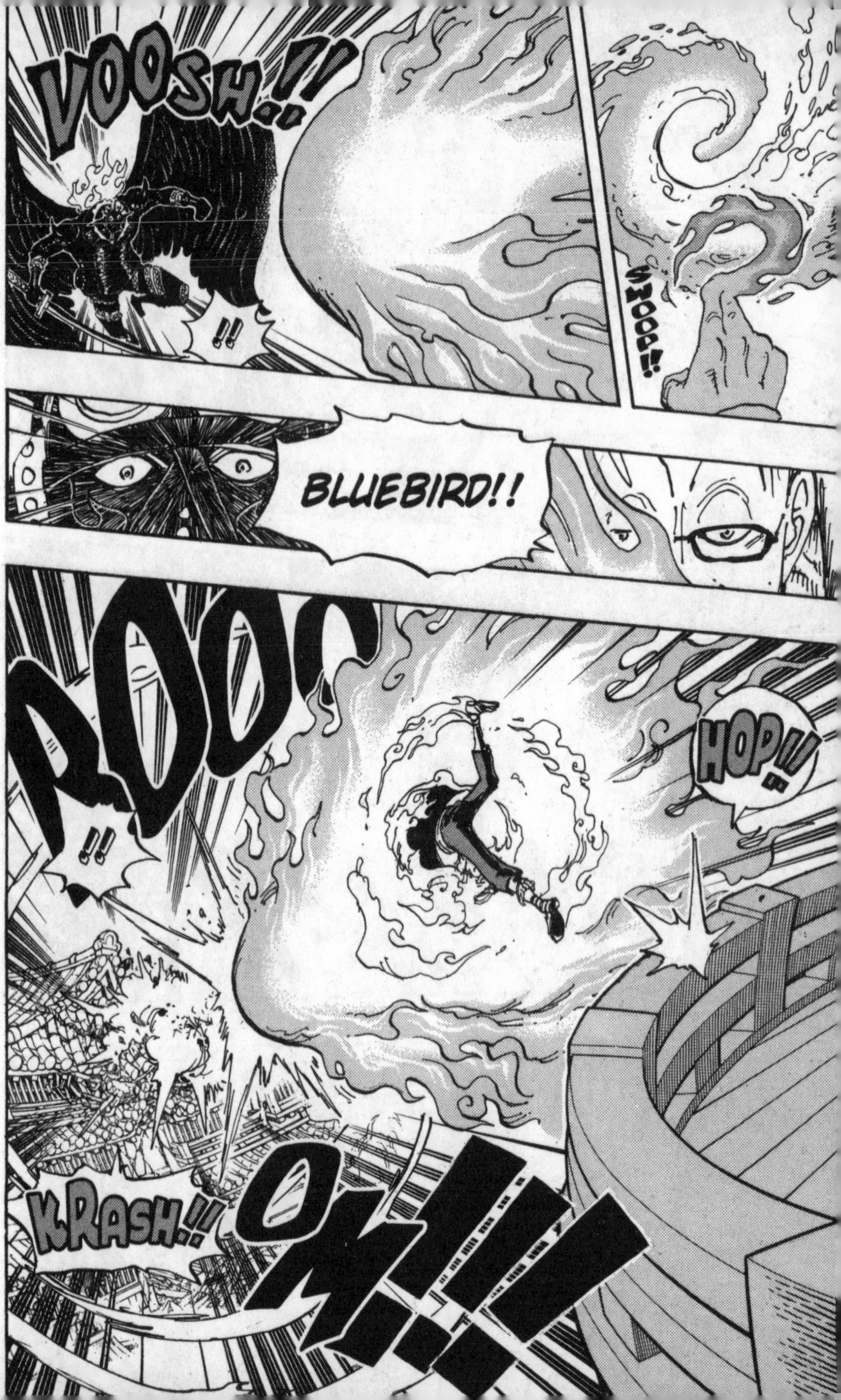

SWOOP!!
VOOSH!!
!!
BLUEBIRD!!
HOP!!
RDOOOM!!!
!!
KRASH!!

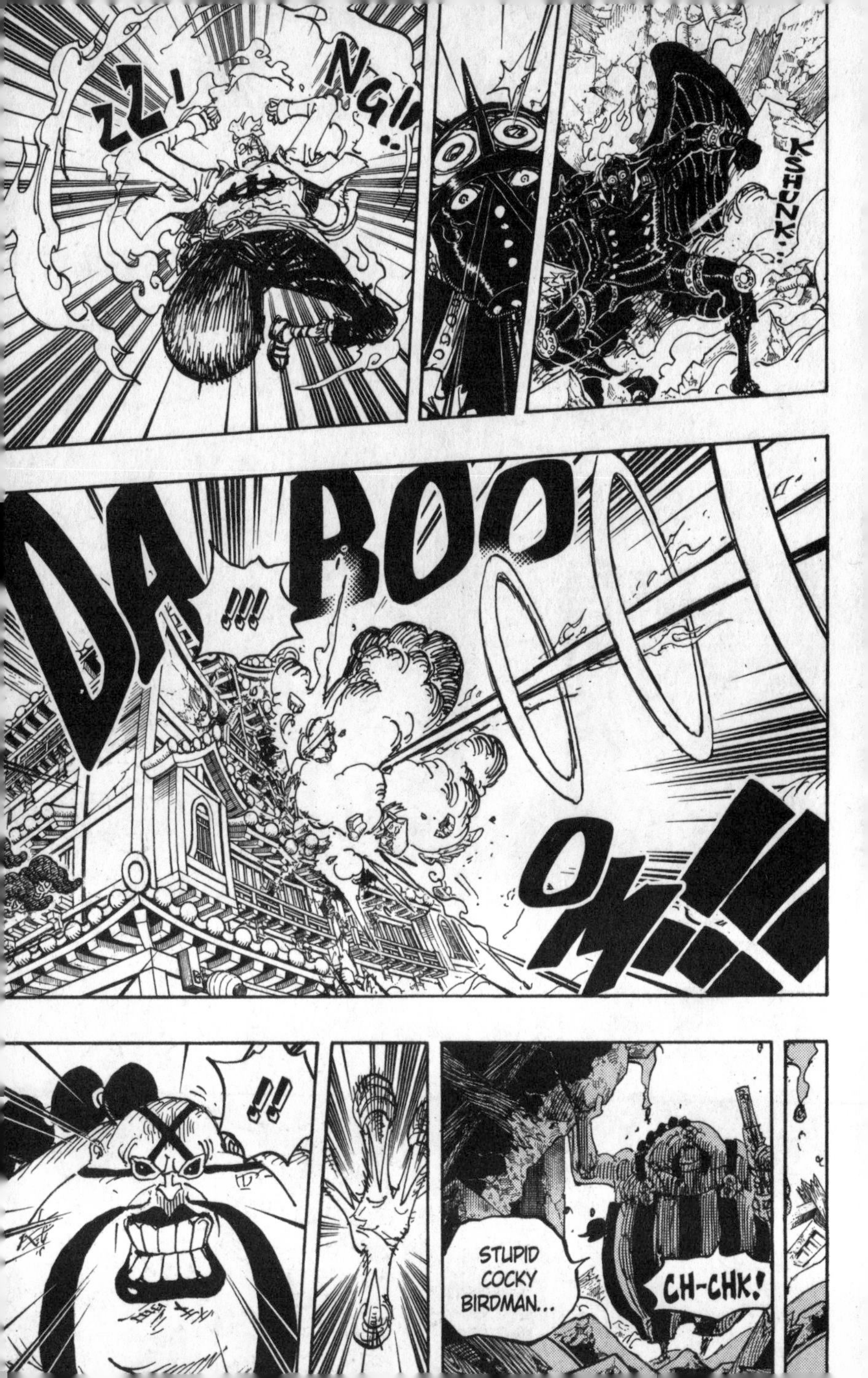
KSHUNK...
ZZI NGII..
DA!!!
BOO
OM!!!
STUPID COCKY BIRDMAN...
CH-CHK!
!!

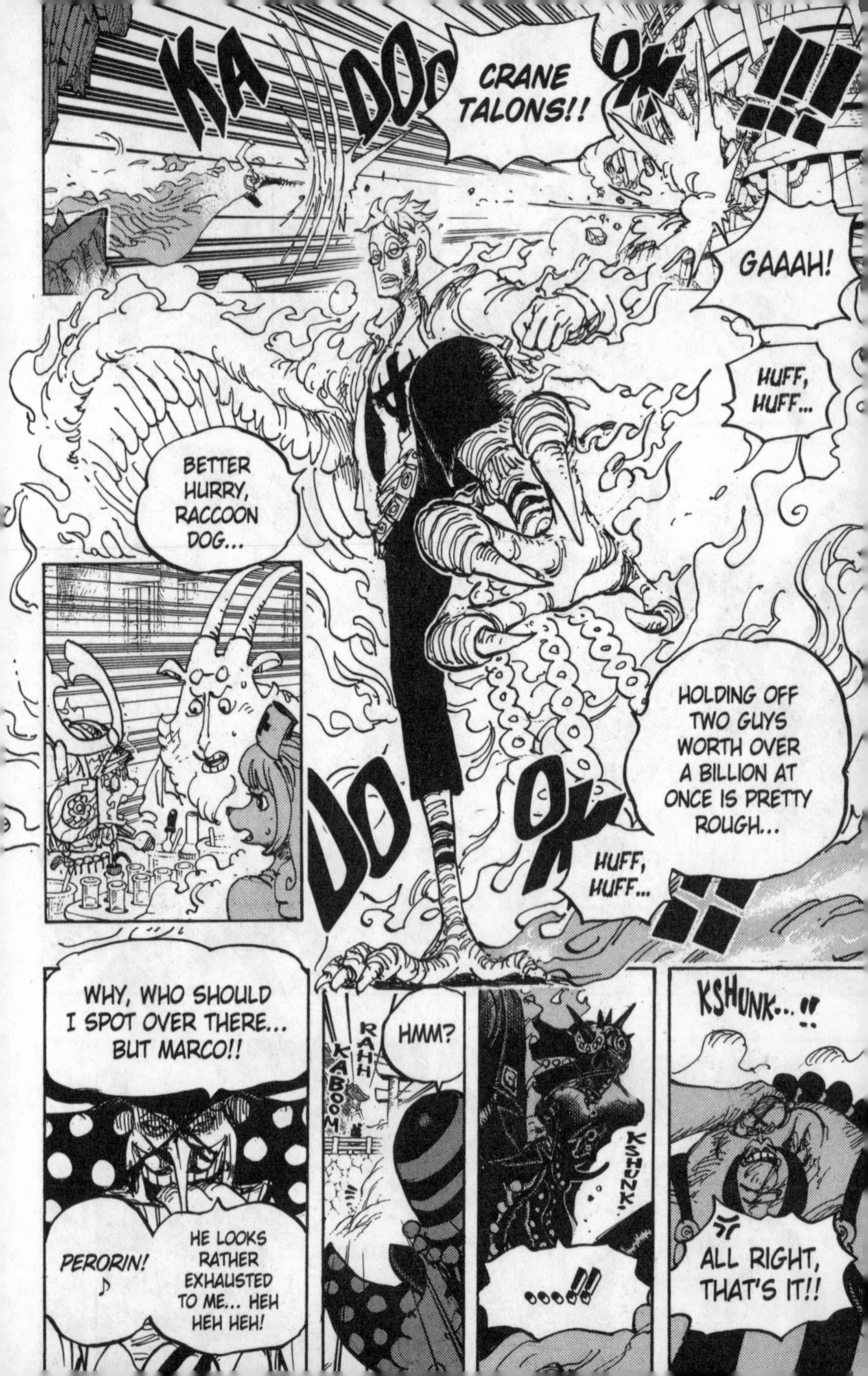
KA-DOOOK!!!
CRANE TALONS!!
GAAAH!
HUFF, HUFF...
BETTER HURRY, RACCOON DOG...
HOLDING OFF TWO GUYS WORTH OVER A BILLION AT ONCE IS PRETTY ROUGH...
DOOK!!
HUFF, HUFF...
KSHUNK...!!
ALL RIGHT, THAT'S IT!!
KSHUNK!
....!!
HMM?
RAHH
KABOOM
WHY, WHO SHOULD I SPOT OVER THERE... BUT MARCO!!
HE LOOKS RATHER EXHAUSTED TO ME... HEH HEH HEH!
PERORIN! ♪

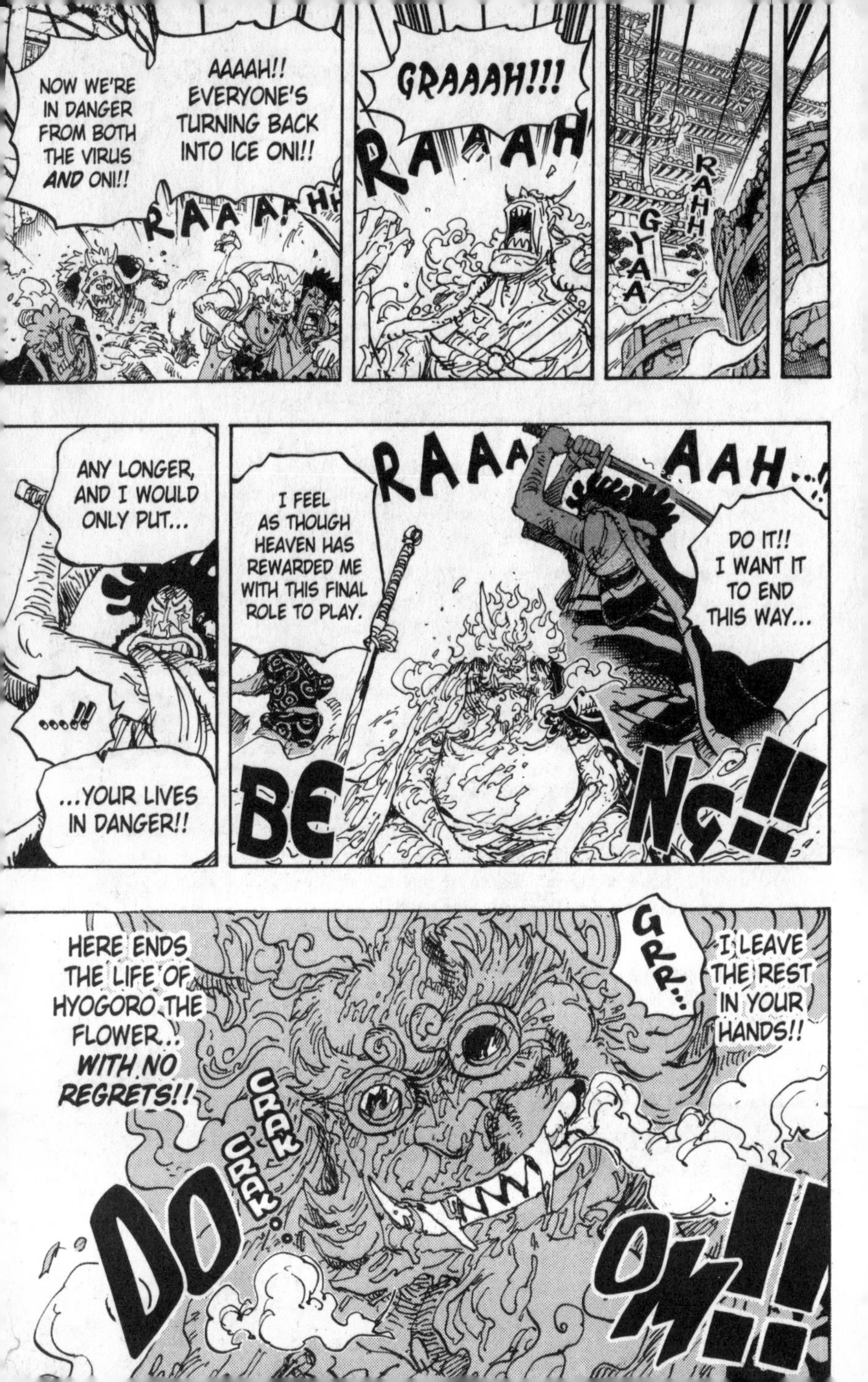
RAHH
GYAA
GRAAAH!!!
RAAAAH
AAAAH!! EVERYONE'S TURNING BACK INTO ICE ONI!!
NOW WE'RE IN DANGER FROM BOTH THE VIRUS AND ONI!!
RAAAAHH
RAAA AAH...!!
DO IT!! I WANT IT TO END THIS WAY...
I FEEL AS THOUGH HEAVEN HAS REWARDED ME WITH THIS FINAL ROLE TO PLAY.
BENG!!
ANY LONGER, AND I WOULD ONLY PUT...
....!!
...YOUR LIVES IN DANGER!!
GRR...
I LEAVE THE REST IN YOUR HANDS!!
HERE ENDS THE LIFE OF HYOGORO THE FLOWER... WITH NO REGRETS!!
CRACK CRACK CRACK
DOOM!!

SBS Question Corner

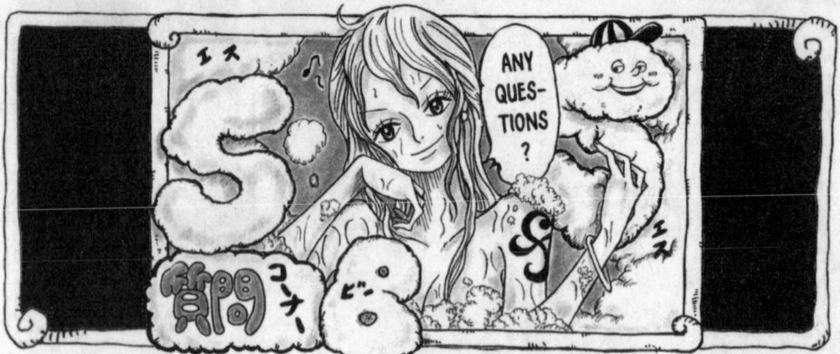
ANY QUES- TIONS ?
質問コーナー

(Sasaaki, Okinawa)

Q: Oda Sensei! There's a hot, stacked babe riding a UFO over there! Okay, now that he's gone, let's kick off the 100-volume milestone and start the SBS!!

--One Hundred

A: Aaaaah!!! It started already!!!
Excuse me! You can't do this! I mean, you gotta let me have this one...right?! It's volume 100, you know?! Weez, weez... Also... there was no hot stacked babe!!

Q: You mentioned that you wanted the PTA to like you in volume 99. This obviously will never happen and it would be pointless to even try, so I think you should draw a personification of Robin's ππ please.

--Doctor Heart Starer

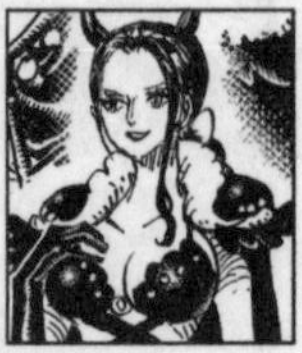

A: I will never!!! And don't talk about boobs in volume 100!! Geez! Okay, all you folks who thought, "Maybe for volume 100, I'll try reading this SBS thing for the very first time"? Please believe me, it's not always like this. Next one is a serious comment!

Q: I was having sleepless nights wondering what the title of chapter 1000 would be. Initially I thought it would be an homage to chapter 100, but it turned out to be chapter 2. "Straw Hat Luffy." It gave me chills! That's a much better title than my idea, "Yamato's Side-boob."

--Wetty

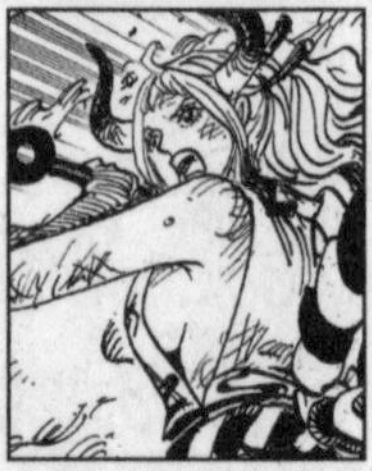

A: I would never!! Oh!! Sorry, I got a little out of sorts!! Hmm, maybe I spoke too early about this comment. Wait a second, I think this next person is going to help fix up this segment!

Q: I'm very worried about the direction this segment is going. So let me straighten things out!
I would like to engage in close contact with Nami!

--Sanadacchi

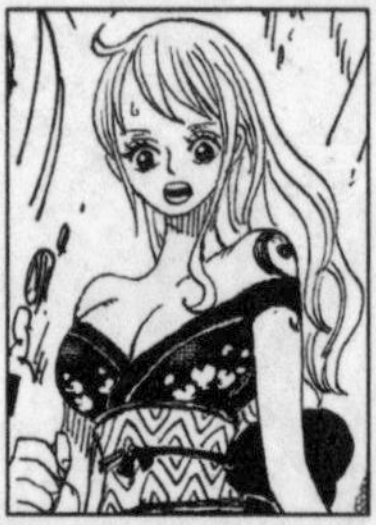

A: Sanadaaaaa!!!
Get out of here, you sickos!!! This is the worst page ever!!

Chapter 1007:
MR. RACCOON DOG

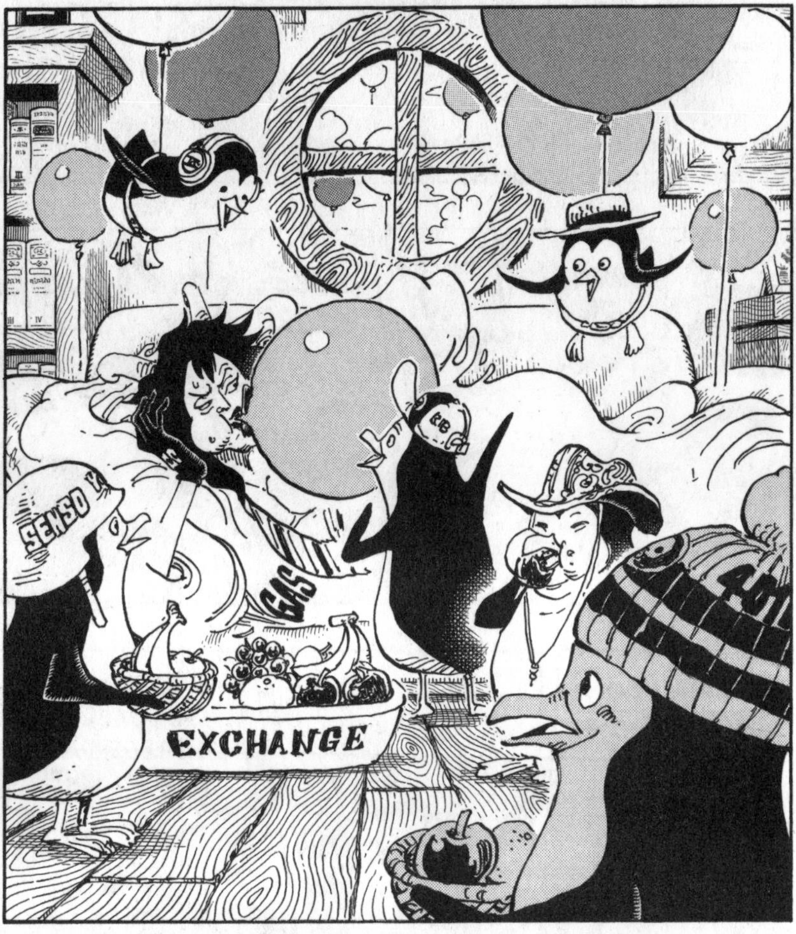
SENSO
GAS
EXCHANGE

READER REQUEST: "CAESAR GIVING PENGUIN CHILDREN GAS-FILLED BALLOONS" BY TKE☆AC

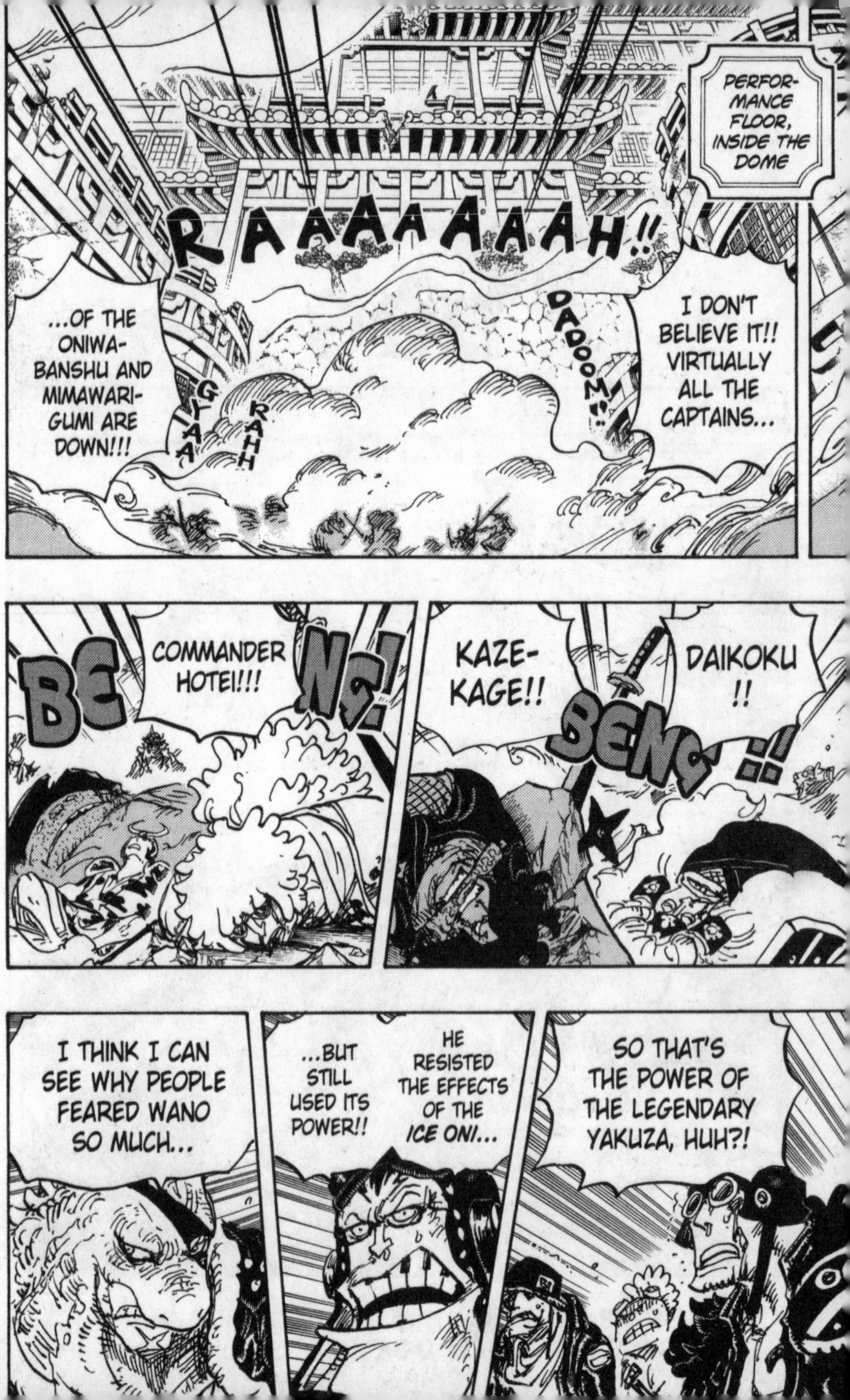
PERFORMANCE FLOOR, INSIDE THE DOME
RAAAAAAAAH!!
I DON'T BELIEVE IT!! VIRTUALLY ALL THE CAPTAINS...
DADOOM!!
...OF THE ONIWABANSHU AND MIMAWARIGUMI ARE DOWN!!!
RAHH
GYAAA
DAIKOKU !!
KAZE-KAGE!!
BENG!!
COMMANDER HOTEI!!!
BENG!
SO THAT'S THE POWER OF THE LEGENDARY YAKUZA, HUH?!
HE RESISTED THE EFFECTS OF THE *ICE ONI*...
...BUT STILL USED ITS POWER!!
I THINK I CAN SEE WHY PEOPLE FEARED WANO SO MUCH...

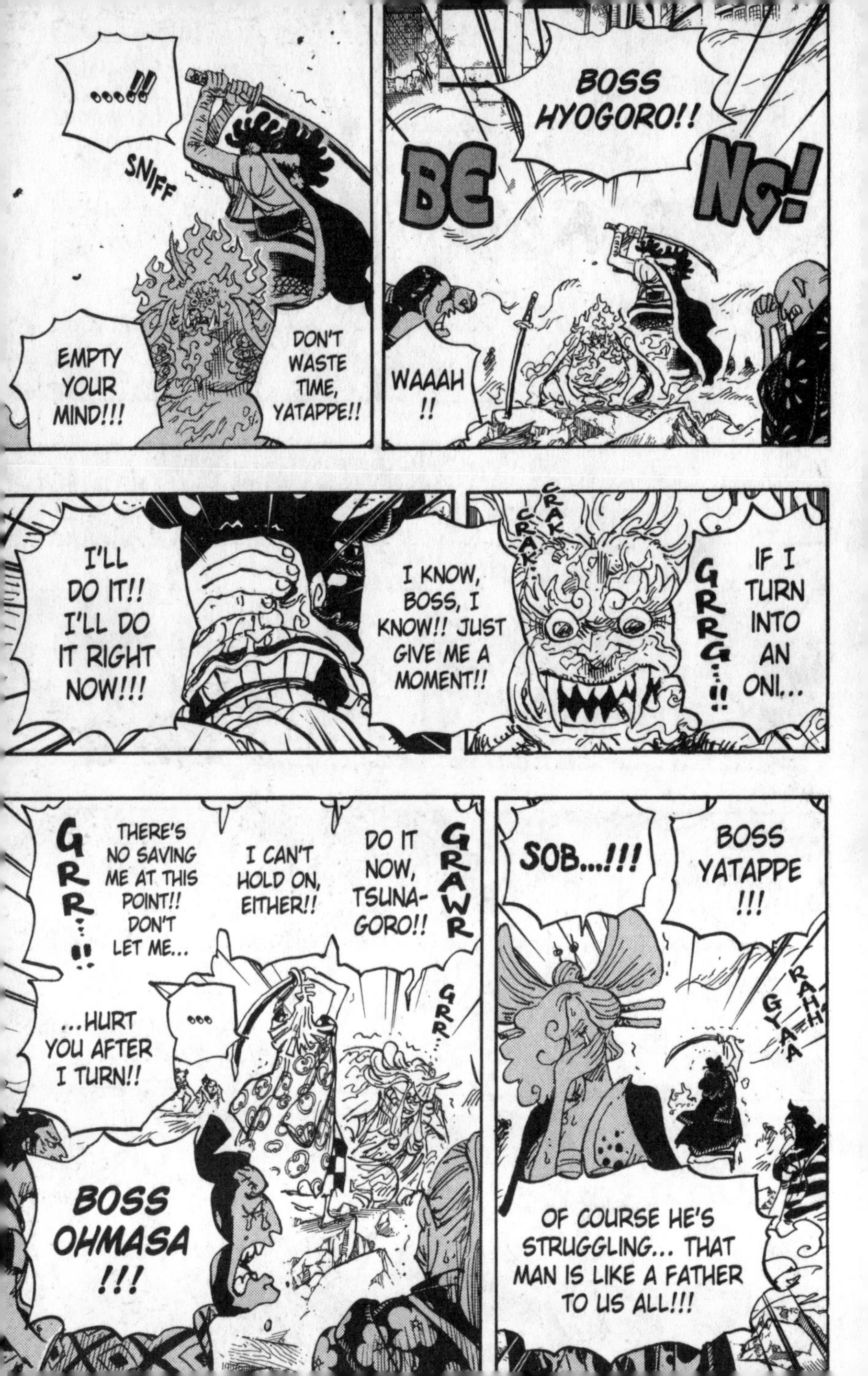
BOSS HYOGORO!!
BENG!
WAAAH!!
...!!
SNIFF
DON'T WASTE TIME, YATAPPE!!
EMPTY YOUR MIND!!!
IF I TURN INTO AN ONI...
GRRG...!!
CRAK CRAK
I KNOW, BOSS, I KNOW!! JUST GIVE ME A MOMENT!!
I'LL DO IT!! I'LL DO IT RIGHT NOW!!!
BOSS YATAPPE!!!
SOB...!!!
GYAAA RAHH
OF COURSE HE'S STRUGGLING... THAT MAN IS LIKE A FATHER TO US ALL!!!
DO IT NOW, TSUNAGORO!!
GRAWR
I CAN'T HOLD ON, EITHER!!
THERE'S NO SAVING ME AT THIS POINT!! DON'T LET ME...
GRR...!!
...HURT YOU AFTER I TURN!!
...
GRR...
BOSS OHMASA!!!

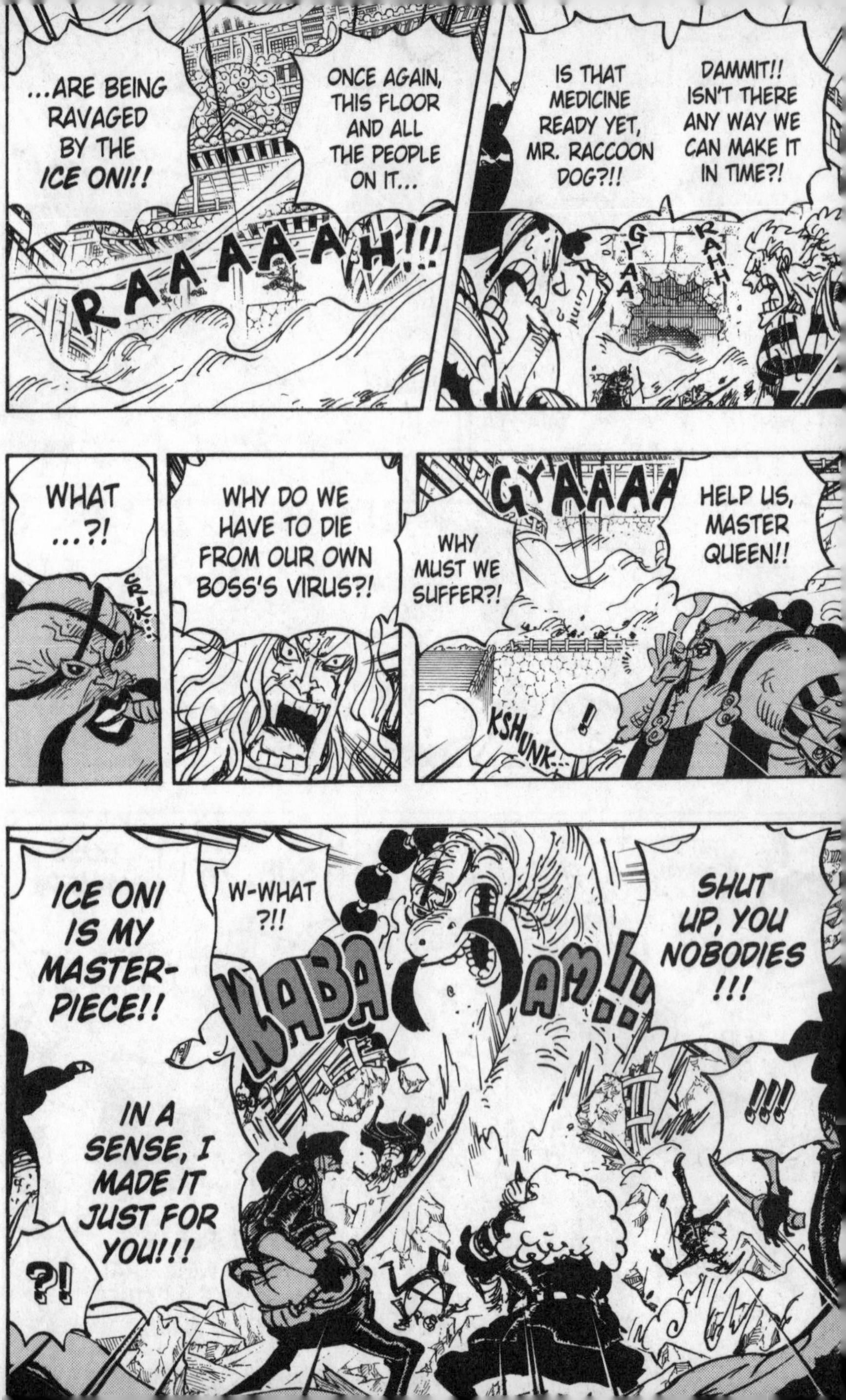
DAMMIT!! ISN'T THERE ANY WAY WE CAN MAKE IT IN TIME?!
IS THAT MEDICINE READY YET, MR. RACCOON DOG?!!
RAHH
GYAA
ONCE AGAIN, THIS FLOOR AND ALL THE PEOPLE ON IT...
...ARE BEING RAVAGED BY THE ICE ONI!!
RAAAAAH!!!
HELP US, MASTER QUEEN!!
GYAAAA
WHY MUST WE SUFFER?!
!
KSHUNK...
WHY DO WE HAVE TO DIE FROM OUR OWN BOSS'S VIRUS?!
WHAT ...?!
CRIK...
SHUT UP, YOU NOBODIES!!!
W-WHAT ?!!
ICE ONI IS MY MASTER-PIECE!!
KABAAM!!
!!!
IN A SENSE, I MADE IT JUST FOR YOU!!!
?!

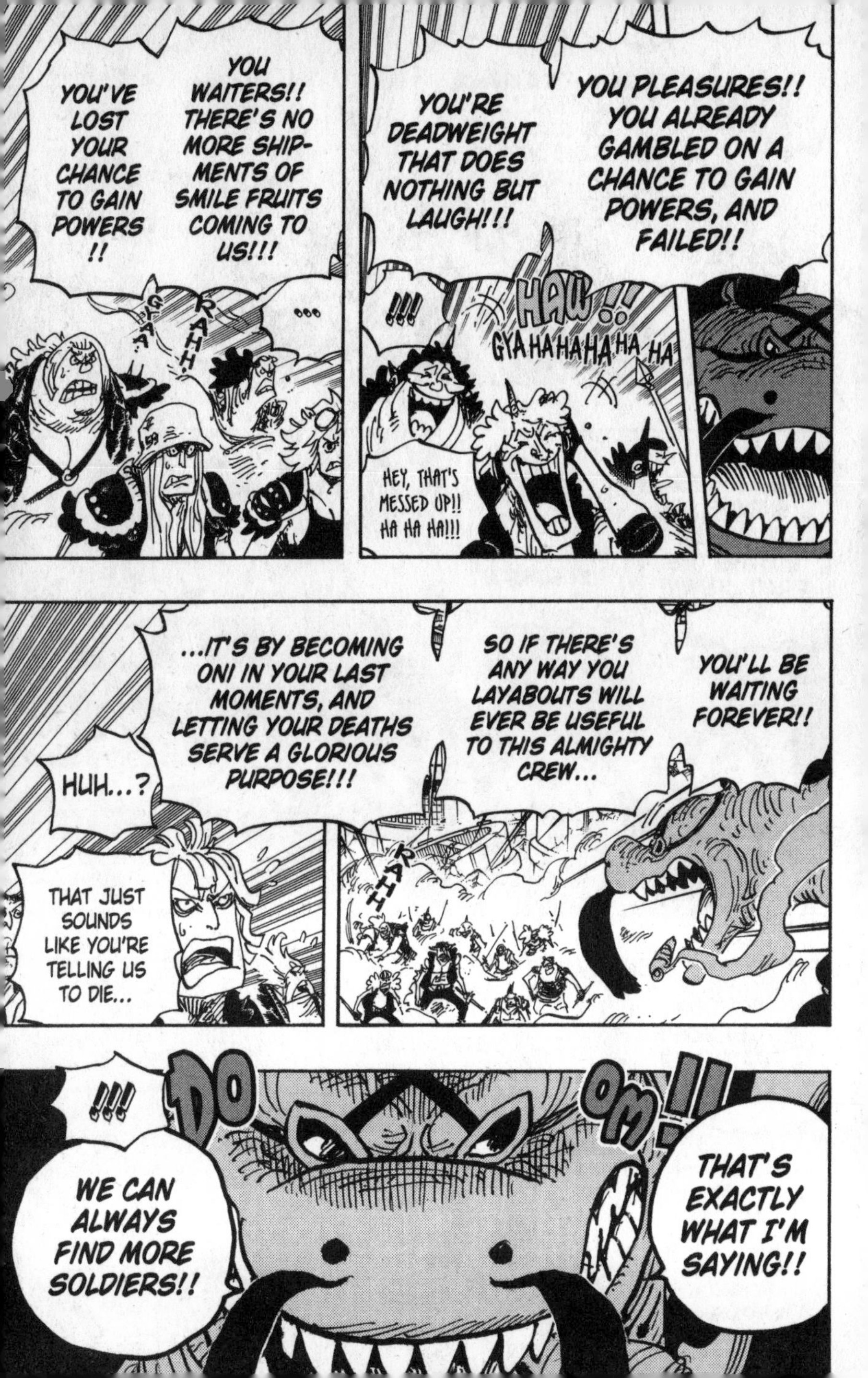
YOU PLEASURES!! YOU ALREADY GAMBLED ON A CHANCE TO GAIN POWERS, AND FAILED!!
YOU'RE DEADWEIGHT THAT DOES NOTHING BUT LAUGH!!!
HAW!!
!!!
GYAHAHAHAHAHA HA
HEY, THAT'S MESSED UP!! HA HA HA!!!
YOU WAITERS!! THERE'S NO MORE SHIPMENTS OF SMILE FRUITS COMING TO US!!!
YOU'VE LOST YOUR CHANCE TO GAIN POWERS!!
...
RAHH!
GYAA
YOU'LL BE WAITING FOREVER!!
SO IF THERE'S ANY WAY YOU LAYABOUTS WILL EVER BE USEFUL TO THIS ALMIGHTY CREW...
...IT'S BY BECOMING ONI IN YOUR LAST MOMENTS, AND LETTING YOUR DEATHS SERVE A GLORIOUS PURPOSE!!!
HUH...?
RAHH
THAT JUST SOUNDS LIKE YOU'RE TELLING US TO DIE...
DOOM!!
THAT'S EXACTLY WHAT I'M SAYING!!
!!!
WE CAN ALWAYS FIND MORE SOLDIERS!!

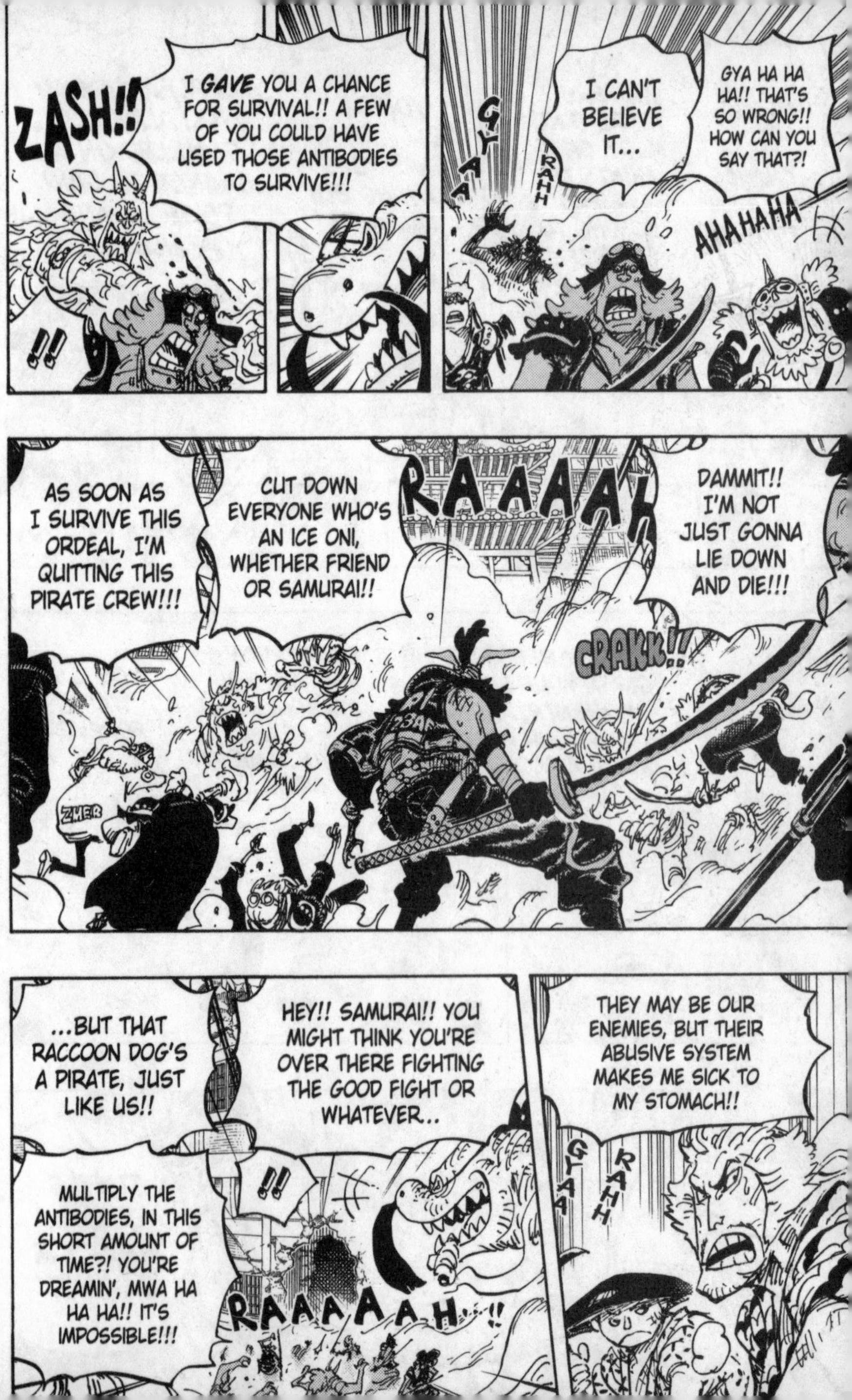
GYA HA HA HA!! THAT'S SO WRONG!! HOW CAN YOU SAY THAT?!
I CAN'T BELIEVE IT...
GYAAA
RAHH
AHAHAHA
I GAVE YOU A CHANCE FOR SURVIVAL!! A FEW OF YOU COULD HAVE USED THOSE ANTIBODIES TO SURVIVE!!!
ZASH!!
!!
DAMMIT!! I'M NOT JUST GONNA LIE DOWN AND DIE!!!
RAAAAH
CUT DOWN EVERYONE WHO'S AN ICE ONI, WHETHER FRIEND OR SAMURAI!!
AS SOON AS I SURVIVE THIS ORDEAL, I'M QUITTING THIS PIRATE CREW!!!
CRAKK!!
ZHER
THEY MAY BE OUR ENEMIES, BUT THEIR ABUSIVE SYSTEM MAKES ME SICK TO MY STOMACH!!
GYAAA
RAHH
HEY!! SAMURAI!! YOU MIGHT THINK YOU'RE OVER THERE FIGHTING THE GOOD FIGHT OR WHATEVER...
...BUT THAT RACCOON DOG'S A PIRATE, JUST LIKE US!!
!!
MULTIPLY THE ANTIBODIES, IN THIS SHORT AMOUNT OF TIME?! YOU'RE DREAMIN', MWA HA HA HA!! IT'S IMPOSSIBLE!!!
RAAAAAH!!

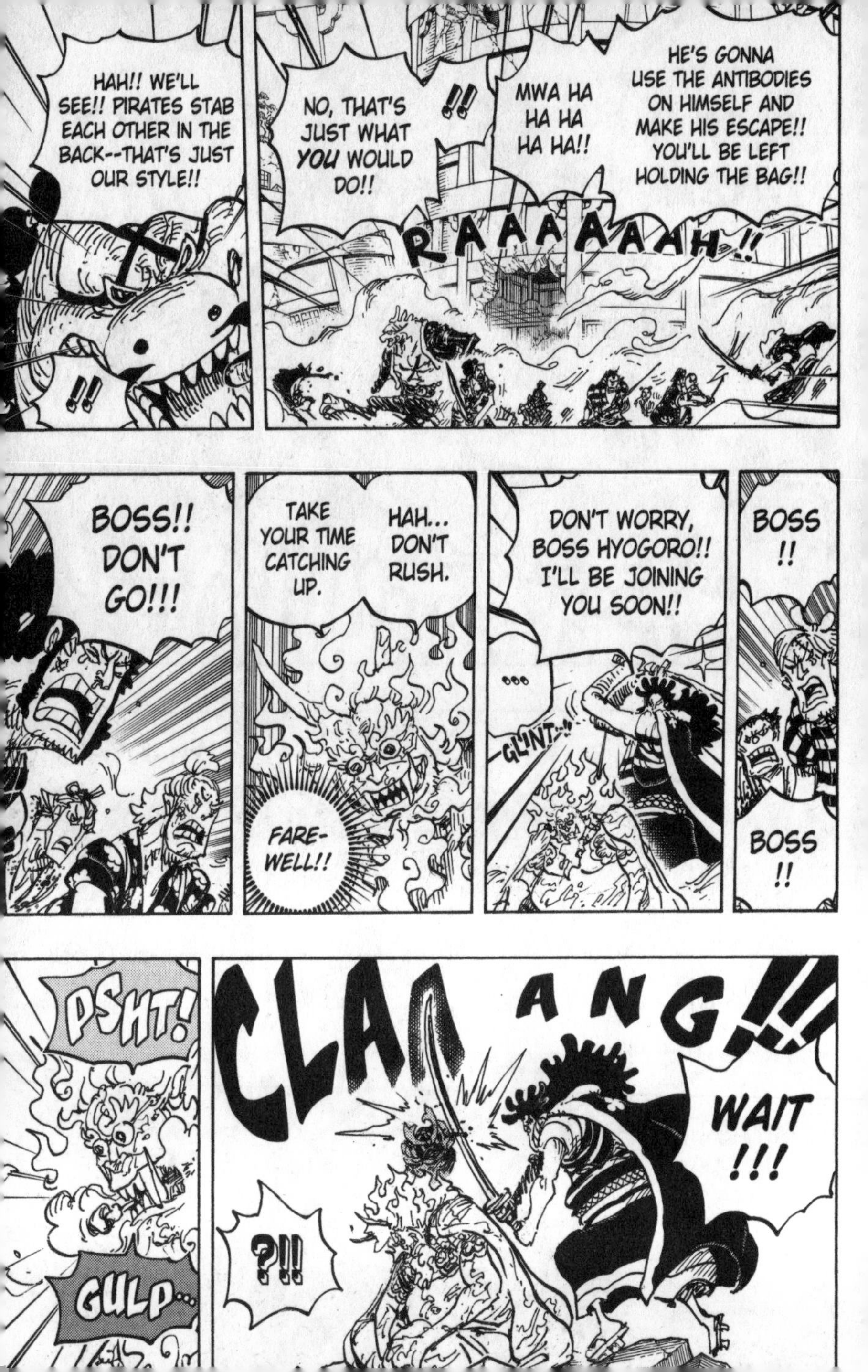
HE'S GONNA USE THE ANTIBODIES ON HIMSELF AND MAKE HIS ESCAPE!! YOU'LL BE LEFT HOLDING THE BAG!!
MWA HA HA HA HA HA!!
!!
NO, THAT'S JUST WHAT YOU WOULD DO!!
RAAAAAAH!!
HAH!! WE'LL SEE!! PIRATES STAB EACH OTHER IN THE BACK--THAT'S JUST OUR STYLE!!
!!
BOSS !!
BOSS !!
DON'T WORRY, BOSS HYOGORO!! I'LL BE JOINING YOU SOON!!
GLINT!!
...
HAH... DON'T RUSH.
TAKE YOUR TIME CATCHING UP.
FARE-WELL!!
BOSS!! DON'T GO!!!
CLAAANG!!!
WAIT !!!
?!!
PSHT!
GULP...

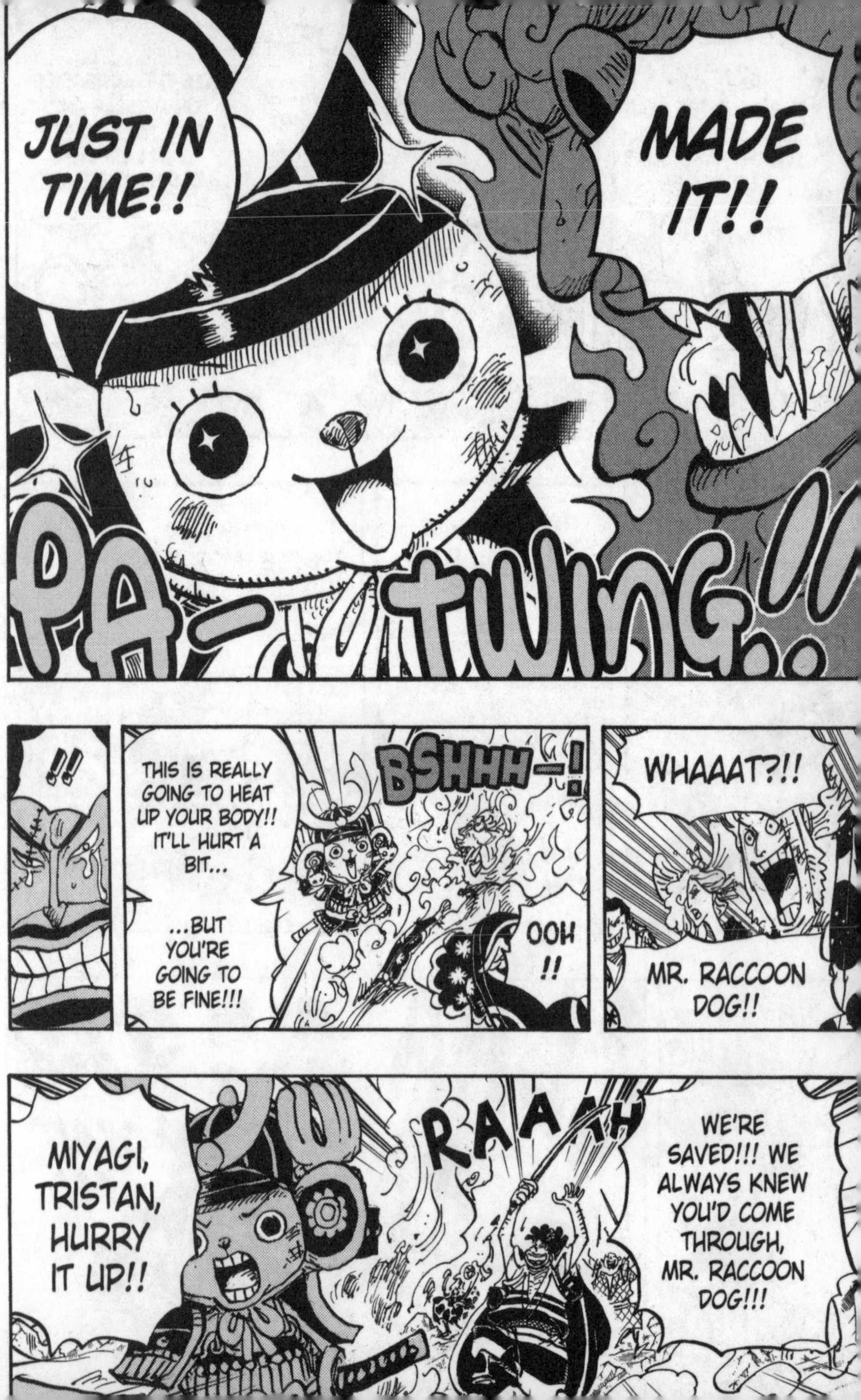
MADE IT!!
JUST IN TIME!!
PA-TWING..!!
WHAAAT?!!
MR. RACCOON DOG!!
BSHHH-!
THIS IS REALLY GOING TO HEAT UP YOUR BODY!! IT'LL HURT A BIT...
OOH!!
...BUT YOU'RE GOING TO BE FINE!!!
!!
WE'RE SAVED!!! WE ALWAYS KNEW YOU'D COME THROUGH, MR. RACCOON DOG!!!
RAAAH
MIYAGI, TRISTAN, HURRY IT UP!!

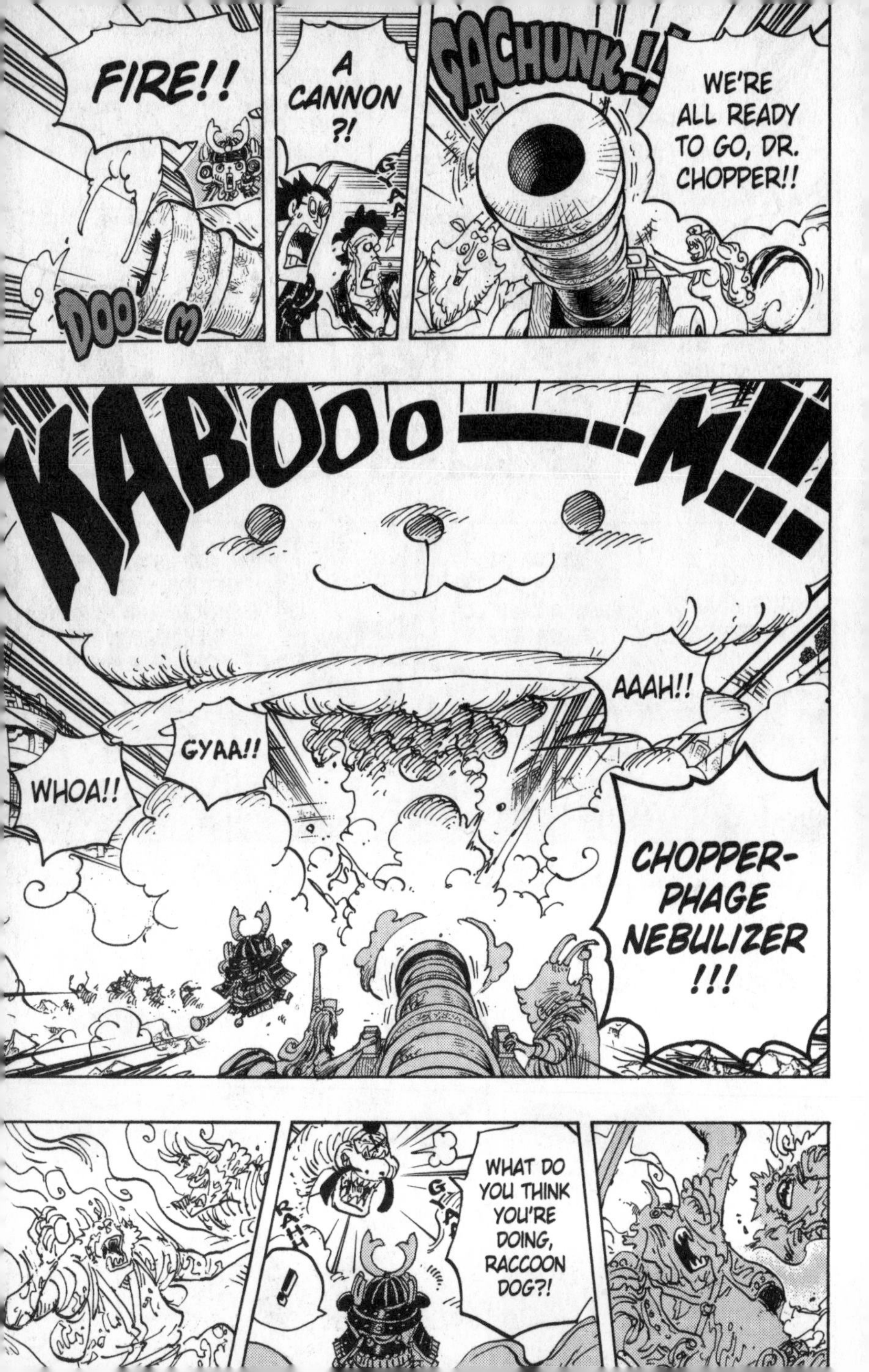
GACHUNK!!
WE'RE ALL READY TO GO, DR. CHOPPER!!
A CANNON ?!
GYAA
FIRE!!
DOOM
KABOOO—M!!
AAAH!!
CHOPPER-PHAGE NEBULIZER !!!
GYAA!!
WHOA!!
WHAT DO YOU THINK YOU'RE DOING, RACCOON DOG?!
GYAA
RAHH!

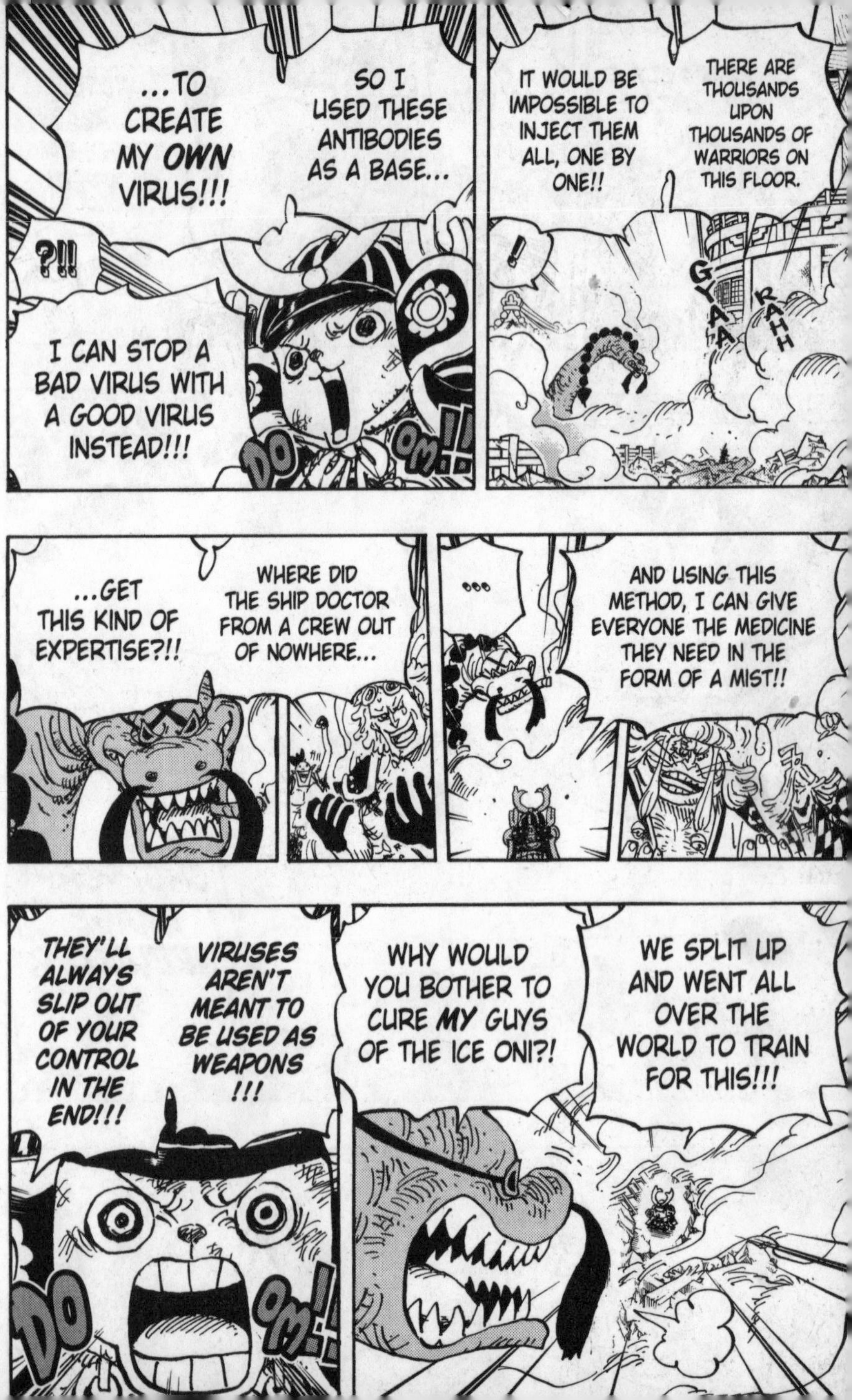
THERE ARE THOUSANDS UPON THOUSANDS OF WARRIORS ON THIS FLOOR.
IT WOULD BE IMPOSSIBLE TO INJECT THEM ALL, ONE BY ONE!!
!
GYAAA
RAHH
SO I USED THESE ANTIBODIES AS A BASE...
...TO CREATE MY OWN VIRUS!!!
?!!
I CAN STOP A BAD VIRUS WITH A GOOD VIRUS INSTEAD!!!
DOOM!!
AND USING THIS METHOD, I CAN GIVE EVERYONE THE MEDICINE THEY NEED IN THE FORM OF A MIST!!
...
WHERE DID THE SHIP DOCTOR FROM A CREW OUT OF NOWHERE...
...GET THIS KIND OF EXPERTISE?!!
WE SPLIT UP AND WENT ALL OVER THE WORLD TO TRAIN FOR THIS!!!
WHY WOULD YOU BOTHER TO CURE MY GUYS OF THE ICE ONI?!
VIRUSES AREN'T MEANT TO BE USED AS WEAPONS!!!
THEY'LL ALWAYS SLIP OUT OF YOUR CONTROL IN THE END!!!
DOOM!!

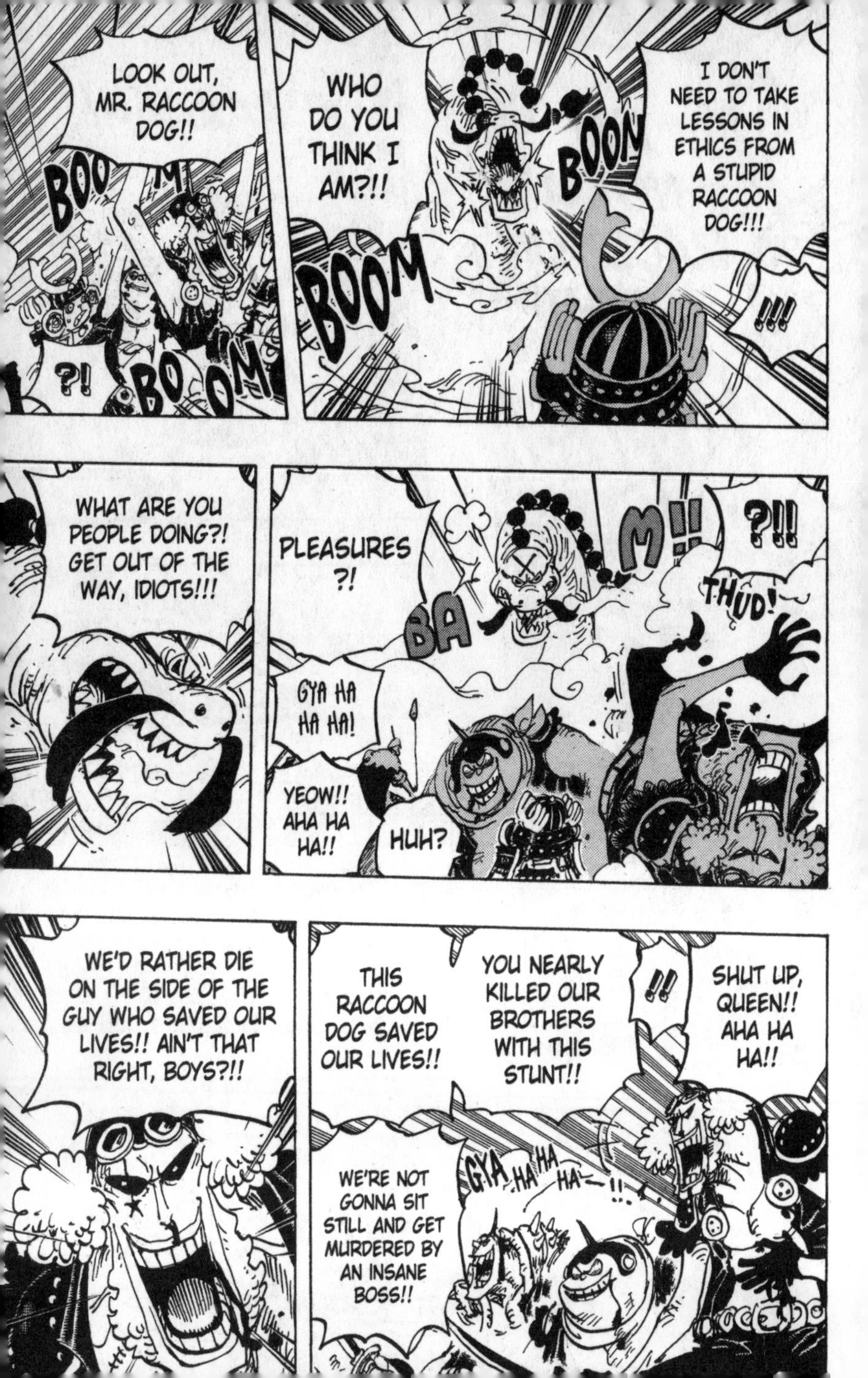
I DON'T NEED TO TAKE LESSONS IN ETHICS FROM A STUPID RACCOON DOG!!!
BOOM
WHO DO YOU THINK I AM?!!
!!!
BOOM
LOOK OUT, MR. RACCOON DOG!!
BOOM
?!
BOOM
?!!
BAM!!
THUD!
PLEASURES ?!
GYA HA HA HA!
HUH?
YEOW!! AHA HA HA!!
WHAT ARE YOU PEOPLE DOING?! GET OUT OF THE WAY, IDIOTS!!!
SHUT UP, QUEEN!! AHA HA HA!!
!!
YOU NEARLY KILLED OUR BROTHERS WITH THIS STUNT!!
THIS RACCOON DOG SAVED OUR LIVES!!
GYA HA HA HA—!!
WE'RE NOT GONNA SIT STILL AND GET MURDERED BY AN INSANE BOSS!!
WE'D RATHER DIE ON THE SIDE OF THE GUY WHO SAVED OUR LIVES!! AIN'T THAT RIGHT, BOYS?!!

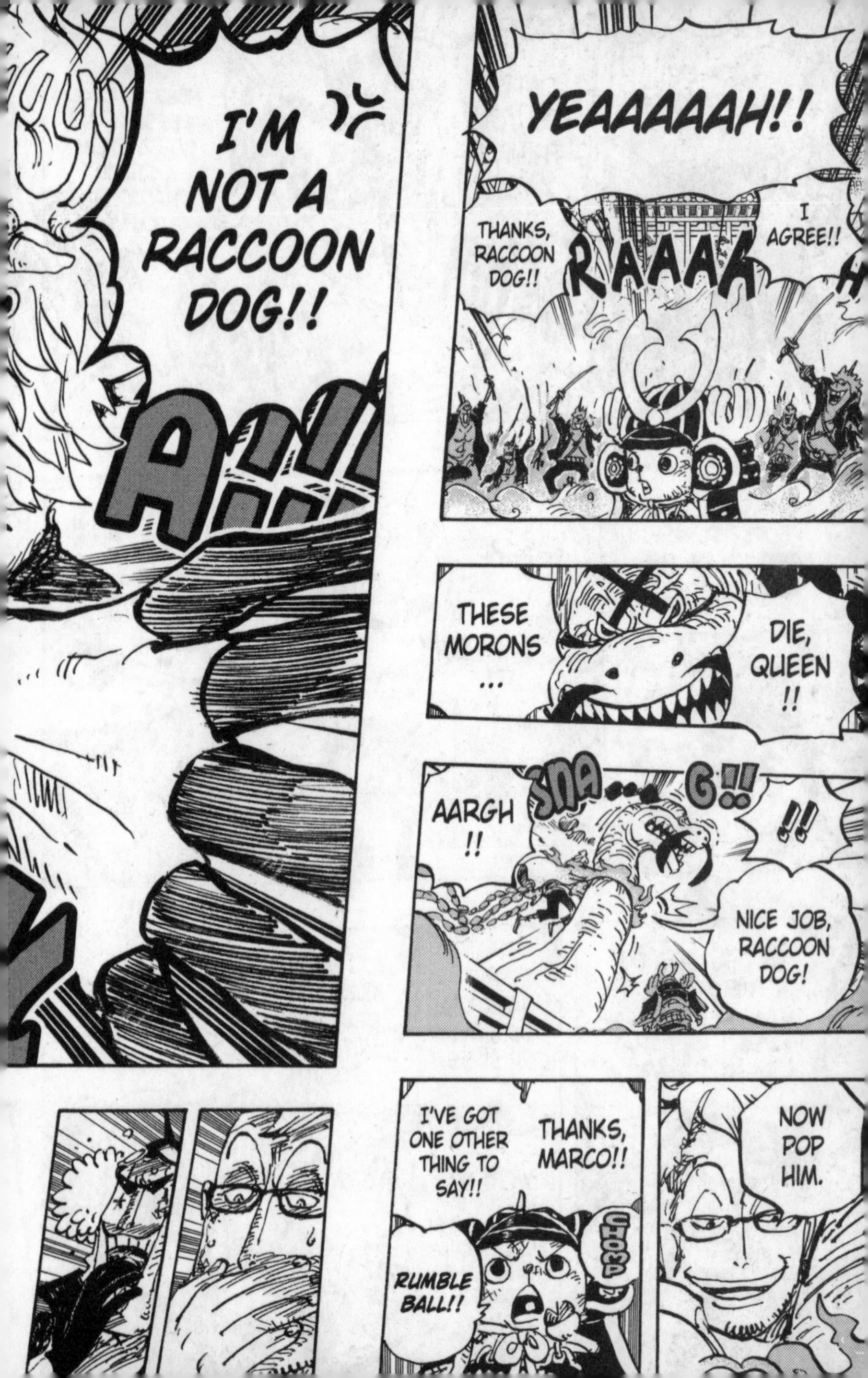
YEAAAAAH!!
I AGREE!!
THANKS, RACCOON DOG!!
DIE, QUEEN!!
THESE MORONS...
SNA...G!!
!!
AARGH!!
NICE JOB, RACCOON DOG!
I'M NOT A RACCOON DOG!!
NOW POP HIM.
THANKS, MARCO!!
I'VE GOT ONE OTHER THING TO SAY!!
CHOMP
RUMBLE BALL!!

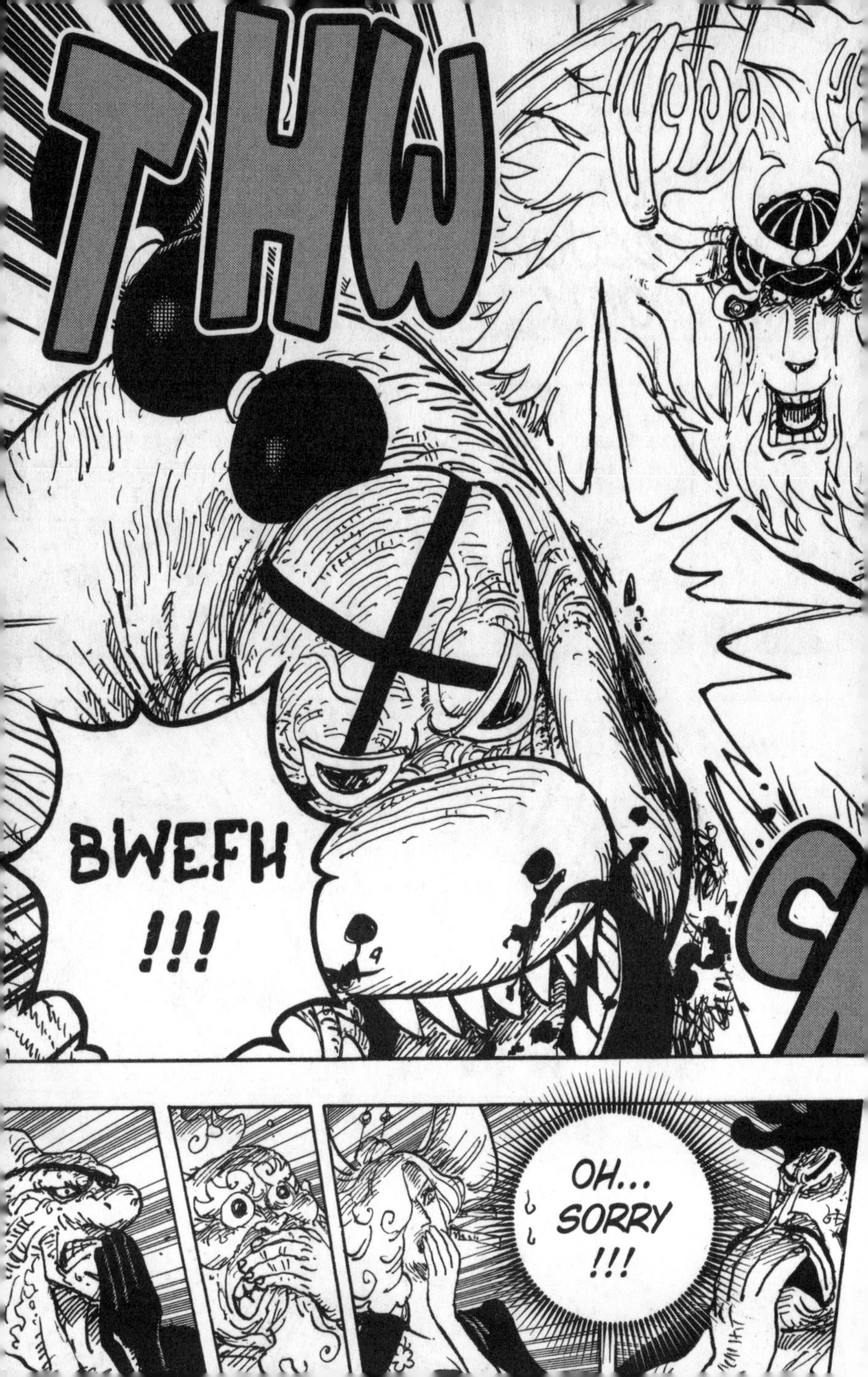
THW
BWEFH !!!
OH... SORRY !!!

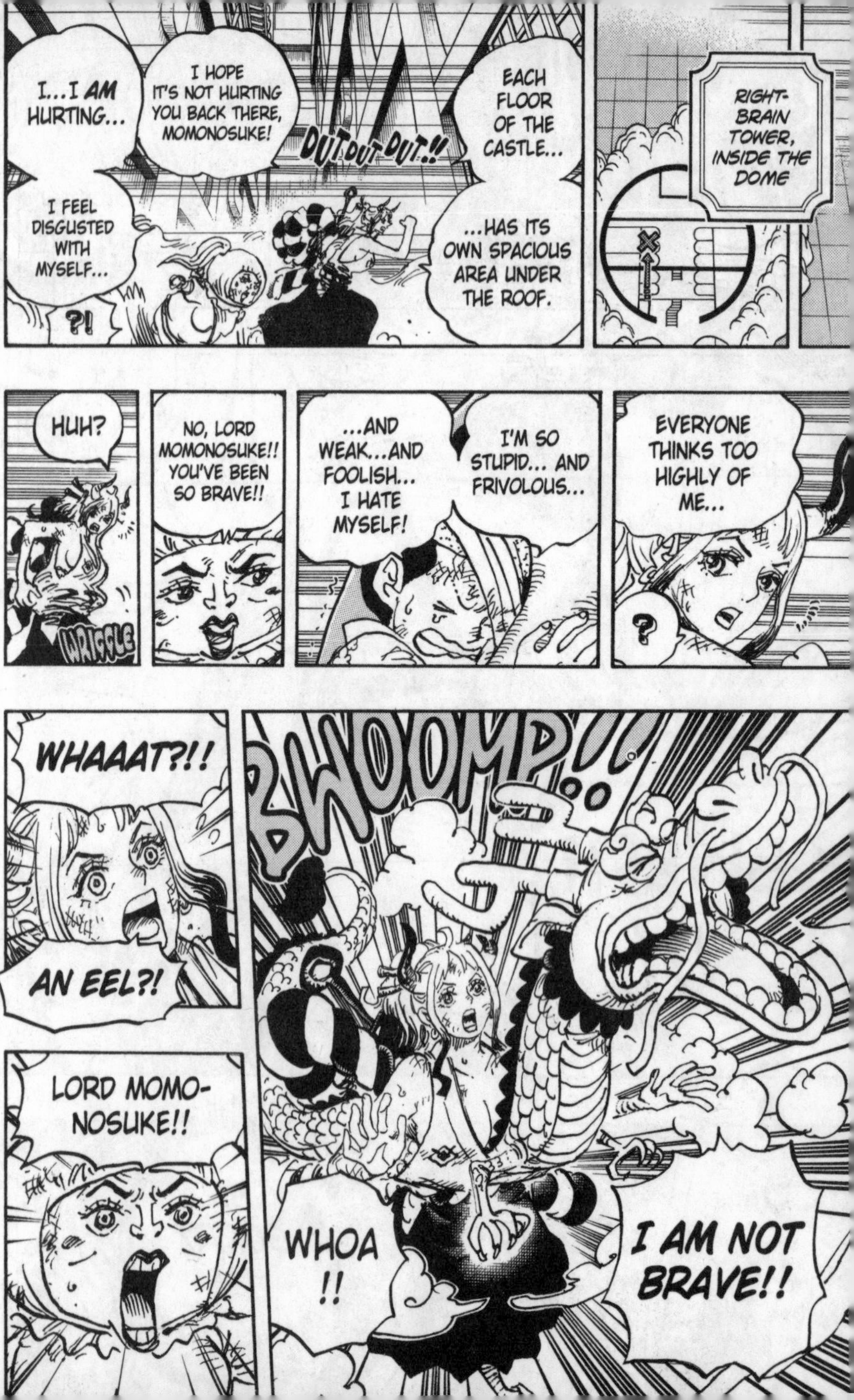
RIGHT-BRAIN TOWER, INSIDE THE DOME
EACH FLOOR OF THE CASTLE...
...HAS ITS OWN SPACIOUS AREA UNDER THE ROOF.
DUT DUT DUT!!
I HOPE IT'S NOT HURTING YOU BACK THERE, MOMONOSUKE!
I...I AM HURTING...
I FEEL DISGUSTED WITH MYSELF...
?!
EVERYONE THINKS TOO HIGHLY OF ME...
?
I'M SO STUPID... AND FRIVOLOUS...
...AND WEAK...AND FOOLISH... I HATE MYSELF!
NO, LORD MOMONOSUKE!! YOU'VE BEEN SO BRAVE!!
HUH?
WRIGGLE
BWOOMP!!
I AM NOT BRAVE!!
WHOA !!
WHAAAT?!!
AN EEL?!
LORD MOMO-NOSUKE!!

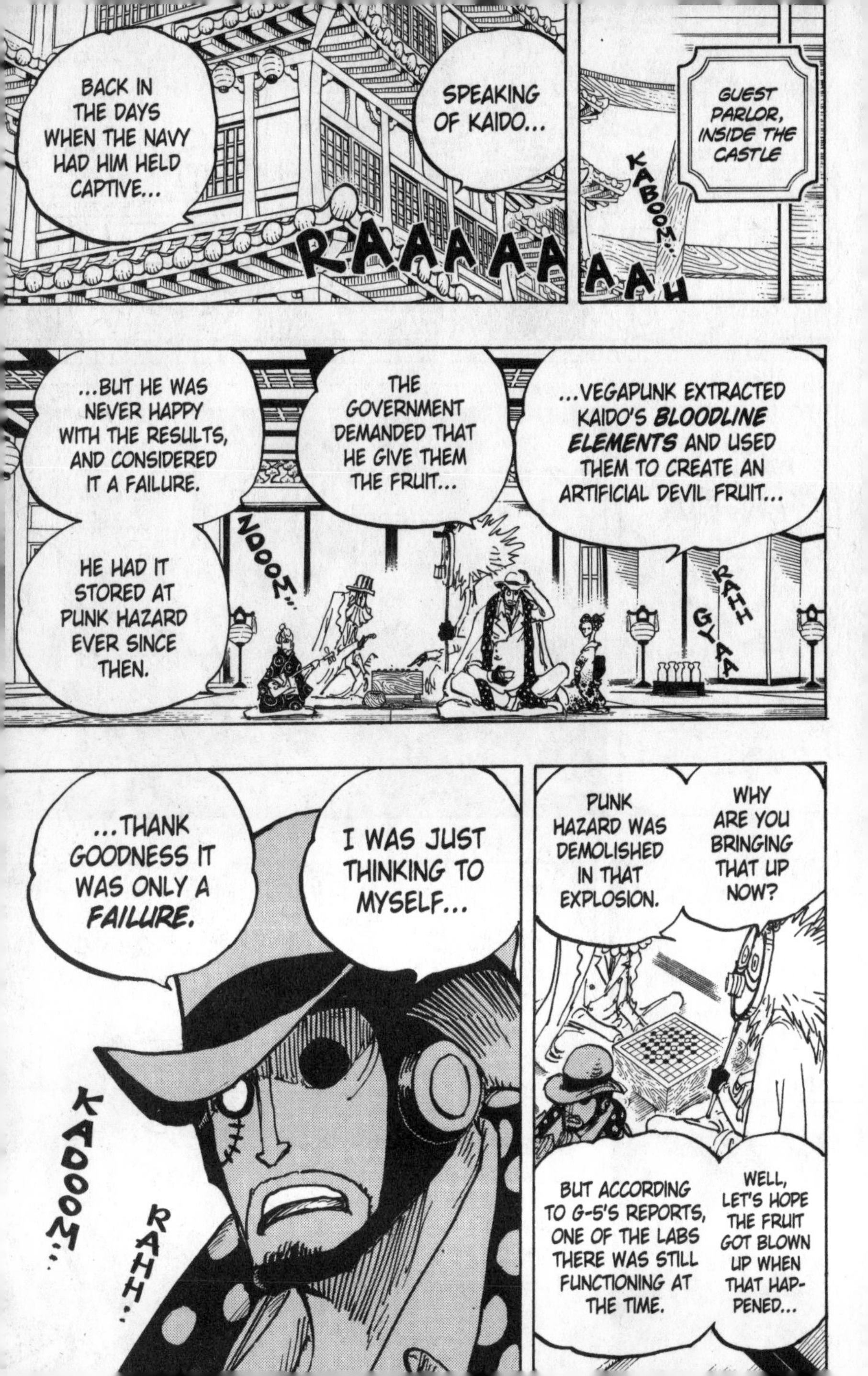
GUEST PARLOR, INSIDE THE CASTLE
KABOOM..
SPEAKING OF KAIDO...
BACK IN THE DAYS WHEN THE NAVY HAD HIM HELD CAPTIVE...
RAAAAAAAH
...VEGAPUNK EXTRACTED KAIDO'S **BLOODLINE ELEMENTS** AND USED THEM TO CREATE AN ARTIFICIAL DEVIL FRUIT...
THE GOVERNMENT DEMANDED THAT HE GIVE THEM THE FRUIT...
...BUT HE WAS NEVER HAPPY WITH THE RESULTS, AND CONSIDERED IT A FAILURE.
HE HAD IT STORED AT PUNK HAZARD EVER SINCE THEN.
RAHH
GYAA
ZDOOOM..
WHY ARE YOU BRINGING THAT UP NOW?
PUNK HAZARD WAS DEMOLISHED IN THAT EXPLOSION.
WELL, LET'S HOPE THE FRUIT GOT BLOWN UP WHEN THAT HAP-PENED...
BUT ACCORDING TO G-5'S REPORTS, ONE OF THE LABS THERE WAS STILL FUNCTIONING AT THE TIME.
I WAS JUST THINKING TO MYSELF...
...THANK GOODNESS IT WAS ONLY A **FAILURE.**
RAHH..
KADOOOM..

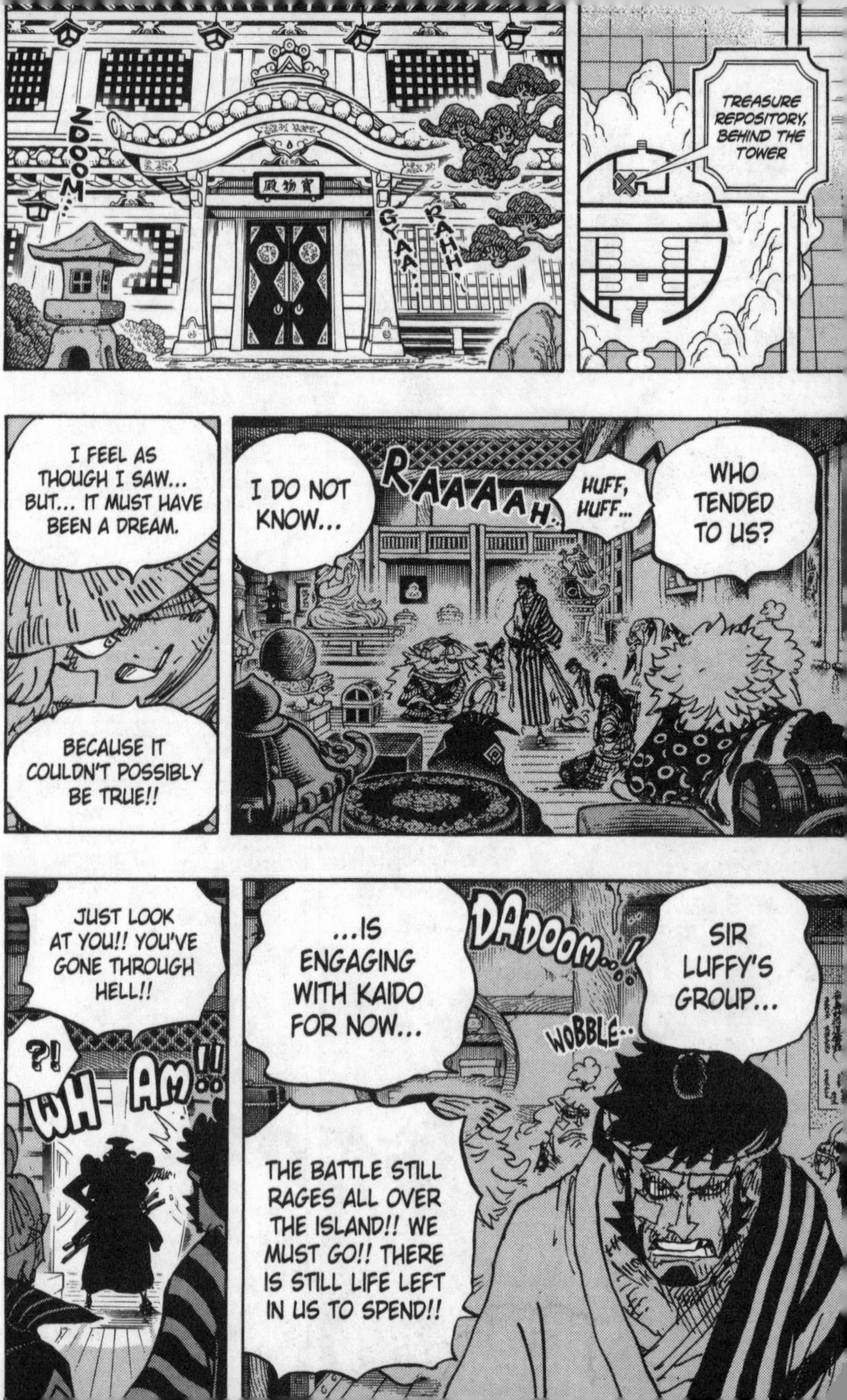
TREASURE REPOSITORY, BEHIND THE TOWER
ZDOOM...
GYAA...
RAHH...
WHO TENDED TO US?
HUFF, HUFF...
RAAAAAH...
I DO NOT KNOW...
I FEEL AS THOUGH I SAW... BUT... IT MUST HAVE BEEN A DREAM.
BECAUSE IT COULDN'T POSSIBLY BE TRUE!!
SIR LUFFY'S GROUP...
DADOOM...!
WOBBLE...
...IS ENGAGING WITH KAIDO FOR NOW...
THE BATTLE STILL RAGES ALL OVER THE ISLAND!! WE MUST GO!! THERE IS STILL LIFE LEFT IN US TO SPEND!!
JUST LOOK AT YOU!! YOU'VE GONE THROUGH HELL!!
?!
WHAM!!

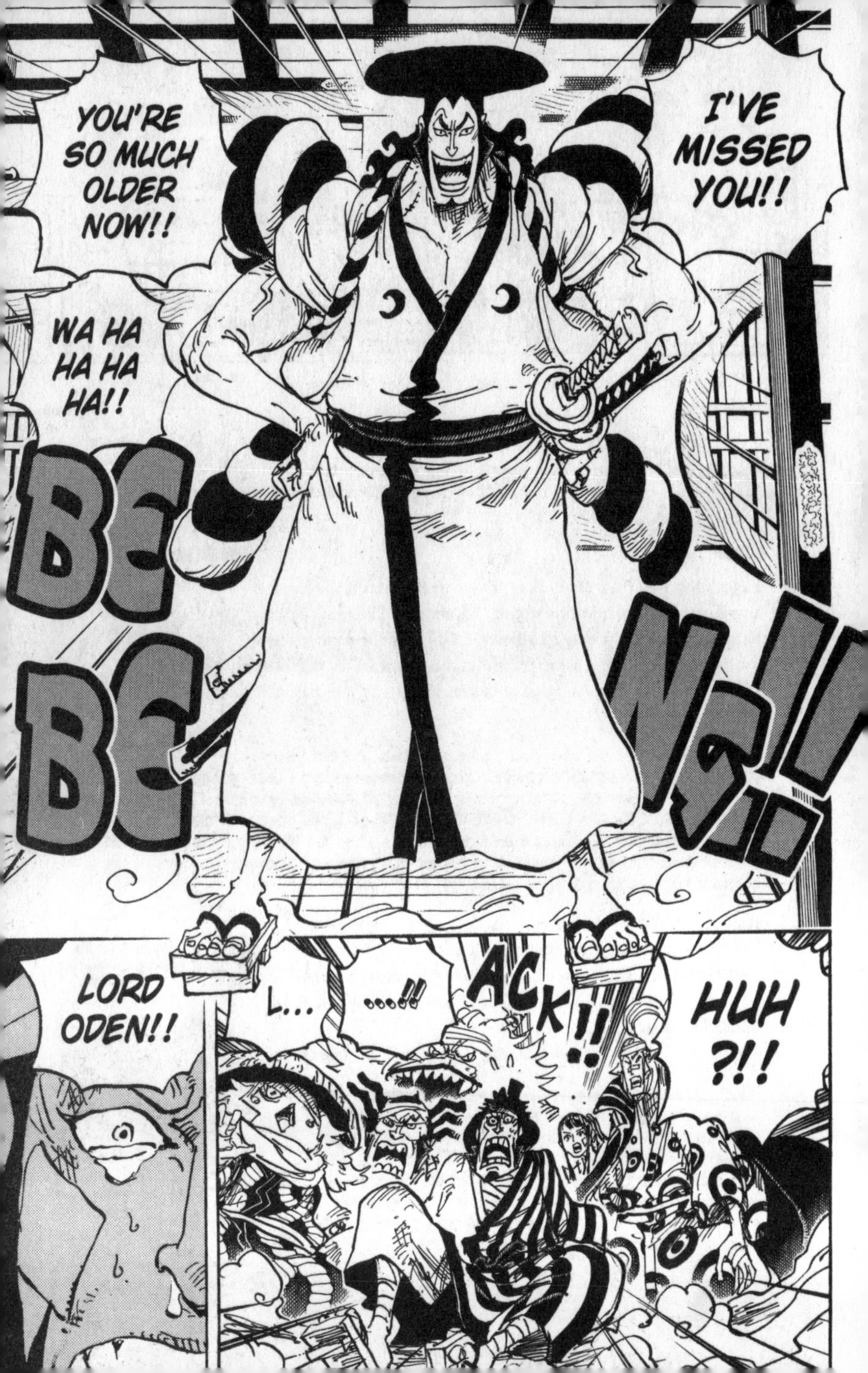
I'VE MISSED YOU!!
YOU'RE SO MUCH OLDER NOW!!
WA HA HA HA HA!!
BE BE
N!!
HUH ?!!
ACK!!
....!!
L...
LORD ODEN!!

SBS Question Corner

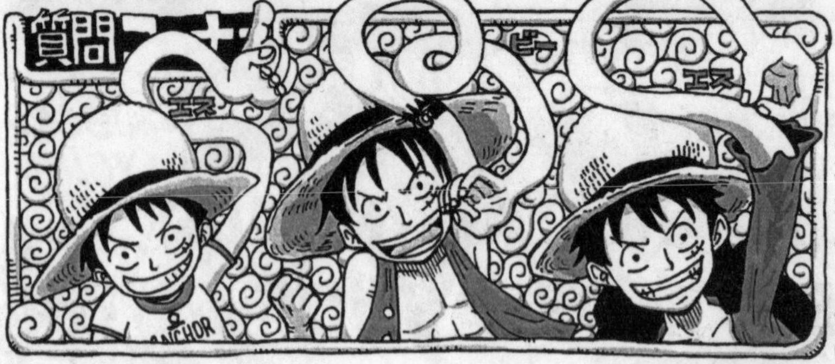

(Buchonosuke, Tochigi)

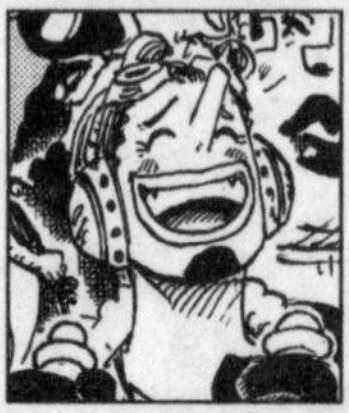

Q: If Usopp wore a mask that covered his nose too, what would it look like?

--Heraclesun

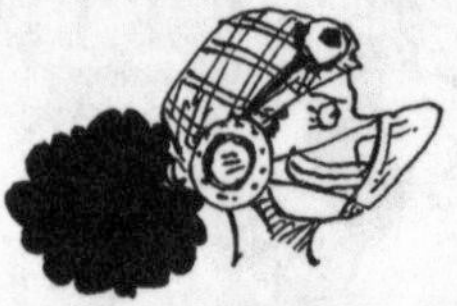

A: Here. Thanks for the postcard. He looks like this.

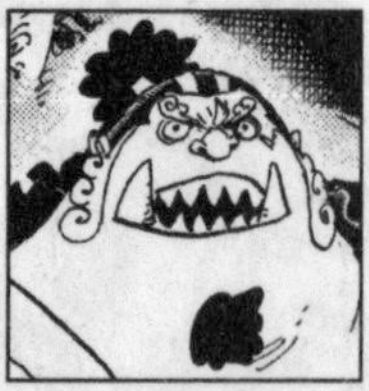

Q: Heya, Odacchi. Boss Jimbei's entrance to the crew was so awesome. I have a question about chapter 976, "Begging Your Pardon!!!" I was listening to a Best-of CD of period piece theme songs, and I heard the same phrase in the theme of an old '60s show called *Tenamonya Sandogasa.* Is that where you got it from?!

--Pay-Pay

A: Well, you didn't write your age on this letter, but you've got old school taste! Just like me when I was young, LOL. Actually, there are a bunch of scenes in samurai movies and old-fashioned yakuza movies that begin with that phrase, "Begging your pardon!!" It's basically just a traditional yakuza greeting. It's kind of like introducing yourself and saying, "I'm so-and-so, and I was born in so-and-so town..." This is called upholding *jingi*, the code of the yakuza.

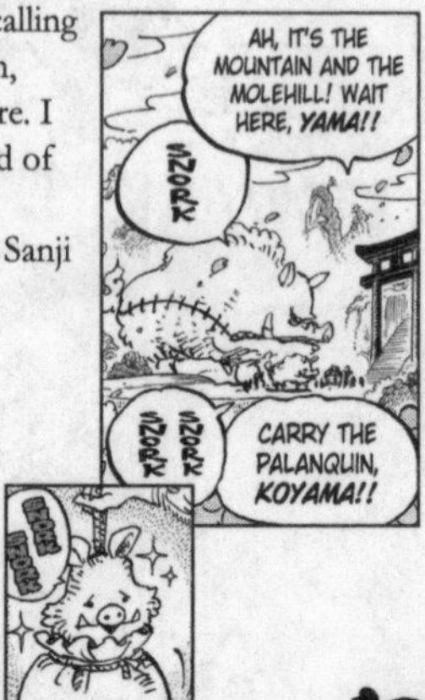
AH, IT'S THE MOUNTAIN AND THE MOLEHILL! WAIT HERE, YAMA!!
SNORK
CARRY THE PALANQUIN, KOYAMA!!
SNORK
SNORK

Q: Hi, Odacchi! On page 173 of volume 95, the one they're calling "Yama" is the giant boar that was the god of the mountain, right? I thought Oden sliced it in two, but it seems fine here. I was really happy to see it alive. Does Wano have some kind of miraculous medical technology?

--Zigzag Shopkeep Who Loves Sanji

A: That's right. The boar is just fine. Haven't you ever heard about arms being severed so cleanly that you can just stitch them back together and they reattach? That's basically it. Oden cut the mountain god so cleanly that it attached back together!! Nice job!! And Koyama was the name of that little piglet, the one they kidnapped earlier.

Chapter 1008: LEADER OF THE ATAMAYAMA THIEVES BRIGADE, ASHURA DOJI

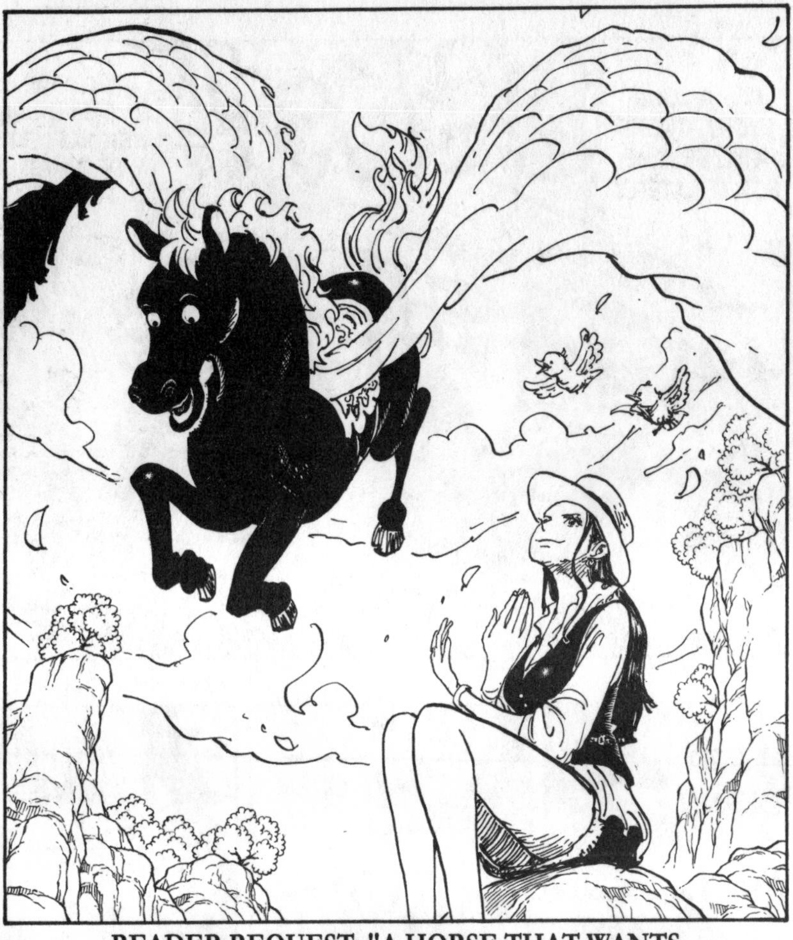

READER REQUEST: "A HORSE THAT WANTS TO FLY GETS TURNED INTO A PEGASUS WITH HELP FROM ROBIN" BY MAICHO CARAMEL

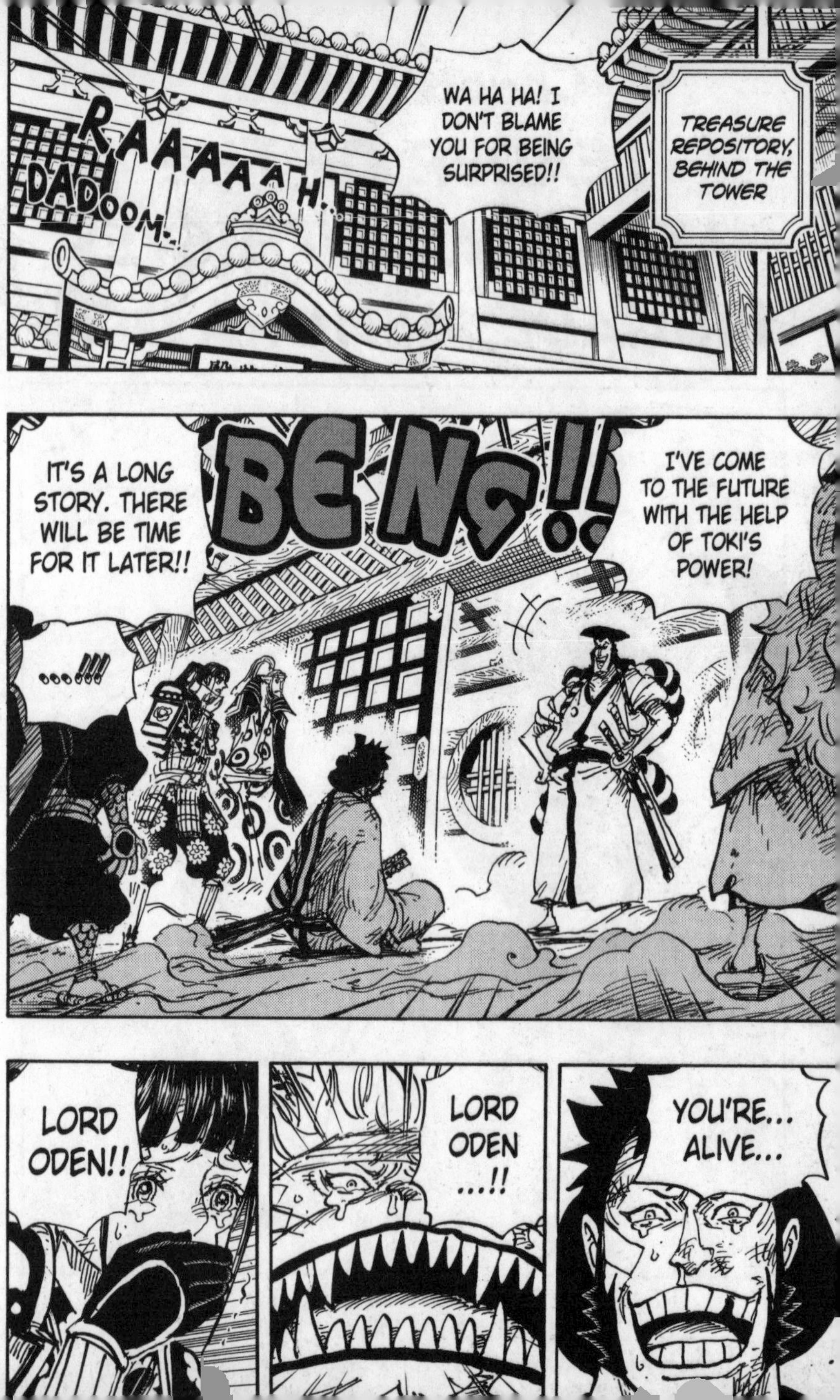
TREASURE REPOSITORY, BEHIND THE TOWER
WA HA HA! I DON'T BLAME YOU FOR BEING SURPRISED!!
RAAAAAAH...
DADOOM...
BENG!!
I'VE COME TO THE FUTURE WITH THE HELP OF TOKI'S POWER!
IT'S A LONG STORY. THERE WILL BE TIME FOR IT LATER!!
...!!!
YOU'RE... ALIVE...
LORD ODEN ...!!
LORD ODEN!!

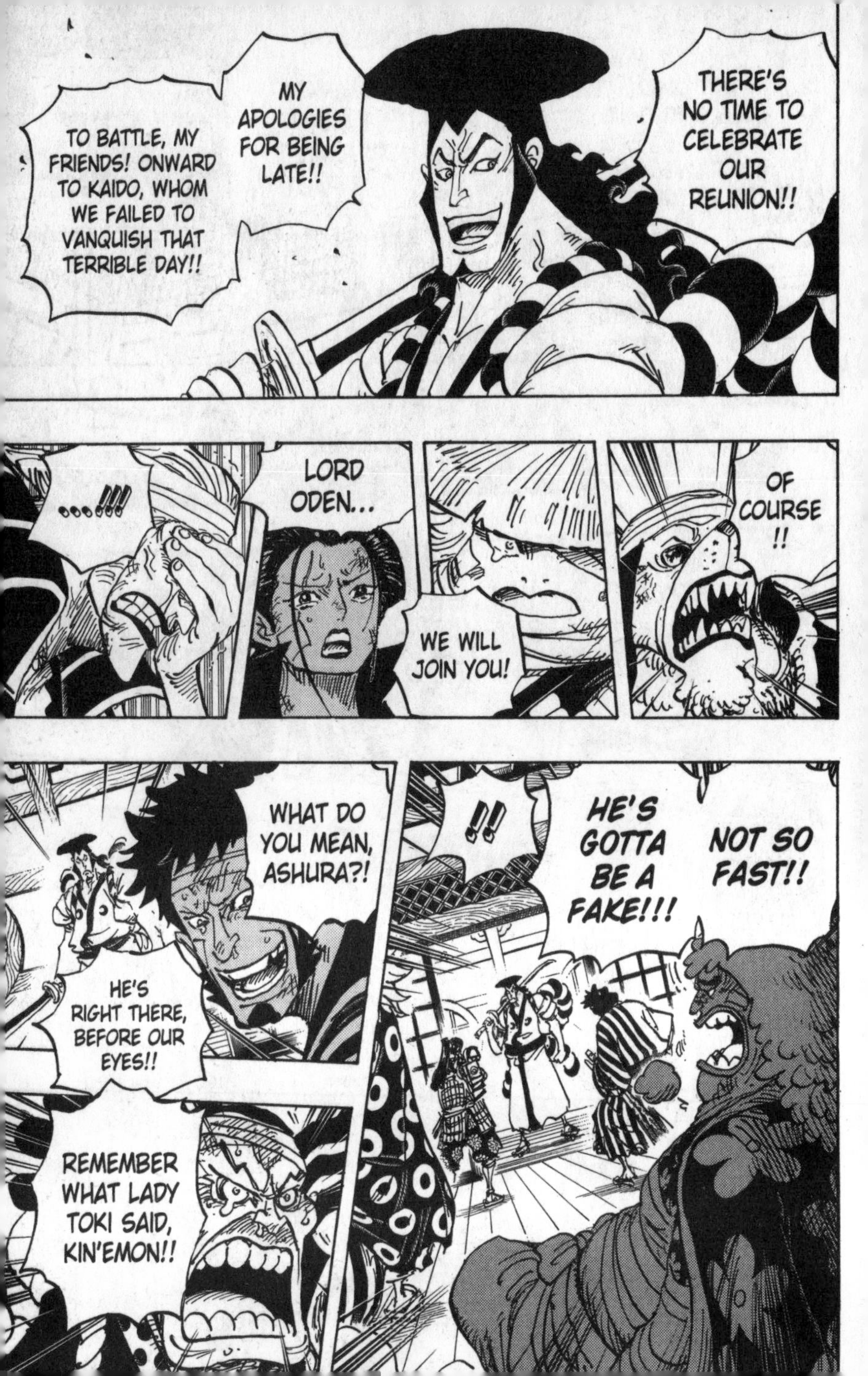
THERE'S NO TIME TO CELEBRATE OUR REUNION!!
MY APOLOGIES FOR BEING LATE!!
TO BATTLE, MY FRIENDS! ONWARD TO KAIDO, WHOM WE FAILED TO VANQUISH THAT TERRIBLE DAY!!
OF COURSE !!
WE WILL JOIN YOU!
LORD ODEN...
...!!!
NOT SO FAST!!
HE'S GOTTA BE A FAKE!!!
!!
WHAT DO YOU MEAN, ASHURA?!
HE'S RIGHT THERE, BEFORE OUR EYES!!
REMEMBER WHAT LADY TOKI SAID, KIN'EMON!!

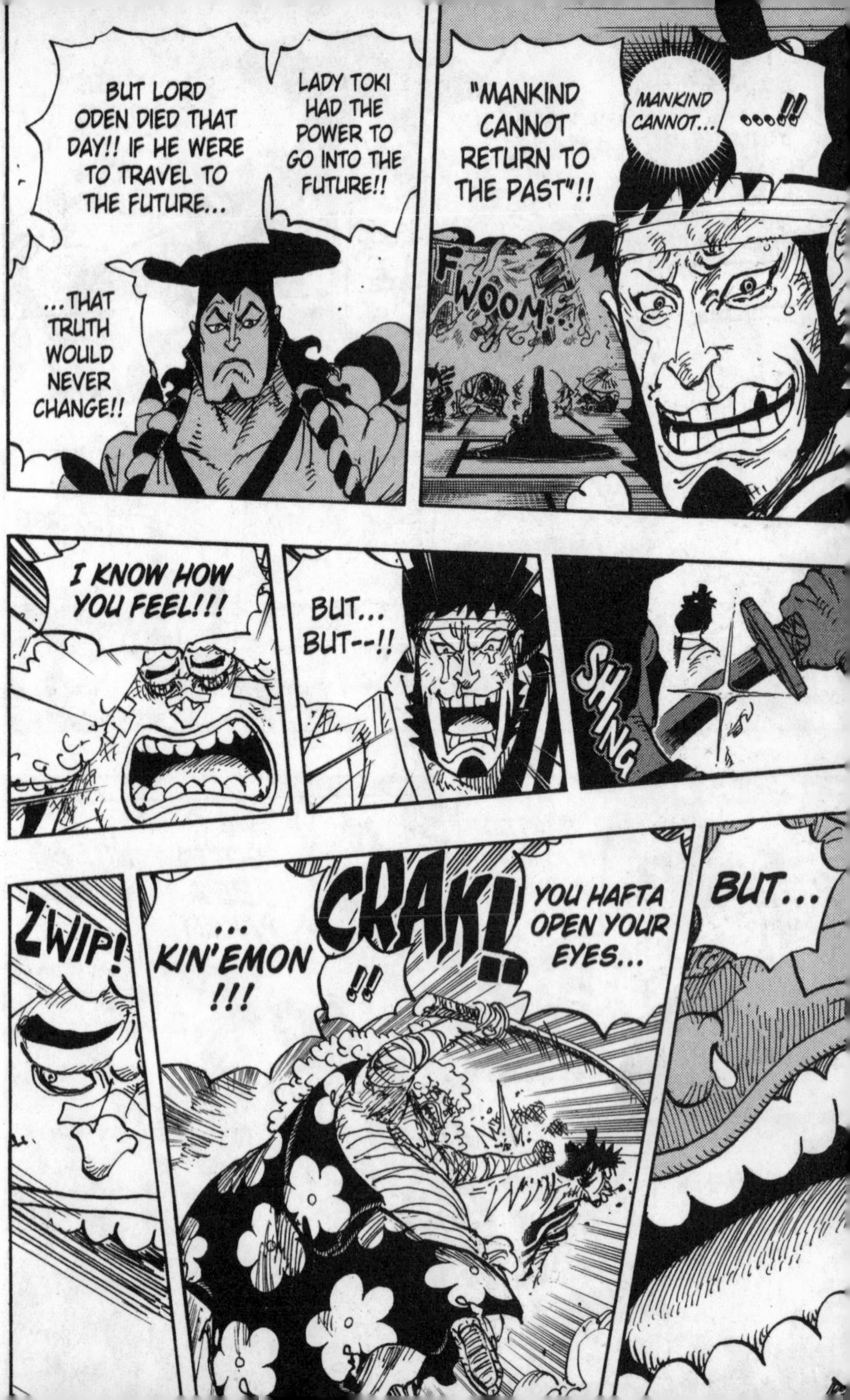
....!!
MANKIND CANNOT...
"MANKIND CANNOT RETURN TO THE PAST"!!
FWOOM
LADY TOKI HAD THE POWER TO GO INTO THE FUTURE!!
BUT LORD ODEN DIED THAT DAY!! IF HE WERE TO TRAVEL TO THE FUTURE...
...THAT TRUTH WOULD NEVER CHANGE!!
SHING
BUT... BUT--!!
I KNOW HOW YOU FEEL!!!
BUT...
YOU HAFTA OPEN YOUR EYES...
CRAK!!
!!
...KIN'EMON!!!
ZWIP!

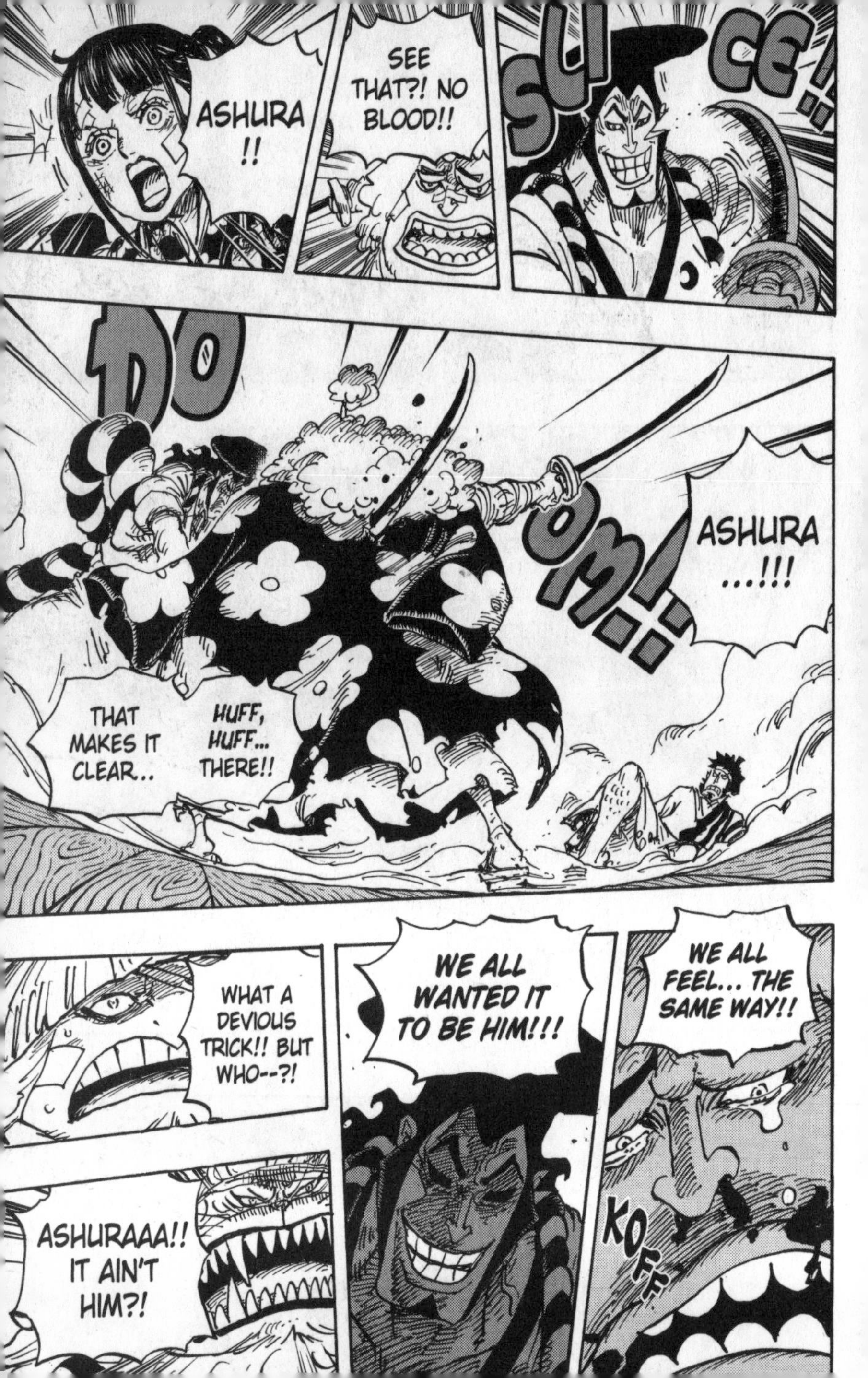
SLICE!!
SEE THAT?! NO BLOOD!!
ASHURA!!
DOOM!!
ASHURA...!!!
HUFF, HUFF... THERE!!
THAT MAKES IT CLEAR...
WE ALL FEEL... THE SAME WAY!!
KOFF
WE ALL WANTED IT TO BE HIM!!!
WHAT A DEVIOUS TRICK!! BUT WHO--?!
ASHURAAA!! IT AIN'T HIM?!

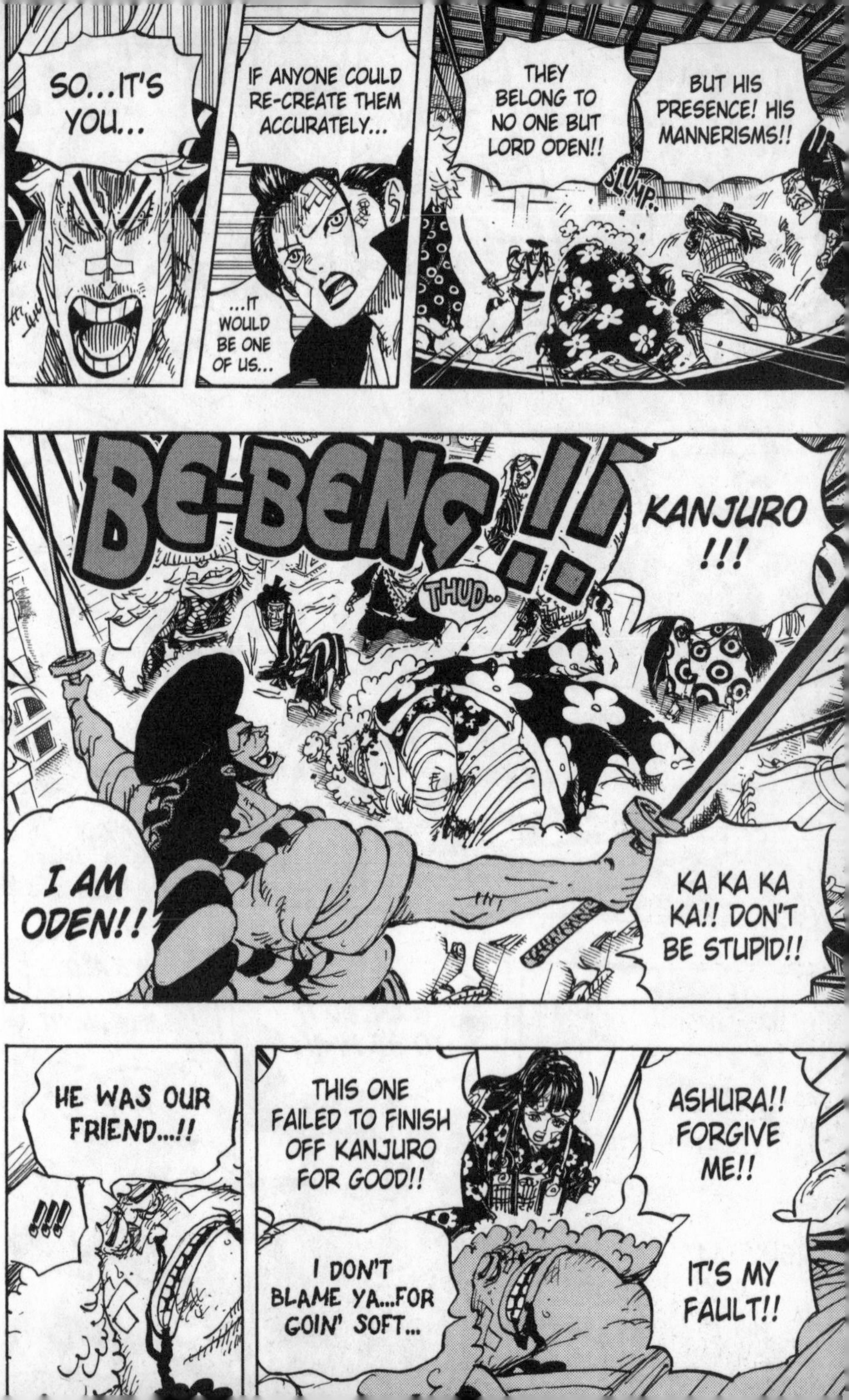
BUT HIS PRESENCE! HIS MANNERISMS!!
THEY BELONG TO NO ONE BUT LORD ODEN!!
SLUMP..
IF ANYONE COULD RE-CREATE THEM ACCURATELY...
...IT WOULD BE ONE OF US...
SO...IT'S YOU...
BE-BENG!!
KANJURO !!!
THUD..
KA KA KA KA!! DON'T BE STUPID!!
I AM ODEN!!
ASHURA!! FORGIVE ME!!
THIS ONE FAILED TO FINISH OFF KANJURO FOR GOOD!!
IT'S MY FAULT!!
I DON'T BLAME YA...FOR GOIN' SOFT...
HE WAS OUR FRIEND...!!
!!!

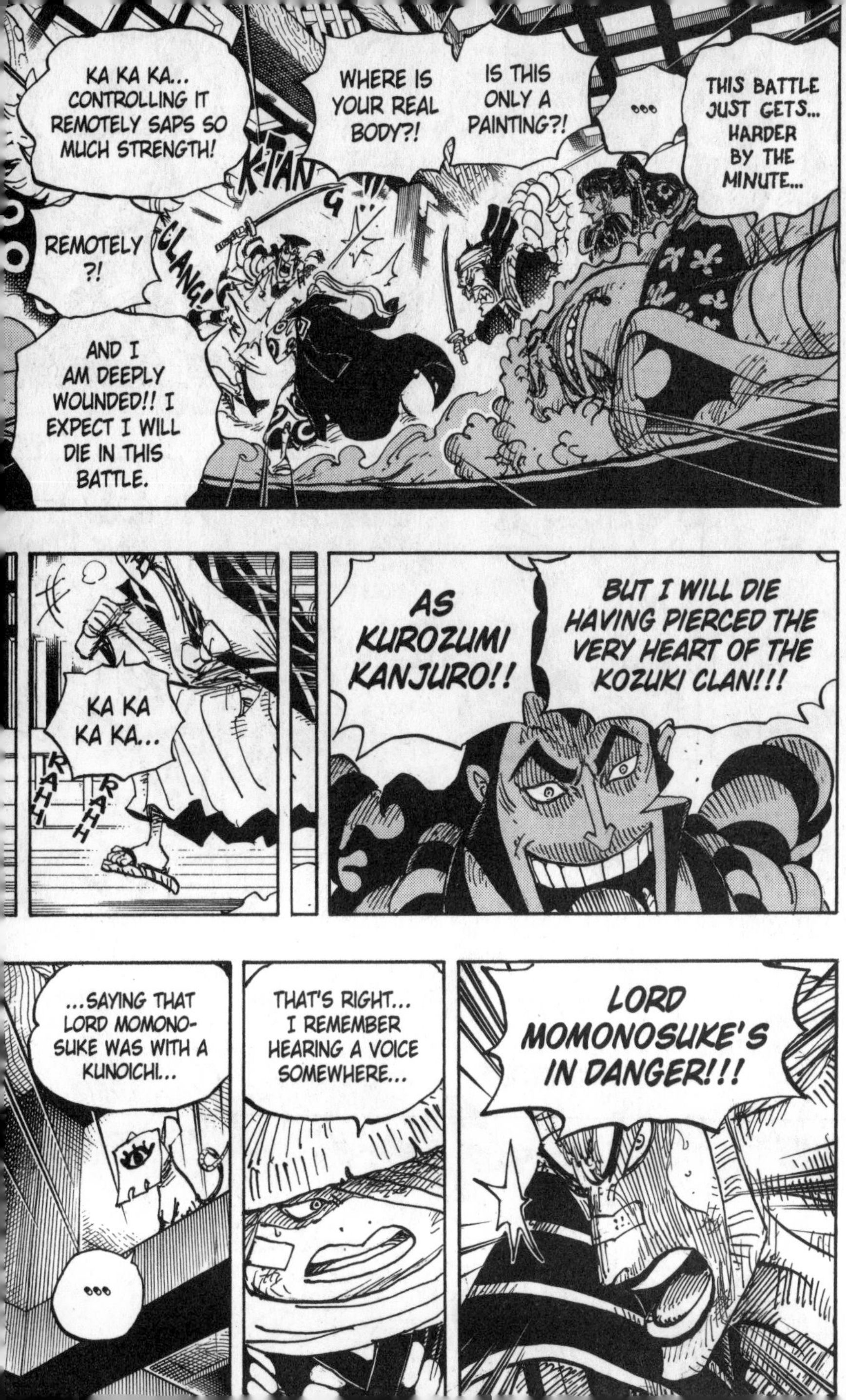
THIS BATTLE JUST GETS... HARDER BY THE MINUTE...
...
IS THIS ONLY A PAINTING?!
WHERE IS YOUR REAL BODY?!
KA KA KA... CONTROLLING IT REMOTELY SAPS SO MUCH STRENGTH!
K-TAN
G
CLANG!
REMOTELY ?!
AND I AM DEEPLY WOUNDED!! I EXPECT I WILL DIE IN THIS BATTLE.
BUT I WILL DIE HAVING PIERCED THE VERY HEART OF THE KOZUKI CLAN!!!
AS KUROZUMI KANJURO!!
KA KA KA KA...
RAHH
RAHH
LORD MOMONOSUKE'S IN DANGER!!!
THAT'S RIGHT... I REMEMBER HEARING A VOICE SOMEWHERE...
...SAYING THAT LORD MOMONOSUKE WAS WITH A KUNOICHI...
...

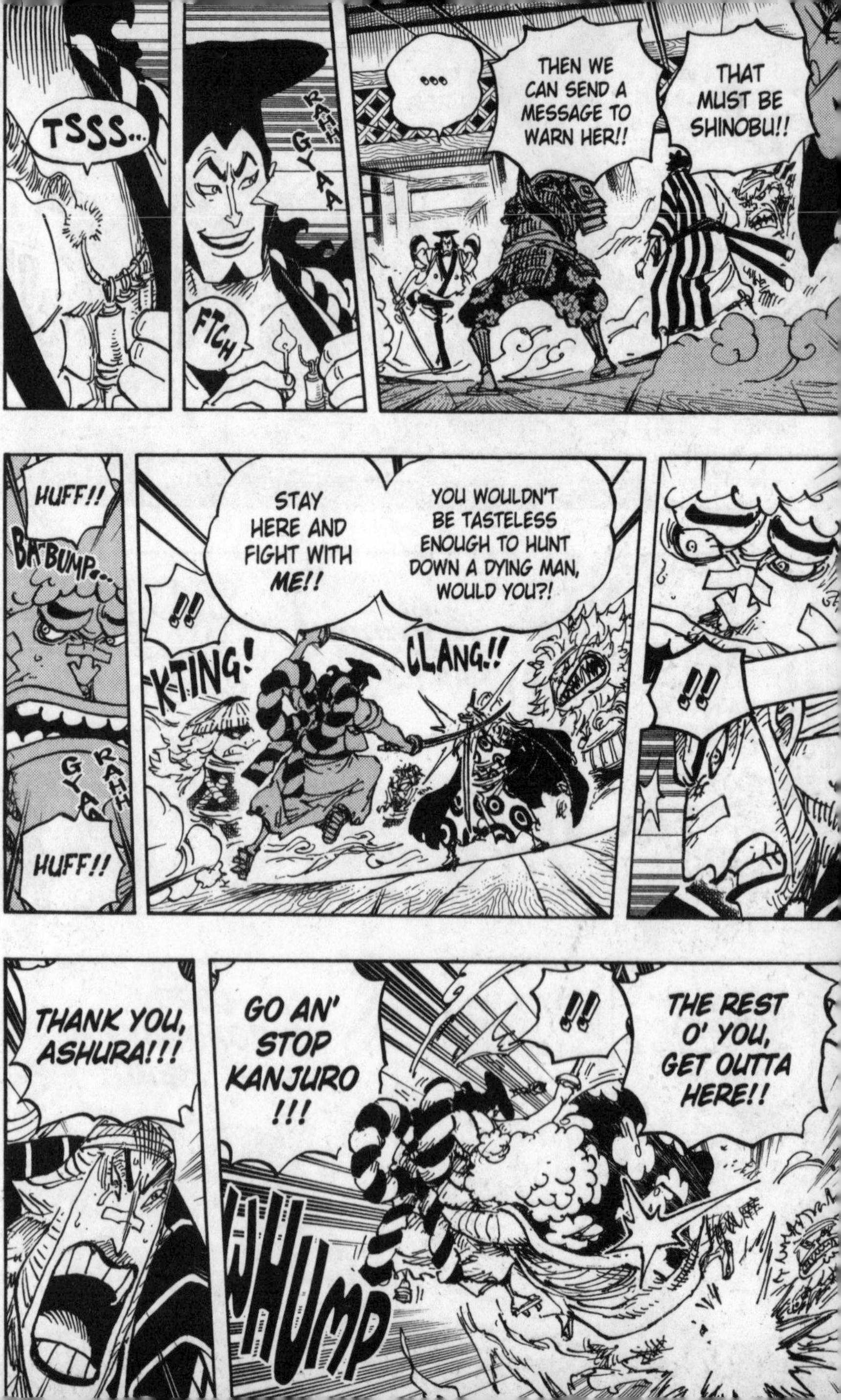
THAT MUST BE SHINOBU!!
THEN WE CAN SEND A MESSAGE TO WARN HER!!
...
RAHH GYAA
FTCH
TSSS...
!!
YOU WOULDN'T BE TASTELESS ENOUGH TO HUNT DOWN A DYING MAN, WOULD YOU?!
STAY HERE AND FIGHT WITH ME!!
CLANG!!
!!
KTING!
HUFF!!
BA-BUMP...
RAHH GYAA
HUFF!!
THE REST O' YOU, GET OUTTA HERE!!
!!
GO AN' STOP KANJURO!!!
WHUMP
THANK YOU, ASHURA!!!

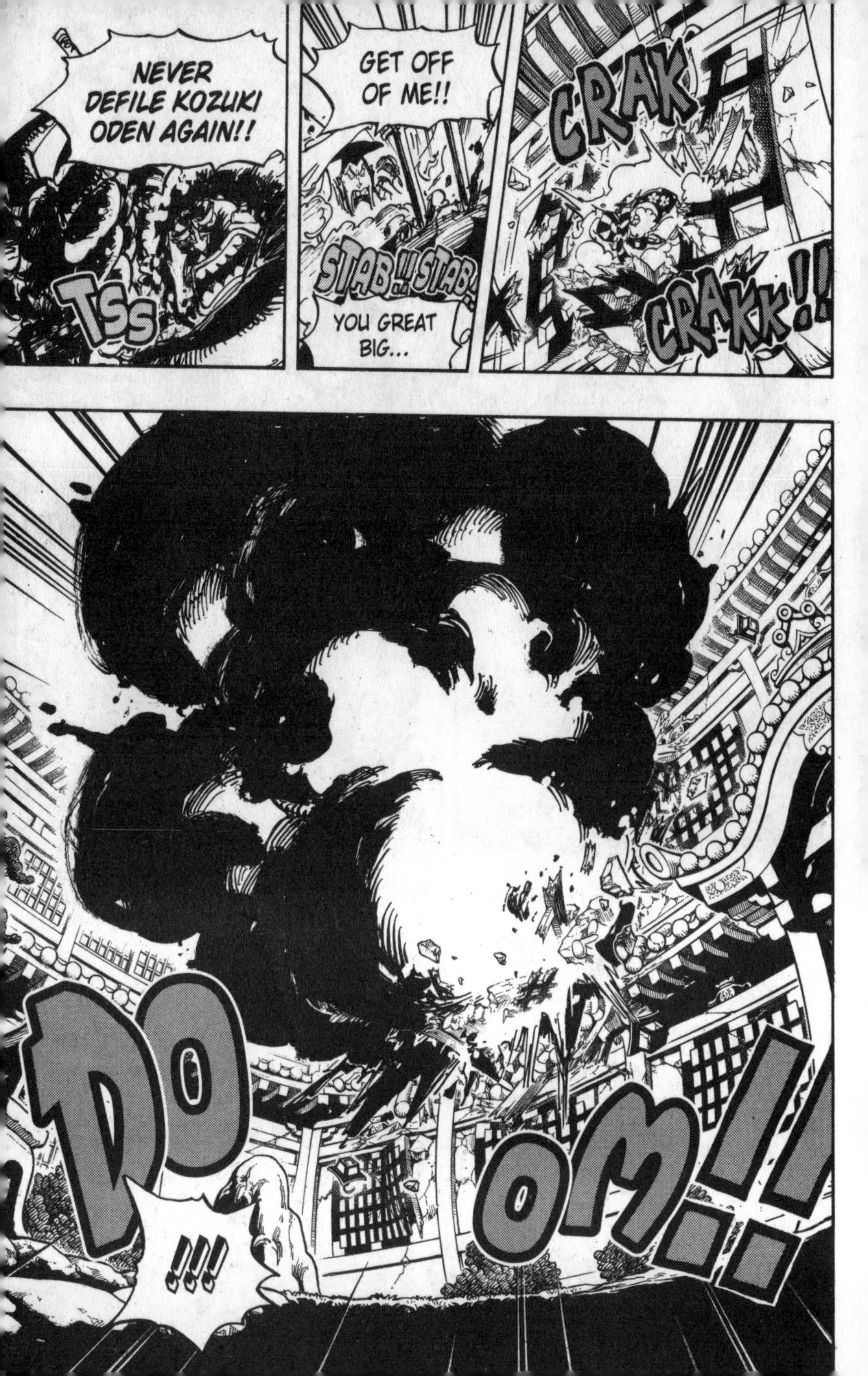
CRAK
CRAKK!!
GET OFF OF ME!!
STAB!! STAB!
YOU GREAT BIG...
NEVER DEFILE KOZUKI ODEN AGAIN!!
TSS
DO
!!!
OM!!

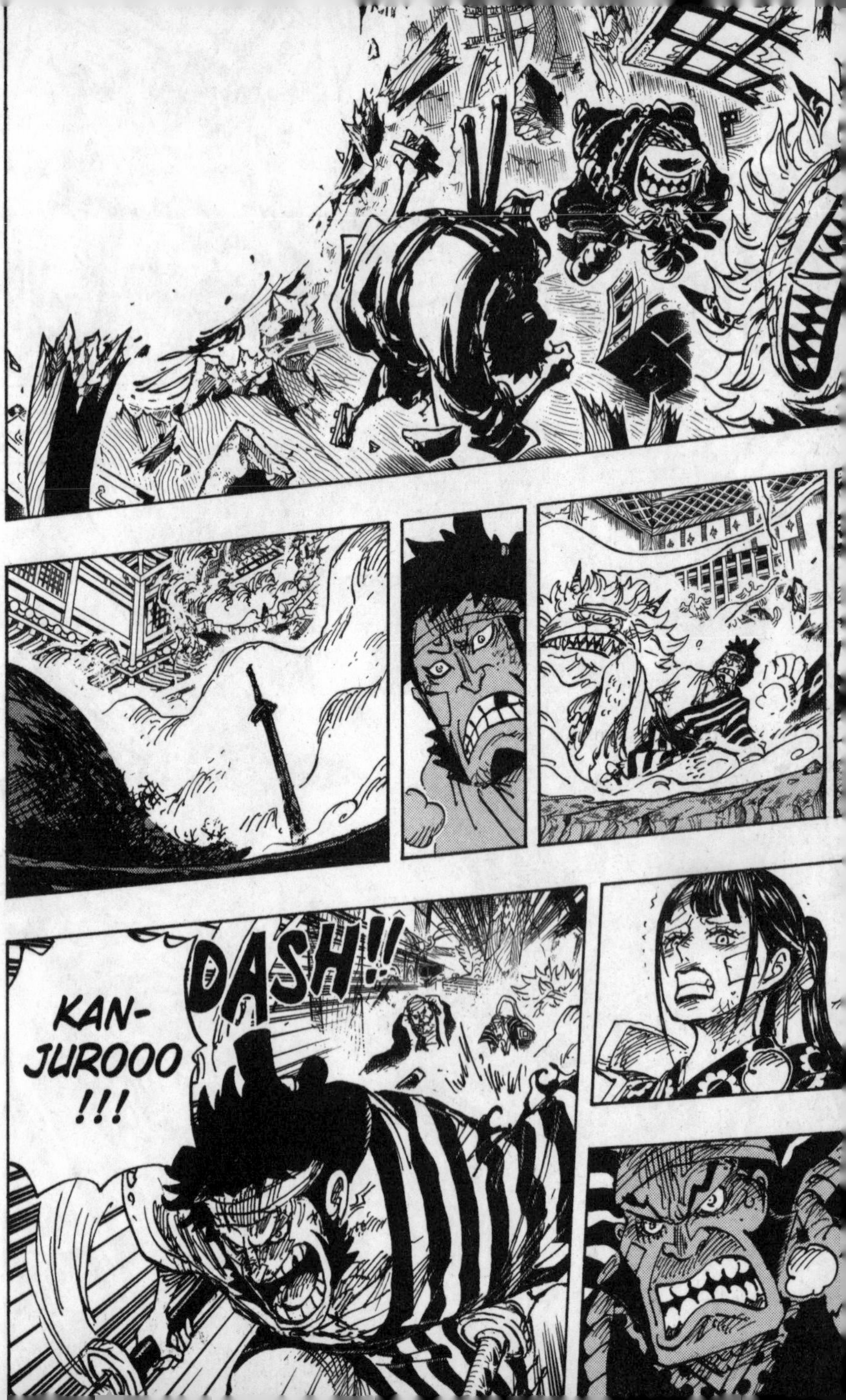
DASH!!
KAN-
JUROOO
!!!

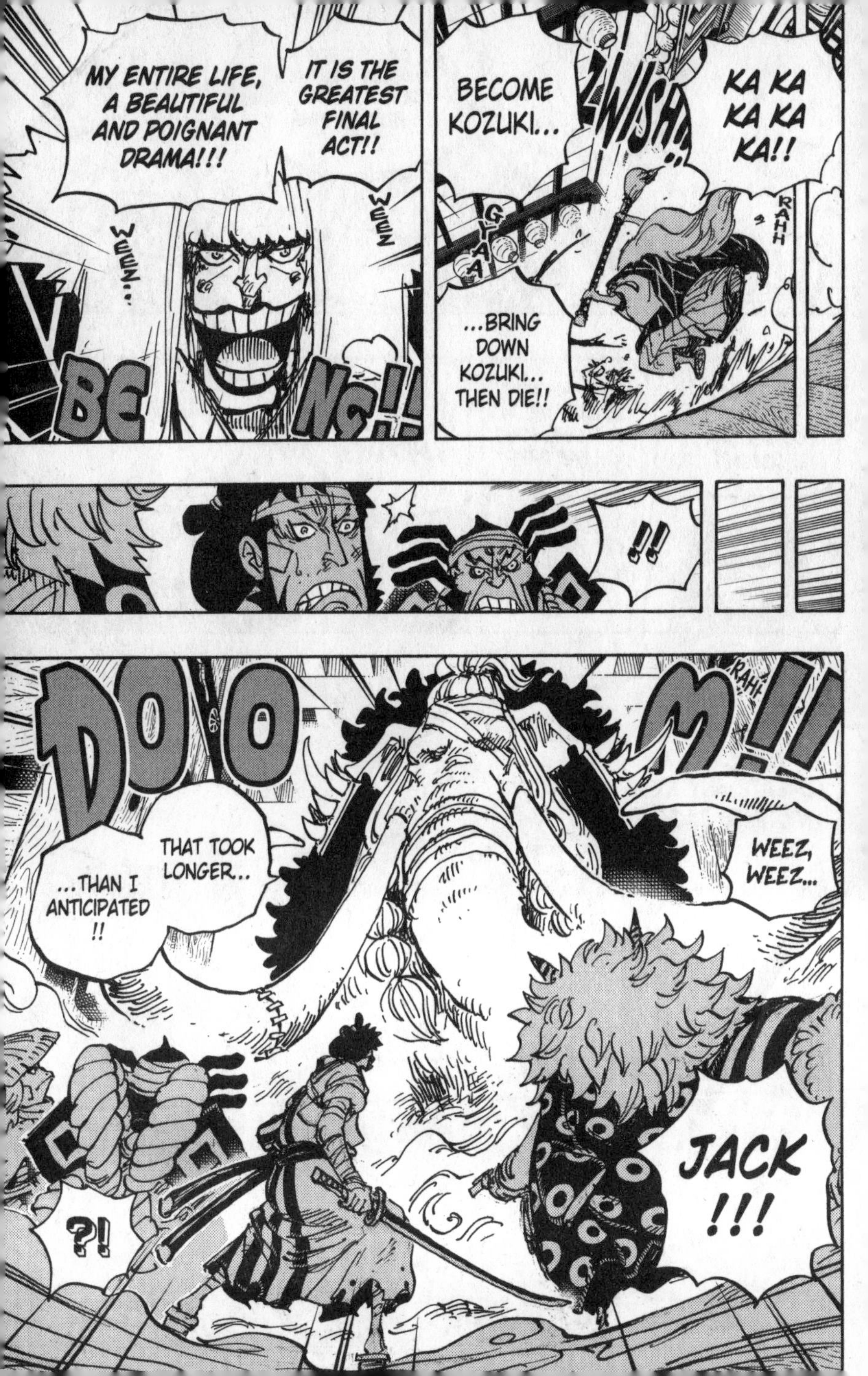
KA KA KA KA KA!!
RAHH
ZWISH
BECOME KOZUKI...
GYAA
...BRING DOWN KOZUKI... THEN DIE!!
IT IS THE GREATEST FINAL ACT!!
MY ENTIRE LIFE, A BEAUTIFUL AND POIGNANT DRAMA!!!
WEEZ
WEEZ..
BENG!!
!!
DOOM!!
RAHH
WEEZ, WEEZ...
THAT TOOK LONGER...
...THAN I ANTICIPATED !!
JACK !!!
?!

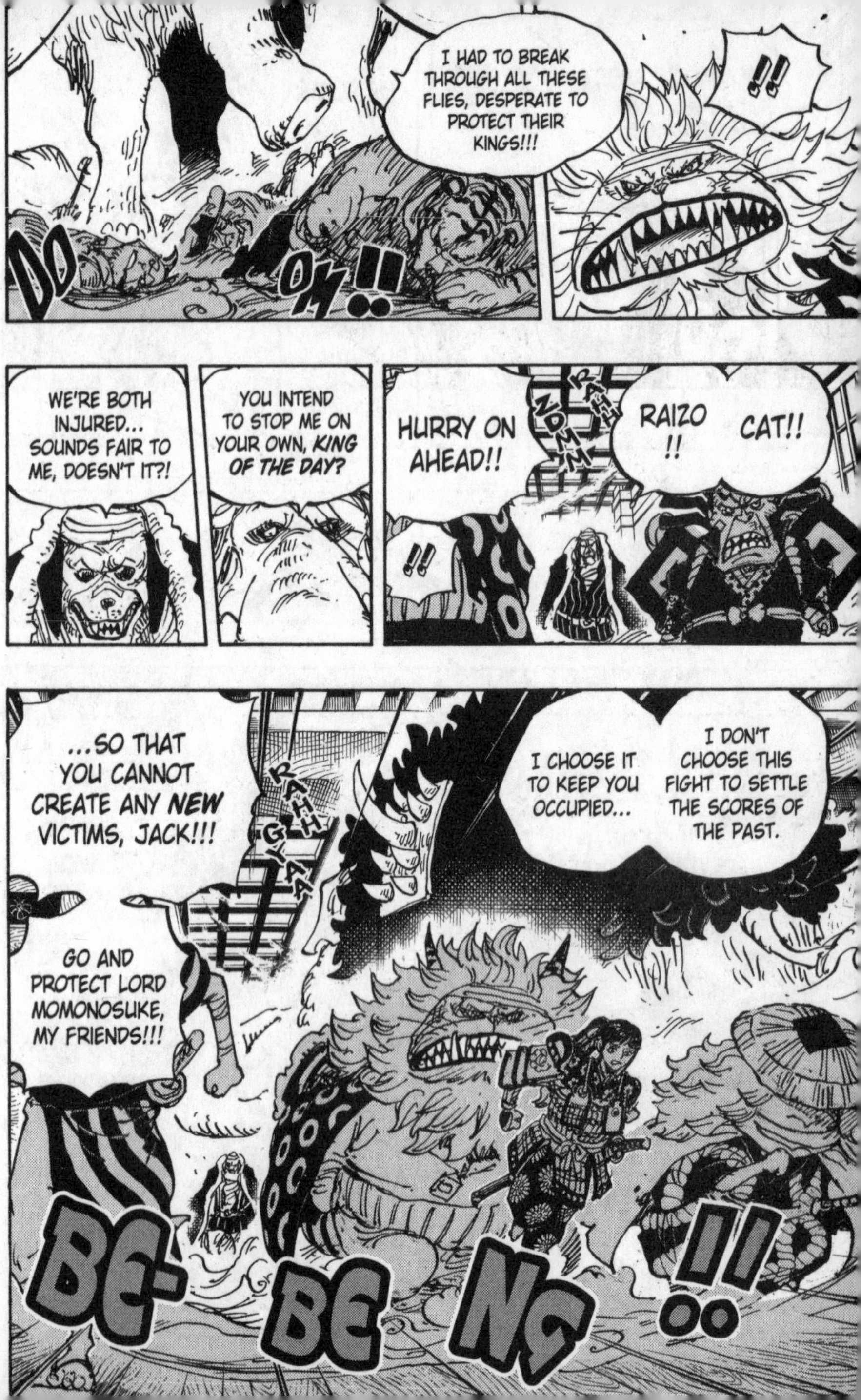
!!
I HAD TO BREAK THROUGH ALL THESE FLIES, DESPERATE TO PROTECT THEIR KINGS!!!
DOOM!!
CAT!!
RAIZO!!
RAHH
ZDMM
HURRY ON AHEAD!!
!!
YOU INTEND TO STOP ME ON YOUR OWN, *KING OF THE DAY?*
WE'RE BOTH INJURED... SOUNDS FAIR TO ME, DOESN'T IT?!
I DON'T CHOOSE THIS FIGHT TO SETTLE THE SCORES OF THE PAST.
I CHOOSE IT TO KEEP YOU OCCUPIED...
...SO THAT YOU CANNOT CREATE ANY *NEW* VICTIMS, JACK!!!
RAHH
GYAA
GO AND PROTECT LORD MOMONOSUKE, MY FRIENDS!!!
BE-BE NG!!

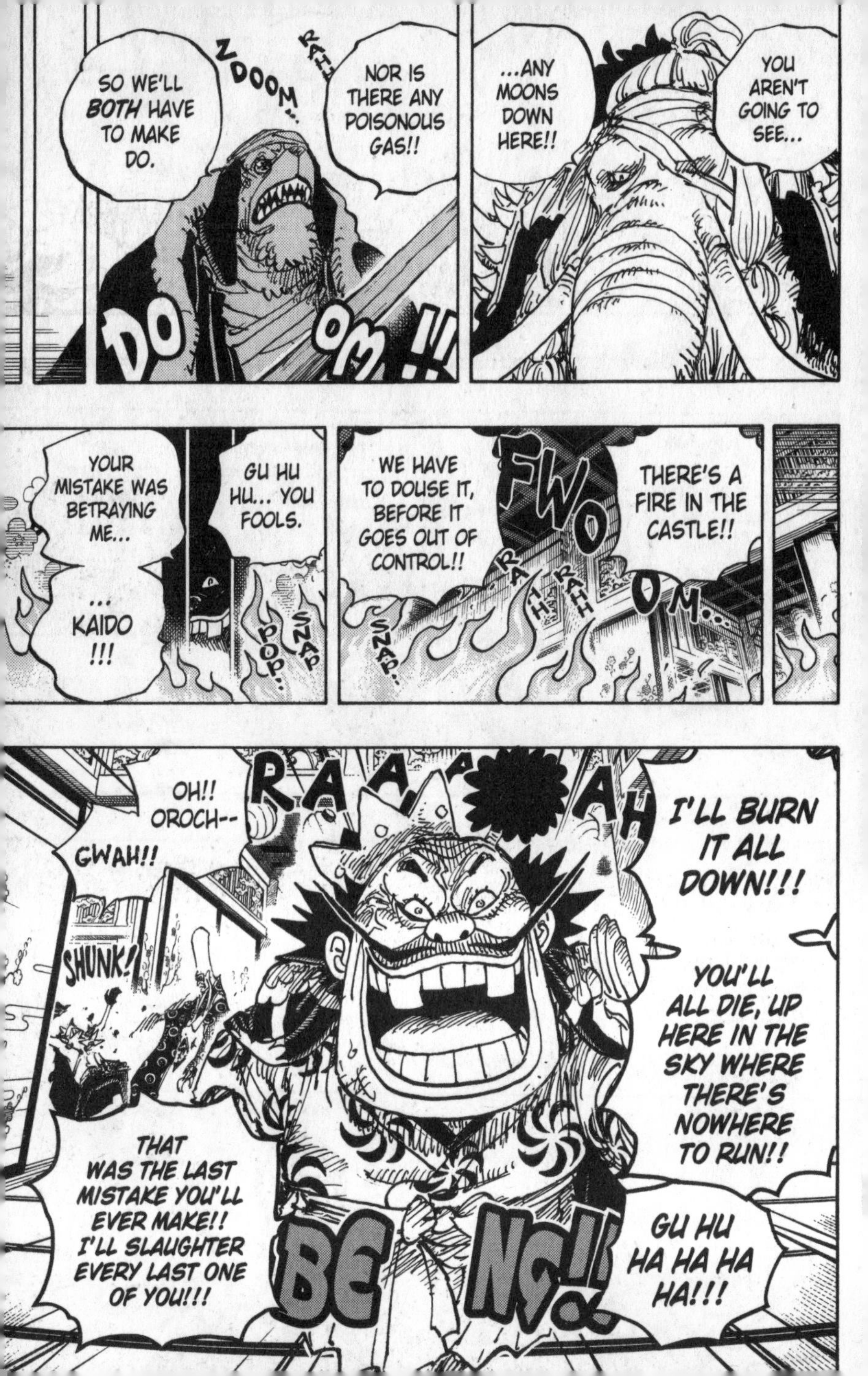
YOU AREN'T GOING TO SEE...
...ANY MOONS DOWN HERE!!
NOR IS THERE ANY POISONOUS GAS!!
RAHH
ZDOOM..
SO WE'LL BOTH HAVE TO MAKE DO.
DOOM!!
THERE'S A FIRE IN THE CASTLE!!
FWOOM...
RAHH
RAHH
WE HAVE TO DOUSE IT, BEFORE IT GOES OUT OF CONTROL!!
SNAP..
GU HU HU... YOU FOOLS.
SNAP
POP..
YOUR MISTAKE WAS BETRAYING ME...
...KAIDO!!!
I'LL BURN IT ALL DOWN!!!
RAAAAH
YOU'LL ALL DIE, UP HERE IN THE SKY WHERE THERE'S NOWHERE TO RUN!!
GU HU HA HA HA HA!!!
OH!! OROCH--
GWAH!!
SHUNK!
THAT WAS THE LAST MISTAKE YOU'LL EVER MAKE!! I'LL SLAUGHTER EVERY LAST ONE OF YOU!!!
BENG!!

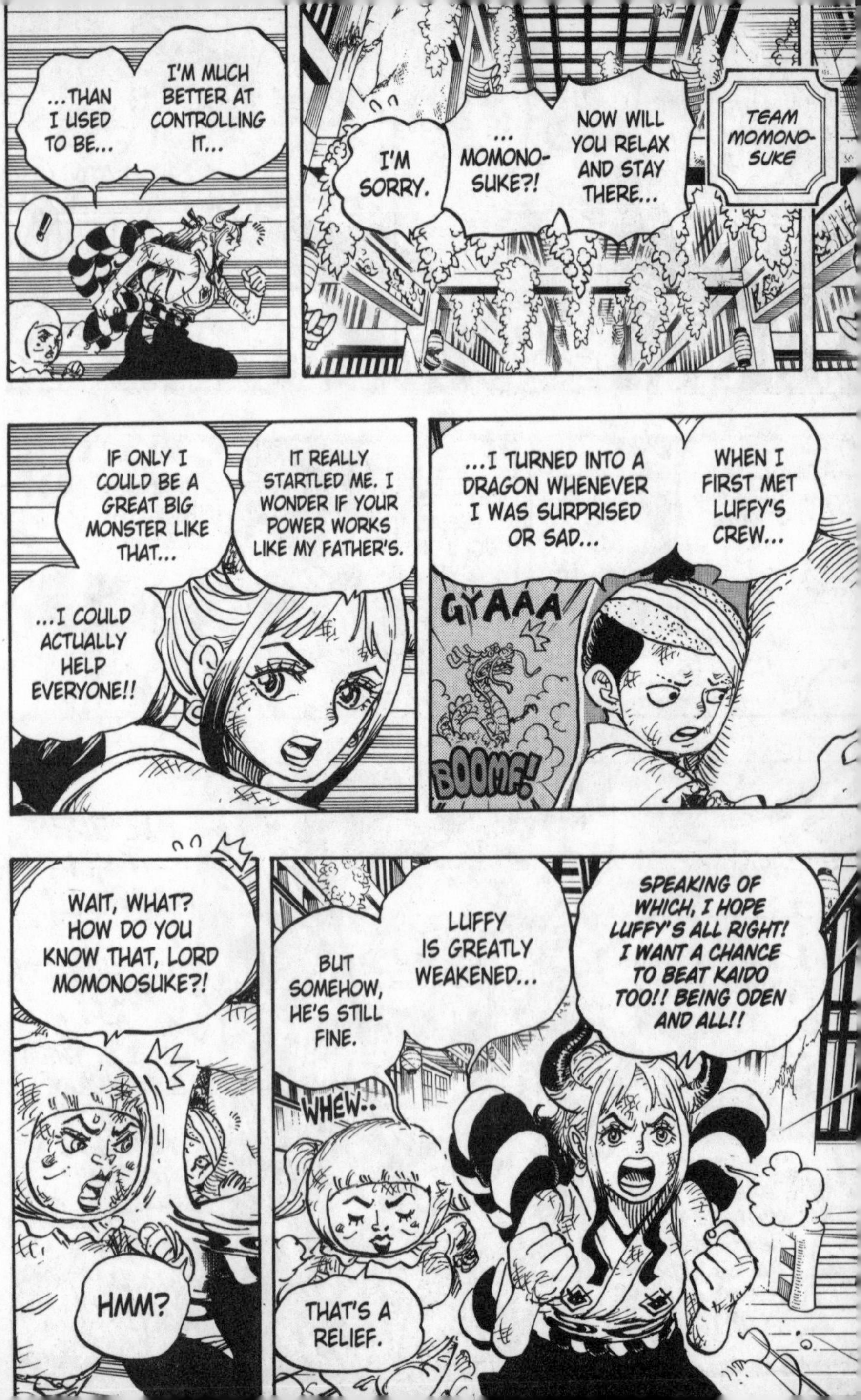
TEAM MOMONOSUKE
NOW WILL YOU RELAX AND STAY THERE...
... MOMONOSUKE?!
I'M SORRY.
I'M MUCH BETTER AT CONTROLLING IT...
...THAN I USED TO BE...
!
WHEN I FIRST MET LUFFY'S CREW...
...I TURNED INTO A DRAGON WHENEVER I WAS SURPRISED OR SAD...
GYAAA
BOOMF!
IT REALLY STARTLED ME. I WONDER IF YOUR POWER WORKS LIKE MY FATHER'S.
IF ONLY I COULD BE A GREAT BIG MONSTER LIKE THAT...
...I COULD ACTUALLY HELP EVERYONE!!
SPEAKING OF WHICH, I HOPE LUFFY'S ALL RIGHT! I WANT A CHANCE TO BEAT KAIDO TOO!! BEING ODEN AND ALL!!
LUFFY IS GREATLY WEAKENED...
BUT SOMEHOW, HE'S STILL FINE.
WHEW..
THAT'S A RELIEF.
WAIT, WHAT? HOW DO YOU KNOW THAT, LORD MOMONOSUKE?!
HMM?

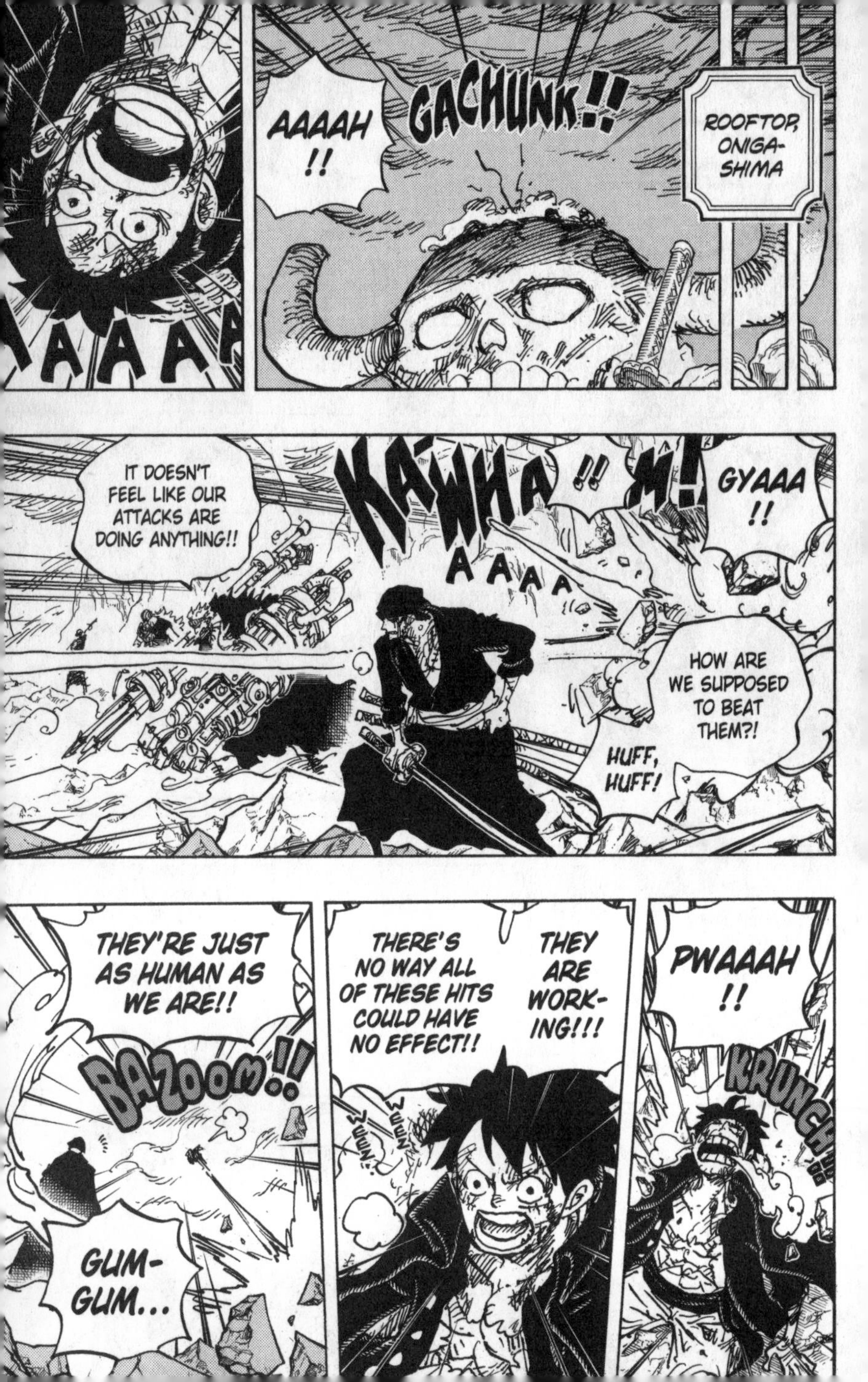
ROOFTOP, ONIGA-SHIMA
GACHUNK!!
AAAAH !!
GYAAA !!
KAWHA !!
M!
AAAA
HOW ARE WE SUPPOSED TO BEAT THEM?!
HUFF, HUFF!
IT DOESN'T FEEL LIKE OUR ATTACKS ARE DOING ANYTHING!!
PWAAAH !!
KRUNCH!!
THEY ARE WORK-ING!!!
THERE'S NO WAY ALL OF THESE HITS COULD HAVE NO EFFECT!!
THEY'RE JUST AS HUMAN AS WE ARE!!
BAZOOM!!
GUM-GUM...

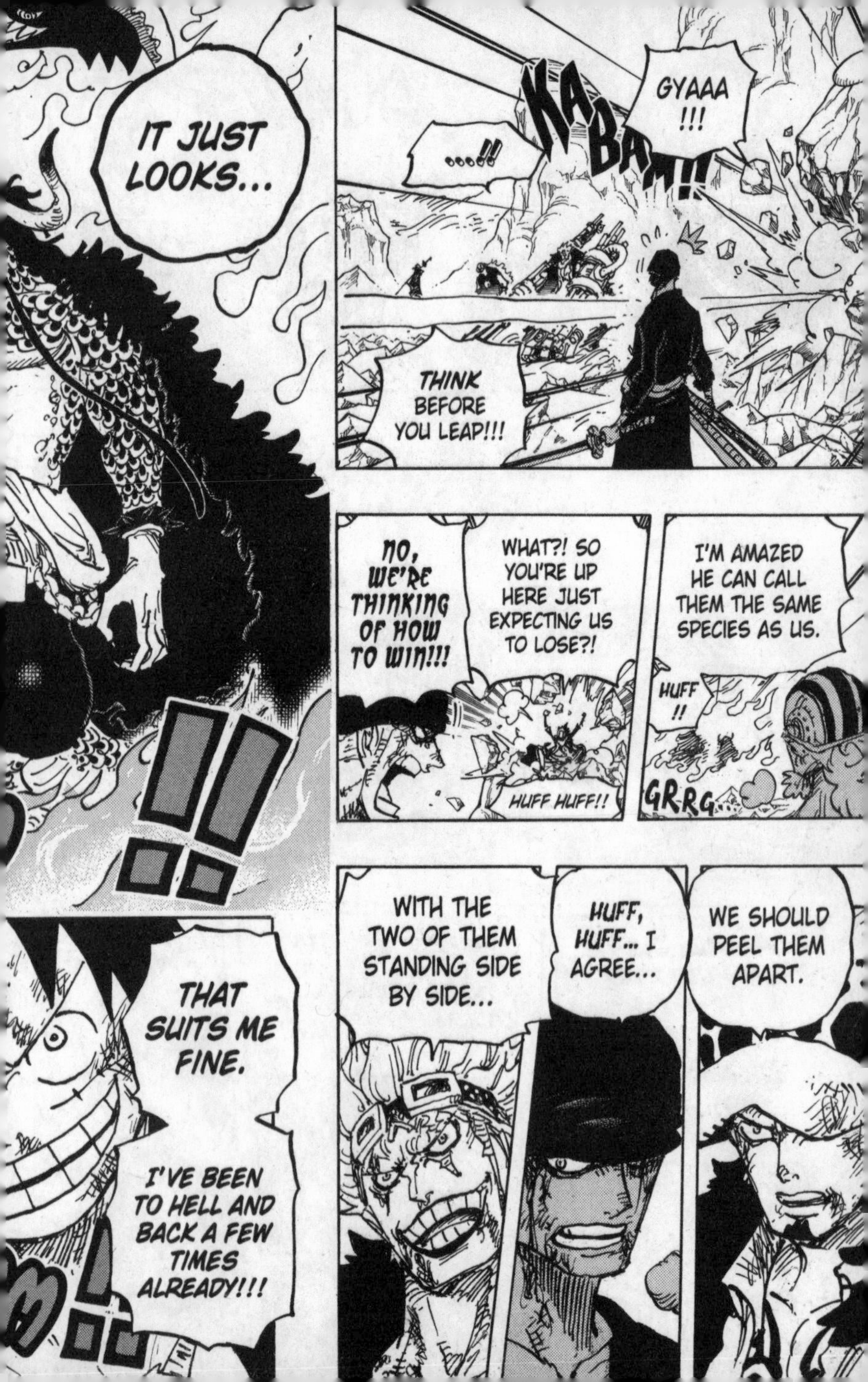
GYAAA !!!
KABAM!!
....!!
THINK BEFORE YOU LEAP!!!
I'M AMAZED HE CAN CALL THEM THE SAME SPECIES AS US.
HUFF !!
GRRG...
WHAT?! SO YOU'RE UP HERE JUST EXPECTING US TO LOSE?!
NO, WE'RE THINKING OF HOW TO WIN!!!
HUFF HUFF!!
IT JUST LOOKS...
WE SHOULD PEEL THEM APART.
HUFF, HUFF... I AGREE...
WITH THE TWO OF THEM STANDING SIDE BY SIDE...
THAT SUITS ME FINE.
I'VE BEEN TO HELL AND BACK A FEW TIMES ALREADY!!!

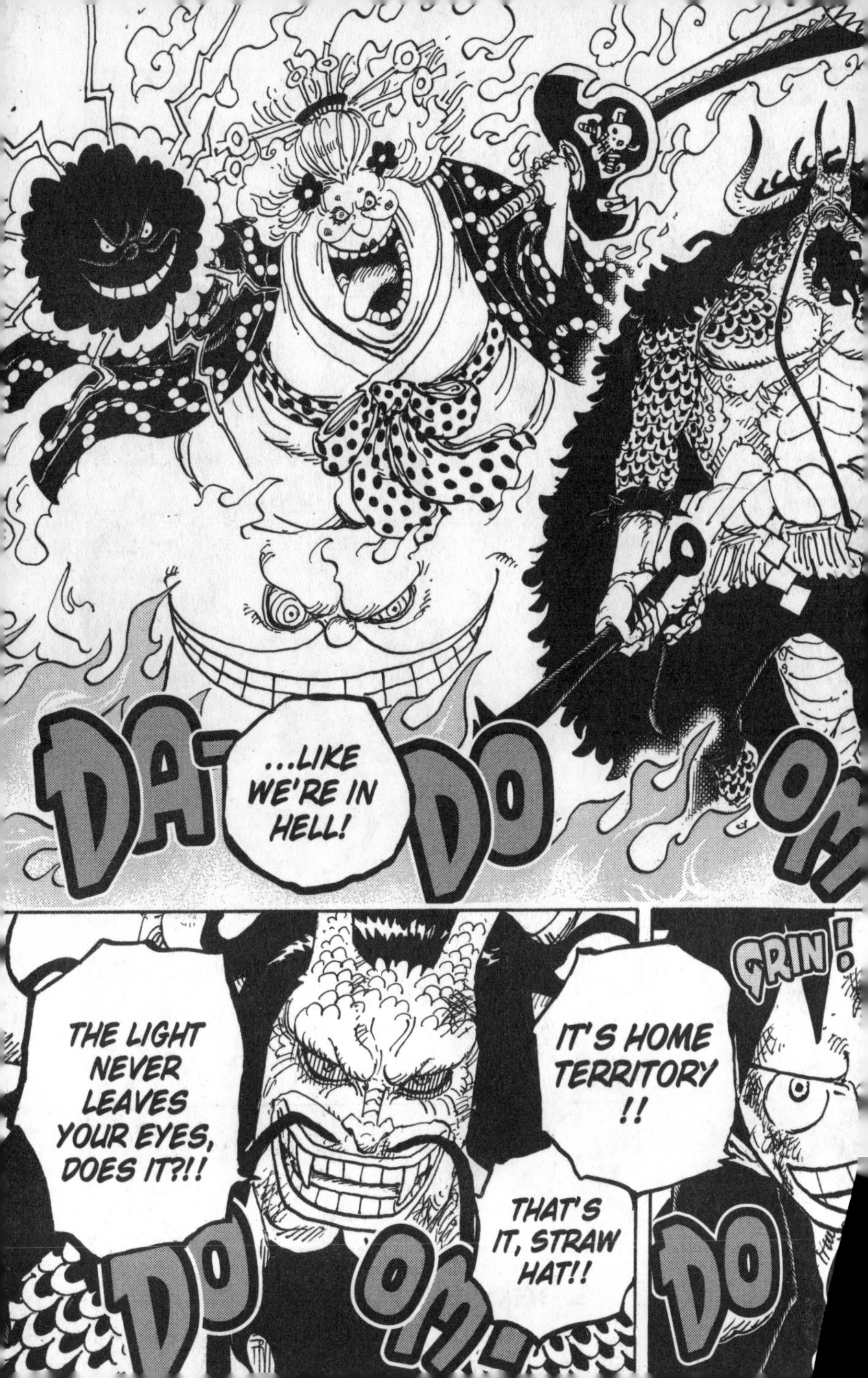
...LIKE WE'RE IN HELL!
DA-DO-OM
GRIN!
DO
IT'S HOME TERRITORY !!
THAT'S IT, STRAW HAT!!
THE LIGHT NEVER LEAVES YOUR EYES, DOES IT?!!
DO OM-

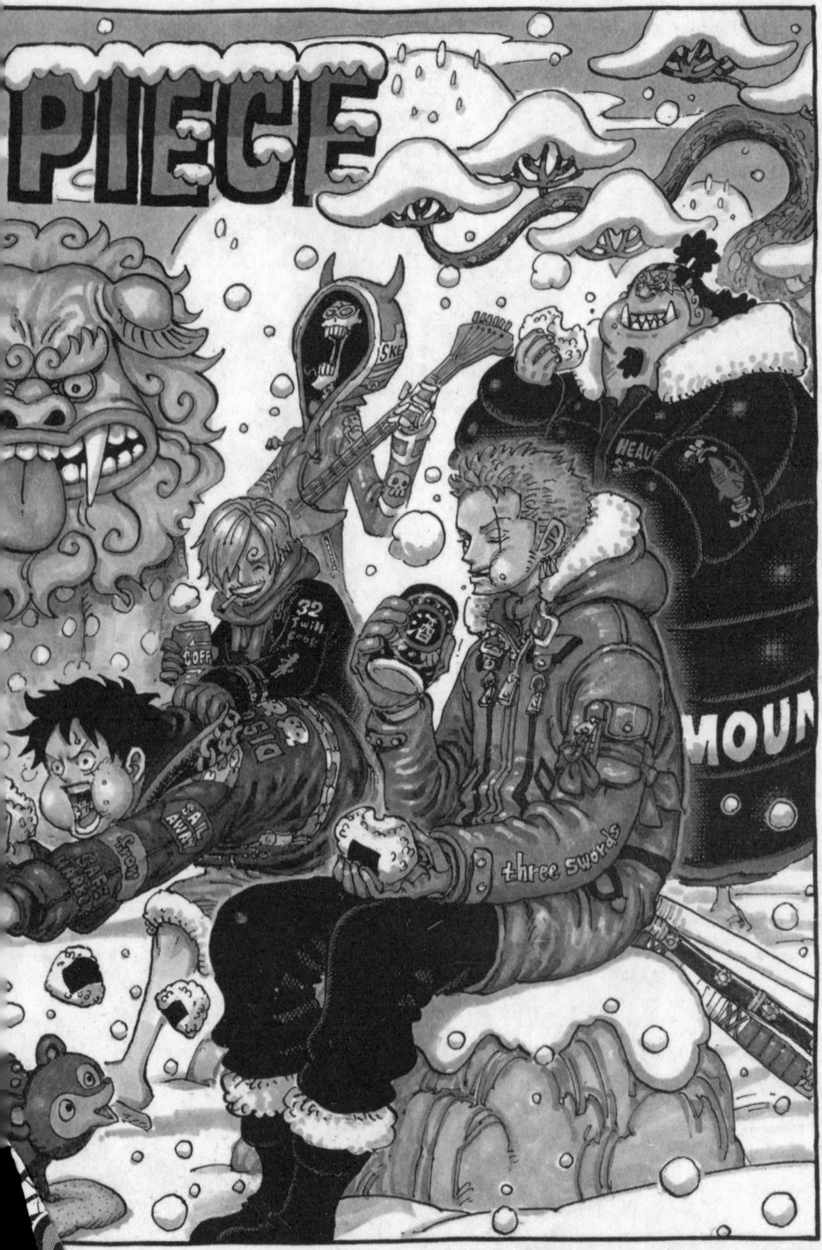
PIECE
32 I will cook
SAIL AWAY
three swords
MOUN

Chapter 1009: NARAKU

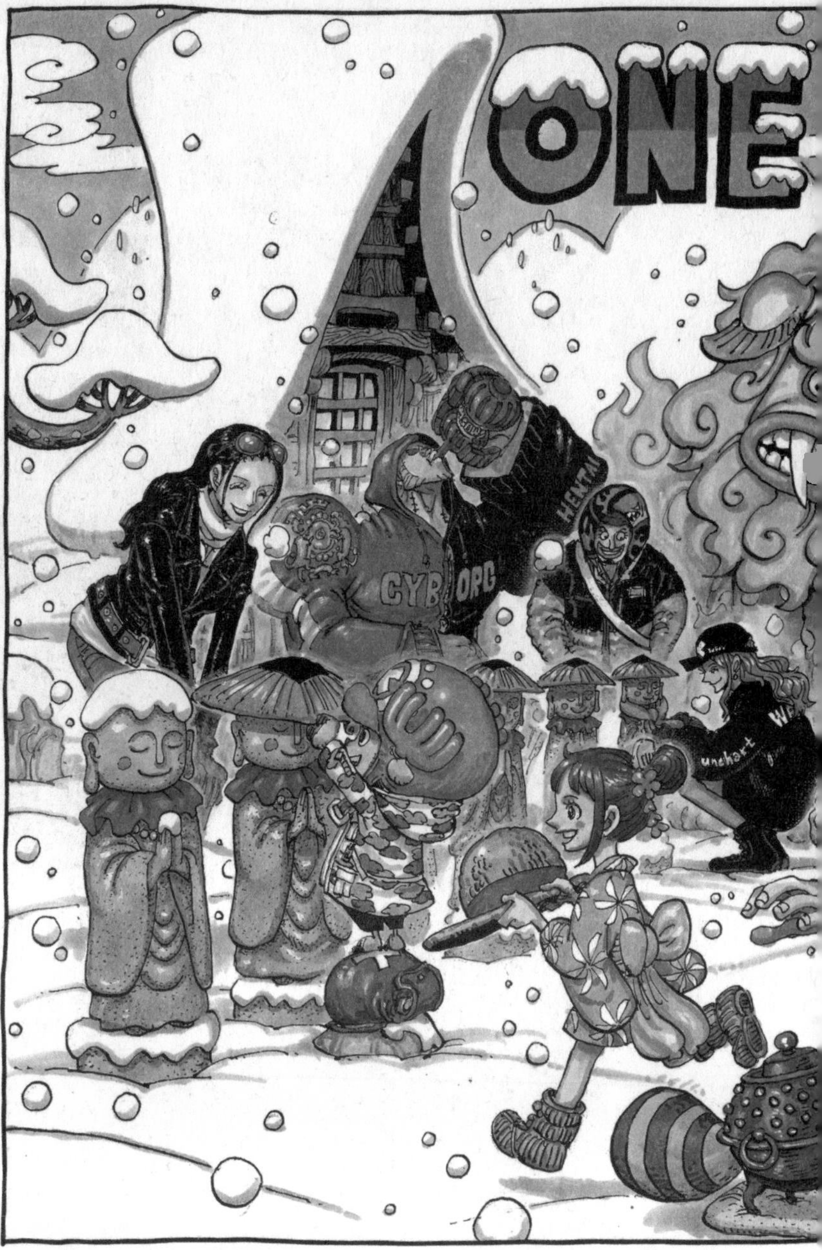
ONE
CYB
ORG
HENTAI
unchart

INSPIRED BY A READER REQUEST: "OTAMA AND KOMACHIYO PUTTING AMIGASA WOVEN HATS ON JIZO STATUES OF THE STRAW HAT CREW ON A RAINY DAY" BY HONEYLICKER

vol.100
ONE PIECE

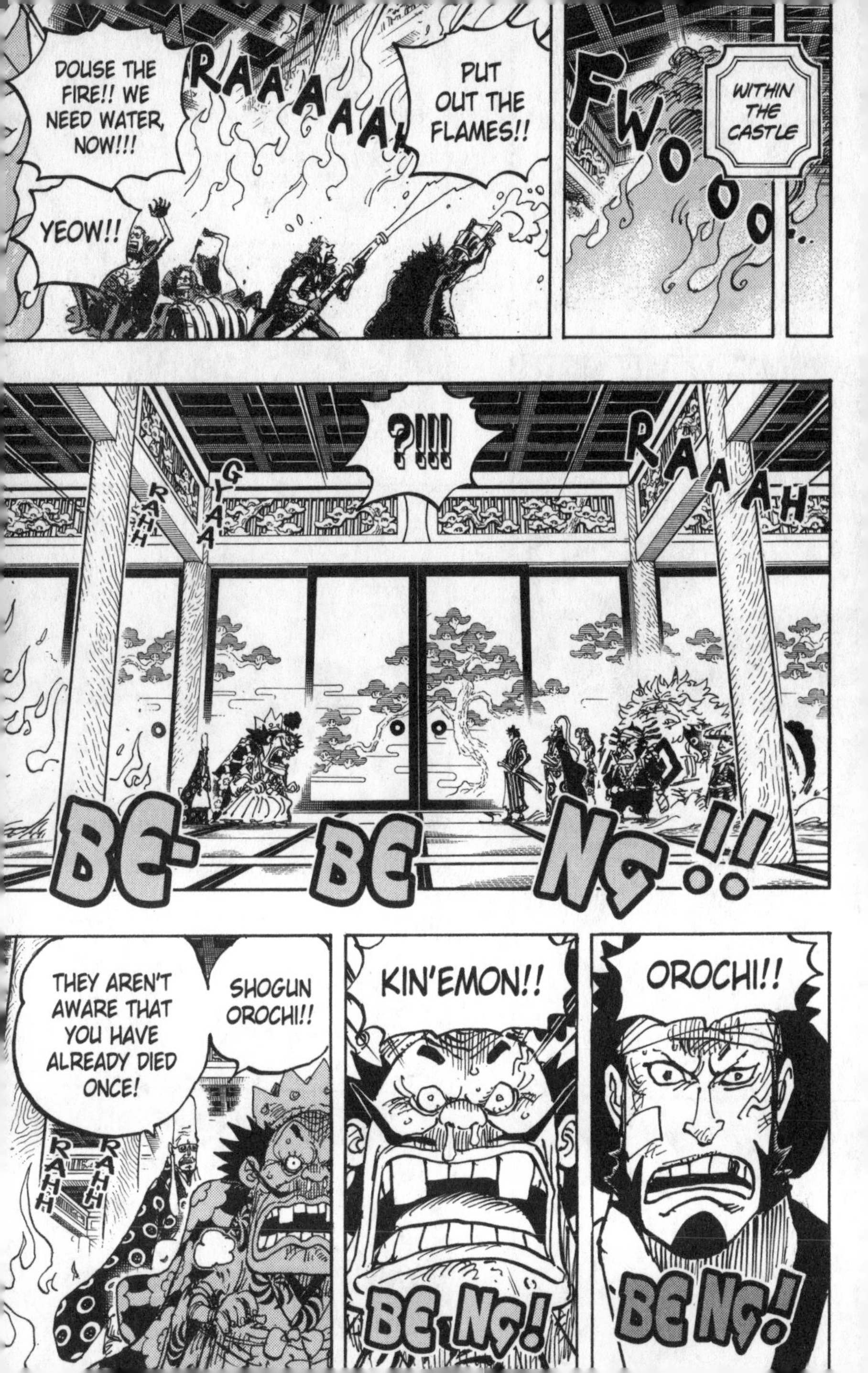

WITHIN THE CASTLE
FWOOOO...
PUT OUT THE FLAMES!!
RAAAAAH
DOUSE THE FIRE!! WE NEED WATER, NOW!!!
YEOW!!
RAAAH
?!!!
GYAA
RAHH
BE-BE-NG..!!
OROCHI!!
BE NG!
KIN'EMON!!
BE NG!
SHOGUN OROCHI!!
THEY AREN'T AWARE THAT YOU HAVE ALREADY DIED ONCE!
RAHH
RAHH

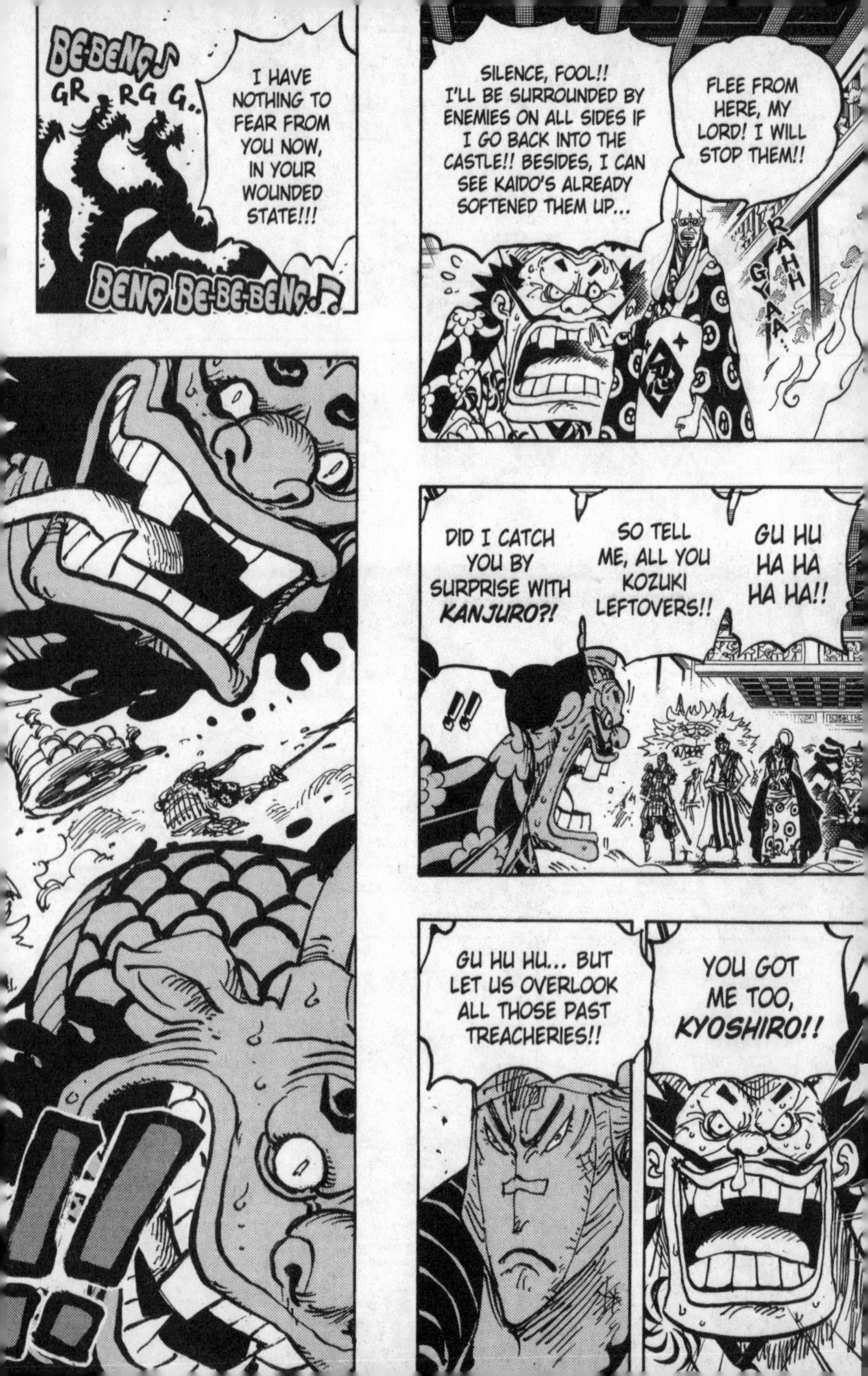
FLEE FROM HERE, MY LORD! I WILL STOP THEM!!
SILENCE, FOOL!! I'LL BE SURROUNDED BY ENEMIES ON ALL SIDES IF I GO BACK INTO THE CASTLE!! BESIDES, I CAN SEE KAIDO'S ALREADY SOFTENED THEM UP...
RAHH
GYAA...
GU HU HA HA HA HA!!
SO TELL ME, ALL YOU KOZUKI LEFTOVERS!!
DID I CATCH YOU BY SURPRISE WITH *KANJURO?!*
!!
YOU GOT ME TOO, *KYOSHIRO!!*
GU HU HU... BUT LET US OVERLOOK ALL THOSE PAST TREACHERIES!!
BE-BENG♪
GR RG G..
I HAVE NOTHING TO FEAR FROM YOU NOW, IN YOUR WOUNDED STATE!!!
BENG BE-BE-BENG♪♪

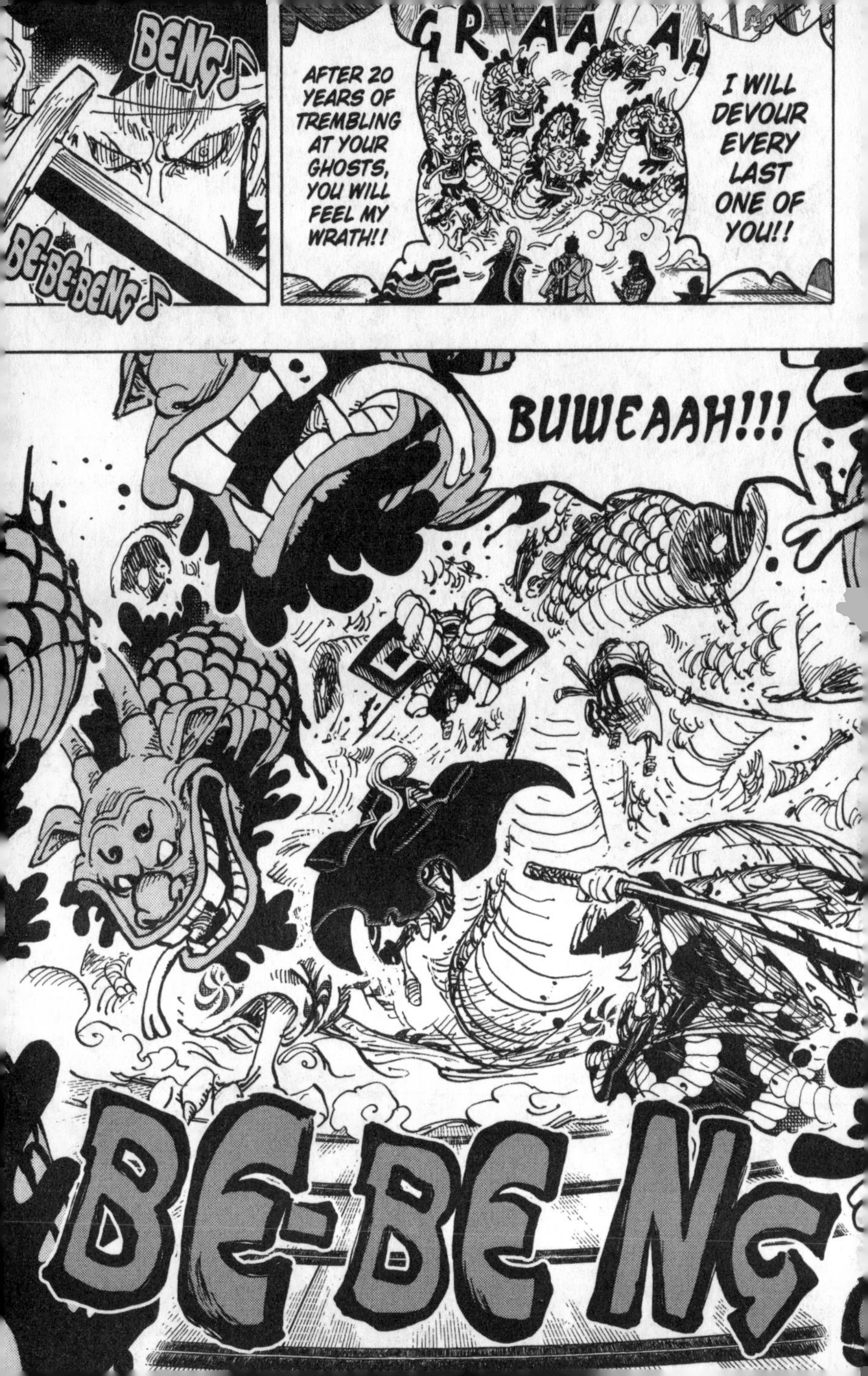
GRAAAH
I WILL DEVOUR EVERY LAST ONE OF YOU!!
AFTER 20 YEARS OF TREMBLING AT YOUR GHOSTS, YOU WILL FEEL MY WRATH!!
BENG♪
BE-BE-BENG♪
BUWEAAH!!!
BE-BE-NG

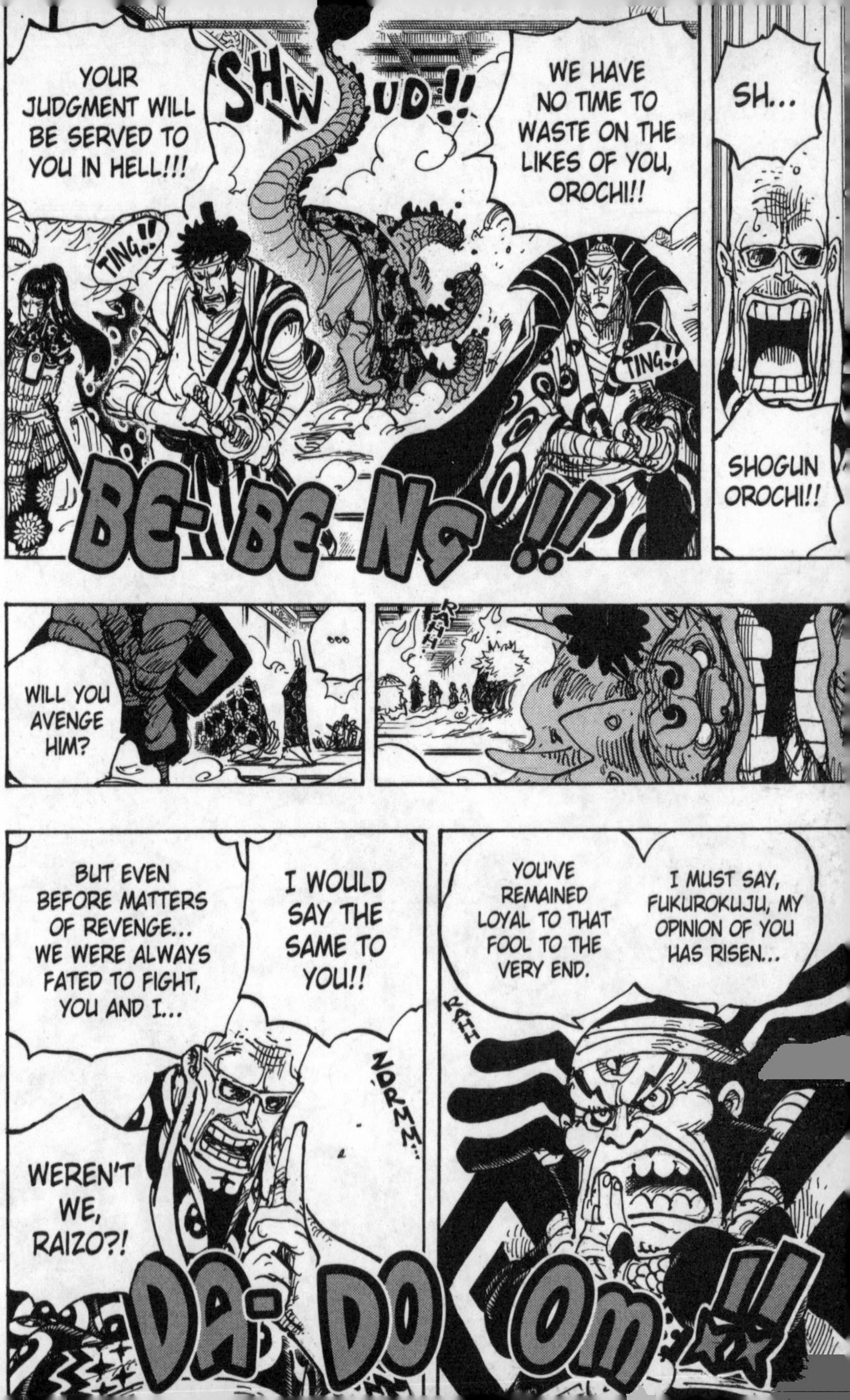
SH...
SHOGUN OROCHI!!
WE HAVE NO TIME TO WASTE ON THE LIKES OF YOU, OROCHI!!
SHWUD!!
YOUR JUDGMENT WILL BE SERVED TO YOU IN HELL!!!
TING!!
TING!!
BE-BE-NG!!
RAHH
...
WILL YOU AVENGE HIM?
I MUST SAY, FUKUROKUJU, MY OPINION OF YOU HAS RISEN...
YOU'VE REMAINED LOYAL TO THAT FOOL TO THE VERY END.
RAHH
I WOULD SAY THE SAME TO YOU!!
BUT EVEN BEFORE MATTERS OF REVENGE... WE WERE ALWAYS FATED TO FIGHT, YOU AND I...
ZDRMM
WEREN'T WE, RAIZO?!
DA-DOOM!!

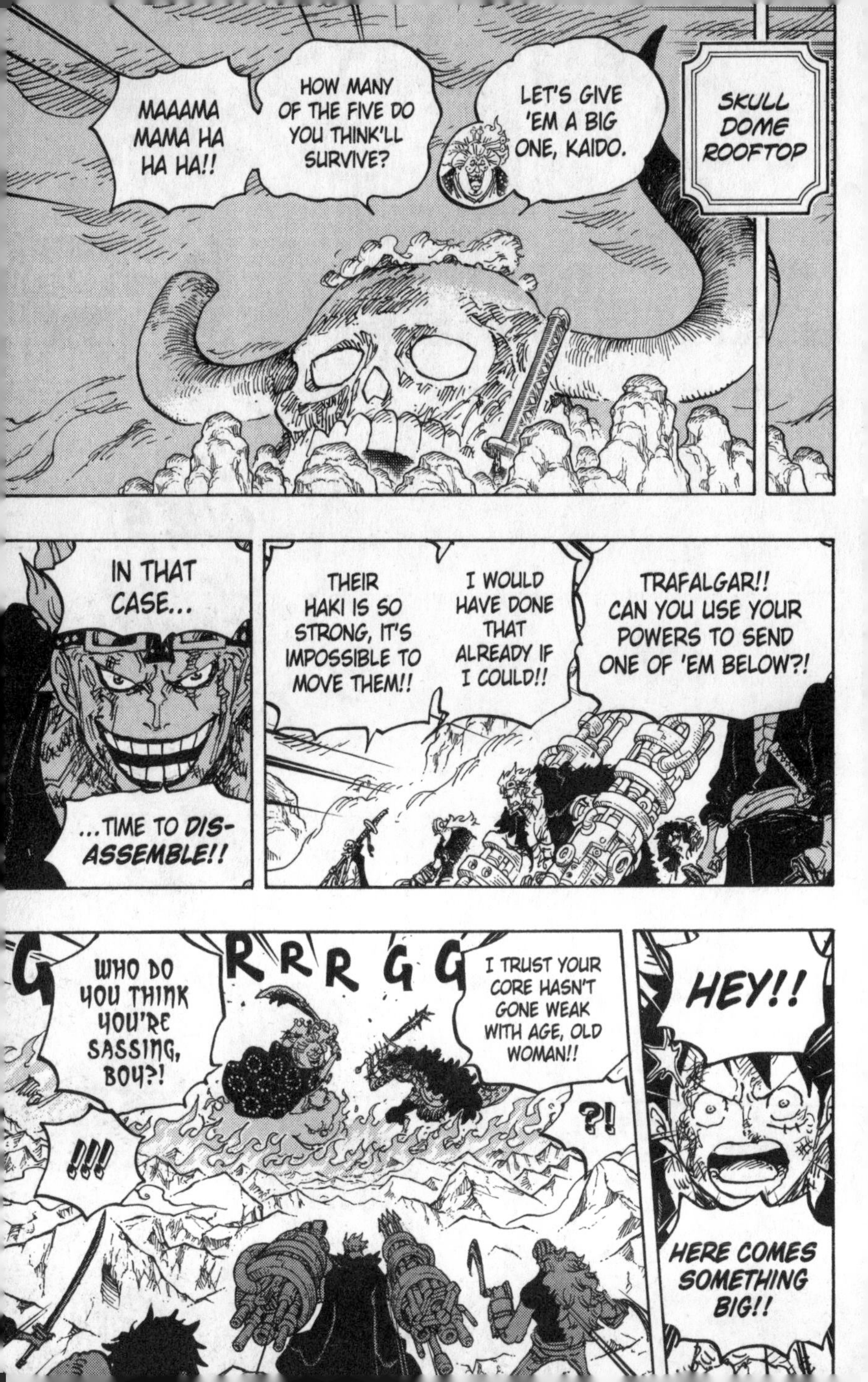
SKULL DOME ROOFTOP
LET'S GIVE 'EM A BIG ONE, KAIDO.
HOW MANY OF THE FIVE DO YOU THINK'LL SURVIVE?
MAAAMA MAMA HA HA HA!!
TRAFALGAR!! CAN YOU USE YOUR POWERS TO SEND ONE OF 'EM BELOW?!
I WOULD HAVE DONE THAT ALREADY IF I COULD!!
THEIR HAKI IS SO STRONG, IT'S IMPOSSIBLE TO MOVE THEM!!
IN THAT CASE...
...TIME TO DIS-ASSEMBLE!!
HEY!!
HERE COMES SOMETHING BIG!!
?!
I TRUST YOUR CORE HASN'T GONE WEAK WITH AGE, OLD WOMAN!!
RRRGG
G
WHO DO YOU THINK YOU'RE SASSING, BOY?!
!!!

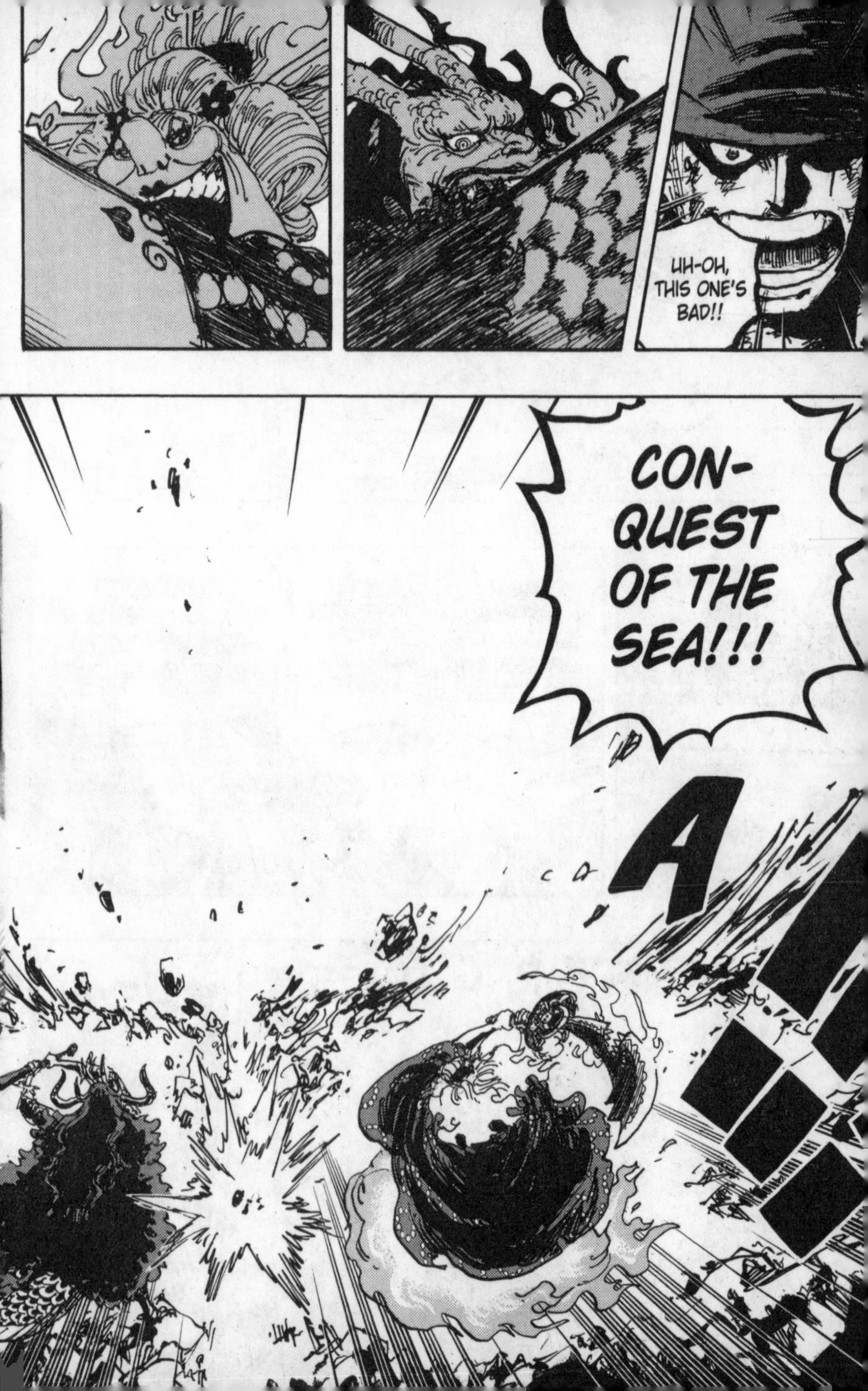
UH-OH, THIS ONE'S BAD!!
CON-QUEST OF THE SEA!!!
A

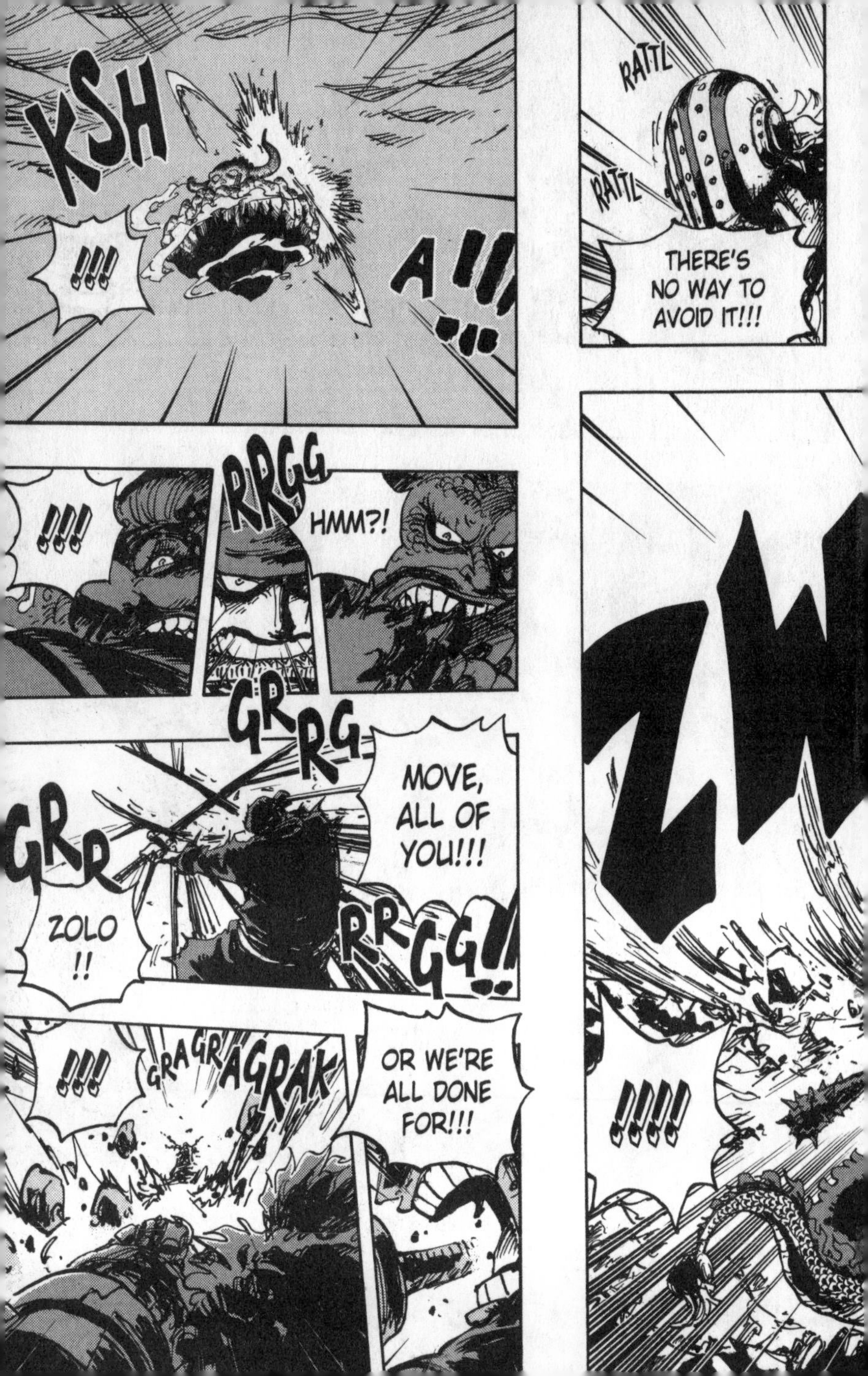
RATTL
RATTL
THERE'S NO WAY TO AVOID IT!!!
KSH
!!!
A!!!
ZW
!!!!
HMM?!
RRGG
!!!
GRRG
MOVE, ALL OF YOU!!!
RRGG!!
ZOLO !!
GRR
OR WE'RE ALL DONE FOR!!!
GRAGRAGRAK
!!!

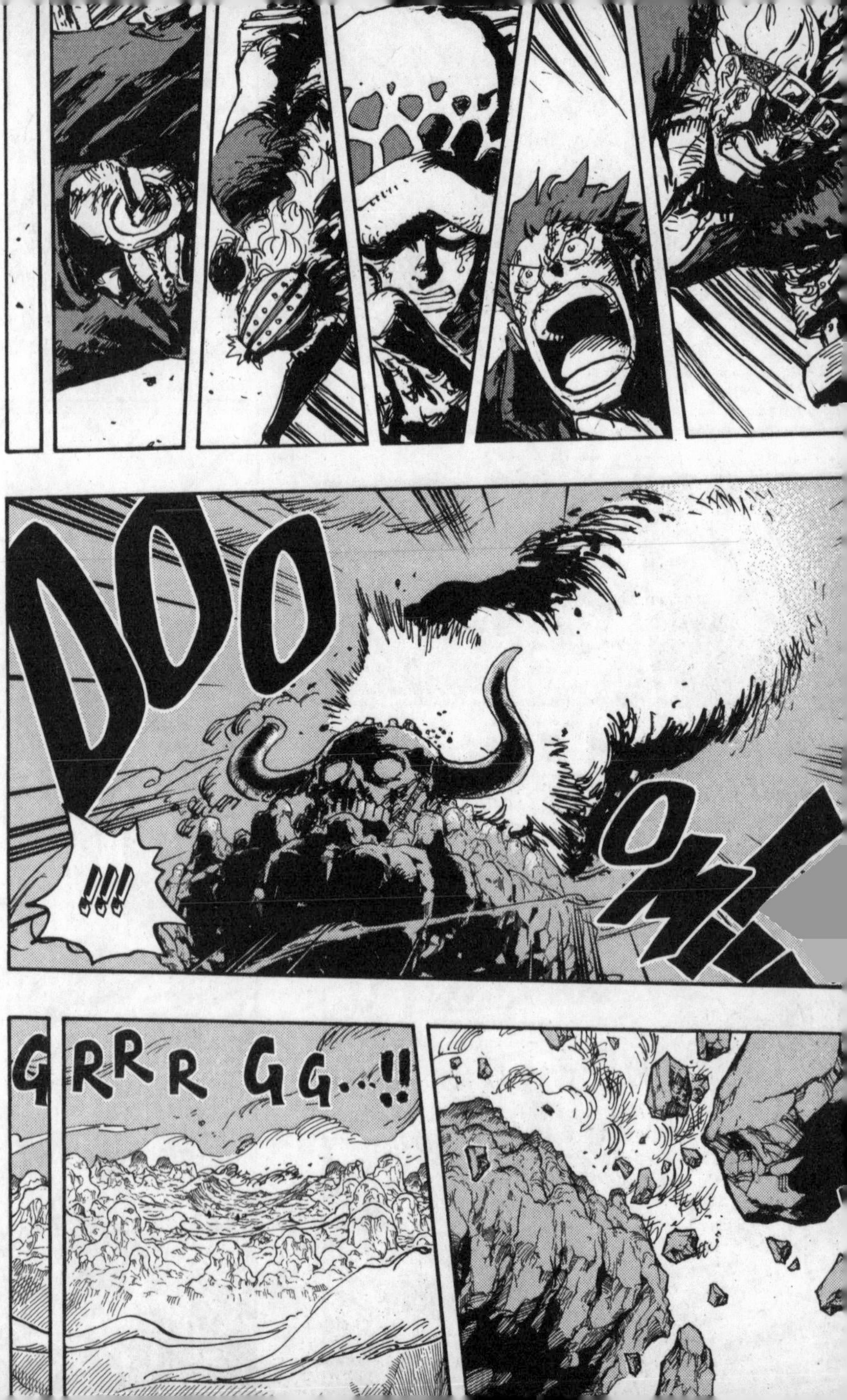
DOOON!!
!!!
GRRRR GG...!!

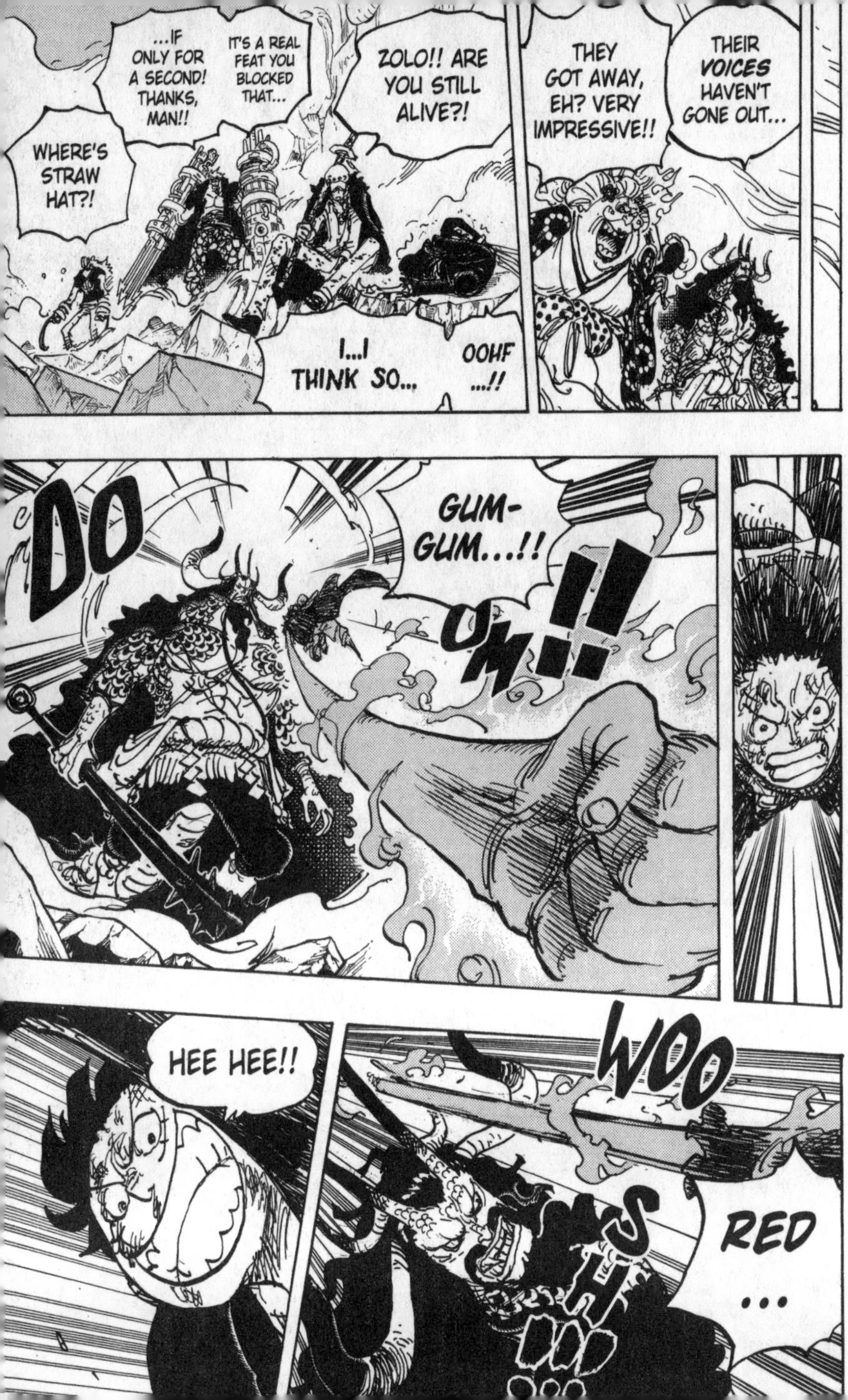
THEIR VOICES HAVEN'T GONE OUT...
THEY GOT AWAY, EH? VERY IMPRESSIVE!!
ZOLO!! ARE YOU STILL ALIVE?!
IT'S A REAL FEAT YOU BLOCKED THAT...
...IF ONLY FOR A SECOND! THANKS, MAN!!
WHERE'S STRAW HAT?!
OOHF ...!!
I...I THINK SO...
GUM-GUM...!!
DO
OM!!
WOO
SH
RED ...
HEE HEE!!

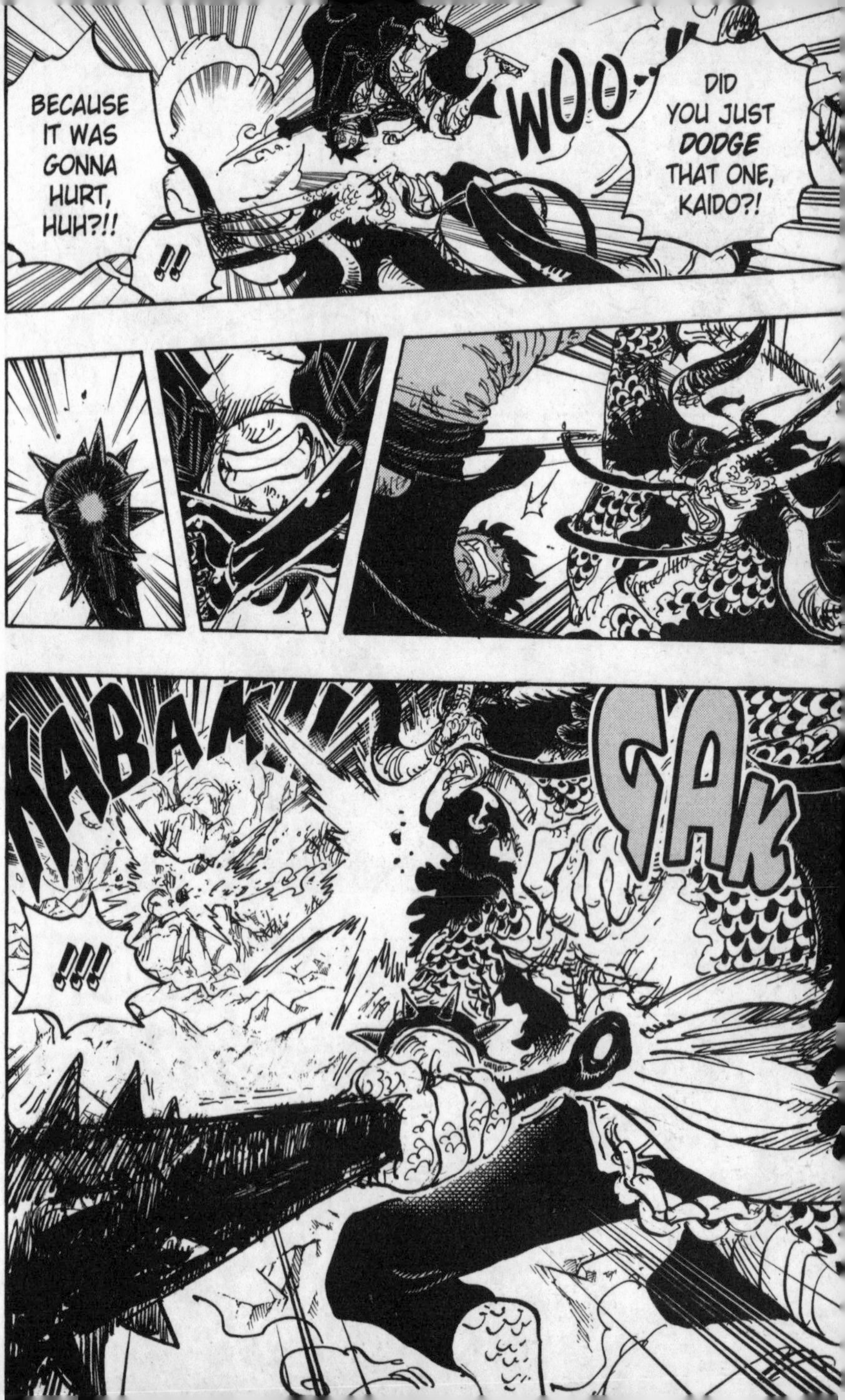
DID YOU JUST DODGE THAT ONE, KAIDO?!
WOO
BECAUSE IT WAS GONNA HURT, HUH?!!
!!
GAK
BABAM
!!!

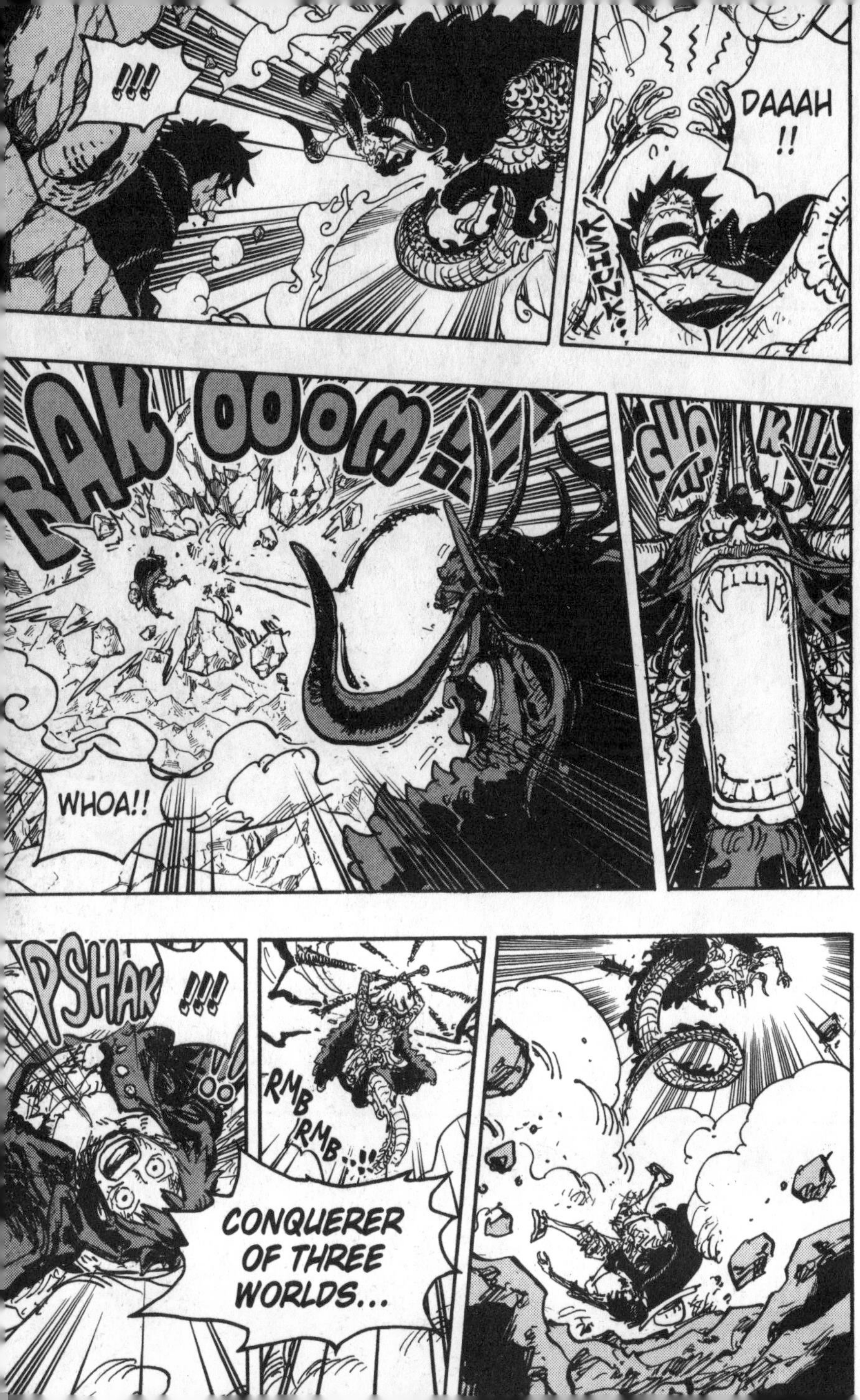
DAAAH!!
KSHUNK...
!!!
SHAK!!
BAKOOOM!!!
WHOA!!
RMB RMB...!!
PSHAK!!!
CONQUERER OF THREE WORLDS...

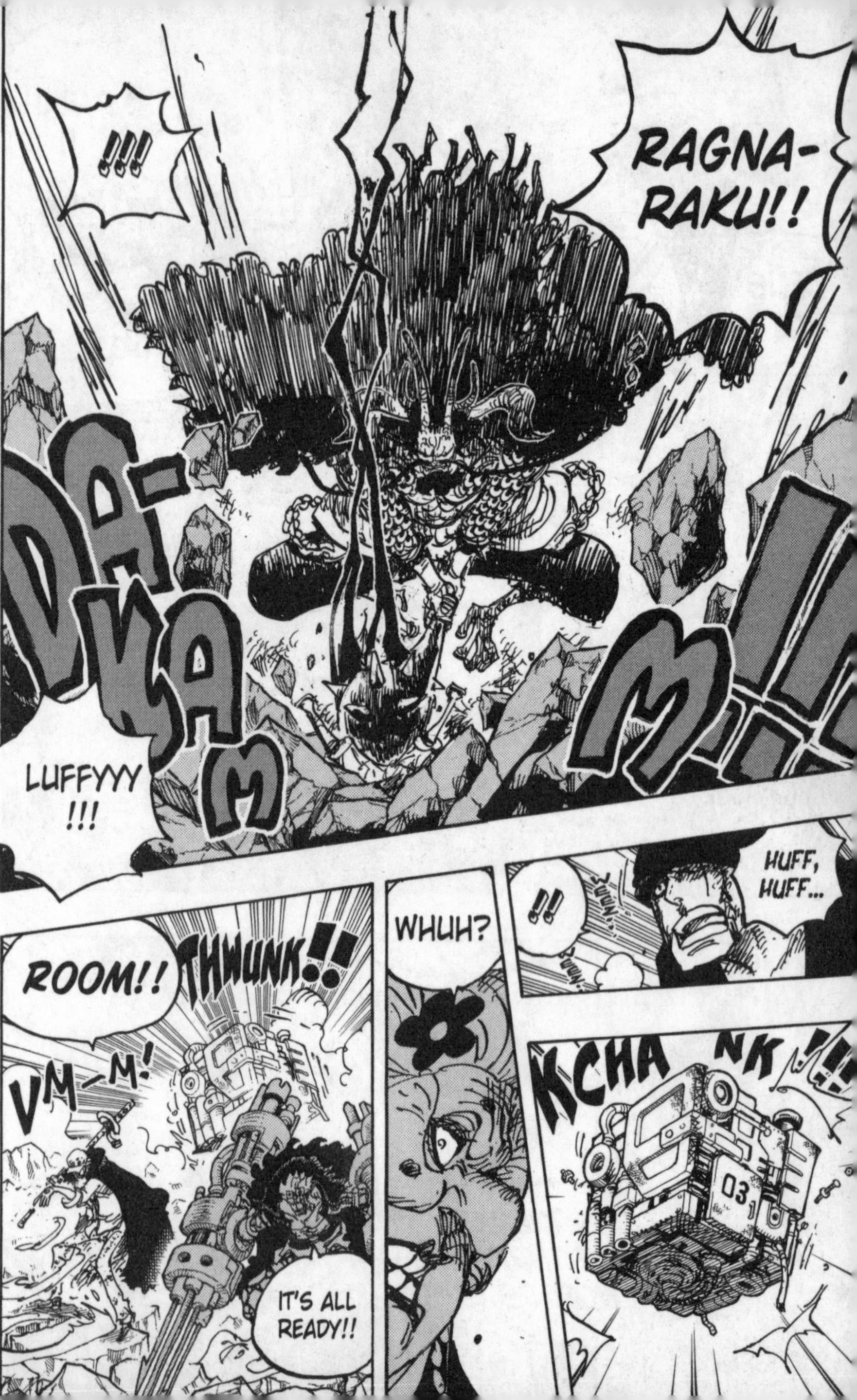
RAGNA-RAKU!!
!!!
DA-KAMM!!
LUFFYYY !!!
HUFF, HUFF...
!!
KCHA NK!!!
WHUH?
ROOM!!
THWUNK!!
VM-M!
IT'S ALL READY!!

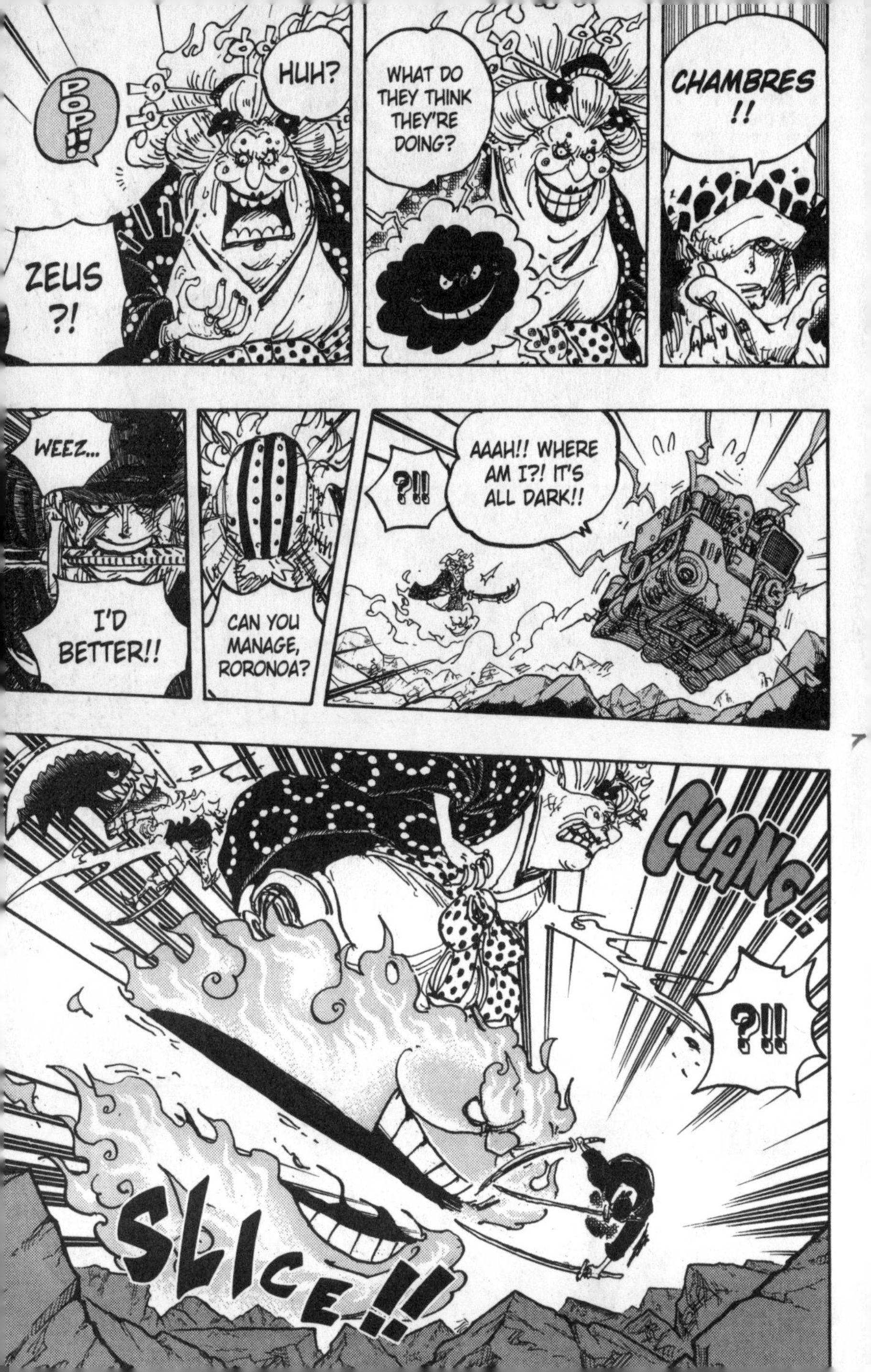
CHAMBRES!!
WHAT DO THEY THINK THEY'RE DOING?
HUH?
POP!!
ZEUS?!
AAAH!! WHERE AM I?! IT'S ALL DARK!!
?!!
CAN YOU MANAGE, RORONOA?
WEEZ...
I'D BETTER!!
CLANG!!
?!!
SLICE!!

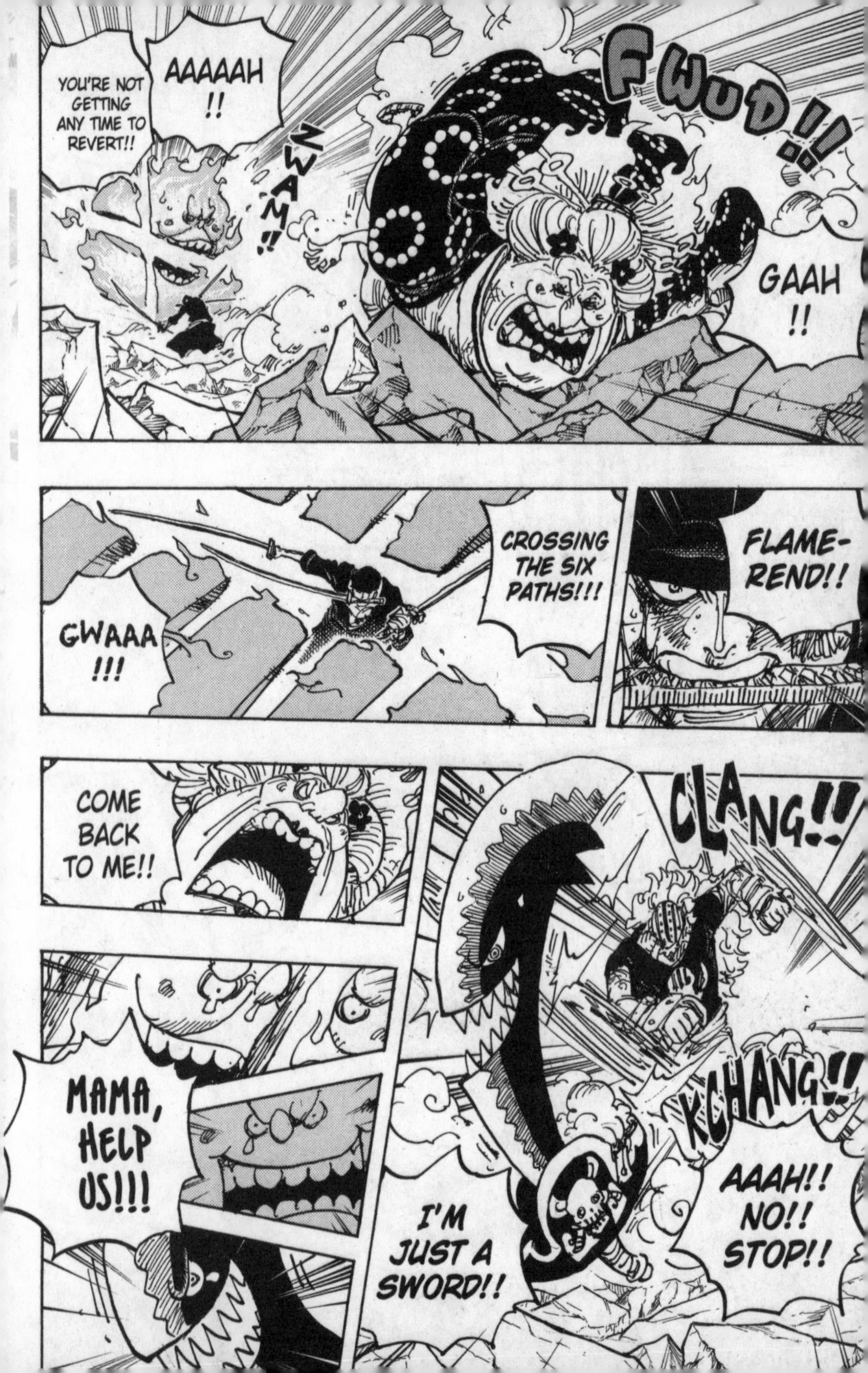
FWUD!!
GAAH!!
ZWAM!!
AAAAAH!!
YOU'RE NOT GETTING ANY TIME TO REVERT!!
FLAME-REND!!
CROSSING THE SIX PATHS!!!
GWAAA!!!
CLANG!!
KCHANG!!
AAAH!! NO!! STOP!!
I'M JUST A SWORD!!
COME BACK TO ME!!
MAMA, HELP US!!!

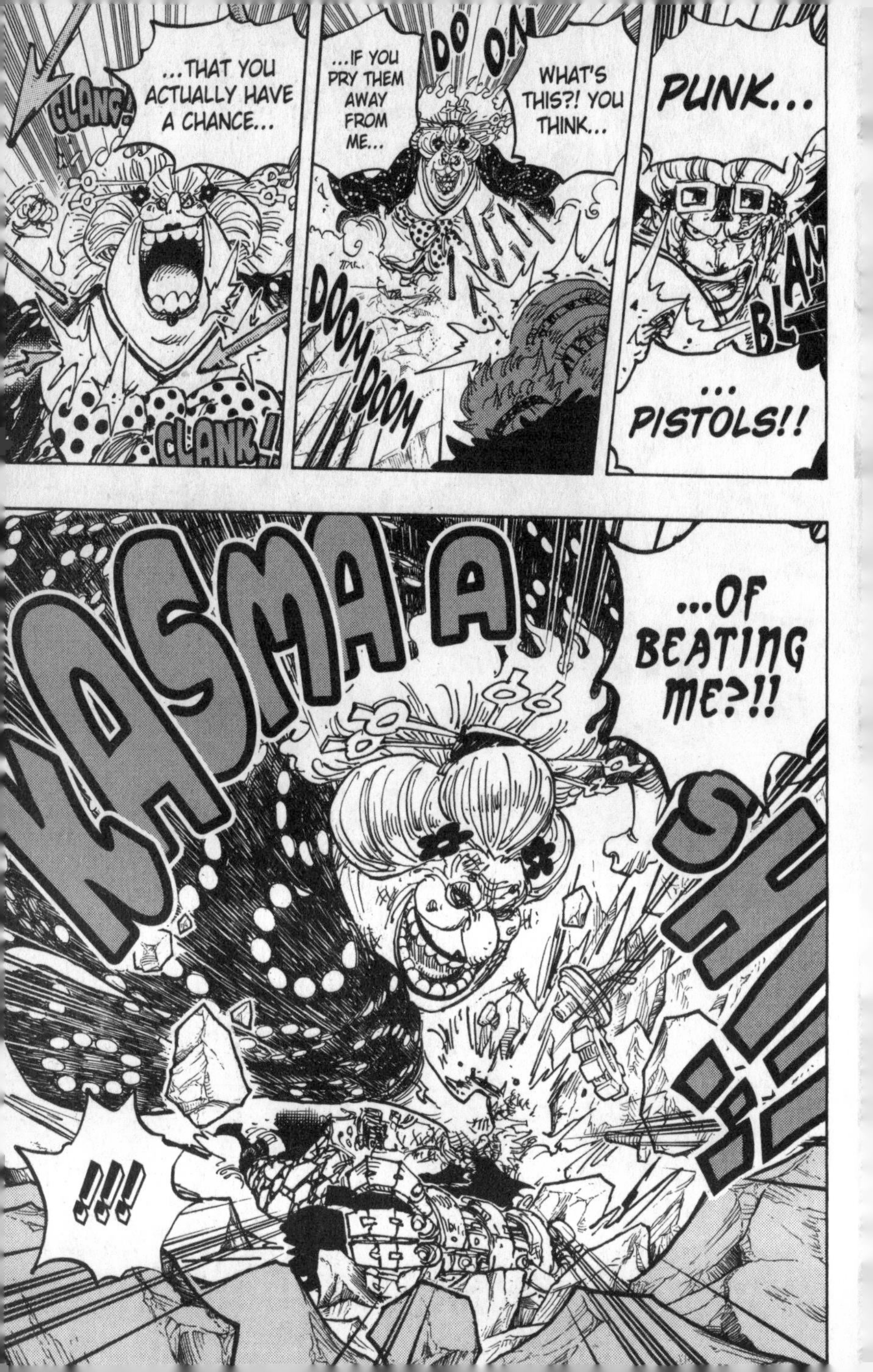
PUNK...
BLAM
... PISTOLS!!
WHAT'S THIS?! YOU THINK...
...IF YOU PRY THEM AWAY FROM ME...
DO ON
DOOM DOOM DOOM
...THAT YOU ACTUALLY HAVE A CHANCE...
CLANG!
CLANK!!
...OF BEATING ME?!!
!!!

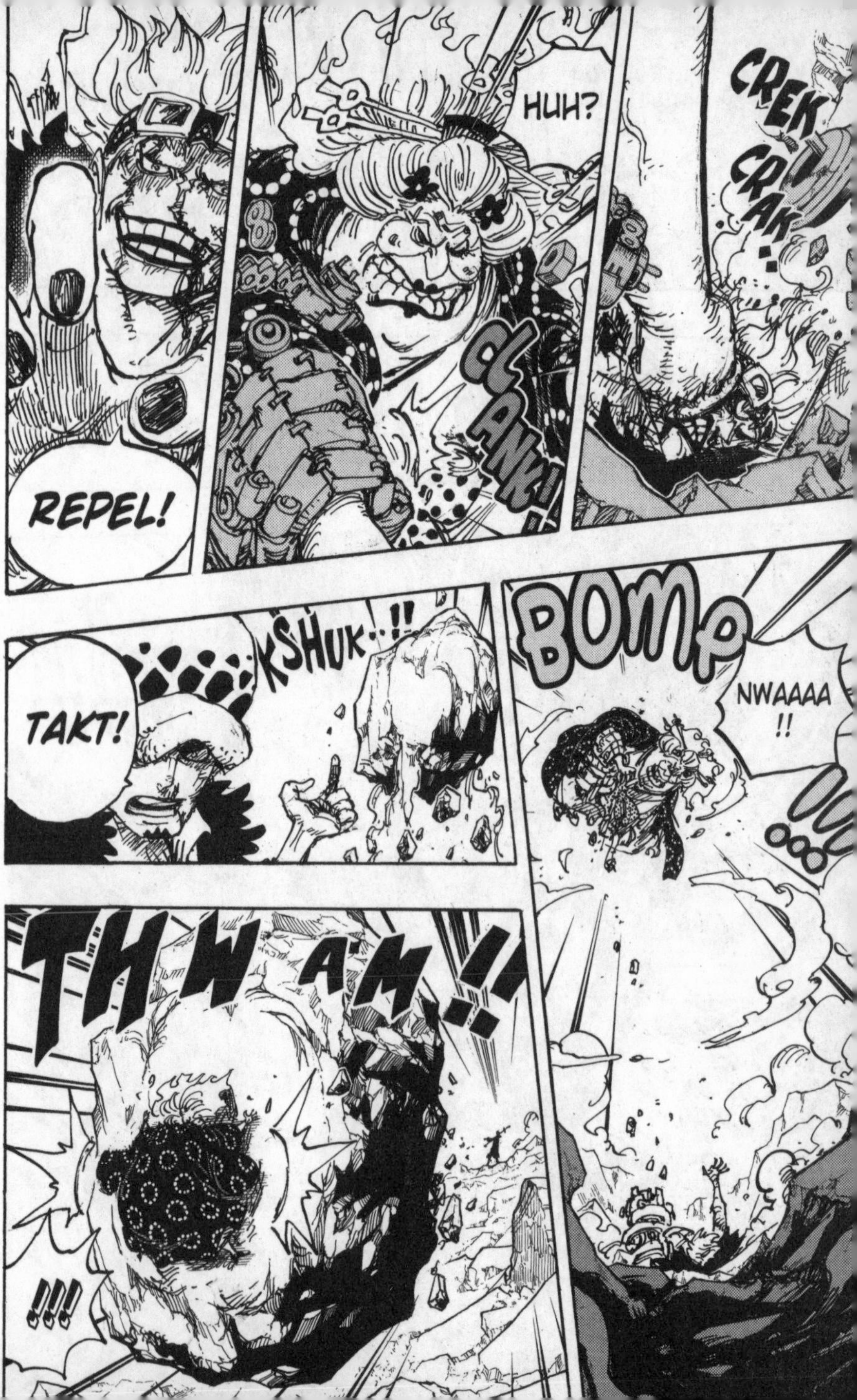
CREK
CRAK...
HUH?
CLANK!!
REPEL!
BOMP
NWAAAA !!
KSHUK..!!
TAKT!
THWAM!!
!!!

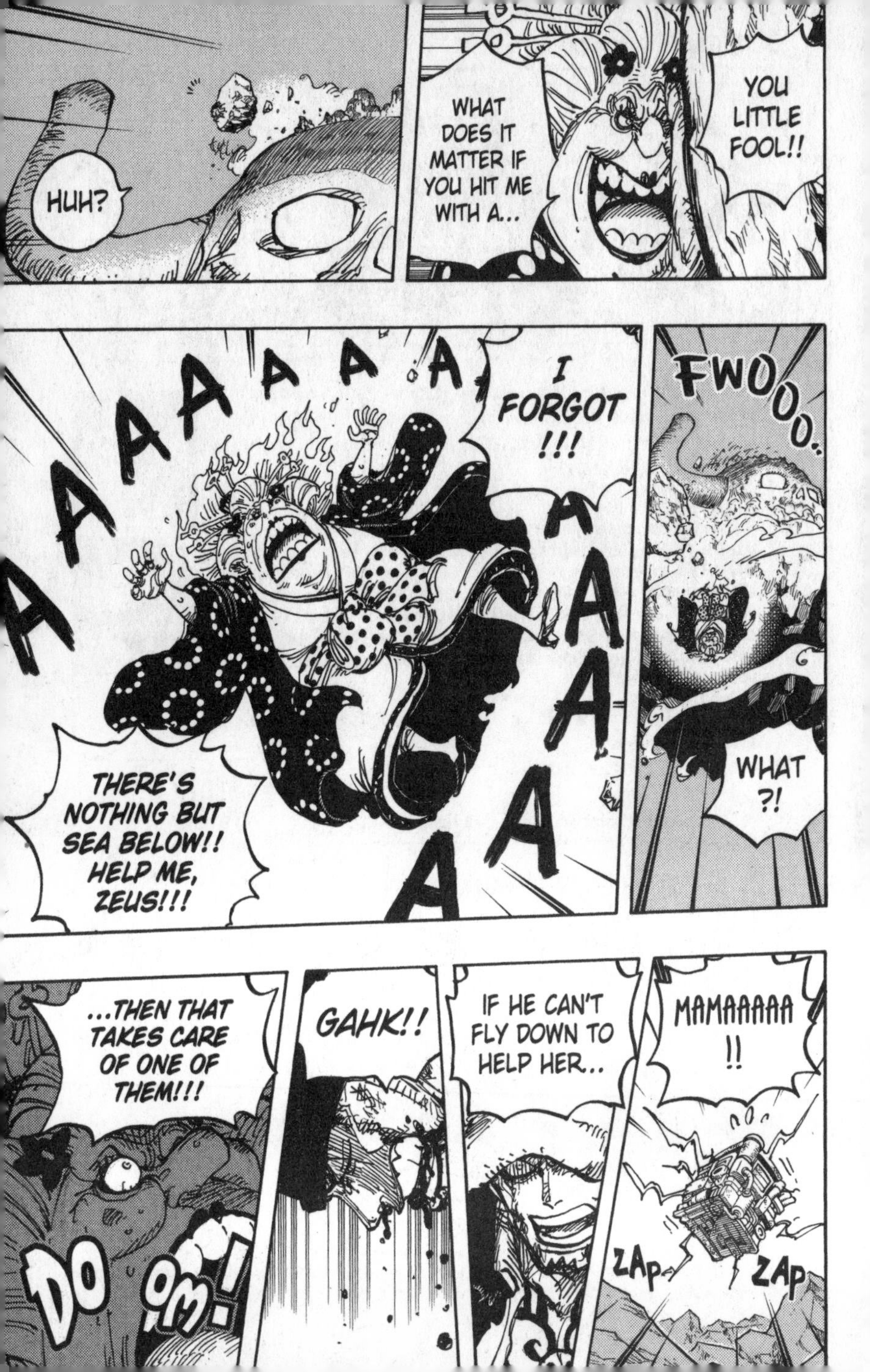
YOU LITTLE FOOL!!
WHAT DOES IT MATTER IF YOU HIT ME WITH A...
HUH?
FWOOOO..
WHAT?!
I FORGOT!!!
AAAAAAAAAAAAA
THERE'S NOTHING BUT SEA BELOW!! HELP ME, ZEUS!!!
MAMAAAAA!!
ZAP
ZAP
IF HE CAN'T FLY DOWN TO HELP HER..
GAHK!!
...THEN THAT TAKES CARE OF ONE OF THEM!!!
DOOOM!

SBS Question Corner

質問コーナー
エス
ビー
エス

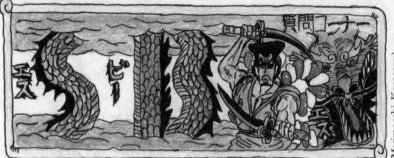

(Marimocchi, Kanagawa)

Q: Are Ulti and Page One actual siblings? I know that sometimes, fellow apprentices will call one another "Sister" or "Brother" out of respect, and they don't look that alike, so I was curious! I love the Ulti-Paypay siblings! ♡♡

--Don (20s)

Ulti

Page One

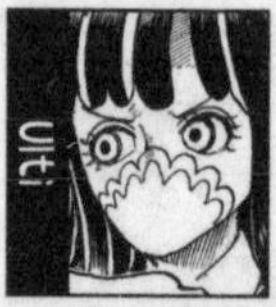

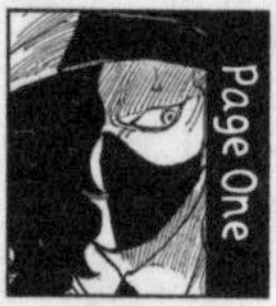

A: Yes, they are actual brother and sister. Their father was a pirate, and after he died, his rival Kaido took them in, or so they've heard. Ulti has always been clever, and she stole two of Kaido's Devil Fruits, which is how she and Page One got their powers. That gave them the strength to thrive in this "survival of the fittest" pirate crew, and helped them claw their way up to the rank of Tobi Roppo.

Q: Question, Odacchi!! Which of the following explains what's going on with Basil Hawkins' eyebrows?!

1. He was born like that
2. He drew them on
3. They're super thick and he shaved them
4. He lost a bet

I love Hawkins' eyebrows!!

--Yashirai

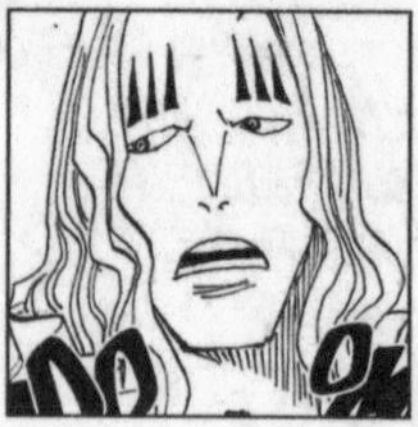

A: Um, it's actually 5. Each triangle is one eyebrow hair. That means Hawkins has six eyebrow hairs.

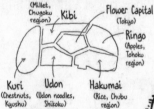

Kibi
(Millet, Chugoku region)
Flower Capital
(Tokyo)
Ringo
(Apples, Tohoku region)
Kuri
(Chestnuts, Kyushu)
Udon
(Udon noodles, Shikoku)
Hakumai
(Rice, Chubu region)

Q: Mr. Oda!! Did you base the regions of Wano on ← these concepts of food and where they come from in Japan?

--Captain Shunya

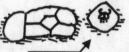

A: Yes, that's right! The names are homophones of types of food, and the regions are based on different areas of the islands of Japan. Originally my arrangement was like this. Onigashima was going to represent Hokkaido, but for story reasons, I moved it to where it is now.

Chapter 1010:
COLOR OF THE SUPREME KING

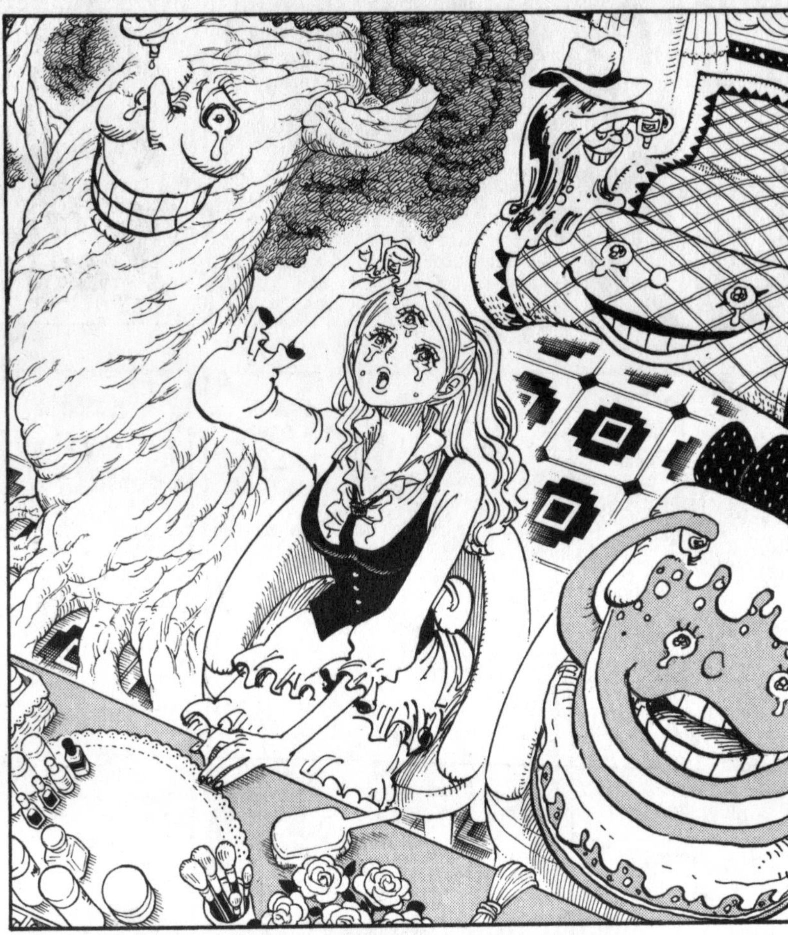

READER REQUEST: "PUDDING PUTTING IN EYE DROPS" BY MATTSU

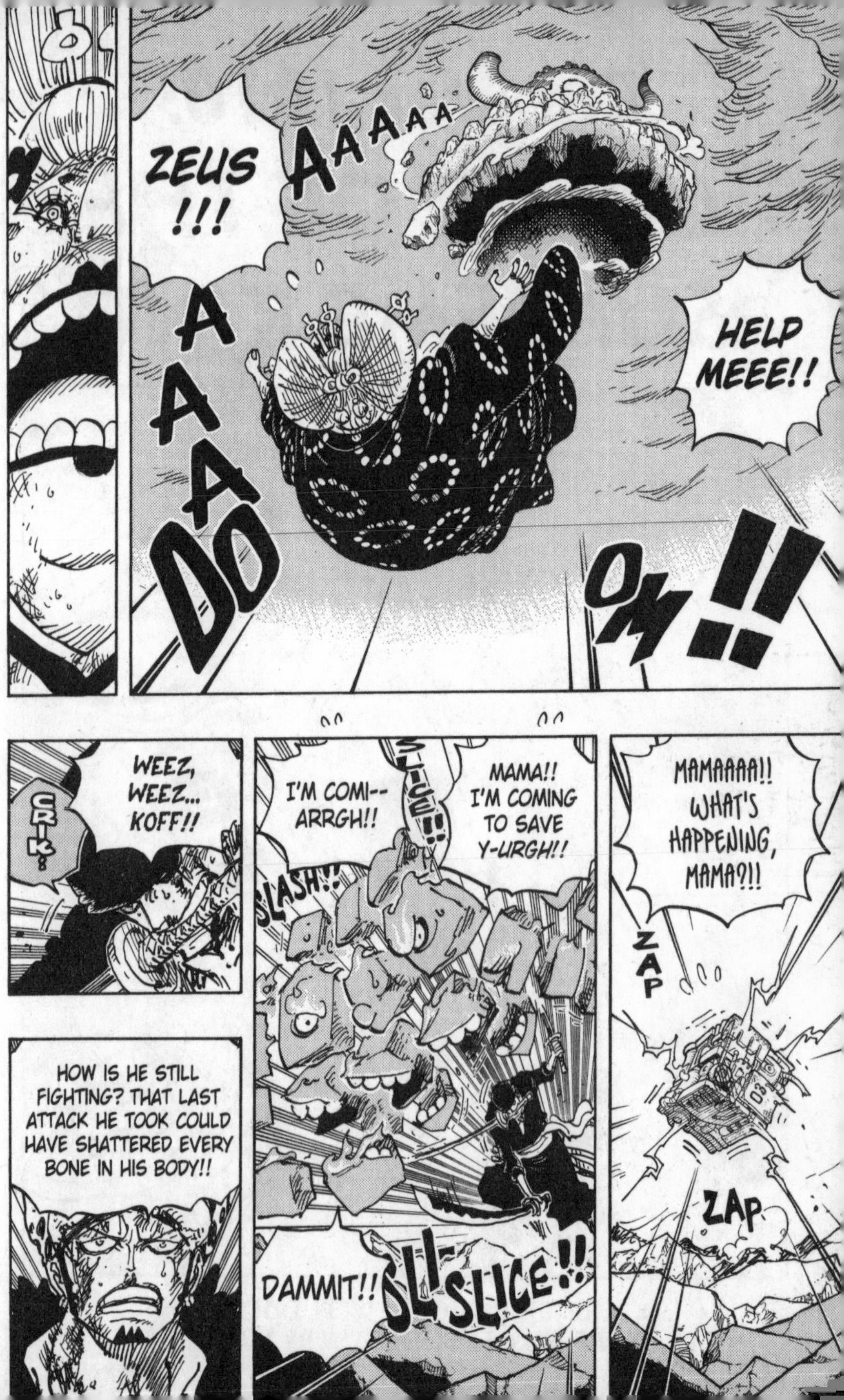
ZEUS!!!
AAAAAAAAAA
HELP MEEE!!
DOOM!!
MAMAAAA!! WHAT'S HAPPENING, MAMA?!!
ZAP
ZAP
MAMA!! I'M COMING TO SAVE Y-URGH!!
SLICE!!
I'M COMI-- ARRGH!!
SLASH!!
DAMMIT!!
SLI-SLICE!!
WEEZ, WEEZ... KOFF!!
CRIK
HOW IS HE STILL FIGHTING? THAT LAST ATTACK HE TOOK COULD HAVE SHATTERED EVERY BONE IN HIS BODY!!

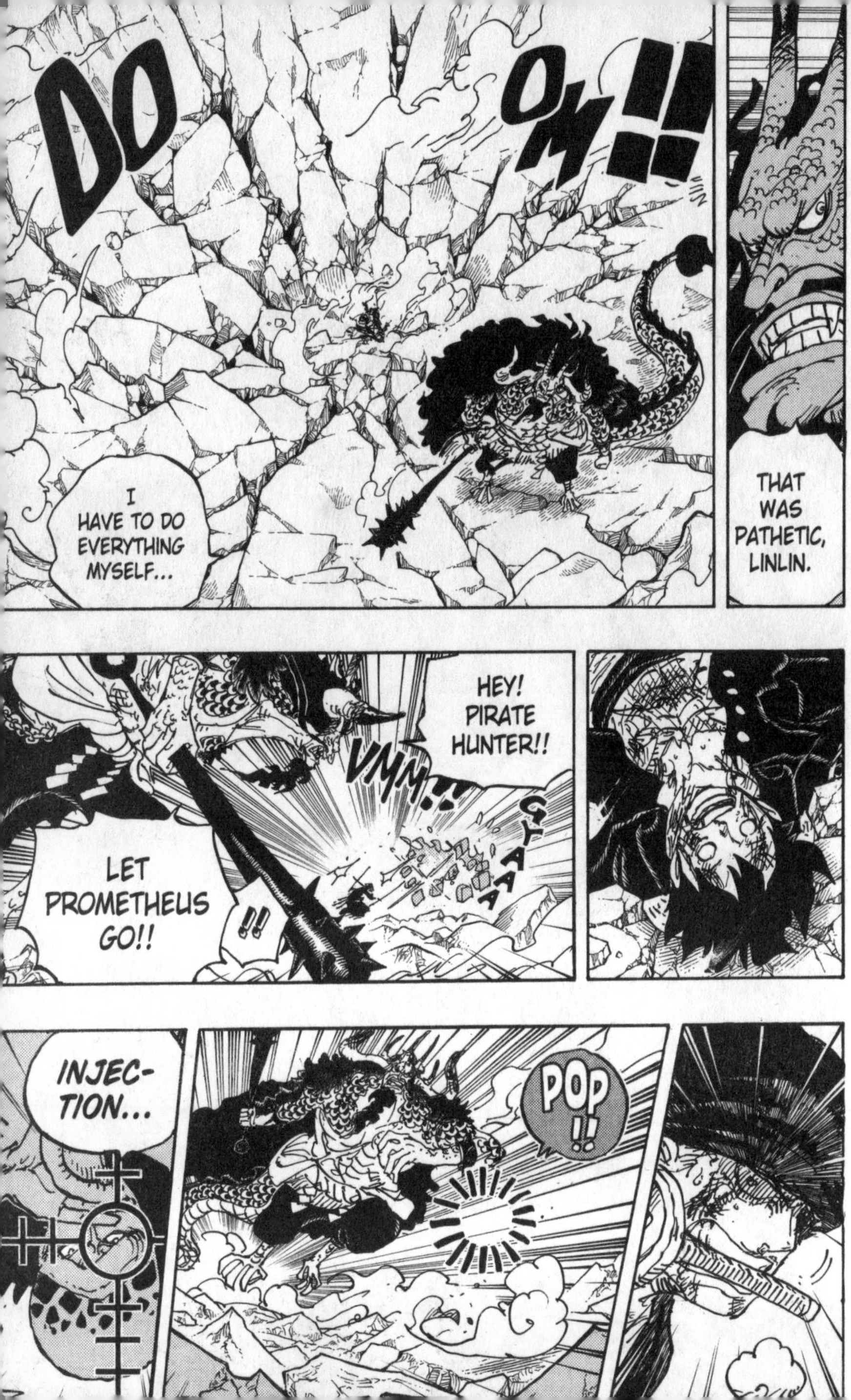
THAT WAS PATHETIC, LINLIN.
DO
OM!!
I HAVE TO DO EVERYTHING MYSELF...
HEY! PIRATE HUNTER!!
VMM!!
GYAAAA
!!
LET PROMETHEUS GO!!
POP!!
INJEC-
TION...

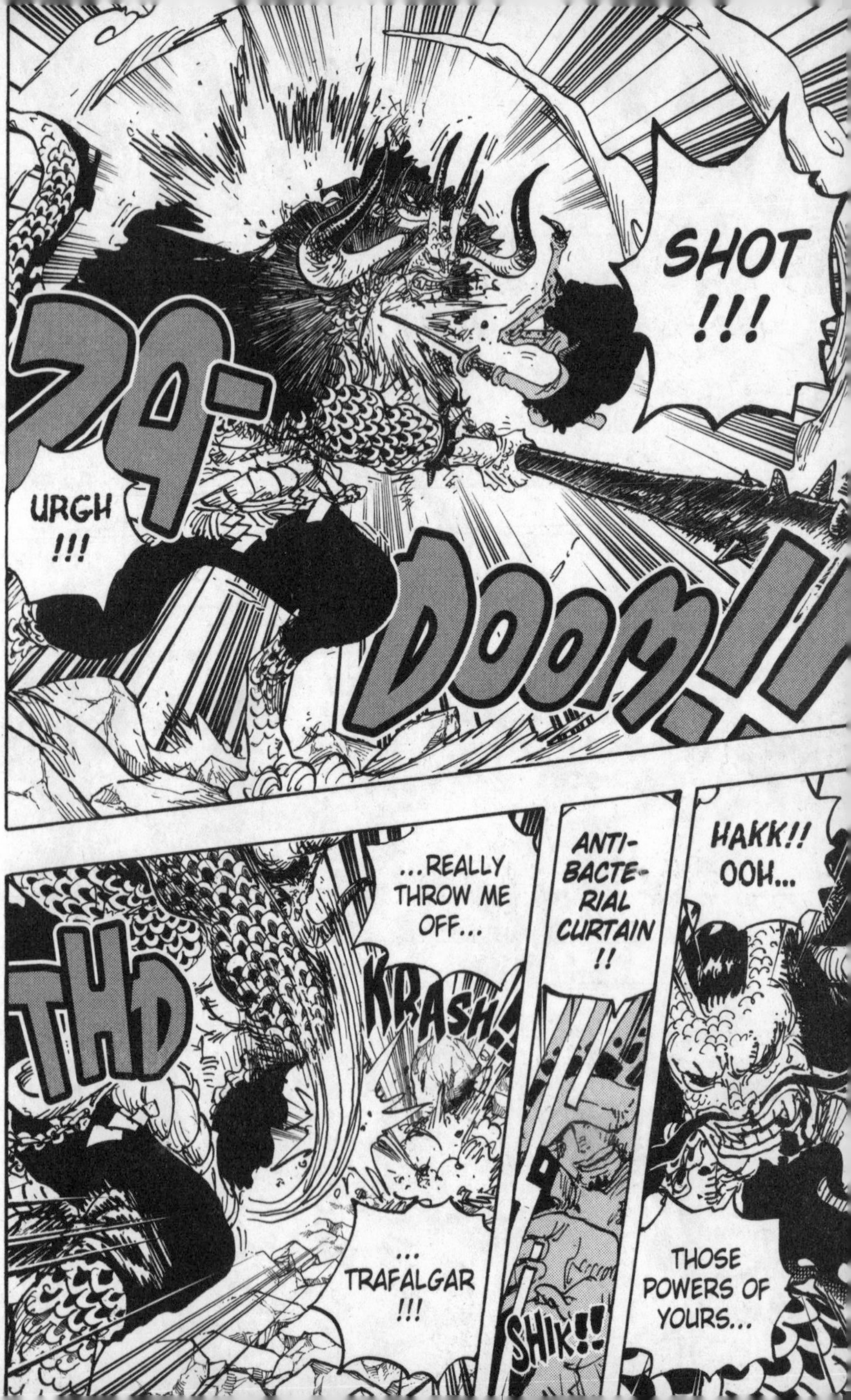
SHOT !!!
DOOM!!
URGH !!!
HAKK!! OOH...
THOSE POWERS OF YOURS...
ANTI-BACTERIAL CURTAIN !!
SHIK!!
...REALLY THROW ME OFF...
KRASH!!
... TRAFALGAR !!!
THD

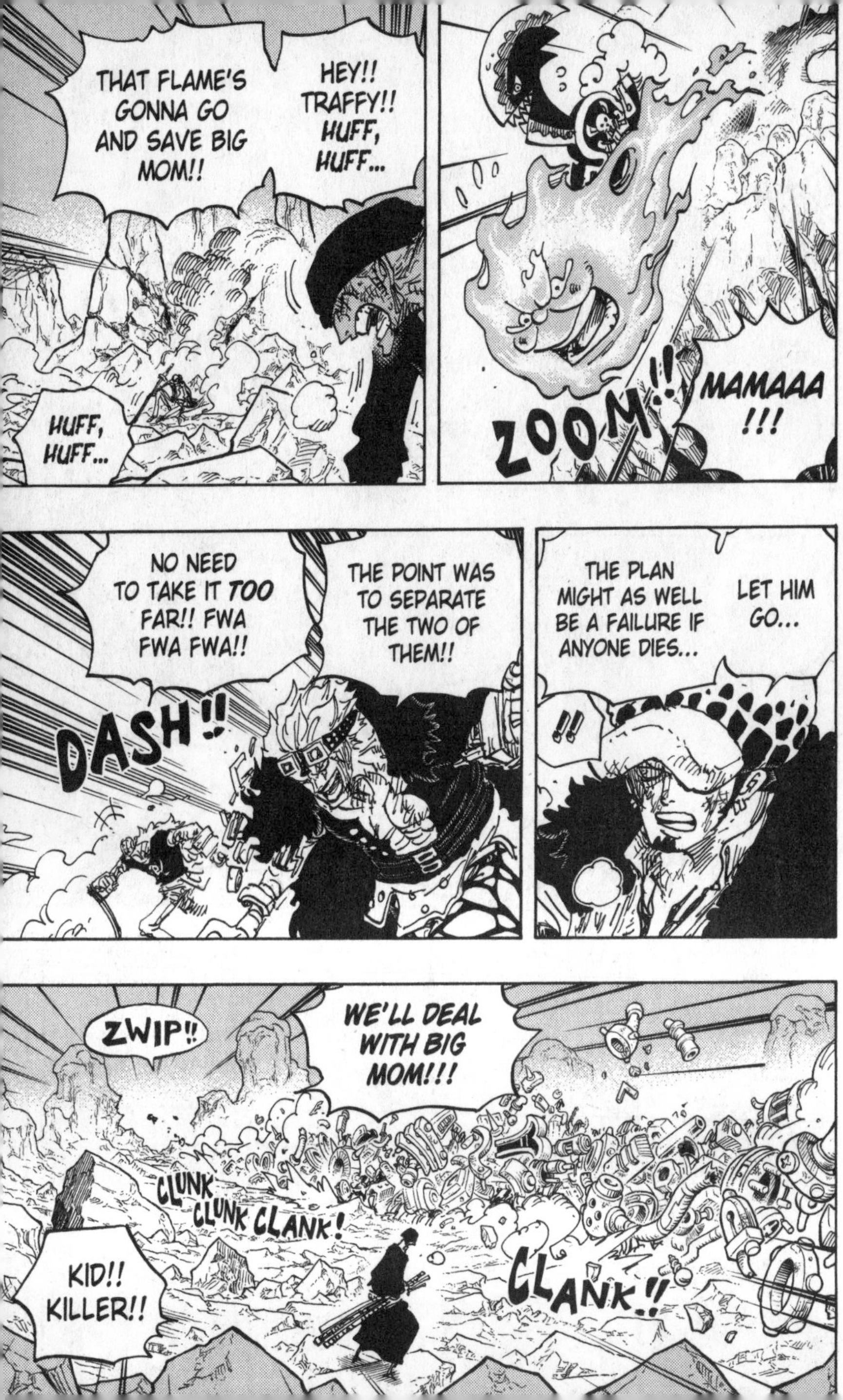
MAMAAA!!!
ZOOM!!
HEY!! TRAFFY!! HUFF, HUFF...
THAT FLAME'S GONNA GO AND SAVE BIG MOM!!
HUFF, HUFF...
LET HIM GO...
THE PLAN MIGHT AS WELL BE A FAILURE IF ANYONE DIES...
!!
THE POINT WAS TO SEPARATE THE TWO OF THEM!!
NO NEED TO TAKE IT *TOO* FAR!! FWA FWA FWA!!
DASH!!
WE'LL DEAL WITH BIG MOM!!!
ZWIP!!
CLANK!!
CLUNK CLUNK CLANK!
KID!! KILLER!!

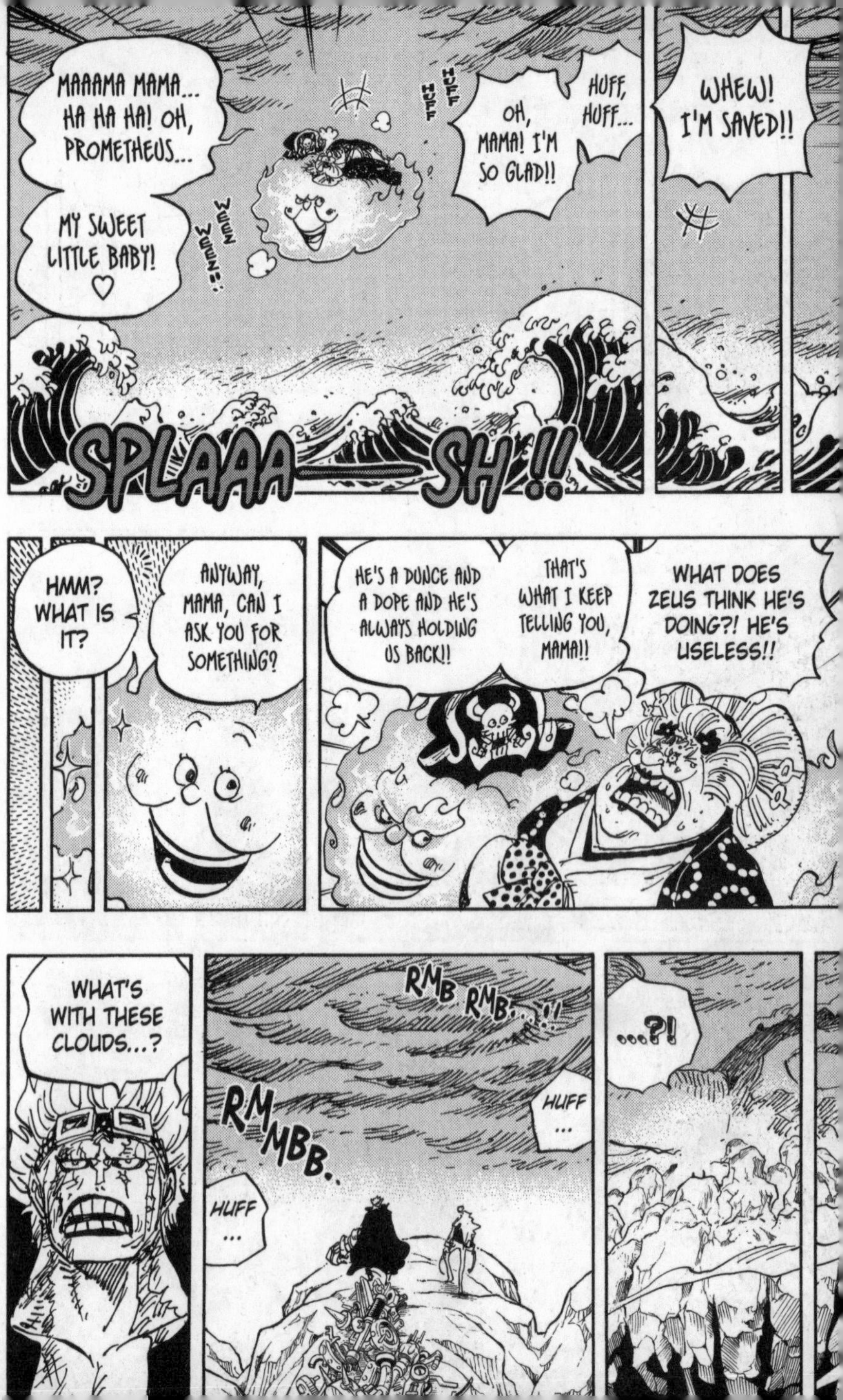
WHEW! I'M SAVED!!
HUFF, HUFF...
OH, MAMA! I'M SO GLAD!!
HUFF HUFF
MAAAMA MAMA... HA HA HA! OH, PROMETHEUS...
WEEN WEEN!!
MY SWEET LITTLE BABY! ♡
SPLAAA—SH!!
WHAT DOES ZEUS THINK HE'S DOING?! HE'S USELESS!!
THAT'S WHAT I KEEP TELLING YOU, MAMA!!
HE'S A DUNCE AND A DOPE AND HE'S ALWAYS HOLDING US BACK!!
ANYWAY, MAMA, CAN I ASK YOU FOR SOMETHING?
HMM? WHAT IS IT?
...?!
RMB RMB...!!
HUFF ...
RMMBB..
HUFF ...
WHAT'S WITH THESE CLOUDS...?

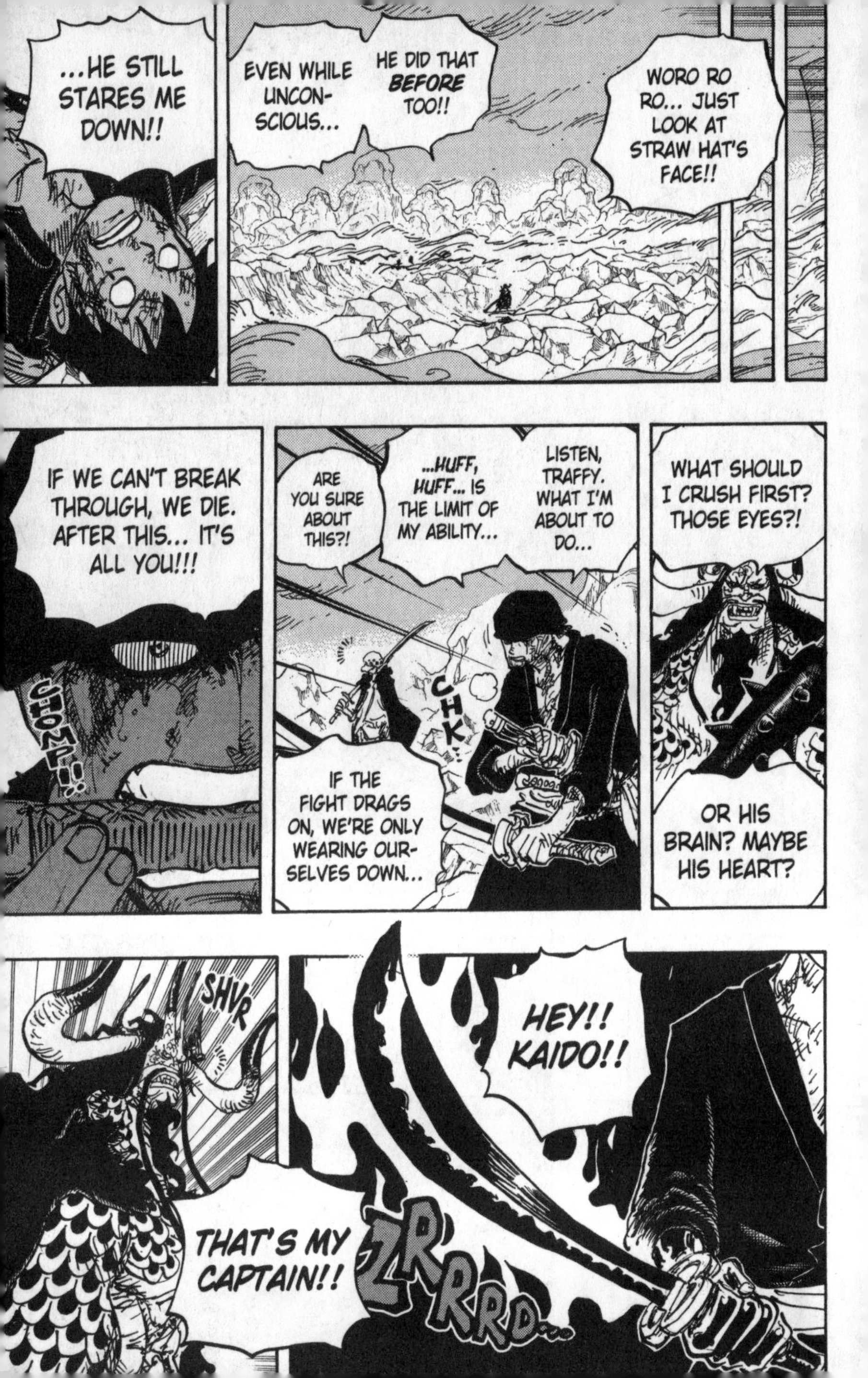
WORO RO RO... JUST LOOK AT STRAW HAT'S FACE!!
HE DID THAT BEFORE TOO!!
EVEN WHILE UNCON-SCIOUS...
...HE STILL STARES ME DOWN!!
WHAT SHOULD I CRUSH FIRST? THOSE EYES?!
OR HIS BRAIN? MAYBE HIS HEART?
LISTEN, TRAFFY. WHAT I'M ABOUT TO DO...
...HUFF, HUFF... IS THE LIMIT OF MY ABILITY...
ARE YOU SURE ABOUT THIS?!
CHK
IF THE FIGHT DRAGS ON, WE'RE ONLY WEARING OUR-SELVES DOWN...
IF WE CAN'T BREAK THROUGH, WE DIE. AFTER THIS... IT'S ALL YOU!!!
CHOMP!!
HEY!! KAIDO!!
ZRRRD...
THAT'S MY CAPTAIN!!
SHVR

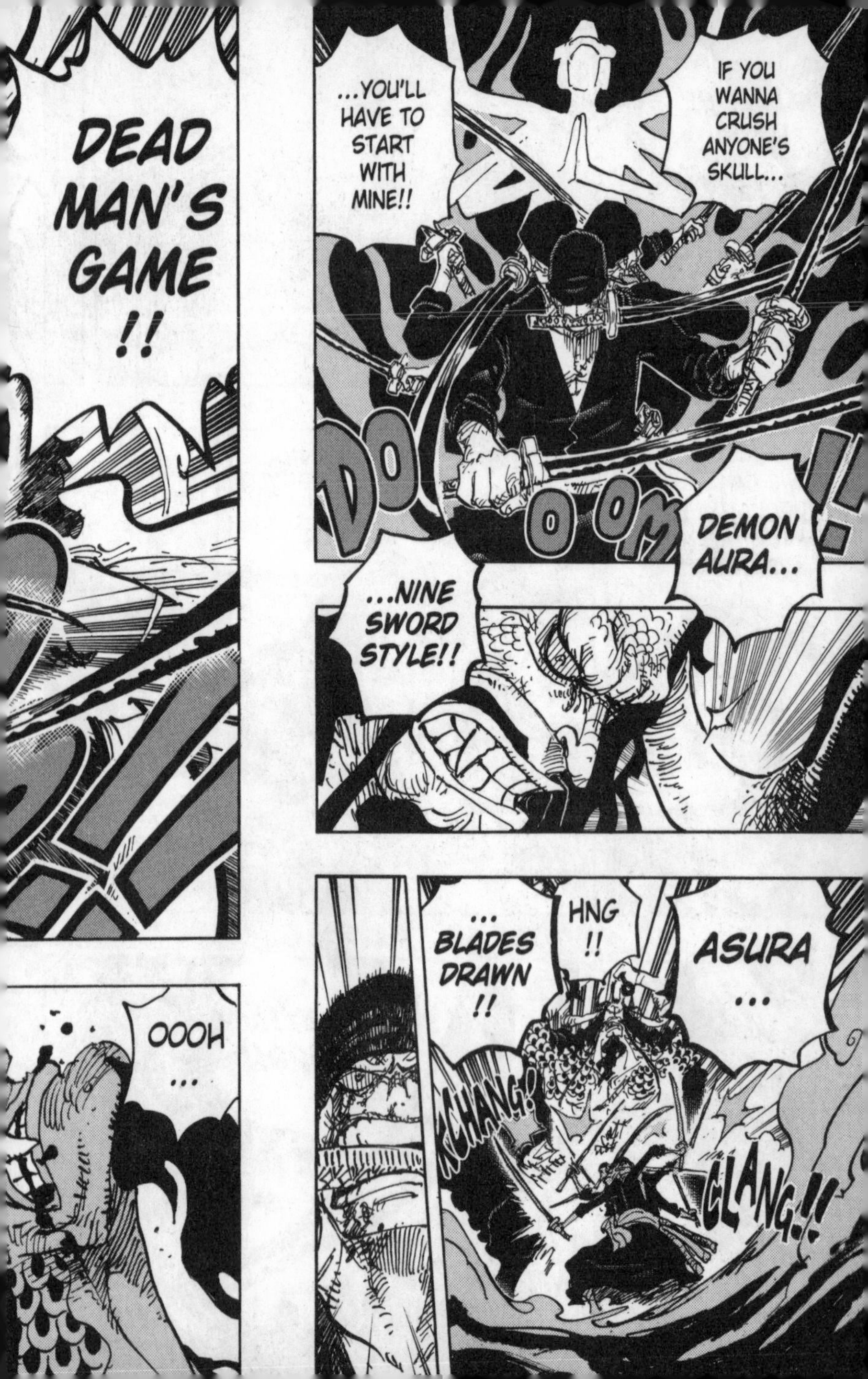
IF YOU WANNA CRUSH ANYONE'S SKULL...
...YOU'LL HAVE TO START WITH MINE!!
DOOOM!!
DEMON AURA...
...NINE SWORD STYLE!!
ASURA...
HNG!!
...BLADES DRAWN!!
CHANG!
CLANG!!
DEAD MAN'S GAME!!
OOOH...

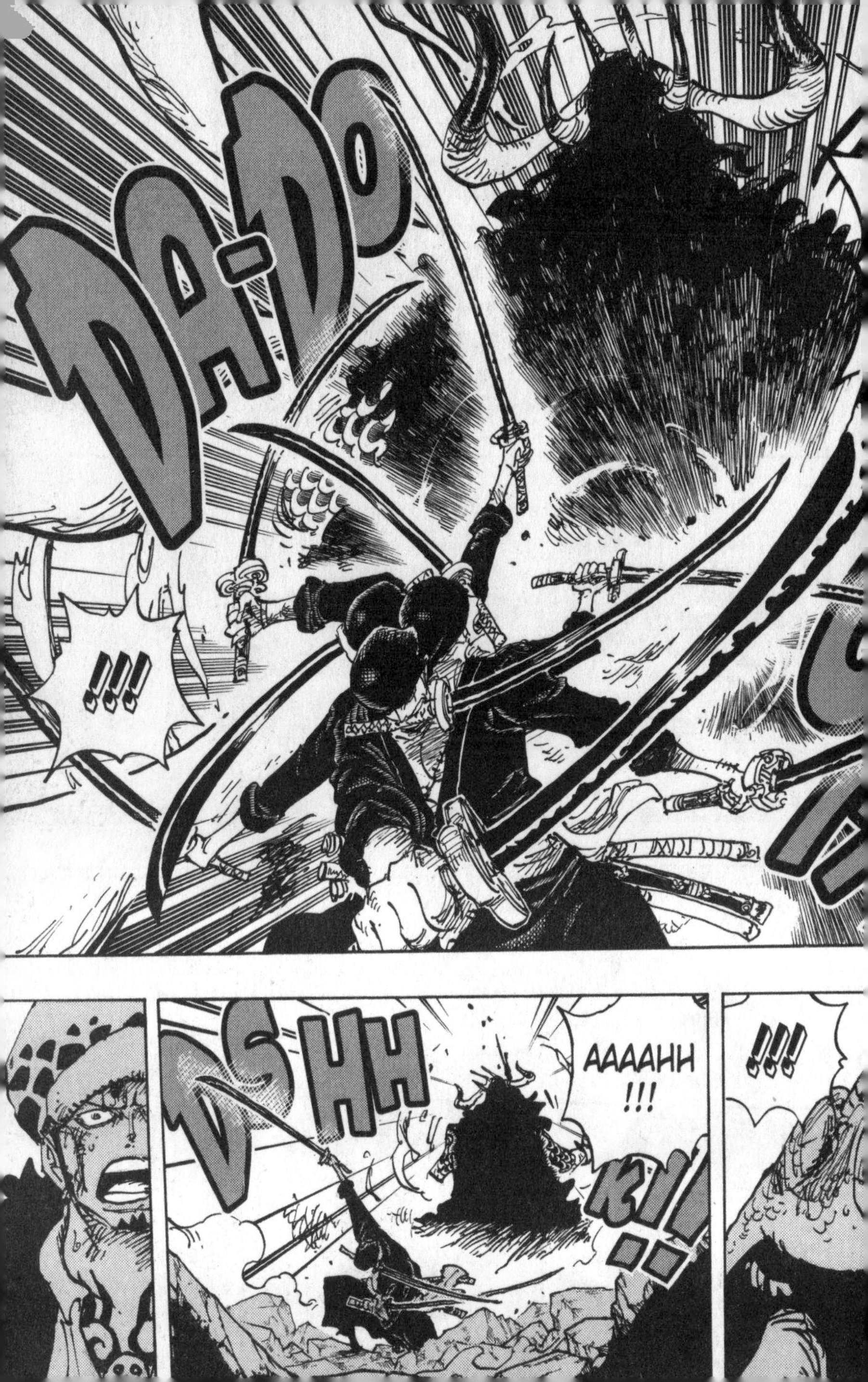
DA-DO
!!!
!!!
AAAAHH
!!!
DSHH

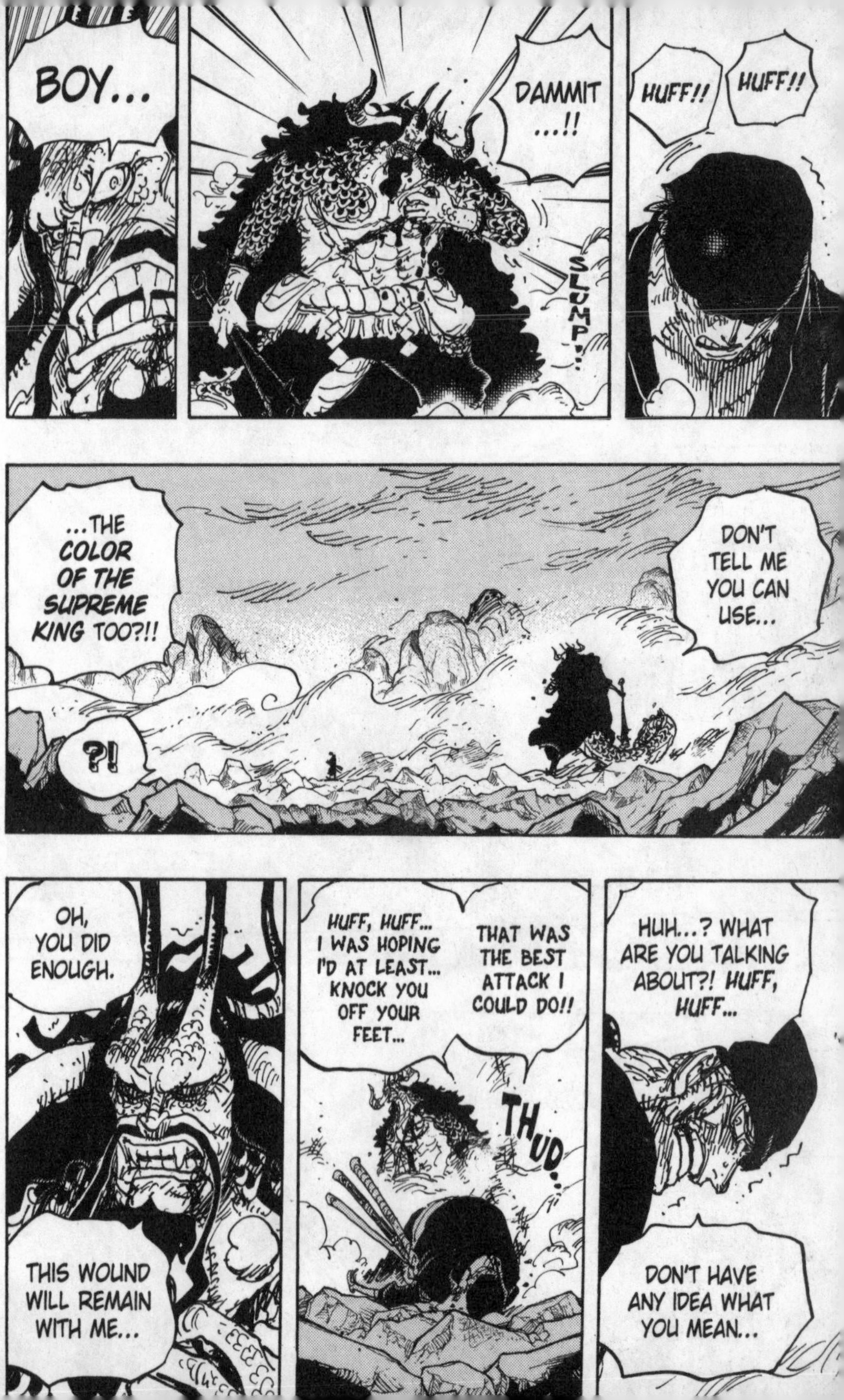
HUFF!!
HUFF!!
DAMMIT ...!!
SLUMP!!
BOY...
DON'T TELL ME YOU CAN USE...
...THE COLOR OF THE SUPREME KING TOO?!!
?!
HUH...? WHAT ARE YOU TALKING ABOUT?! HUFF, HUFF...
DON'T HAVE ANY IDEA WHAT YOU MEAN...
THAT WAS THE BEST ATTACK I COULD DO!!
HUFF, HUFF... I WAS HOPING I'D AT LEAST... KNOCK YOU OFF YOUR FEET...
THUD
OH, YOU DID ENOUGH.
THIS WOUND WILL REMAIN WITH ME...

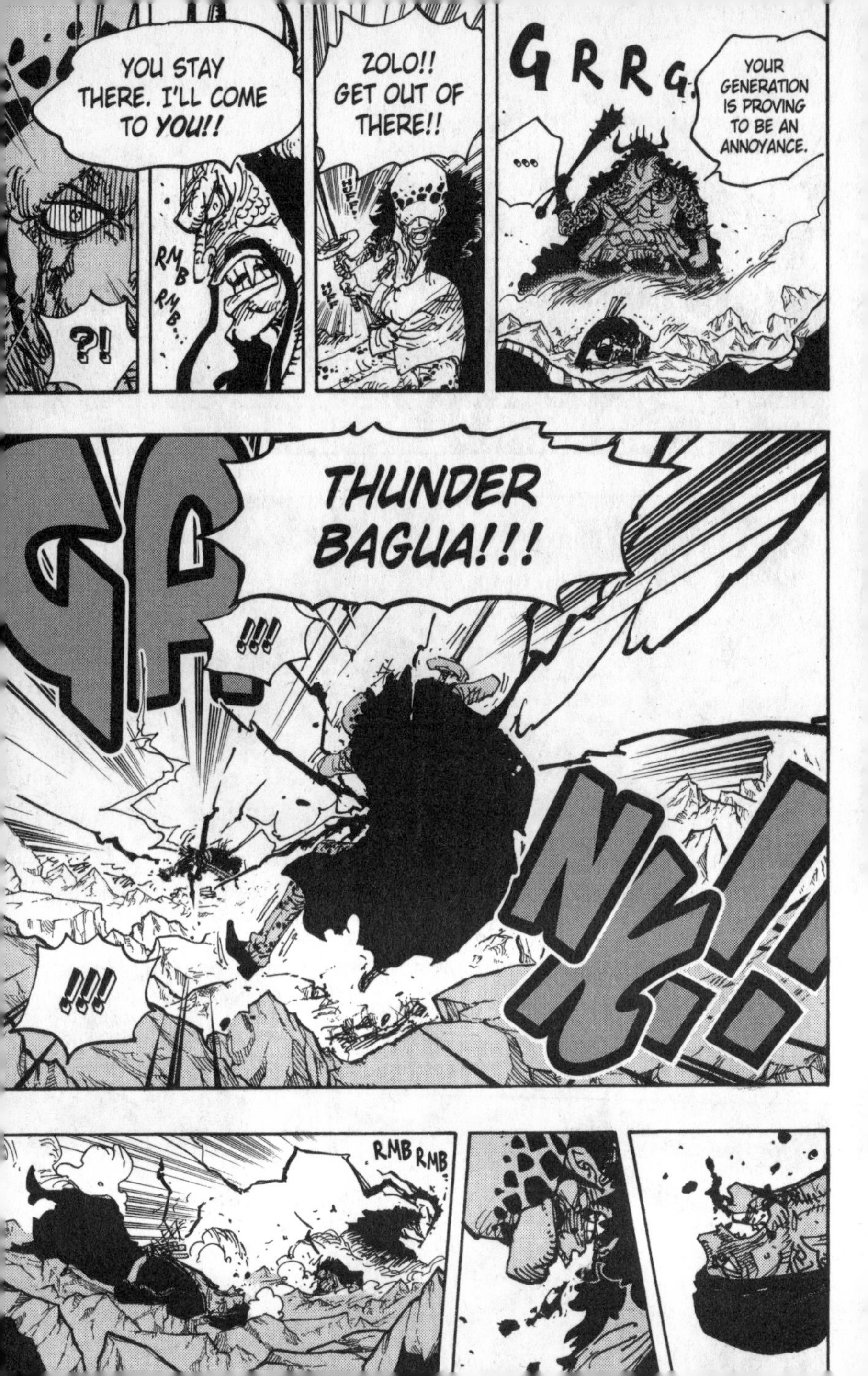
GRRRG.
YOUR GENERATION IS PROVING TO BE AN ANNOYANCE.
...
ZOLO!! GET OUT OF THERE!!
HUFF
HUFF
RMB RMB...
YOU STAY THERE. I'LL COME TO YOU!!
?!
THUNDER BAGUA!!!
!!!
!!!
RMB RMB

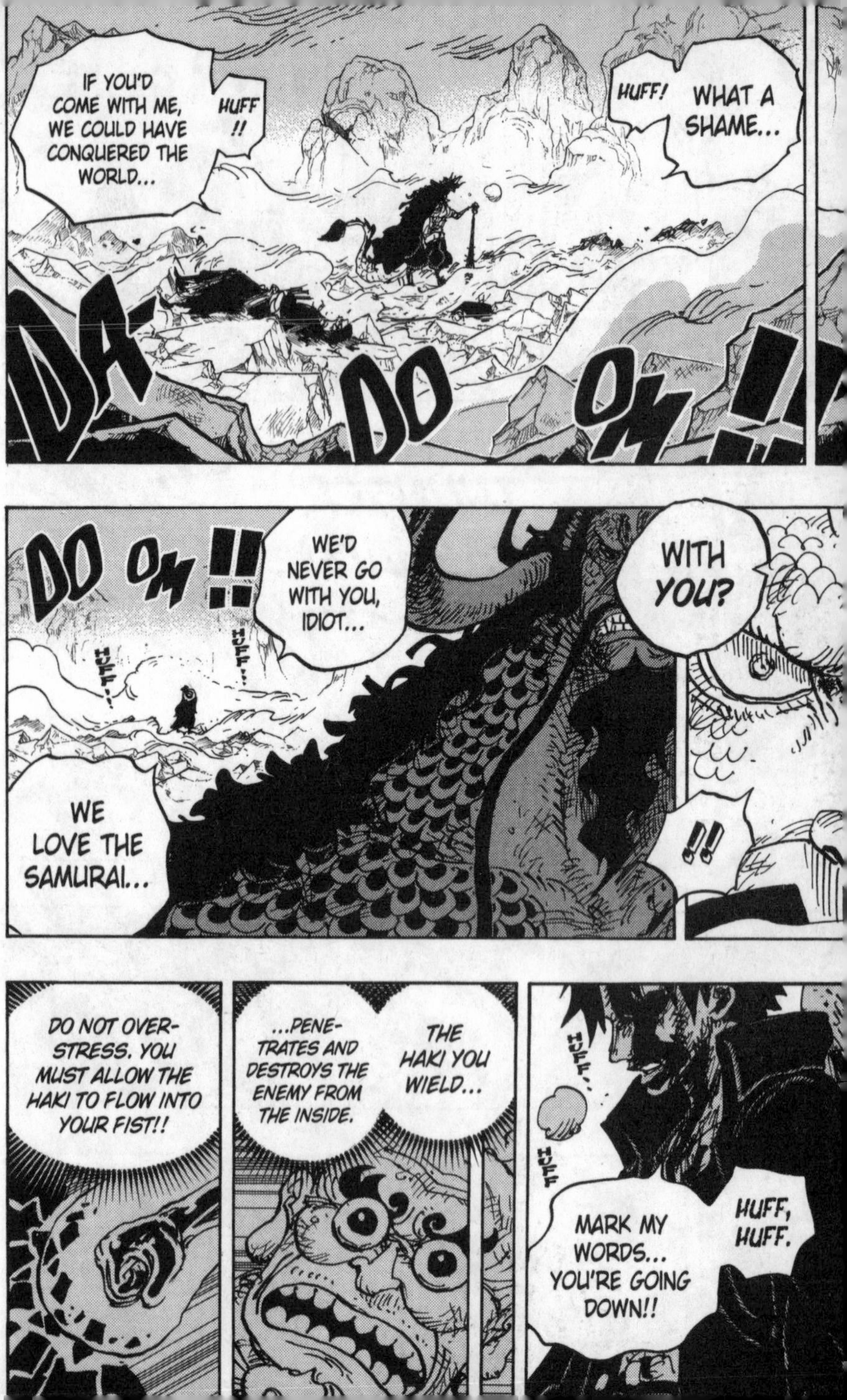
HUFF!
WHAT A SHAME...
HUFF !!
IF YOU'D COME WITH ME, WE COULD HAVE CONQUERED THE WORLD...
DA-DO OM!!
WITH YOU?
!!
WE'D NEVER GO WITH YOU, IDIOT...
DO OM!!
HUFF...
HUFF...
WE LOVE THE SAMURAI...
HUFF...
HUFF
HUFF, HUFF.
MARK MY WORDS... YOU'RE GOING DOWN!!
THE HAKI YOU WIELD...
...PENE-TRATES AND DESTROYS THE ENEMY FROM THE INSIDE.
DO NOT OVER-STRESS. YOU MUST ALLOW THE HAKI TO FLOW INTO YOUR FIST!!

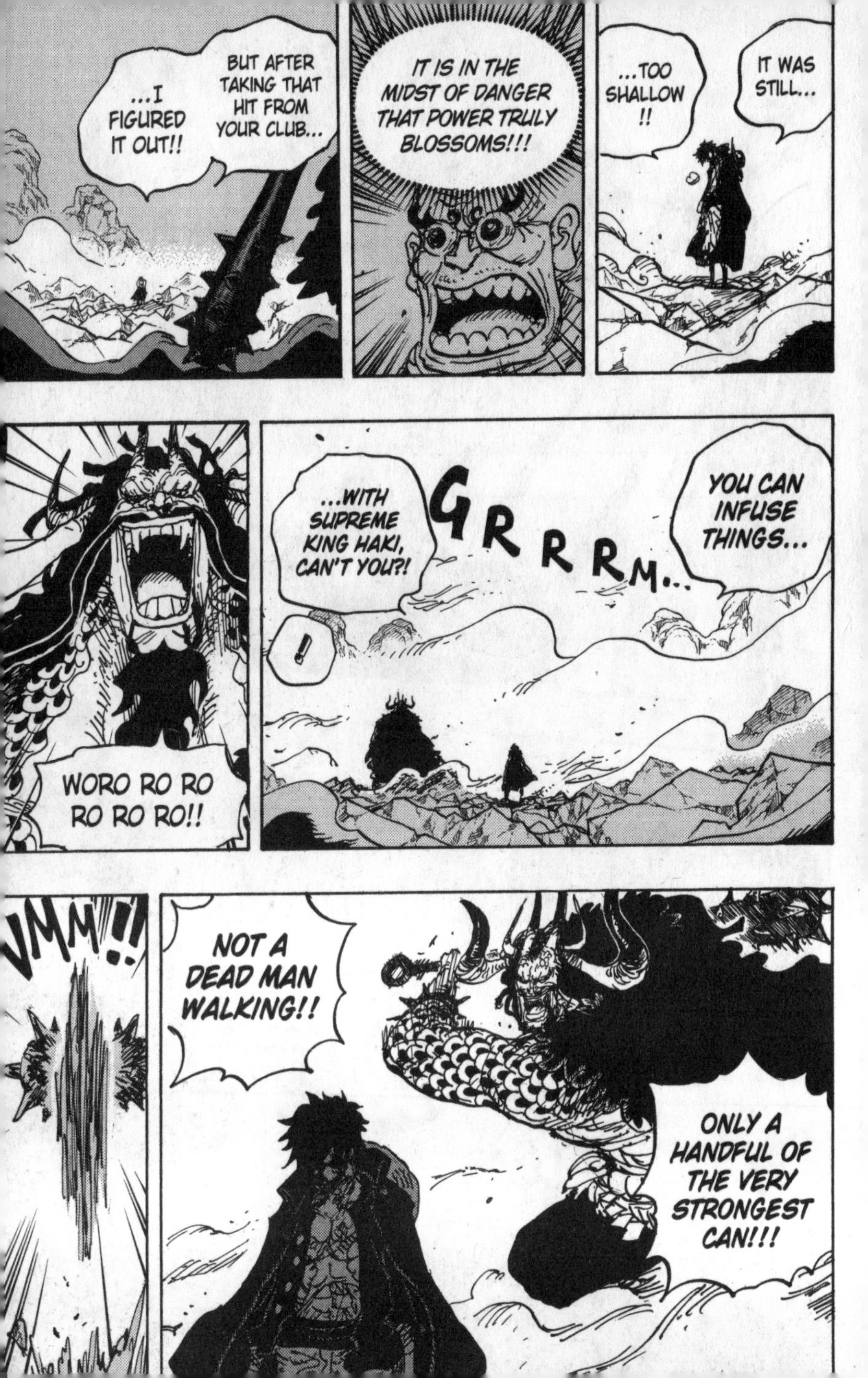
IT WAS STILL...
...TOO SHALLOW !!
IT IS IN THE MIDST OF DANGER THAT POWER TRULY BLOSSOMS!!!
BUT AFTER TAKING THAT HIT FROM YOUR CLUB...
...I FIGURED IT OUT!!
YOU CAN INFUSE THINGS...
GRRRRM...
...WITH SUPREME KING HAKI, CAN'T YOU?!
!
WORO RO RO RO RO RO!!
ONLY A HANDFUL OF THE VERY STRONGEST CAN!!!
NOT A DEAD MAN WALKING!!
VMM!!

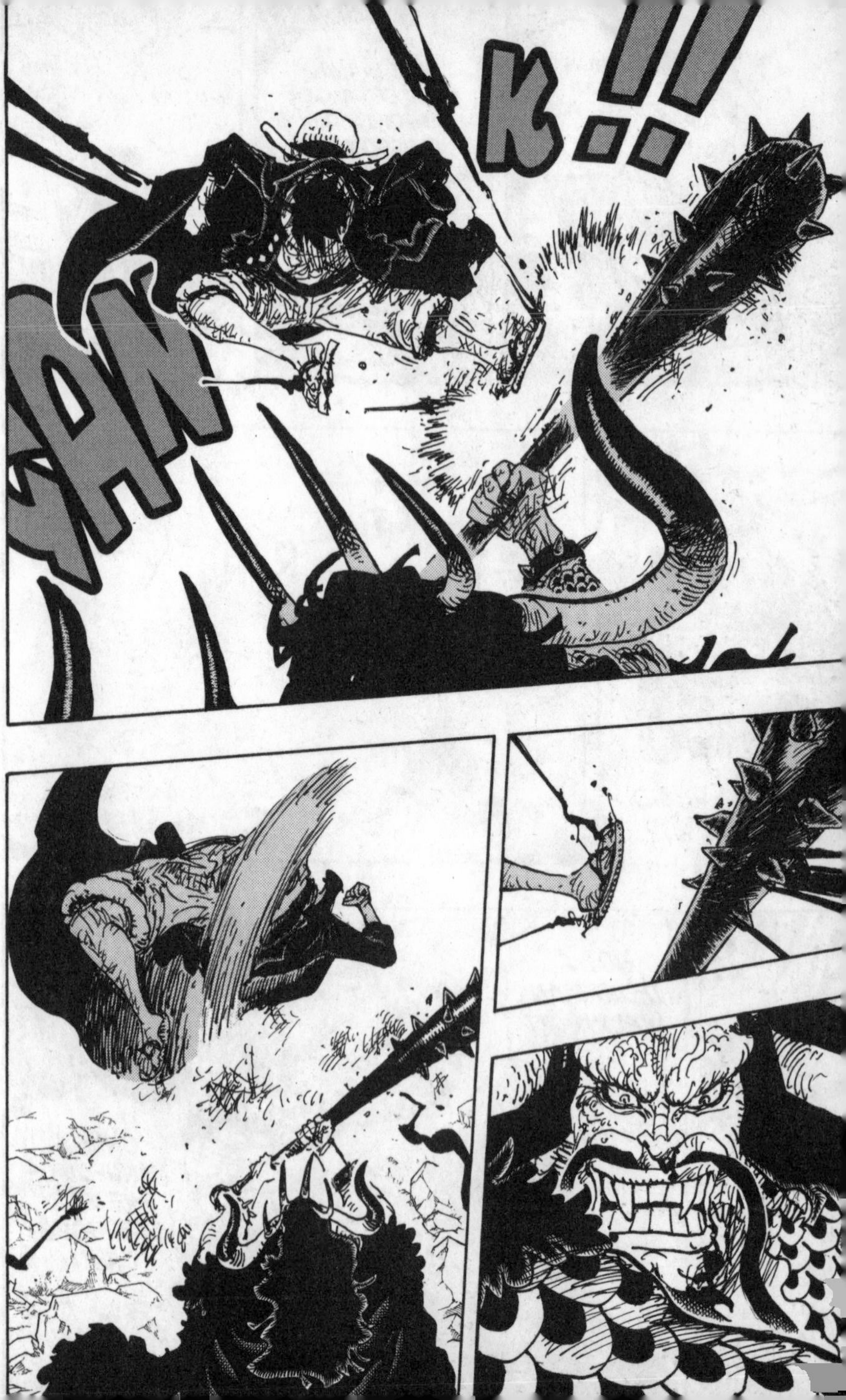
K..!!
GAN

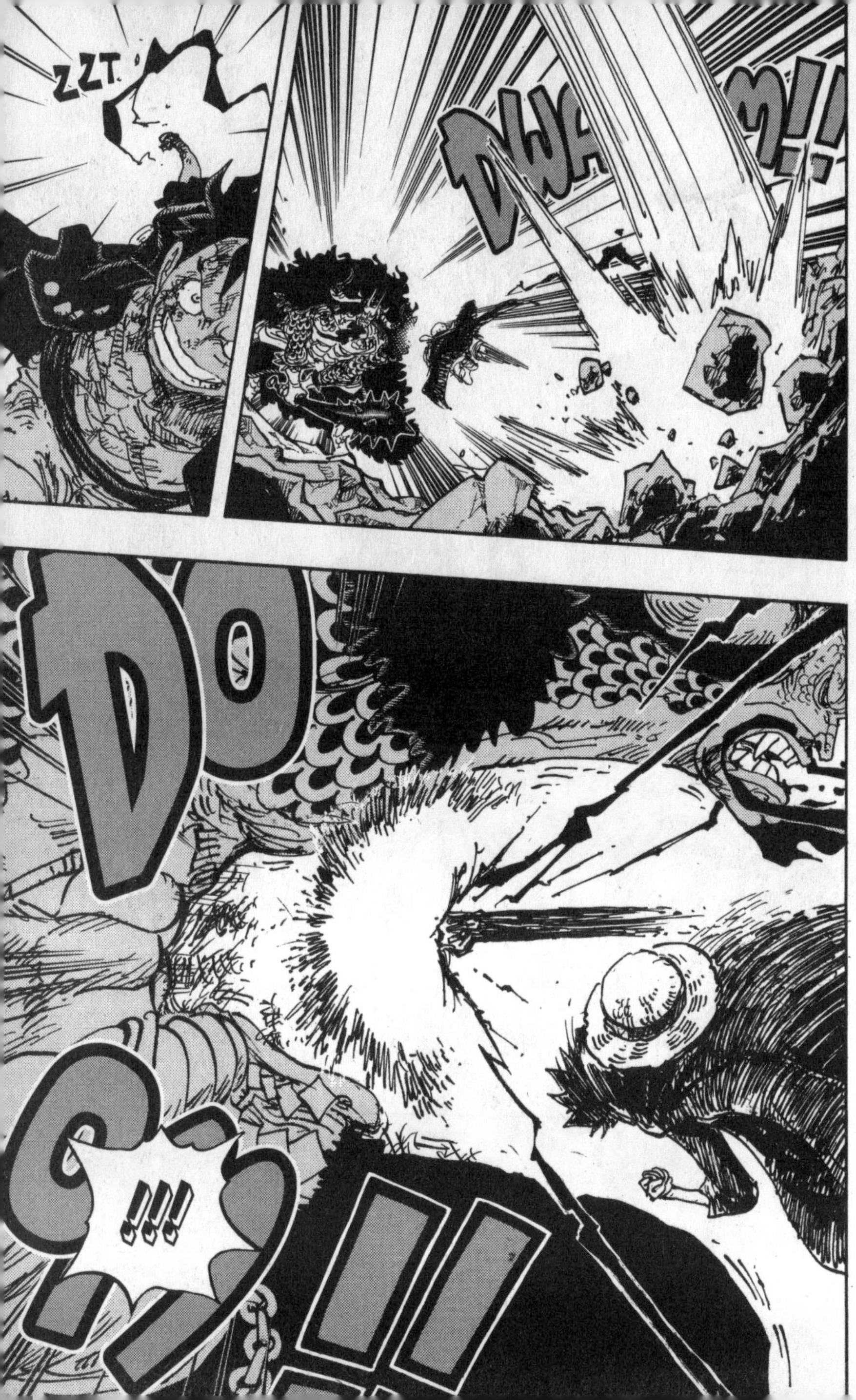
ZZT

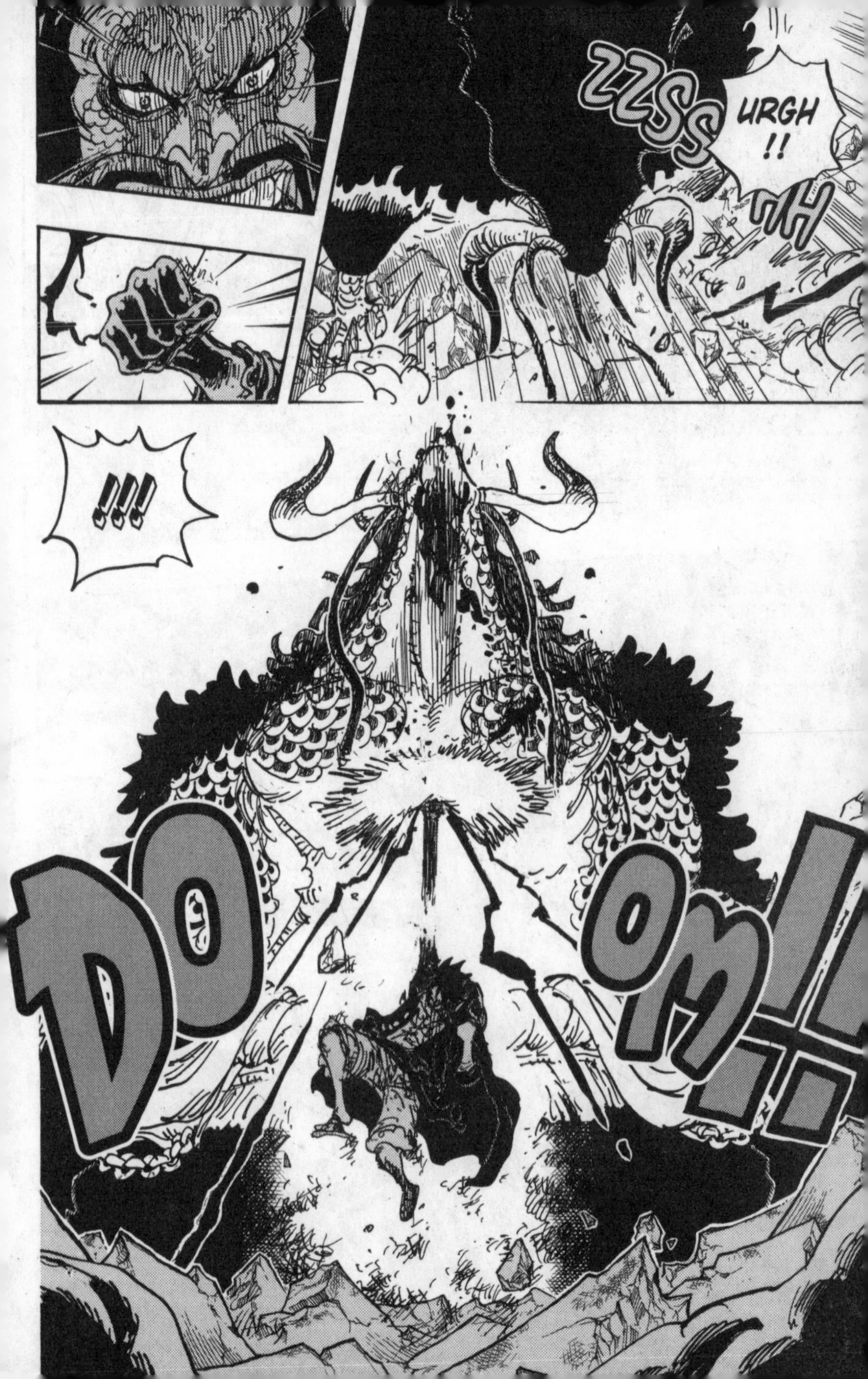
URGH !!
ZZSS
HH
!!!
DOOM!!

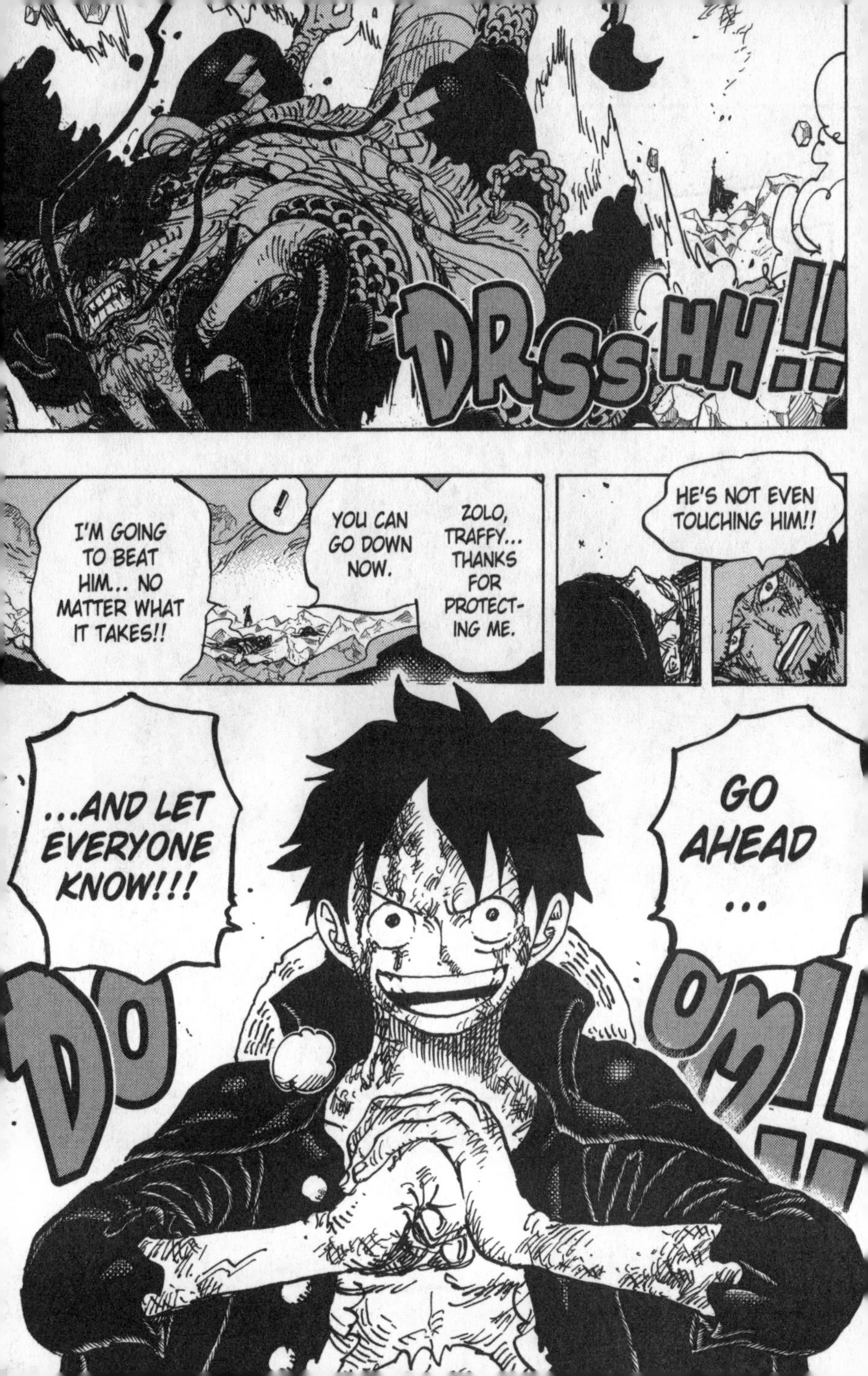
DRSSHH!!
HE'S NOT EVEN TOUCHING HIM!!
ZOLO, TRAFFY... THANKS FOR PROTECTING ME.
!
YOU CAN GO DOWN NOW.
I'M GOING TO BEAT HIM... NO MATTER WHAT IT TAKES!!
GO AHEAD ...
...AND LET EVERYONE KNOW!!!
DOOM!!

THE CODE OF SWEET BEANS

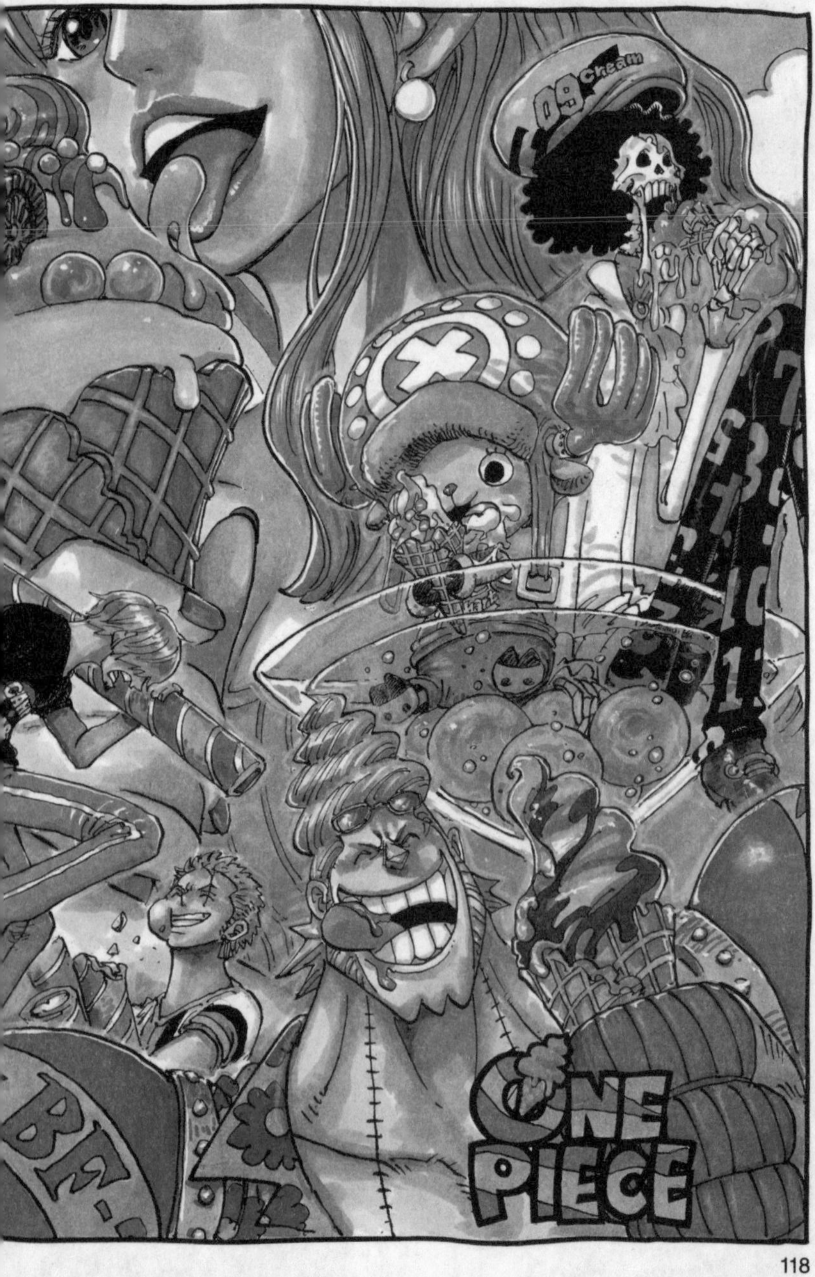
09 cream
ONE PIECE

Chapter 1011:

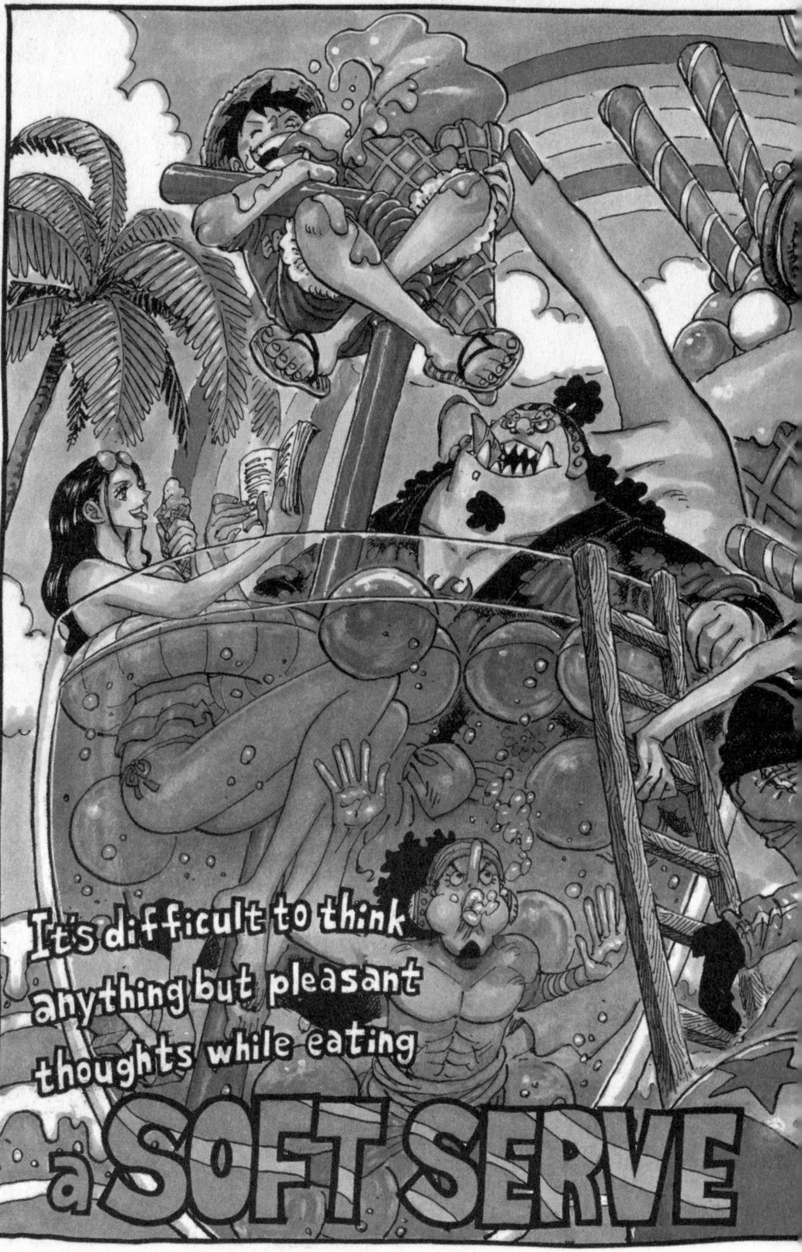
It's difficult to think anything but pleasant thoughts while eating
a SOFT SERVE

vol.100
ONE PIECE

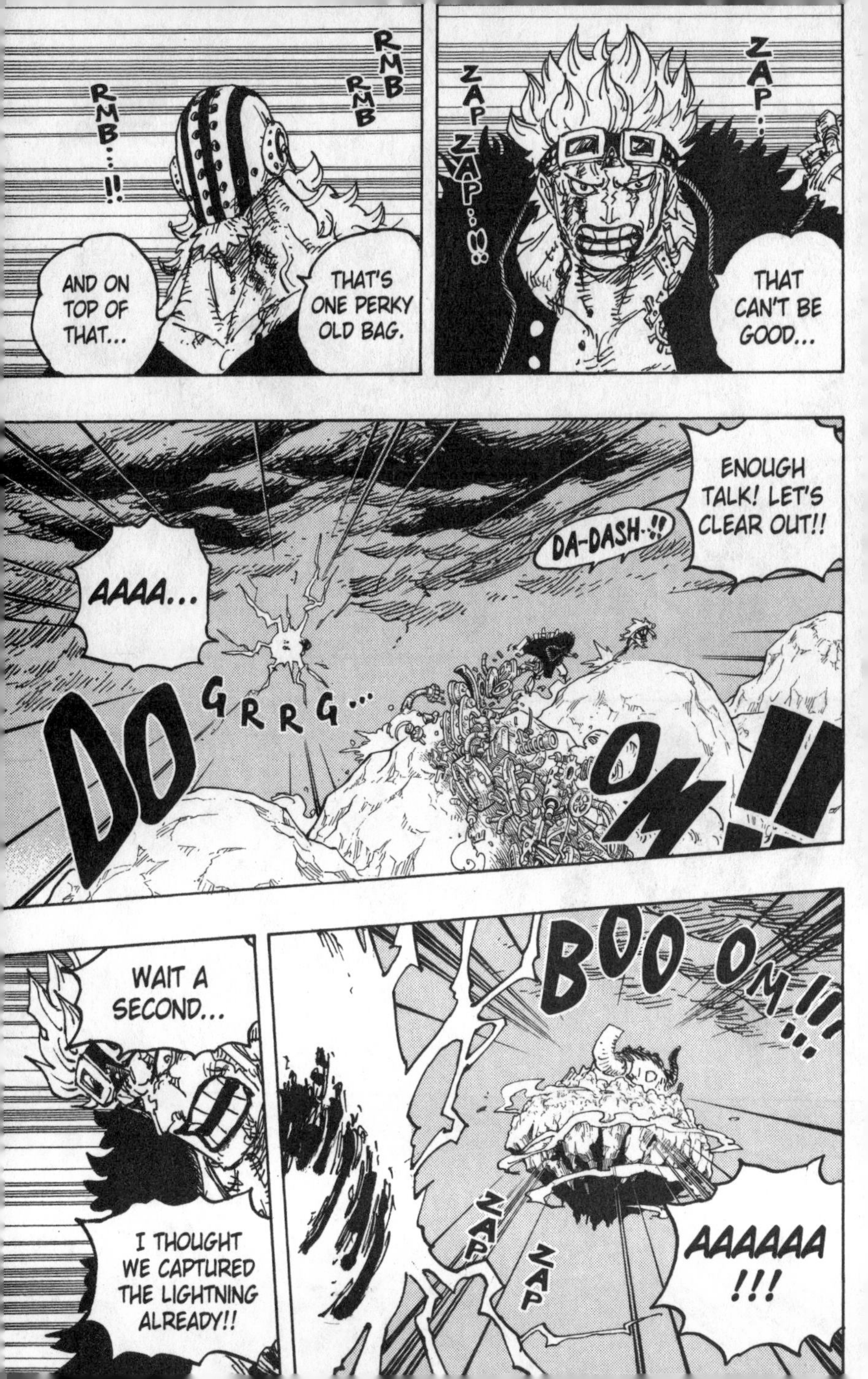
ZAP...
ZAP ZAP ZAP..!!
THAT CAN'T BE GOOD...
RMB RMB
RMB...!!
THAT'S ONE PERKY OLD BAG.
AND ON TOP OF THAT...
ENOUGH TALK! LET'S CLEAR OUT!!
DA-DASH..!!
AAAA...
DO
GRRG...
OM!!
BOOOM!!!
ZAP
ZAP
AAAAAA !!!
WAIT A SECOND...
I THOUGHT WE CAPTURED THE LIGHTNING ALREADY!!

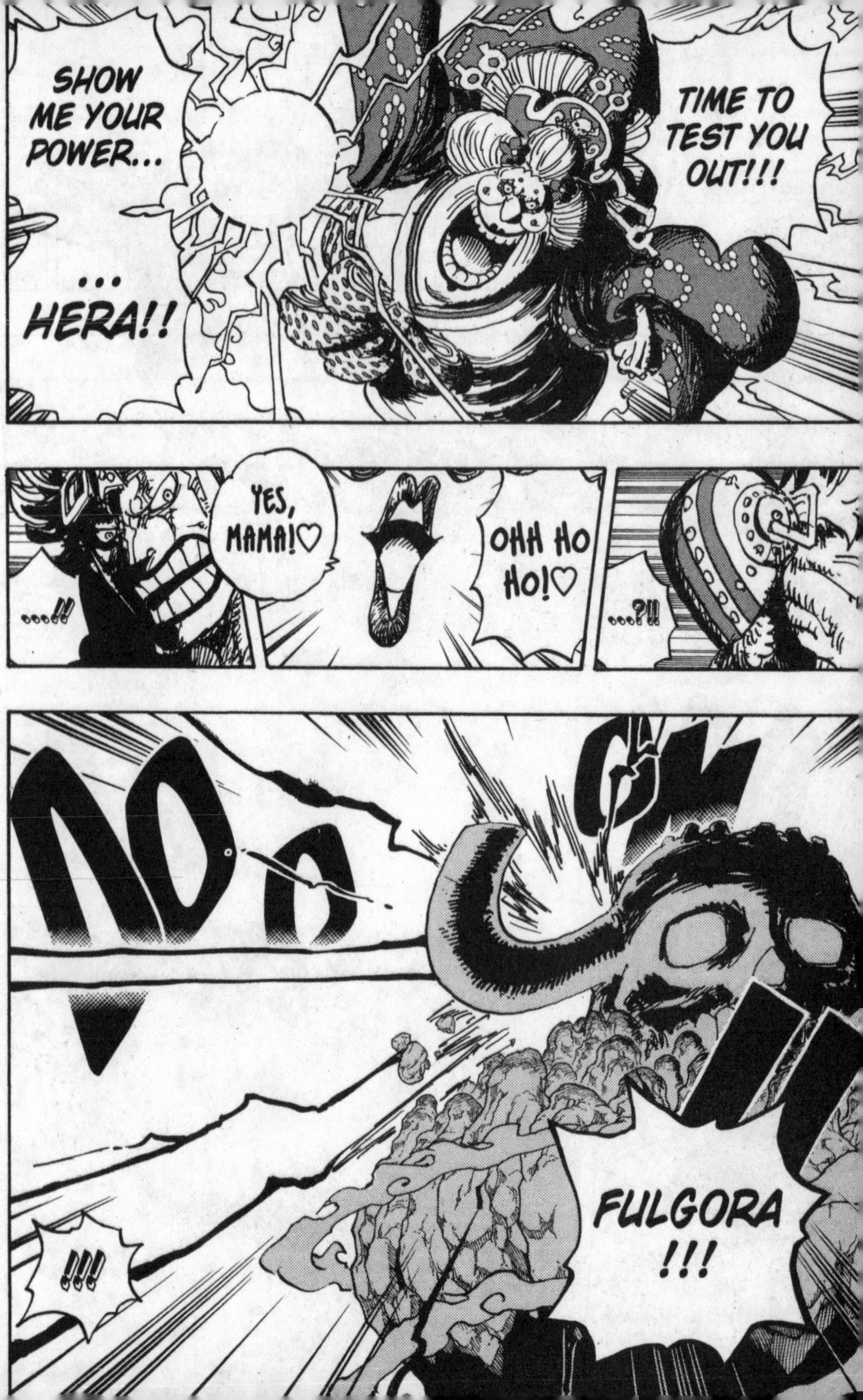
TIME TO TEST YOU OUT!!!
SHOW ME YOUR POWER...
... HERA!!
...?!!
OHH HO HO!♡
YES, MAMA!♡
...!!
DOOOM
FULGORA !!!
!!!

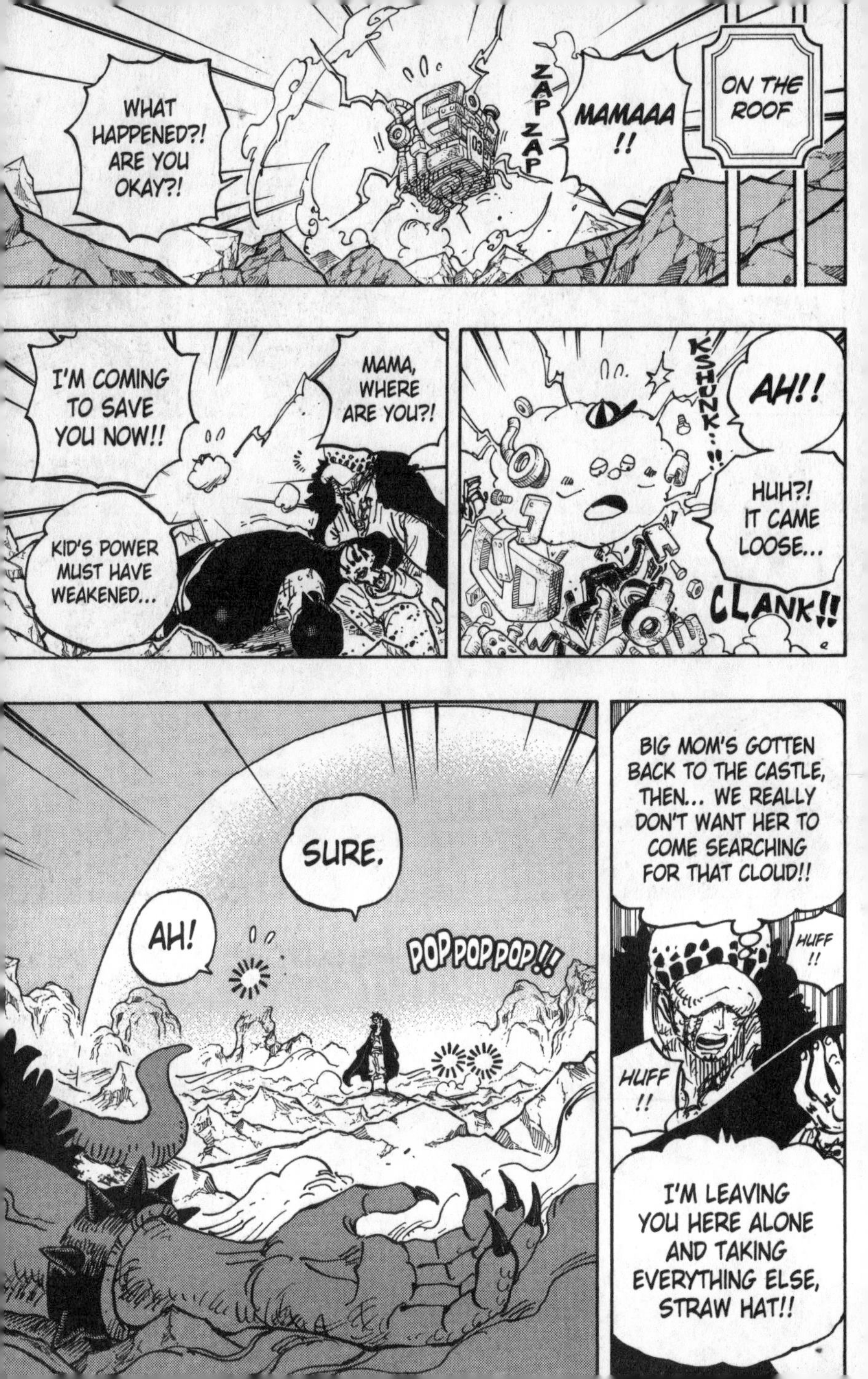
ON THE ROOF
MAMAAA !!
ZAP ZAP
WHAT HAPPENED?! ARE YOU OKAY?!
AH!!
KSHUNK...!!
HUH?! IT CAME LOOSE...
CLANK!!
MAMA, WHERE ARE YOU?!
I'M COMING TO SAVE YOU NOW!!
KID'S POWER MUST HAVE WEAKENED...
BIG MOM'S GOTTEN BACK TO THE CASTLE, THEN... WE REALLY DON'T WANT HER TO COME SEARCHING FOR THAT CLOUD!!
HUFF !!
HUFF !!
I'M LEAVING YOU HERE ALONE AND TAKING EVERYTHING ELSE, STRAW HAT!!
SURE.
POP POP POP!!
AH!

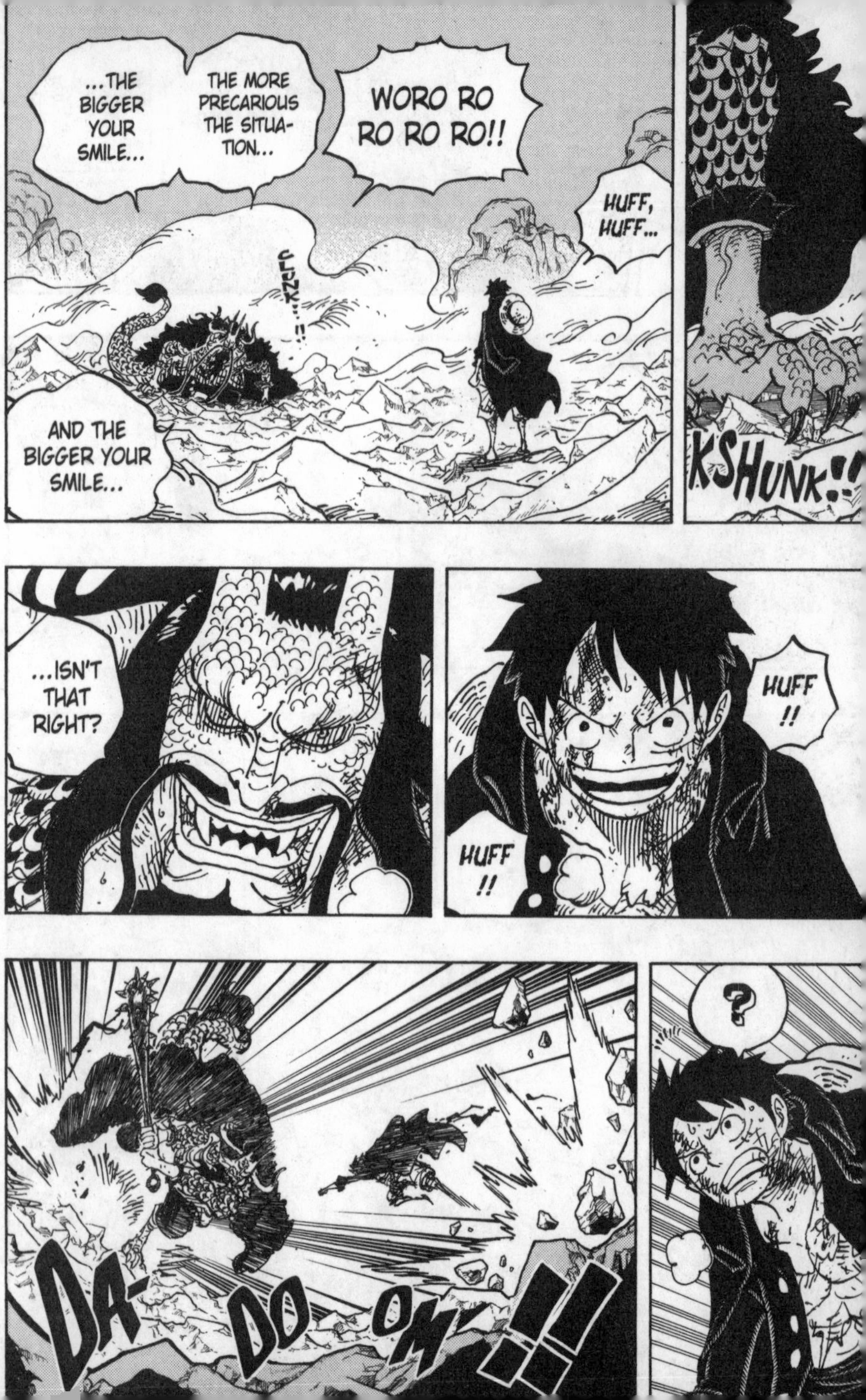
KSHUNK!!
WORO RO RO RO RO!!
HUFF, HUFF...
THE MORE PRECARIOUS THE SITUATION...
...THE BIGGER YOUR SMILE...
CLUNK...!!
AND THE BIGGER YOUR SMILE...
HUFF !!
HUFF !!
...ISN'T THAT RIGHT?
?
DA-DO-OM!!

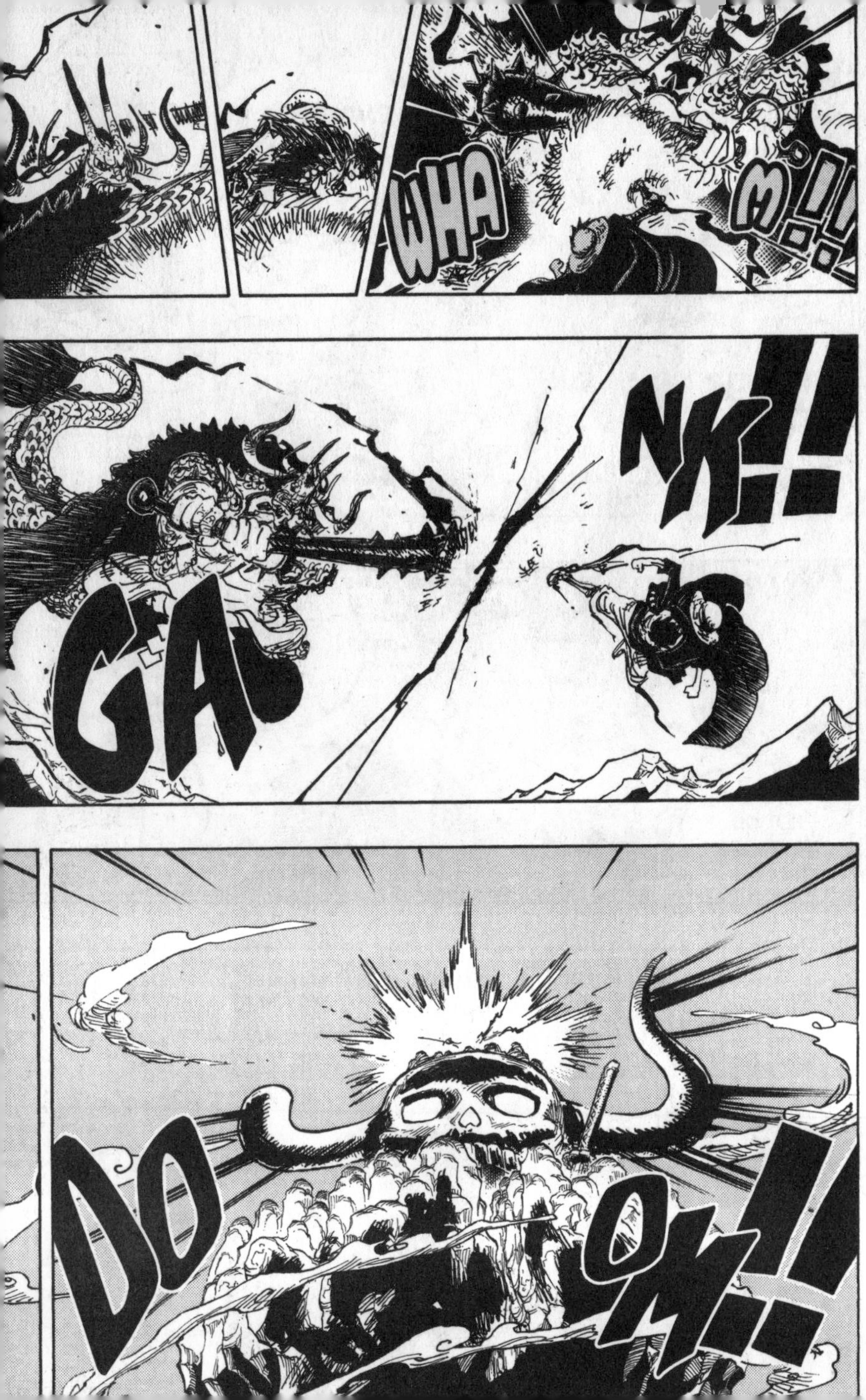
WHA
M..!!
NK!!
GA
DO
OM..!!

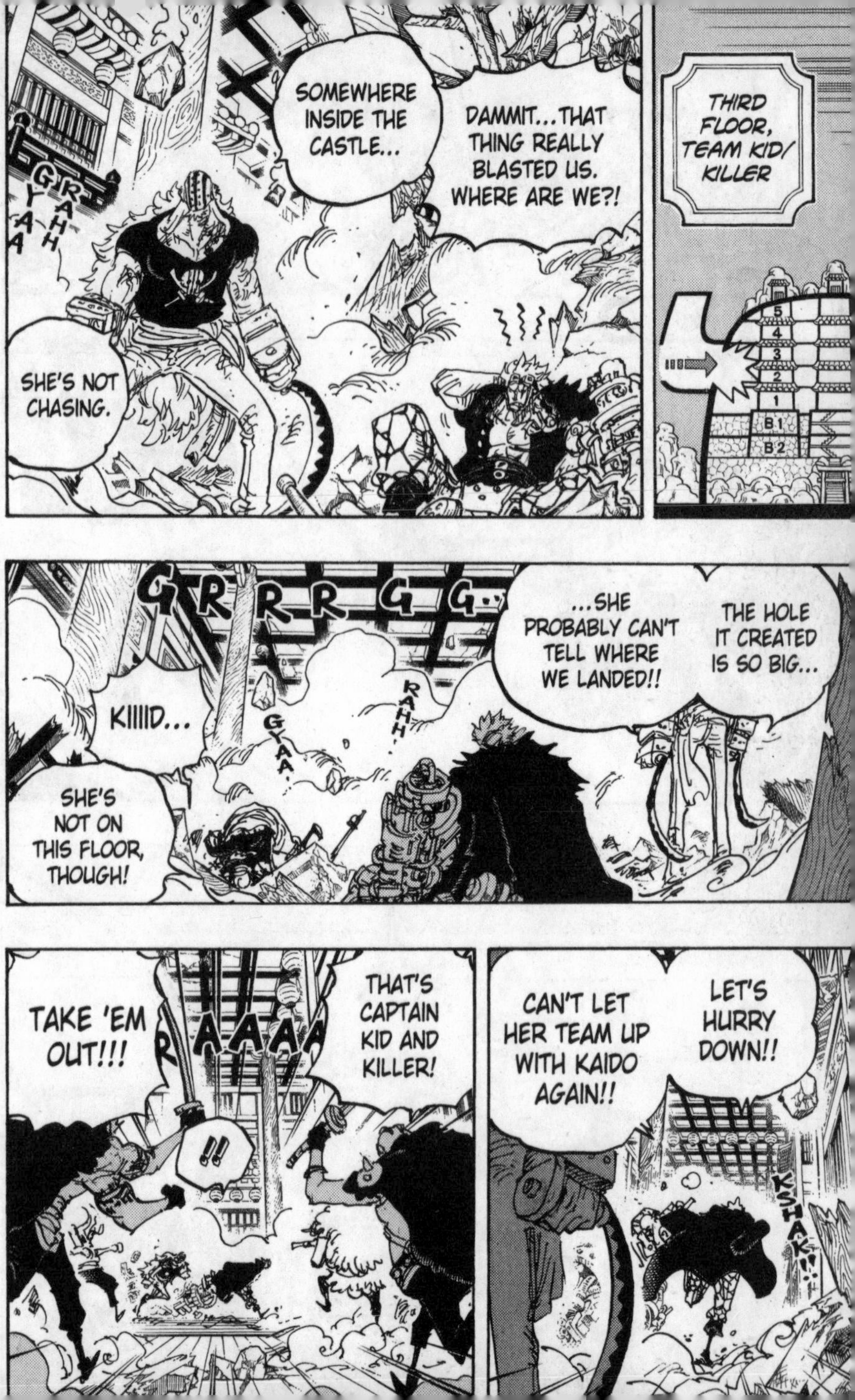
THIRD FLOOR, TEAM KID/KILLER
5
4
3
2
1
B1
B2
DAMMIT...THAT THING REALLY BLASTED US. WHERE ARE WE?!
SOMEWHERE INSIDE THE CASTLE...
GRRAHH
GYAA
SHE'S NOT CHASING.
THE HOLE IT CREATED IS SO BIG...
...SHE PROBABLY CAN'T TELL WHERE WE LANDED!!
GRRRGG...
RAHH
GYAA
KIIIID...
SHE'S NOT ON THIS FLOOR, THOUGH!
LET'S HURRY DOWN!!
CAN'T LET HER TEAM UP WITH KAIDO AGAIN!!
KSHAK!!
THAT'S CAPTAIN KID AND KILLER!
RAAAAA
TAKE 'EM OUT!!!
!!

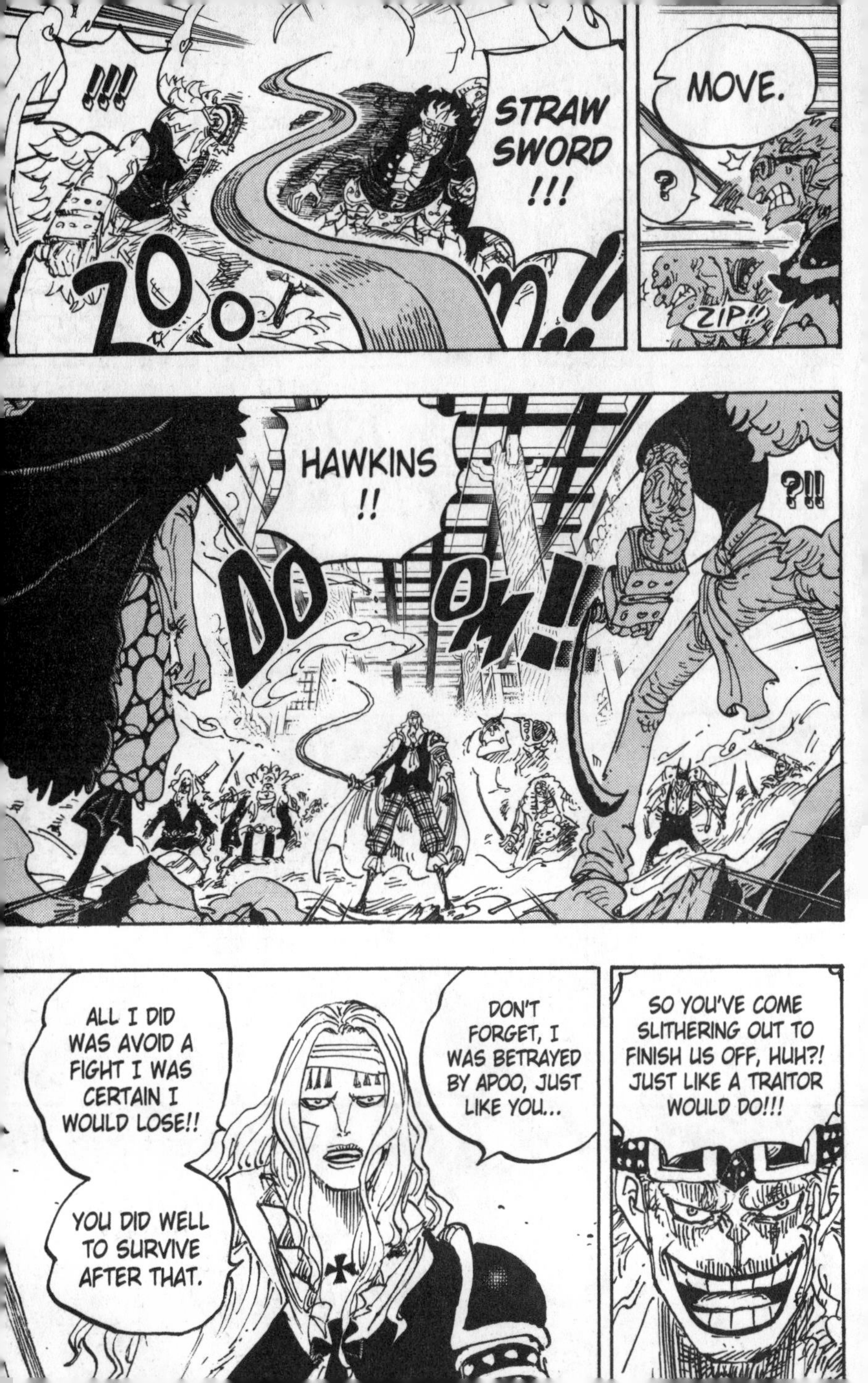
MOVE.
?
ZIP!!
!!!
STRAW SWORD !!!
ZOOOM!!
?!!
HAWKINS !!
DOOM!!
SO YOU'VE COME SLITHERING OUT TO FINISH US OFF, HUH?! JUST LIKE A TRAITOR WOULD DO!!!
DON'T FORGET, I WAS BETRAYED BY APOO, JUST LIKE YOU...
ALL I DID WAS AVOID A FIGHT I WAS CERTAIN I WOULD LOSE!!
YOU DID WELL TO SURVIVE AFTER THAT.

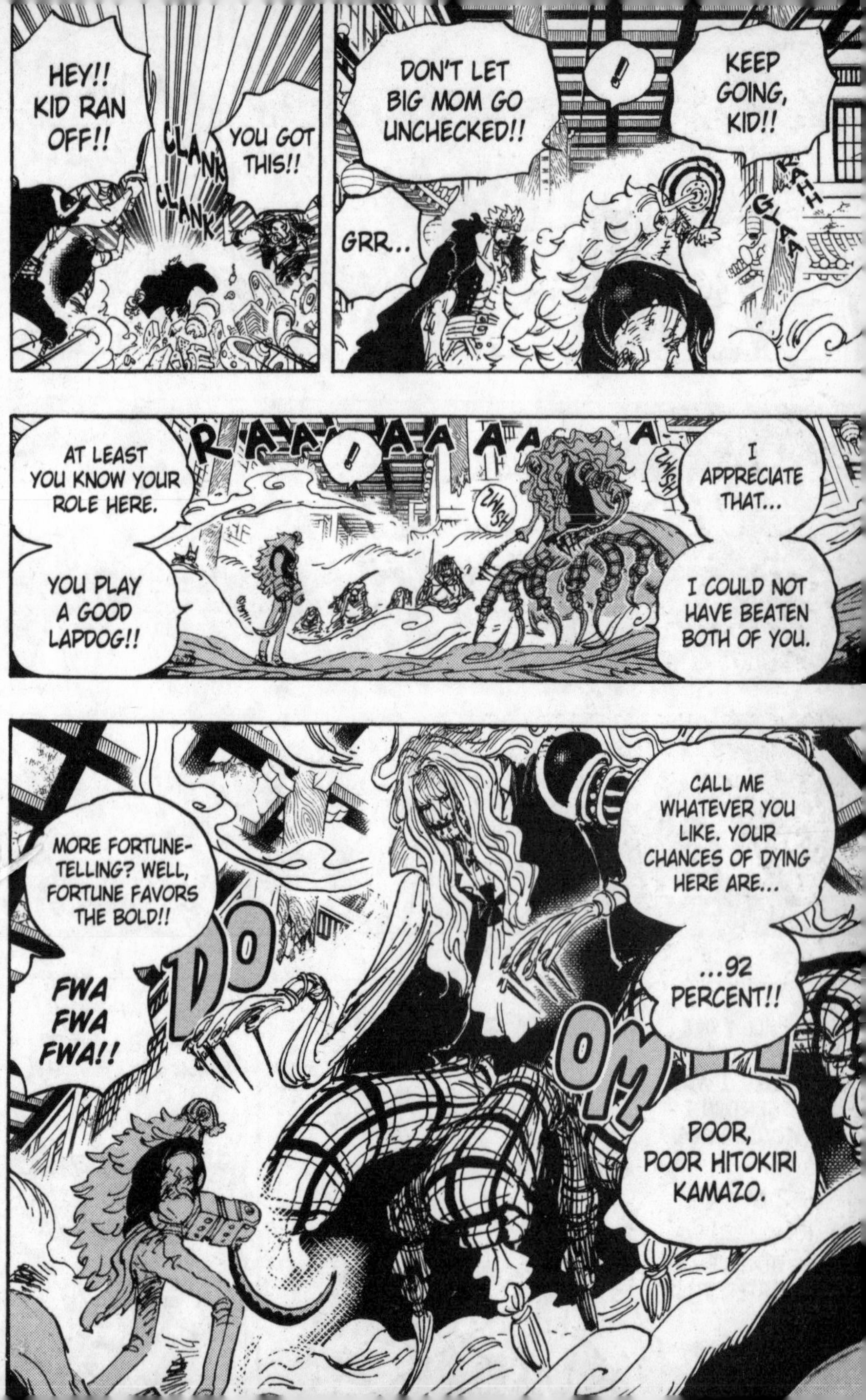
KEEP GOING, KID!!
KAHH GYAA
!
DON'T LET BIG MOM GO UNCHECKED!!
GRR...
HEY!! KID RAN OFF!!
CLANK CLANK
YOU GOT THIS!!
I APPRECIATE THAT...
I COULD NOT HAVE BEATEN BOTH OF YOU.
ZWISH
ZWISH
RAAAAAA
!
AT LEAST YOU KNOW YOUR ROLE HERE.
YOU PLAY A GOOD LAPDOG!!
CALL ME WHATEVER YOU LIKE. YOUR CHANCES OF DYING HERE ARE...
...92 PERCENT!!
POOR, POOR HITOKIRI KAMAZO.
DOOM
MORE FORTUNE-TELLING? WELL, FORTUNE FAVORS THE BOLD!!
FWA FWA FWA!!

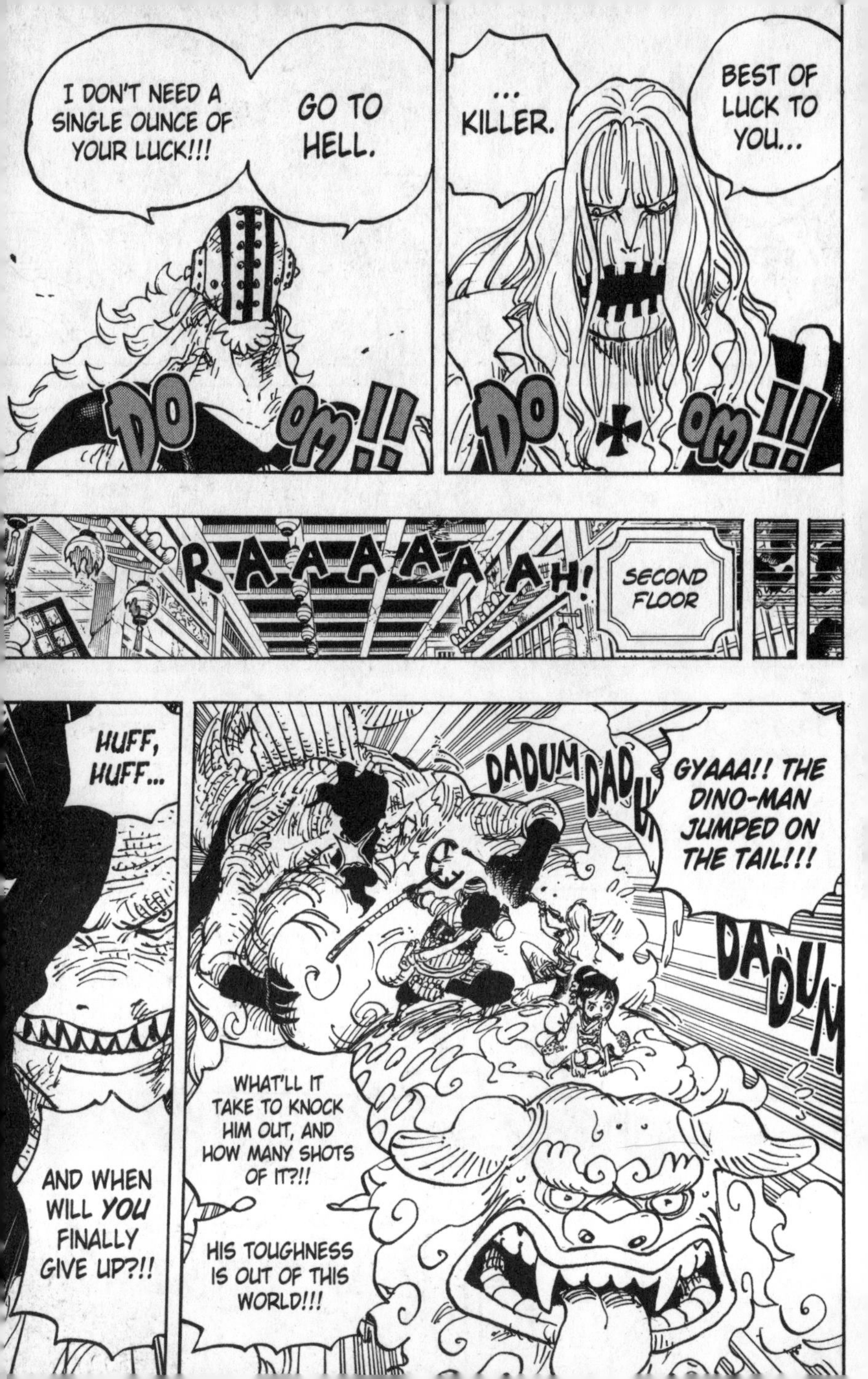
BEST OF LUCK TO YOU...
... KILLER.
DOOM!!
GO TO HELL.
I DON'T NEED A SINGLE OUNCE OF YOUR LUCK!!!
DOOM!!
SECOND FLOOR
RAAAAAAAH!
GYAAA!! THE DINO-MAN JUMPED ON THE TAIL!!!
DADUM DADU
DADUM
WHAT'LL IT TAKE TO KNOCK HIM OUT, AND HOW MANY SHOTS OF IT?!!
HIS TOUGHNESS IS OUT OF THIS WORLD!!!
HUFF, HUFF...
AND WHEN WILL *YOU* FINALLY GIVE UP?!!

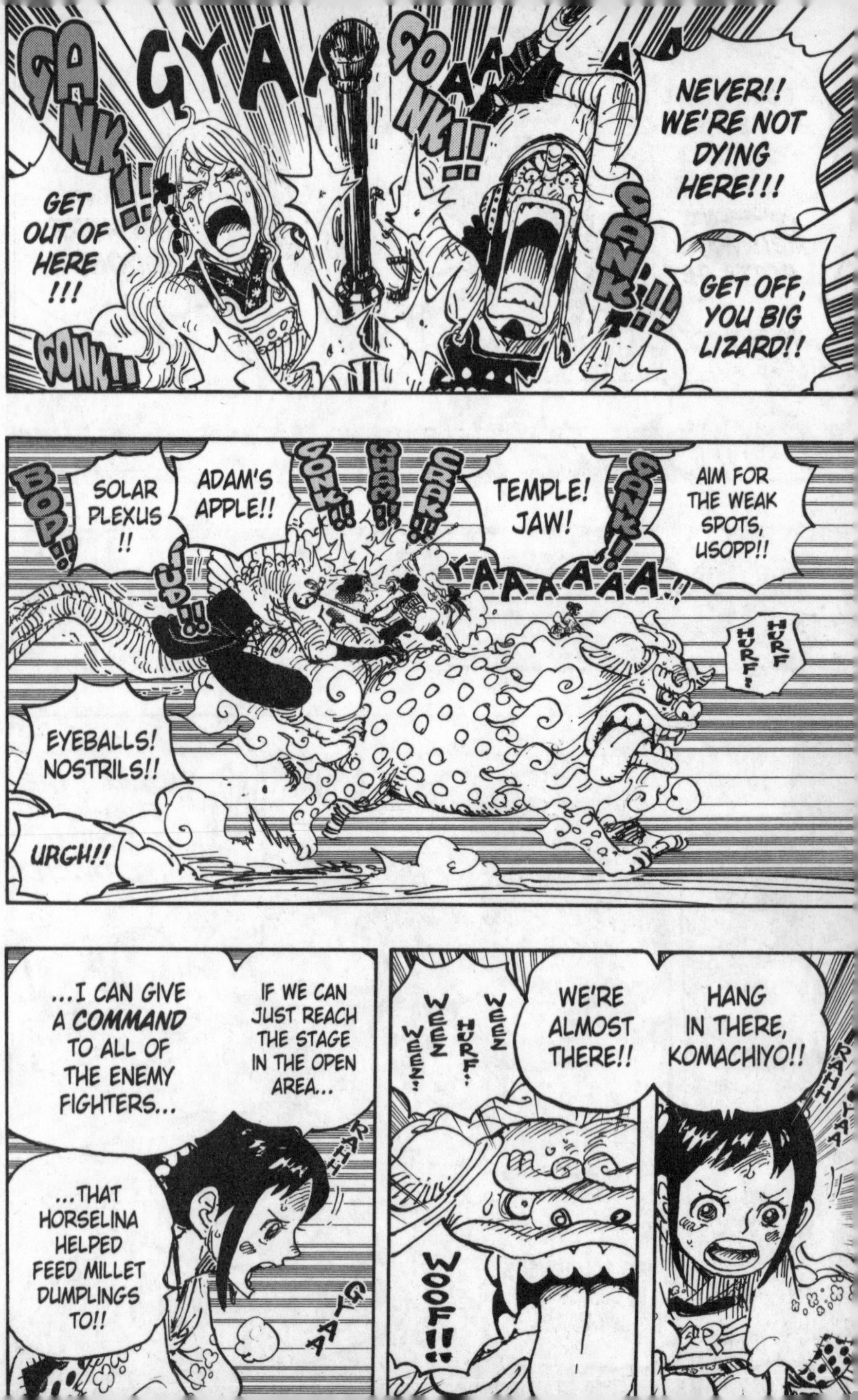

NEVER!! WE'RE NOT DYING HERE!!!
GET OFF, YOU BIG LIZARD!!
GONK!!
GOAANK!!
GYAA
GANK!!
GET OUT OF HERE!!!
GONK!!
AIM FOR THE WEAK SPOTS, USOPP!!
GONK!!
TEMPLE! JAW!
CRAK!!
WHAM!!
GONK!!
ADAM'S APPLE!!
SOLAR PLEXUS!!
BOP!!
THUD!!
YAAAAAA!!
HURF HURF
EYEBALLS! NOSTRILS!!
URGH!!
HANG IN THERE, KOMACHIYO!!
RAHHYAA
WE'RE ALMOST THERE!!
WEEZ HURF WEEZ WEEZ
WOOF!!
IF WE CAN JUST REACH THE STAGE IN THE OPEN AREA...
...I CAN GIVE A *COMMAND* TO ALL OF THE ENEMY FIGHTERS...
RAHH
...THAT HORSELINA HELPED FEED MILLET DUMPLINGS TO!!
GYAA

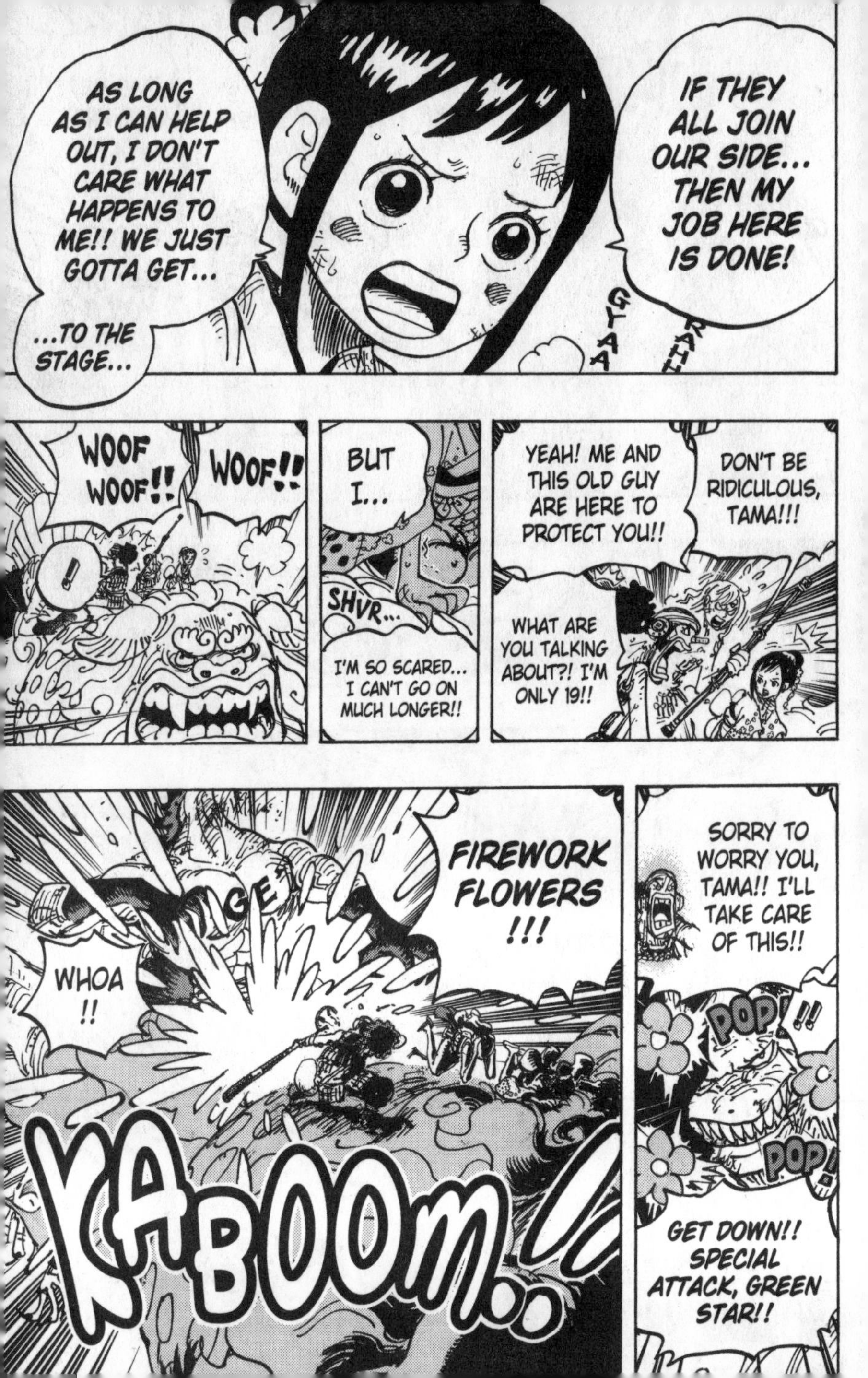
IF THEY ALL JOIN OUR SIDE... THEN MY JOB HERE IS DONE!
GYAA
RAHH
AS LONG AS I CAN HELP OUT, I DON'T CARE WHAT HAPPENS TO ME!! WE JUST GOTTA GET...
...TO THE STAGE...
DON'T BE RIDICULOUS, TAMA!!!
YEAH! ME AND THIS OLD GUY ARE HERE TO PROTECT YOU!!
WHAT ARE YOU TALKING ABOUT?! I'M ONLY 19!!
BUT I...
SHVR...
I'M SO SCARED... I CAN'T GO ON MUCH LONGER!!
WOOF!!
WOOF WOOF!!
!
SORRY TO WORRY YOU, TAMA!! I'LL TAKE CARE OF THIS!!
POP!!!
POP!
GET DOWN!! SPECIAL ATTACK, GREEN STAR!!
FIREWORK FLOWERS !!!
GE
WHOA !!
KABOOM..!!

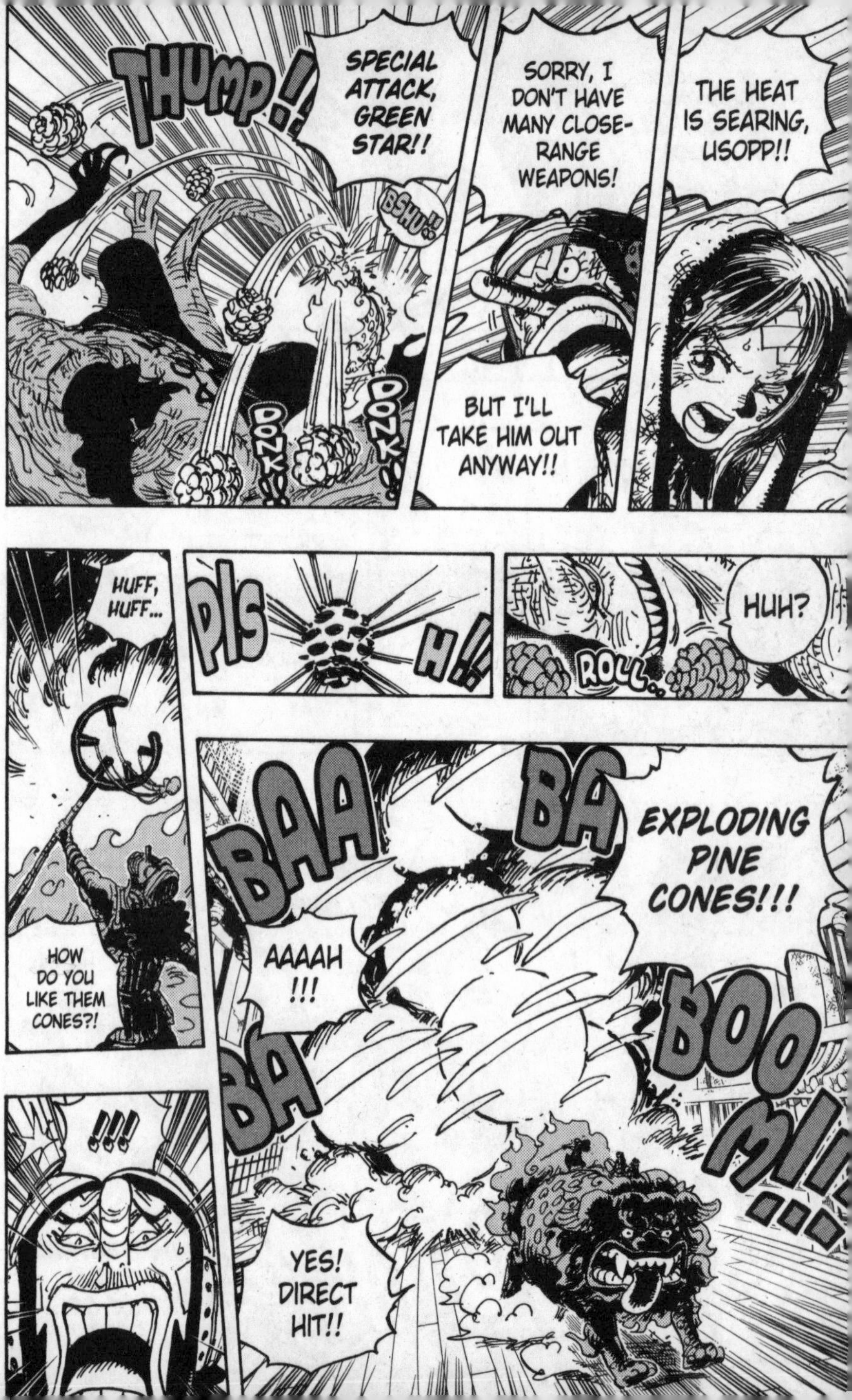
THE HEAT IS SEARING, USOPP!!
SORRY, I DON'T HAVE MANY CLOSE-RANGE WEAPONS!
BUT I'LL TAKE HIM OUT ANYWAY!!
SPECIAL ATTACK, GREEN STAR!!
THUMP!!
BSHU!!
DONK!!
DONK!!
HUH?
ROLL...
PISH!!
EXPLODING PINE CONES!!!
BAA
BA
BA
AAAAH!!!
BOOM!!...
YES! DIRECT HIT!!
HUFF, HUFF...
HOW DO YOU LIKE THEM CONES?!
!!!

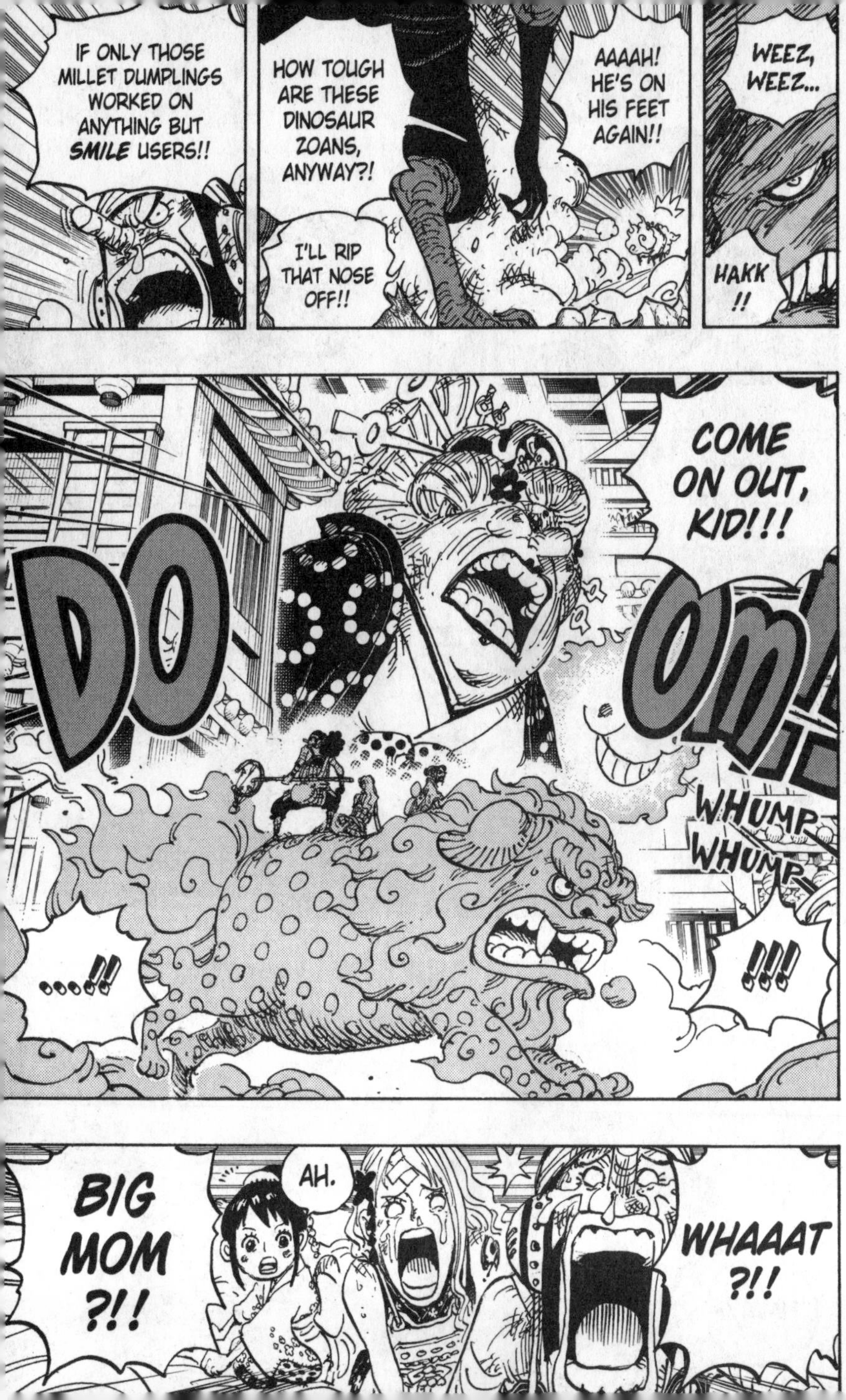
WEEZ, WEEZ...
HAKK !!
AAAAH! HE'S ON HIS FEET AGAIN!!
HOW TOUGH ARE THESE DINOSAUR ZOANS, ANYWAY?!
I'LL RIP THAT NOSE OFF!!
IF ONLY THOSE MILLET DUMPLINGS WORKED ON ANYTHING BUT SMILE USERS!!
COME ON OUT, KID!!!
DOOM!
WHUMP WHUMP
!!!
....!!
WHAAAT ?!!
AH.
BIG MOM ?!!

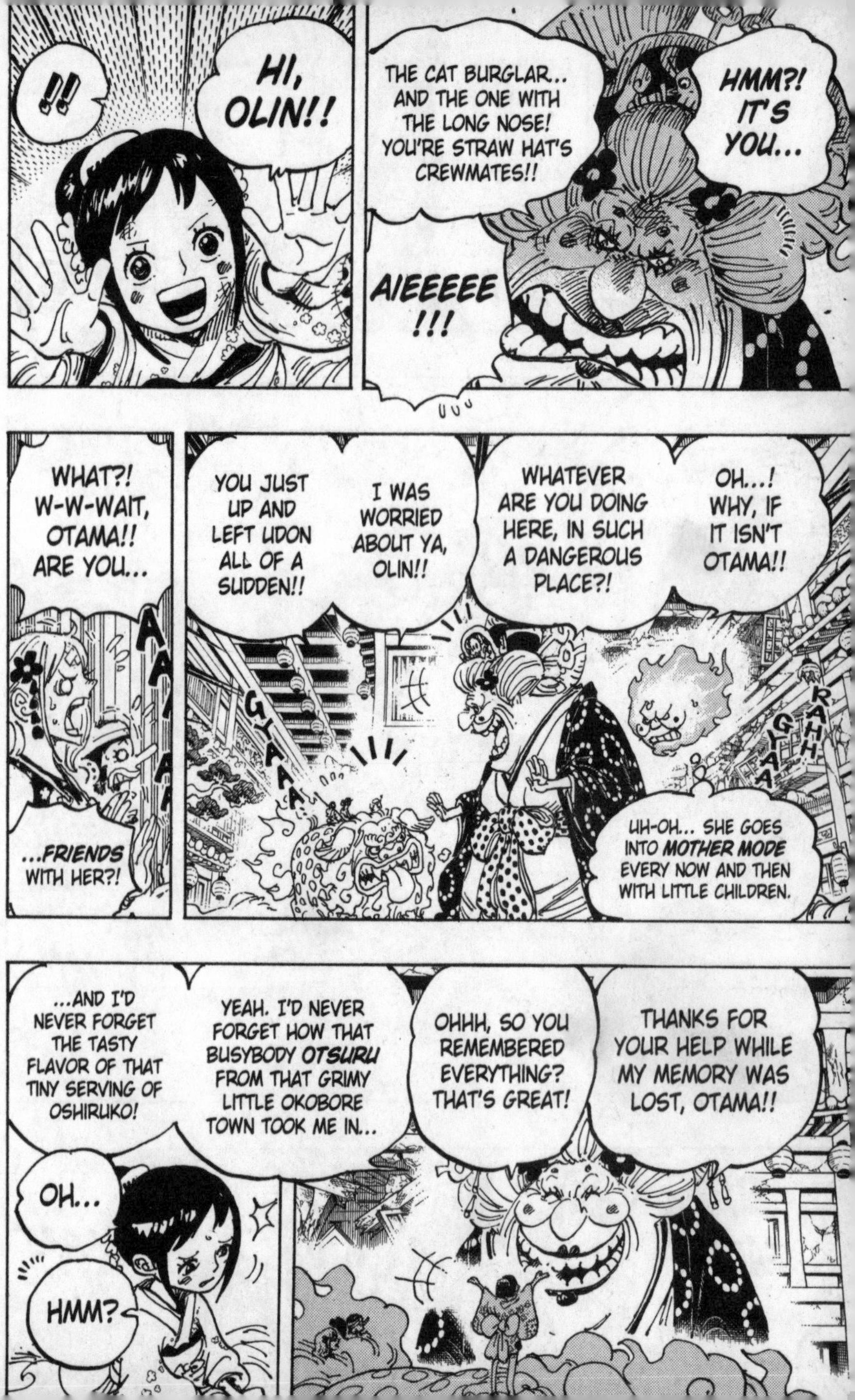
HMM?! IT'S YOU...
THE CAT BURGLAR... AND THE ONE WITH THE LONG NOSE! YOU'RE STRAW HAT'S CREWMATES!!
AIEEEEE !!!
HI, OLIN!!
!!
OH...! WHY, IF IT ISN'T OTAMA!!
WHATEVER ARE YOU DOING HERE, IN SUCH A DANGEROUS PLACE?!
RAHH
GYAA
I WAS WORRIED ABOUT YA, OLIN!!
YOU JUST UP AND LEFT UDON ALL OF A SUDDEN!!
GYAAA
UH-OH... SHE GOES INTO *MOTHER MODE* EVERY NOW AND THEN WITH LITTLE CHILDREN.
WHAT?! W-W-WAIT, OTAMA!! ARE YOU...
...*FRIENDS* WITH HER?!
THANKS FOR YOUR HELP WHILE MY MEMORY WAS LOST, OTAMA!!
OHHH, SO YOU REMEMBERED EVERYTHING? THAT'S GREAT!
YEAH. I'D NEVER FORGET HOW THAT BUSYBODY *OTSURU* FROM THAT GRIMY LITTLE OKOBORE TOWN TOOK ME IN...
...AND I'D NEVER FORGET THE TASTY FLAVOR OF THAT TINY SERVING OF OSHIRUKO!
OH...
HMM?

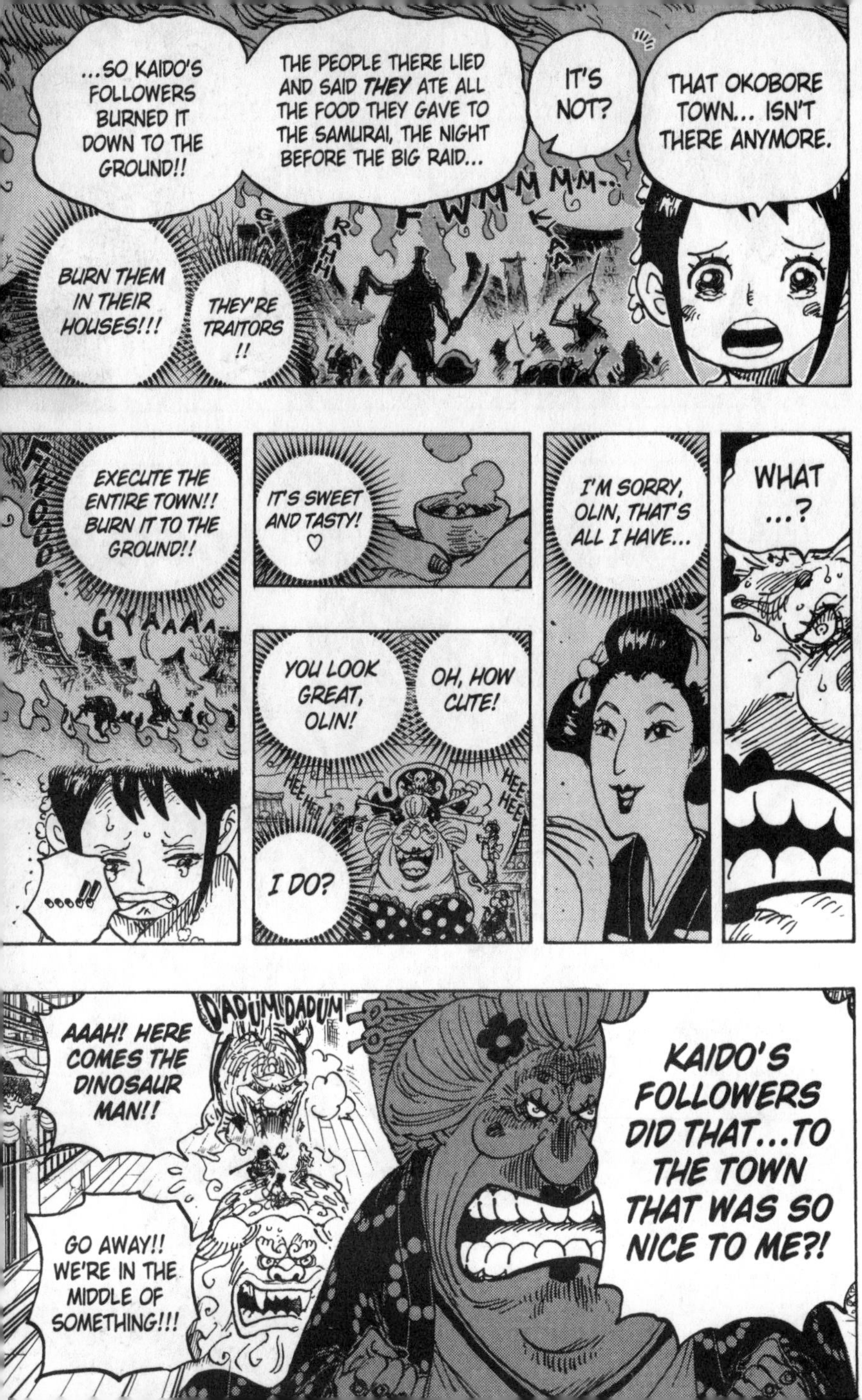

THAT OKOBORE TOWN... ISN'T THERE ANYMORE.
IT'S NOT?
THE PEOPLE THERE LIED AND SAID *THEY* ATE ALL THE FOOD THEY GAVE TO THE SAMURAI, THE NIGHT BEFORE THE BIG RAID...
...SO KAIDO'S FOLLOWERS BURNED IT DOWN TO THE GROUND!!
FWMMMMM...
THEY'RE TRAITORS!!
BURN THEM IN THEIR HOUSES!!!
WHAT ...?
I'M SORRY, OLIN, THAT'S ALL I HAVE...
IT'S SWEET AND TASTY! ♡
OH, HOW CUTE!
YOU LOOK GREAT, OLIN!
HEE HEE
HEE HEE
I DO?
EXECUTE THE ENTIRE TOWN!! BURN IT TO THE GROUND!!
GYAAAA
....!!
KAIDO'S FOLLOWERS DID THAT...TO THE TOWN THAT WAS SO NICE TO ME?!
DADUM DADUM
AAAH! HERE COMES THE DINOSAUR MAN!!
GO AWAY!! WE'RE IN THE MIDDLE OF SOMETHING!!!

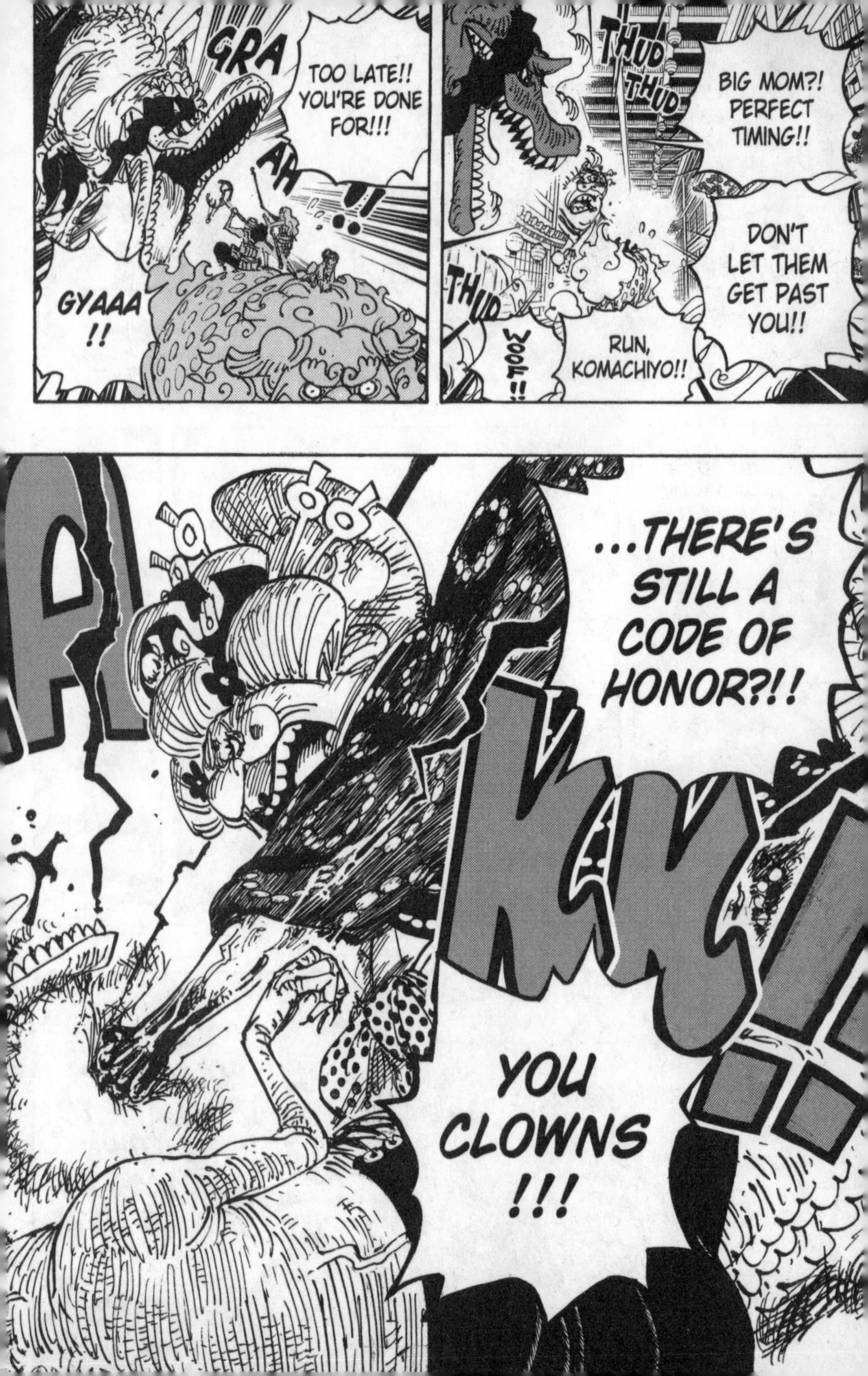
THUD THUD
BIG MOM?! PERFECT TIMING!!
DON'T LET THEM GET PAST YOU!!
RUN, KOMACHIYO!!
THUD
WOOF!!
GRA
TOO LATE!! YOU'RE DONE FOR!!!
AH!!
GYAAA!!
...THERE'S STILL A CODE OF HONOR?!!
YOU CLOWNS!!!

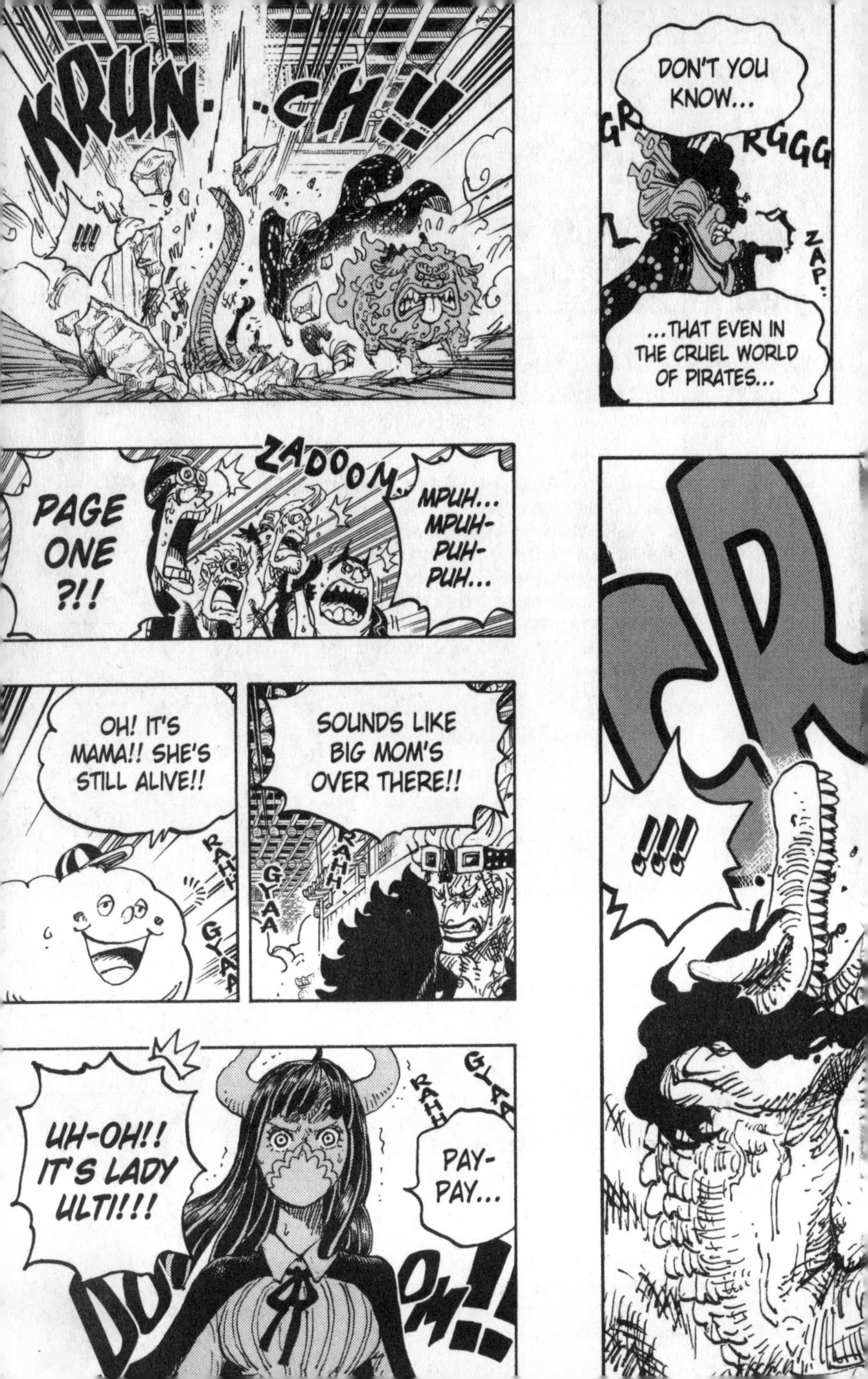
DON'T YOU KNOW...
GRRRGGG
ZAP
...THAT EVEN IN THE CRUEL WORLD OF PIRATES...
KRUN-...CH!!
!!!
!!!
MPUH... MPUH-PUH-PUH...
ZADOOOM
PAGE ONE ?!!
SOUNDS LIKE BIG MOM'S OVER THERE!!
RAHH
GYAA
OH! IT'S MAMA!! SHE'S STILL ALIVE!!
RAHH
GYAA
GYAA
RAHH
PAY-PAY...
UH-OH!! IT'S LADY ULTI!!!
DOOM!!

SBS Question Corner

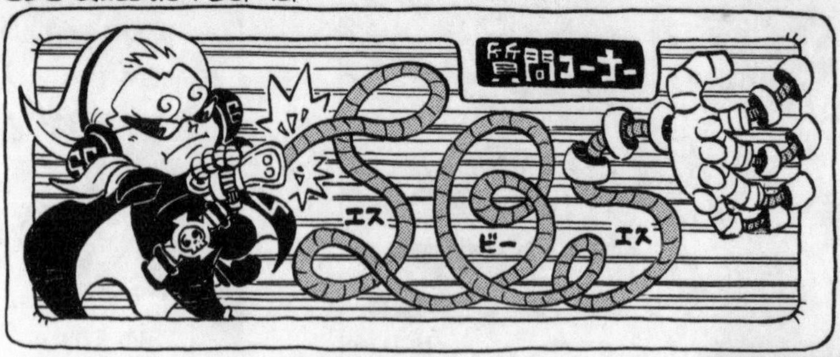
質問コーナー
エス
ビー
エス

(I ♡ OP, Ishikawa)

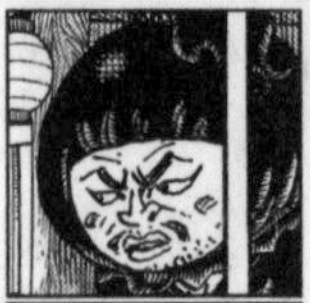

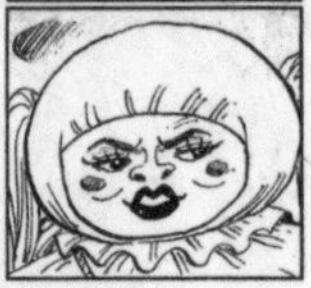

Q: Question for Oda Sensei! On page 33 of volume 95 of *One Piece,* is that person in Rasetsu Town…actually Shinobu without her makeup on?

--Yamatoro

A: Wow, good catch! And hey, that's really rude to Shinobu! That's actually her older brother. His name is Shinosuke. After Shinobu left the Oniwabanshu, she became a "nuke-nin," meaning her life was danger from her former colleagues. As a caring brother, he became a nuke-nin too, and serves as a Kozuki samurai, protecting Shinobu from the shadows.

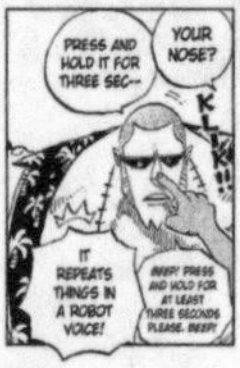
YOUR NOSE?
PRESS AND HOLD IT FOR THREE SEC--
KLIK!!
BEEP! PRESS AND HOLD FOR AT LEAST THREE SECONDS PLEASE. BEEP!
IT REPEATS THINGS IN A ROBOT VOICE!

Q: When he comes across those "I'm not a robot" captcha tests, does Franky click on the box?

--Takataka

A: Well, he's a cyborg, not a robot, so...... huh?⬆

Q: Oda Sensei! Can you please explain the strength and importance of the different Cipher Pols?! I think the strongest is CP0 and then it goes CP9, CP8, CP7, and so on… Is that right? Also, this guy sucks, but can you put him in CP0 please? ➡

--Boy Who Thinks Wapol Is Hilarious

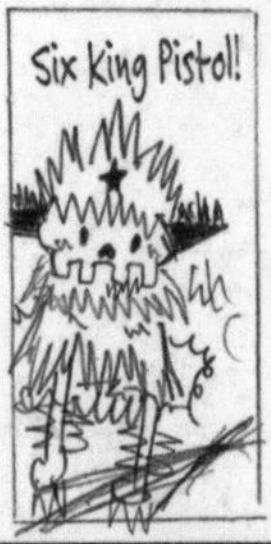
Six King Pistol!

A: First off, I'm going to ignore Six King Pistol there.
Cipher Pol is a spy agency. They do dirty government work in the shadows. The public only knows about CP1 through CP8. The higher the number gets, the more important the duties. The legendary CP9, which officially does not exist, is a group of assassins given the right to eliminate those the government finds inconvenient. CP0 (Cipher Pol "Aigis" Zero) is on a different level entirely. They offer personal protection to Celestial Dragons and act on their orders, so they are the strongest of all. That means Mr. Six King Pistol cannot join. Please get out of here.

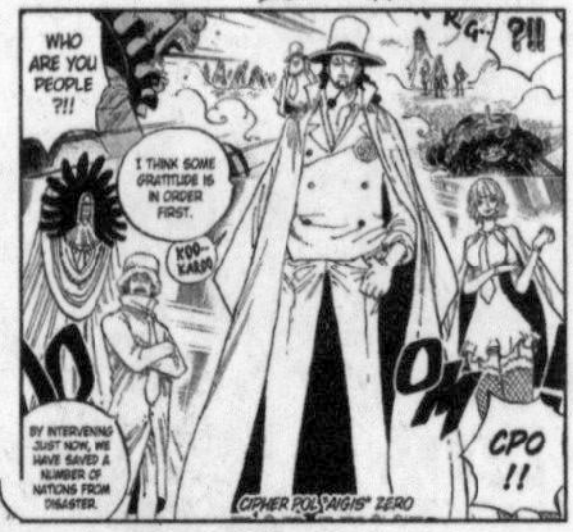
?!!
CPO !!
I THINK SOME GRATITUDE IS IN ORDER FIRST.
KOO-KAROO
WHO ARE YOU PEOPLE ?!!
BY INTERVENING JUST NOW, WE HAVE SAVED A NUMBER OF NATIONS FROM DISASTER.
CIPHER POL "AIGIS" ZERO

Chapter 1012: ITCH

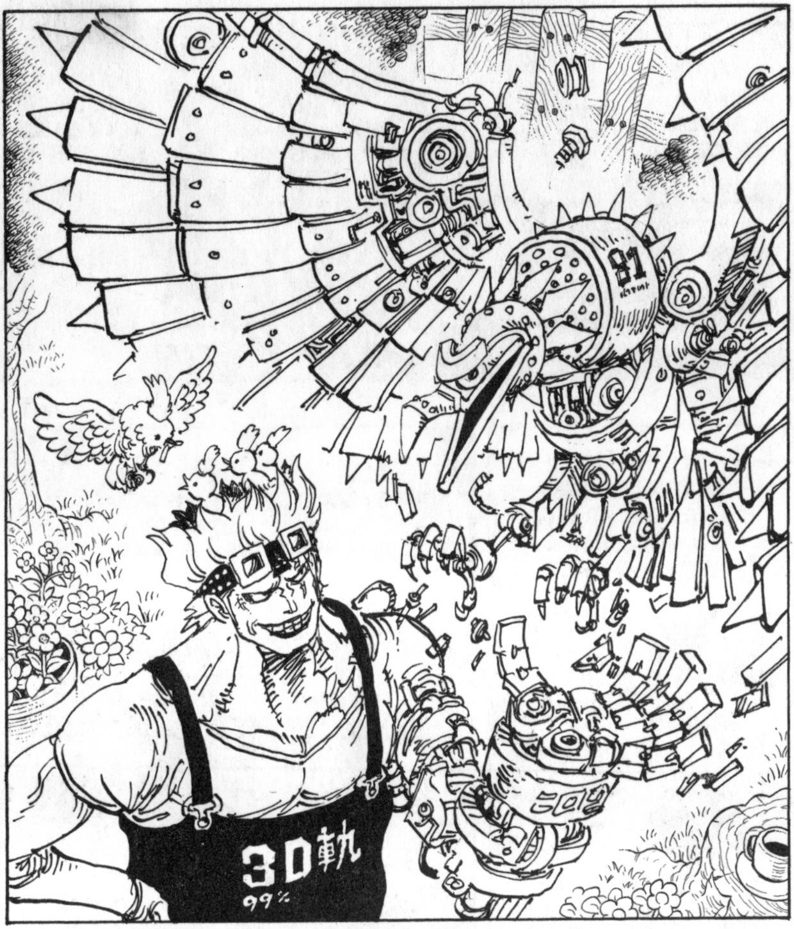

81
30軌
99%
*3D PATH

READER REQUEST: "KID SO FOCUSED ON BUILDING A BIRD OUT OF SCRAP METAL, HE DOESN'T REALIZE HIS HEAD GOT TURNED INTO A BIRD'S NEST" BY ATSUKI

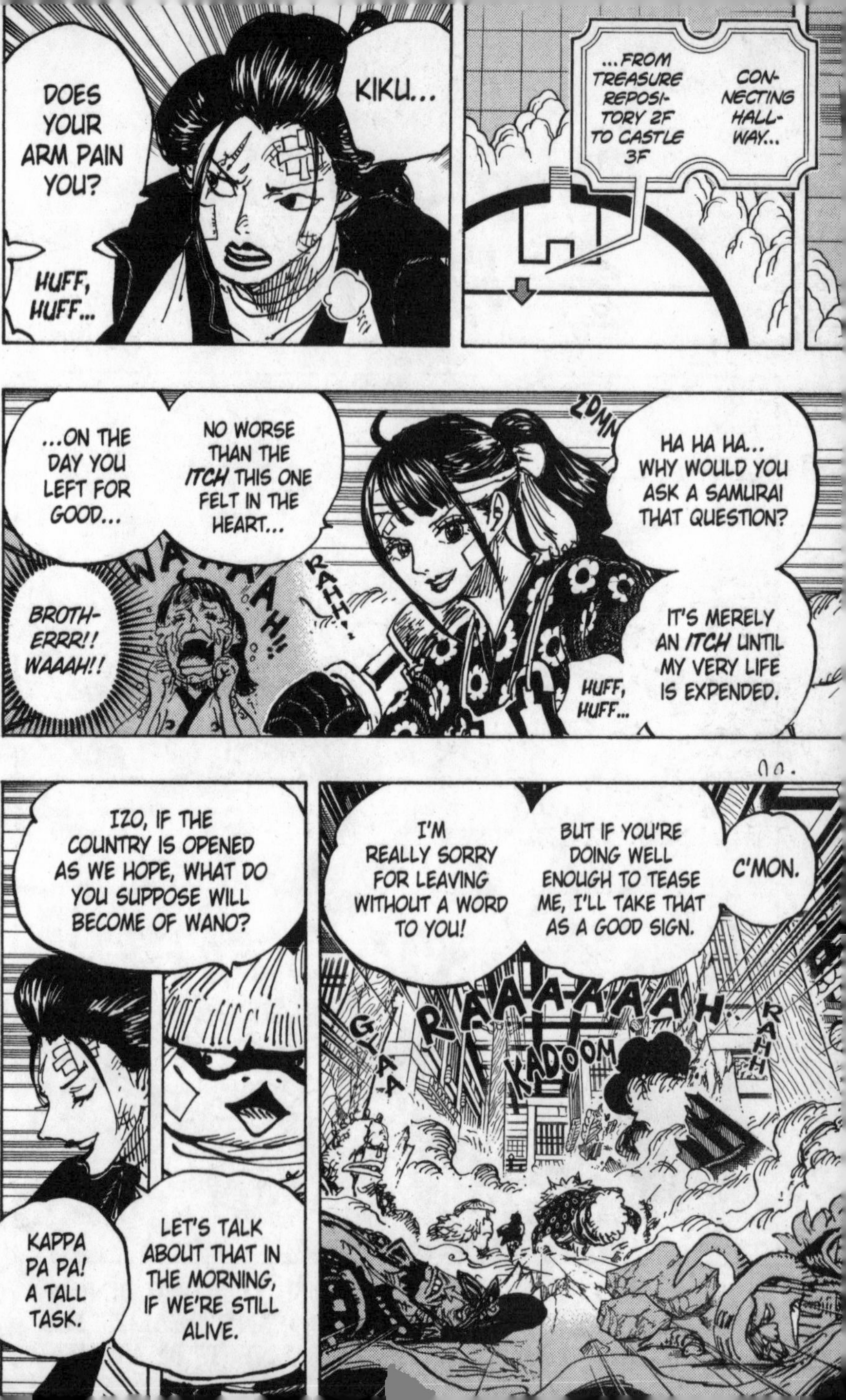
CONNECTING HALLWAY...
...FROM TREASURE REPOSITORY 2F TO CASTLE 3F
KIKU...
DOES YOUR ARM PAIN YOU?
HUFF, HUFF...
ZDMN
HA HA HA... WHY WOULD YOU ASK A SAMURAI THAT QUESTION?
IT'S MERELY AN *ITCH* UNTIL MY VERY LIFE IS EXPENDED.
HUFF, HUFF...
NO WORSE THAN THE *ITCH* THIS ONE FELT IN THE HEART...
...ON THE DAY YOU LEFT FOR GOOD...
RAHH!
WAAAAH!!
BROTH-ERRR!! WAAAH!!
C'MON.
BUT IF YOU'RE DOING WELL ENOUGH TO TEASE ME, I'LL TAKE THAT AS A GOOD SIGN.
I'M REALLY SORRY FOR LEAVING WITHOUT A WORD TO YOU!
RAHH
RAAAAAAAH
KADOOM
GYAA
IZO, IF THE COUNTRY IS OPENED AS WE HOPE, WHAT DO YOU SUPPOSE WILL BECOME OF WANO?
LET'S TALK ABOUT THAT IN THE MORNING, IF WE'RE STILL ALIVE.
KAPPA PA PA! A TALL TASK.

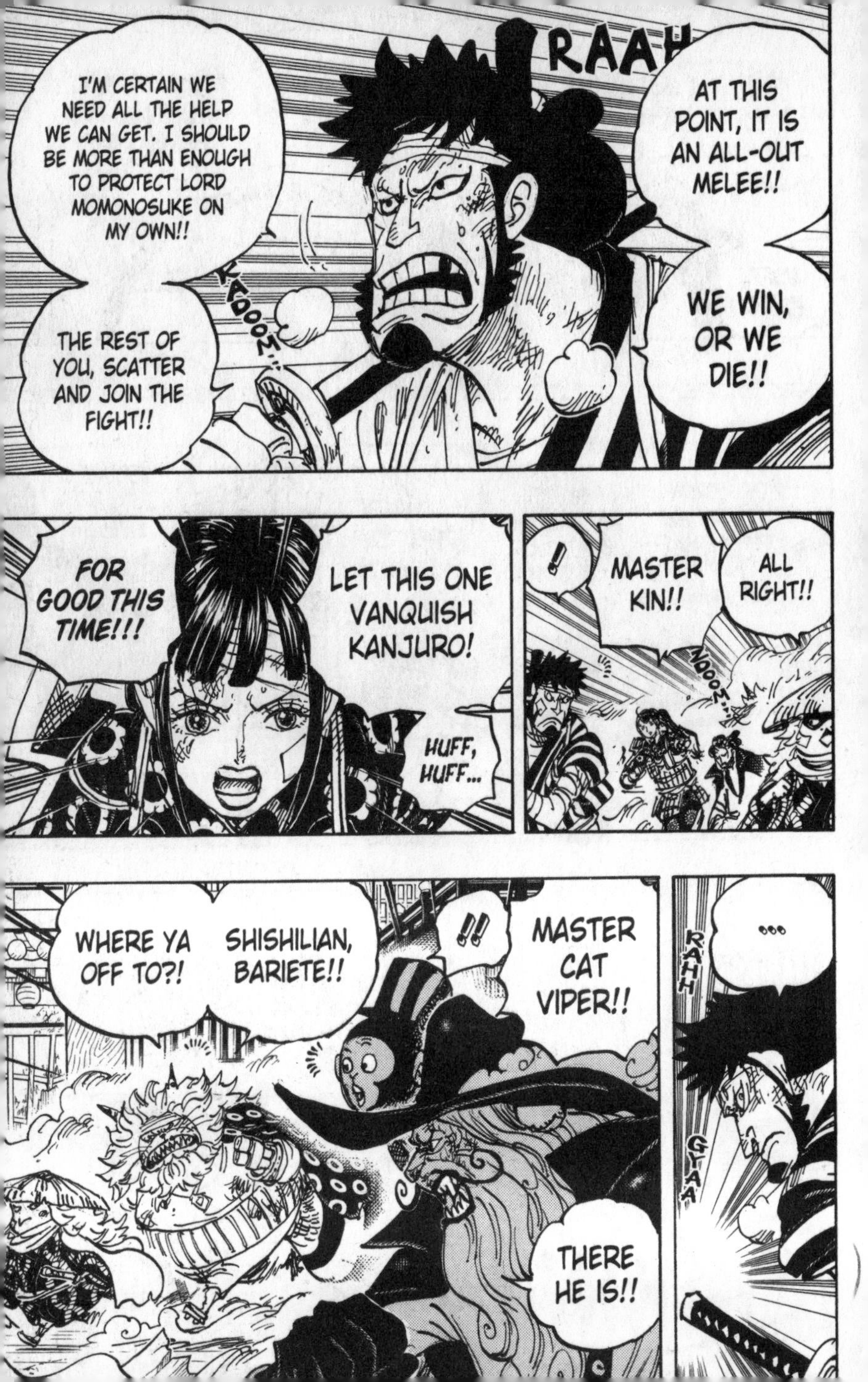
RAAH
AT THIS POINT, IT IS AN ALL-OUT MELEE!!
WE WIN, OR WE DIE!!
I'M CERTAIN WE NEED ALL THE HELP WE CAN GET. I SHOULD BE MORE THAN ENOUGH TO PROTECT LORD MOMONOSUKE ON MY OWN!!
THE REST OF YOU, SCATTER AND JOIN THE FIGHT!!
KADOOM
ALL RIGHT!!
MASTER KIN!!
!
LET THIS ONE VANQUISH KANJURO!
FOR GOOD THIS TIME!!!
HUFF, HUFF...
...
RAHH
GYAA
MASTER CAT VIPER!!
!!
SHISHILIAN, BARIETE!!
WHERE YA OFF TO?!
THERE HE IS!!

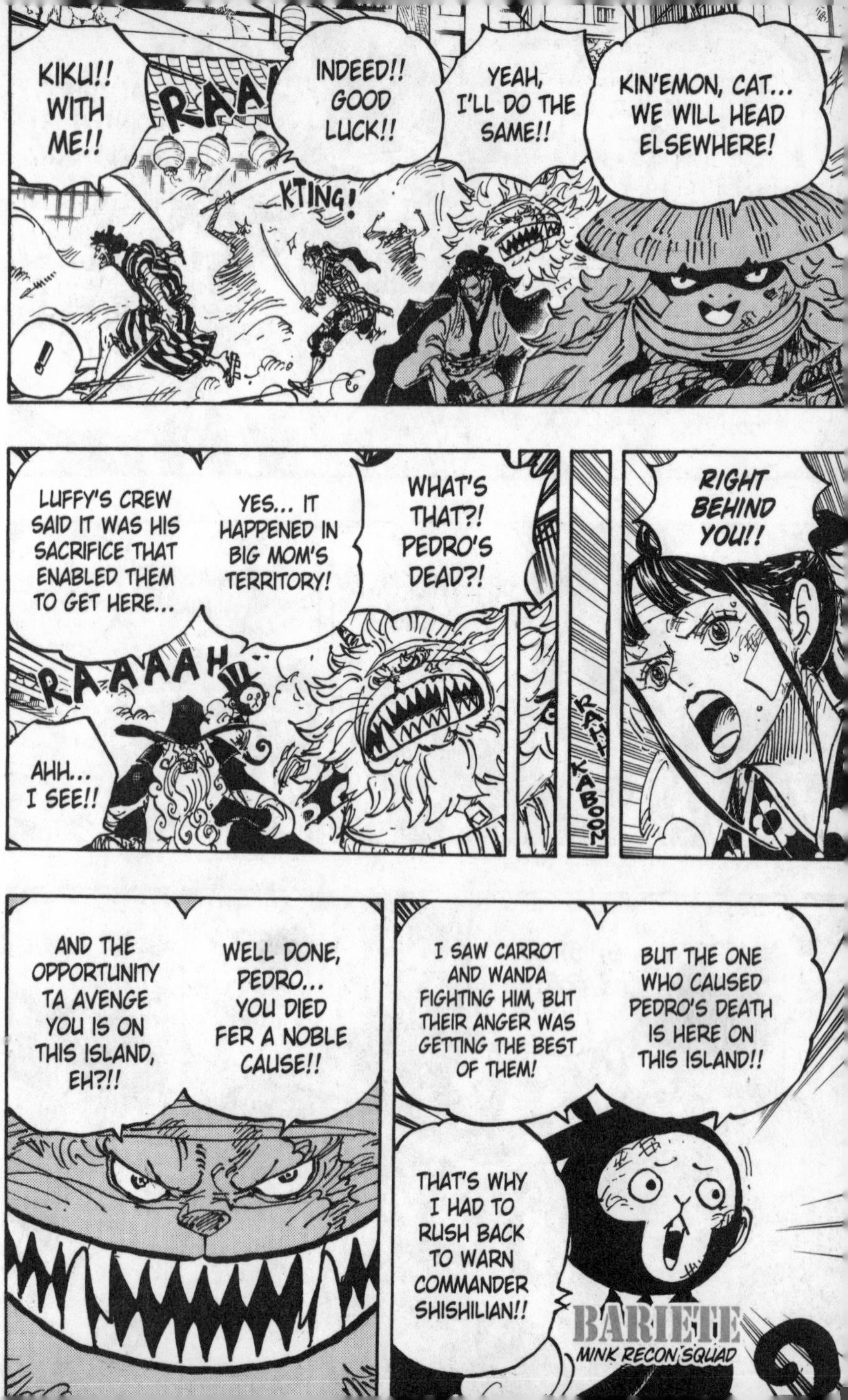
KIN'EMON, CAT... WE WILL HEAD ELSEWHERE!
YEAH, I'LL DO THE SAME!!
INDEED!! GOOD LUCK!!
KIKU!! WITH ME!!
RAA
KTING!
!
RIGHT BEHIND YOU!!
RAH
KABOON
WHAT'S THAT?! PEDRO'S DEAD?!
YES... IT HAPPENED IN BIG MOM'S TERRITORY!
LUFFY'S CREW SAID IT WAS HIS SACRIFICE THAT ENABLED THEM TO GET HERE...
RAAAAH
AHH... I SEE!!
BUT THE ONE WHO CAUSED PEDRO'S DEATH IS HERE ON THIS ISLAND!!
I SAW CARROT AND WANDA FIGHTING HIM, BUT THEIR ANGER WAS GETTING THE BEST OF THEM!
THAT'S WHY I HAD TO RUSH BACK TO WARN COMMANDER SHISHILIAN!!
BARIETE
MINK RECON SQUAD
WELL DONE, PEDRO... YOU DIED FER A NOBLE CAUSE!!
AND THE OPPORTUNITY TA AVENGE YOU IS ON THIS ISLAND, EH?!!

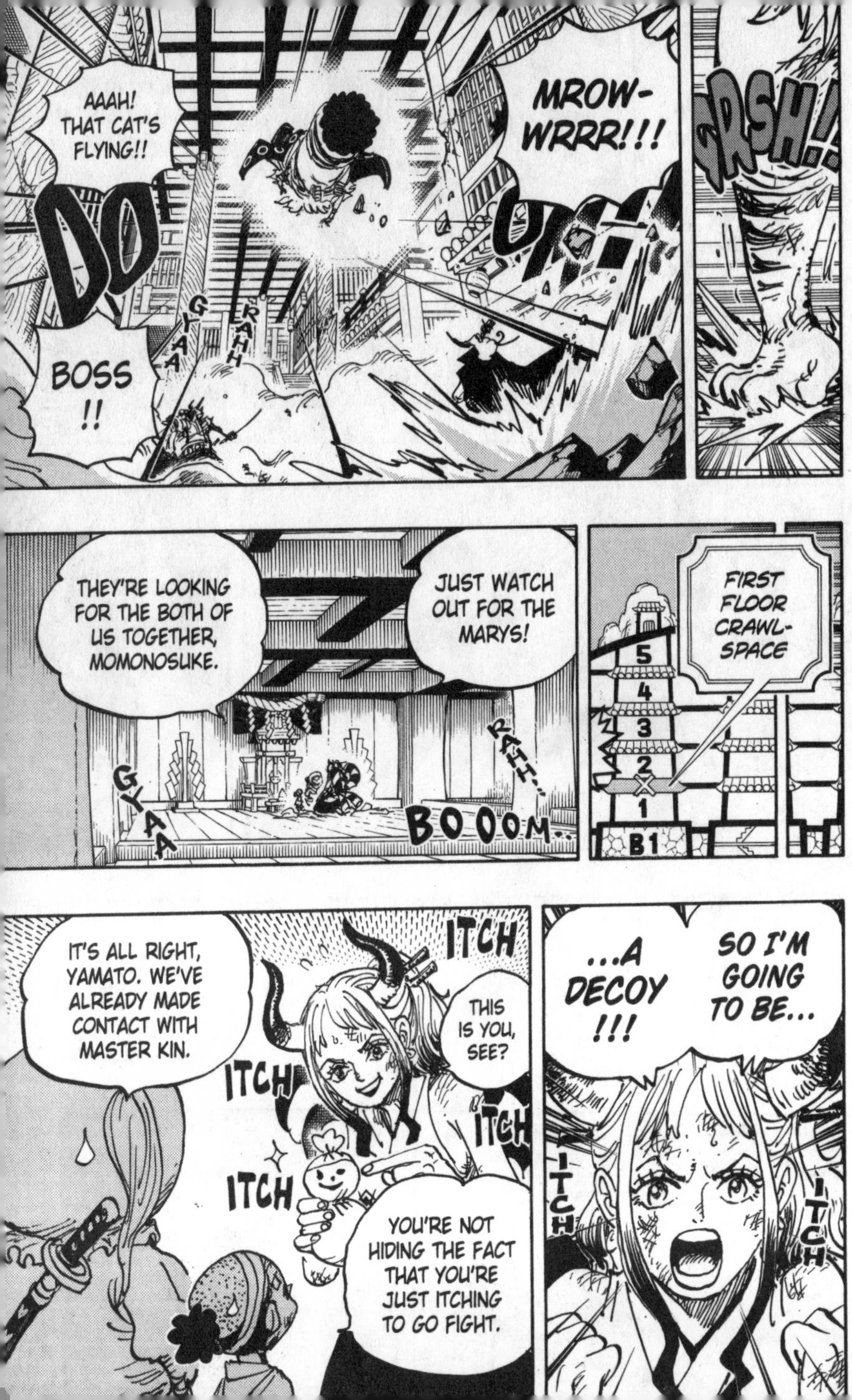
MROW-WRRR!!!
AAAH! THAT CAT'S FLYING!!
DO
GYAA
RAHH
BOSS!!
FIRST FLOOR CRAWL-SPACE
5
4
3
2
1
B1
JUST WATCH OUT FOR THE MARYS!
THEY'RE LOOKING FOR THE BOTH OF US TOGETHER, MOMONOSUKE.
RAHH...
BOOOM...
GYAA
SO I'M GOING TO BE...
...A DECOY!!!
ITCH
ITCH
ITCH
THIS IS YOU, SEE?
IT'S ALL RIGHT, YAMATO. WE'VE ALREADY MADE CONTACT WITH MASTER KIN.
ITCH
ITCH
ITCH
YOU'RE NOT HIDING THE FACT THAT YOU'RE JUST ITCHING TO GO FIGHT.

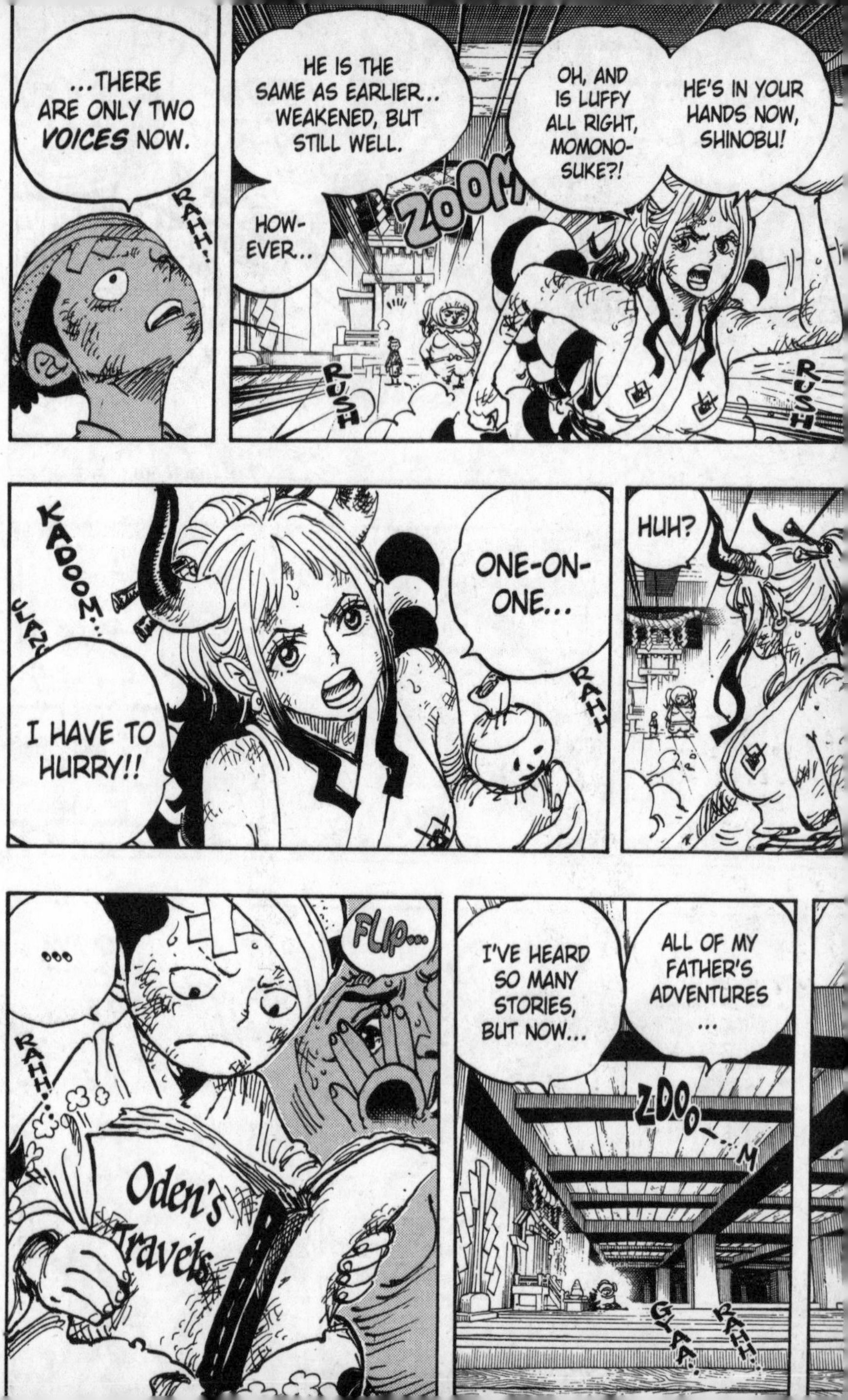
HE'S IN YOUR HANDS NOW, SHINOBU!
OH, AND IS LUFFY ALL RIGHT, MOMONOSUKE?!
ZOOM
HE IS THE SAME AS EARLIER... WEAKENED, BUT STILL WELL.
HOW-EVER...
RUSH
RUSH
...THERE ARE ONLY TWO *VOICES* NOW.
RAHH!
HUH?
ONE-ON-ONE...
RAHH
KADOOOM...
I HAVE TO HURRY!!
ALL OF MY FATHER'S ADVENTURES ...
I'VE HEARD SO MANY STORIES, BUT NOW...
ZDOO-...M
RAHH
GYAA
FLIP...
...
RAHH...
Oden's Travels

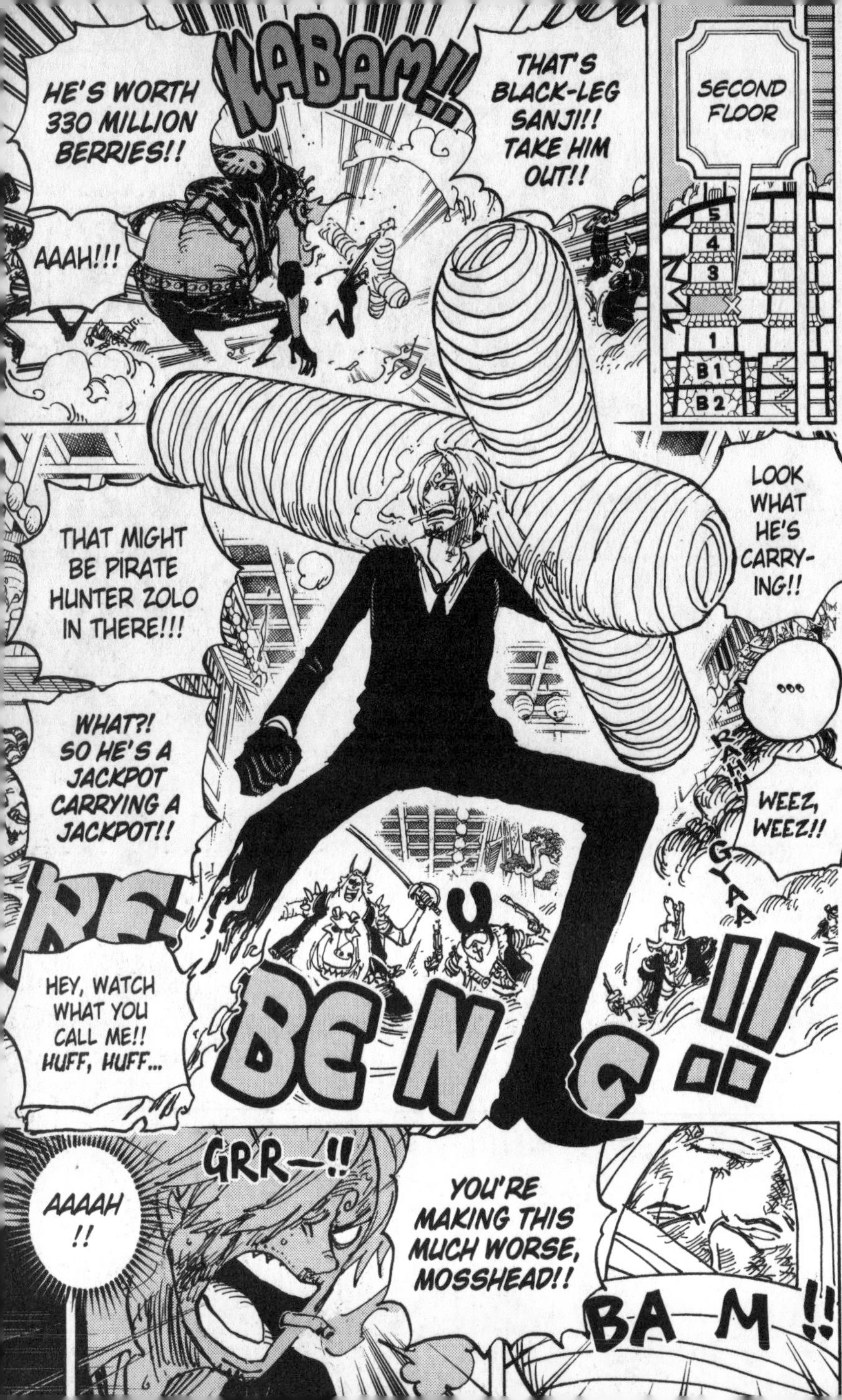
SECOND FLOOR
5
4
3
1
B1
B2
THAT'S BLACK-LEG SANJI!! TAKE HIM OUT!!
KABAM!!
HE'S WORTH 330 MILLION BERRIES!!
AAAH!!!
LOOK WHAT HE'S CARRYING!!
THAT MIGHT BE PIRATE HUNTER ZOLO IN THERE!!!
...
WEEZ, WEEZ!!
WHAT?! SO HE'S A JACKPOT CARRYING A JACKPOT!!
GYAA
BENG!!
HEY, WATCH WHAT YOU CALL ME!! HUFF, HUFF...
BAM!!
YOU'RE MAKING THIS MUCH WORSE, MOSSHEAD!!
GRR—!!
AAAAH!!

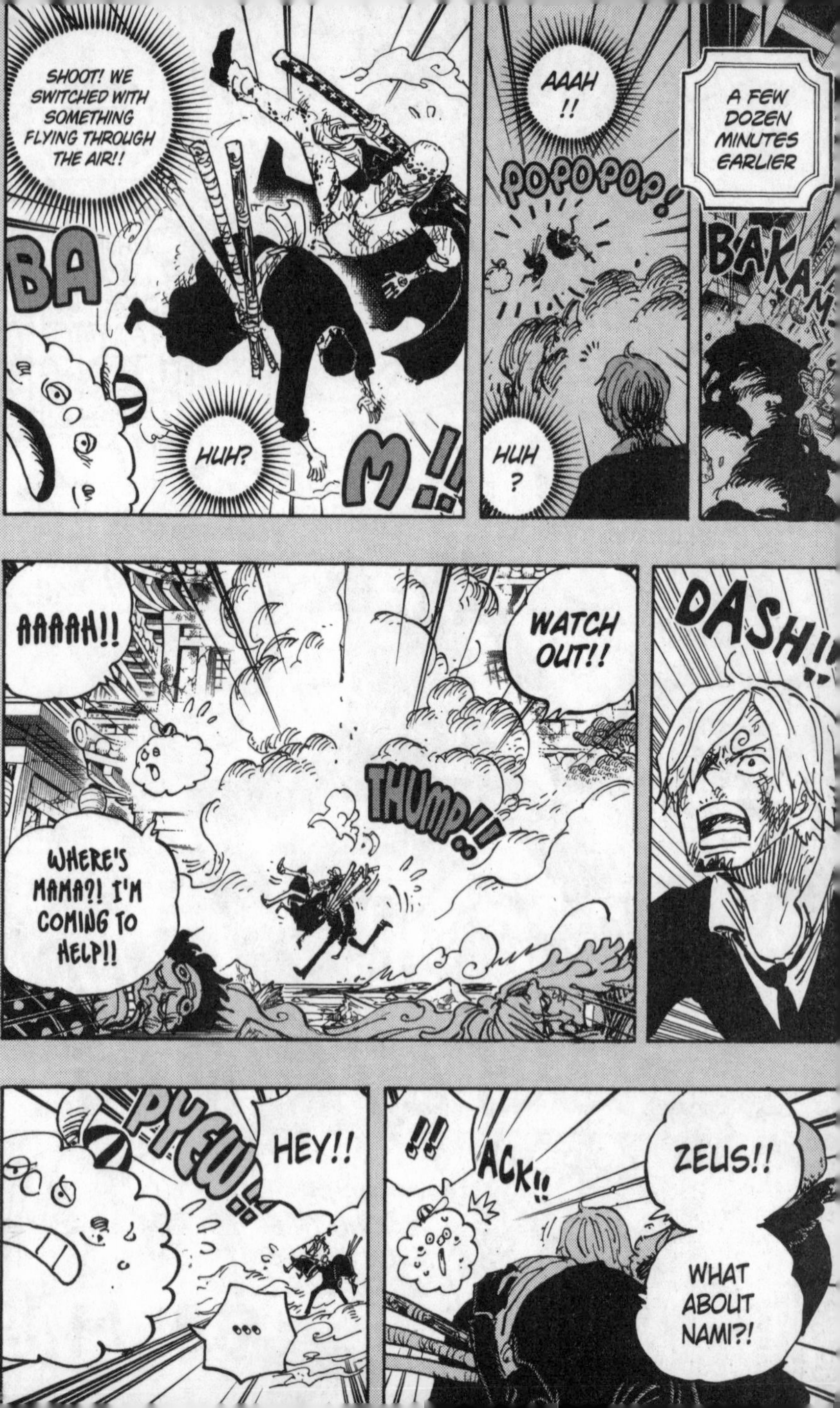
A FEW DOZEN MINUTES EARLIER
BAKAM
AAAH!!
POPOPOP
HUH?
SHOOT! WE SWITCHED WITH SOMETHING FLYING THROUGH THE AIR!!
BA
M!!
HUH?
DASH!!
WATCH OUT!!
AAAAH!!
THUMP!!
WHERE'S MAMA?! I'M COMING TO HELP!!
ZEUS!!
!!
ACK!!
WHAT ABOUT NAMI?!
HEY!!
PYEW
...

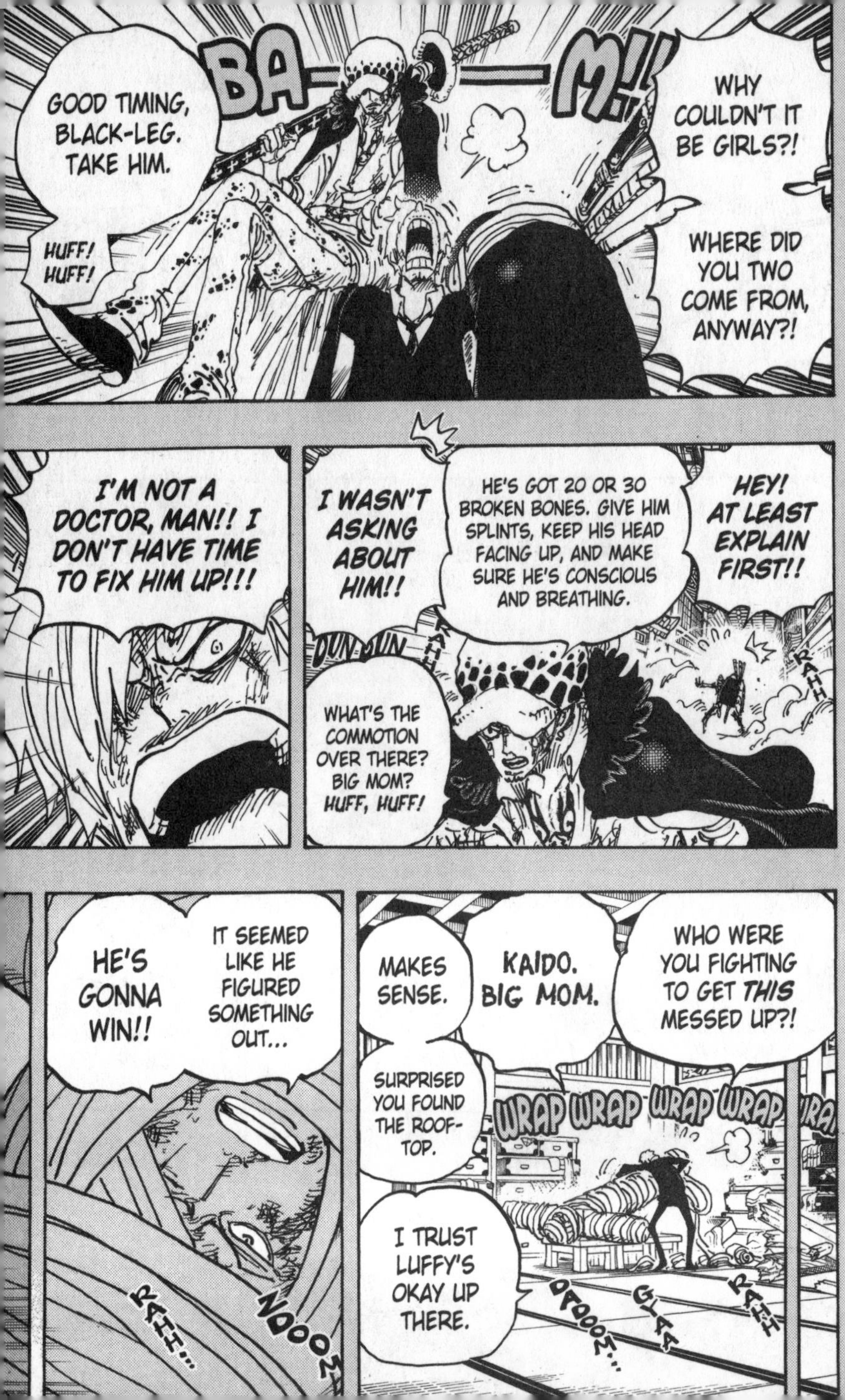
BA—M!!
WHY COULDN'T IT BE GIRLS?!
GOOD TIMING, BLACK-LEG. TAKE HIM.
WHERE DID YOU TWO COME FROM, ANYWAY?!
HUFF! HUFF!
HEY! AT LEAST EXPLAIN FIRST!!
HE'S GOT 20 OR 30 BROKEN BONES. GIVE HIM SPLINTS, KEEP HIS HEAD FACING UP, AND MAKE SURE HE'S CONSCIOUS AND BREATHING.
I WASN'T ASKING ABOUT HIM!!
RAHH
RAHH
DUN DUN
WHAT'S THE COMMOTION OVER THERE? BIG MOM? HUFF, HUFF!
I'M NOT A DOCTOR, MAN!! I DON'T HAVE TIME TO FIX HIM UP!!!
WHO WERE YOU FIGHTING TO GET THIS MESSED UP?!
KAIDO. BIG MOM.
MAKES SENSE.
SURPRISED YOU FOUND THE ROOF-TOP.
WRAP WRAP WRAP WRAP
I TRUST LUFFY'S OKAY UP THERE.
RAHH
GYAA
DOOOOM...
IT SEEMED LIKE HE FIGURED SOMETHING OUT...
HE'S GONNA WIN!!
RAHH...

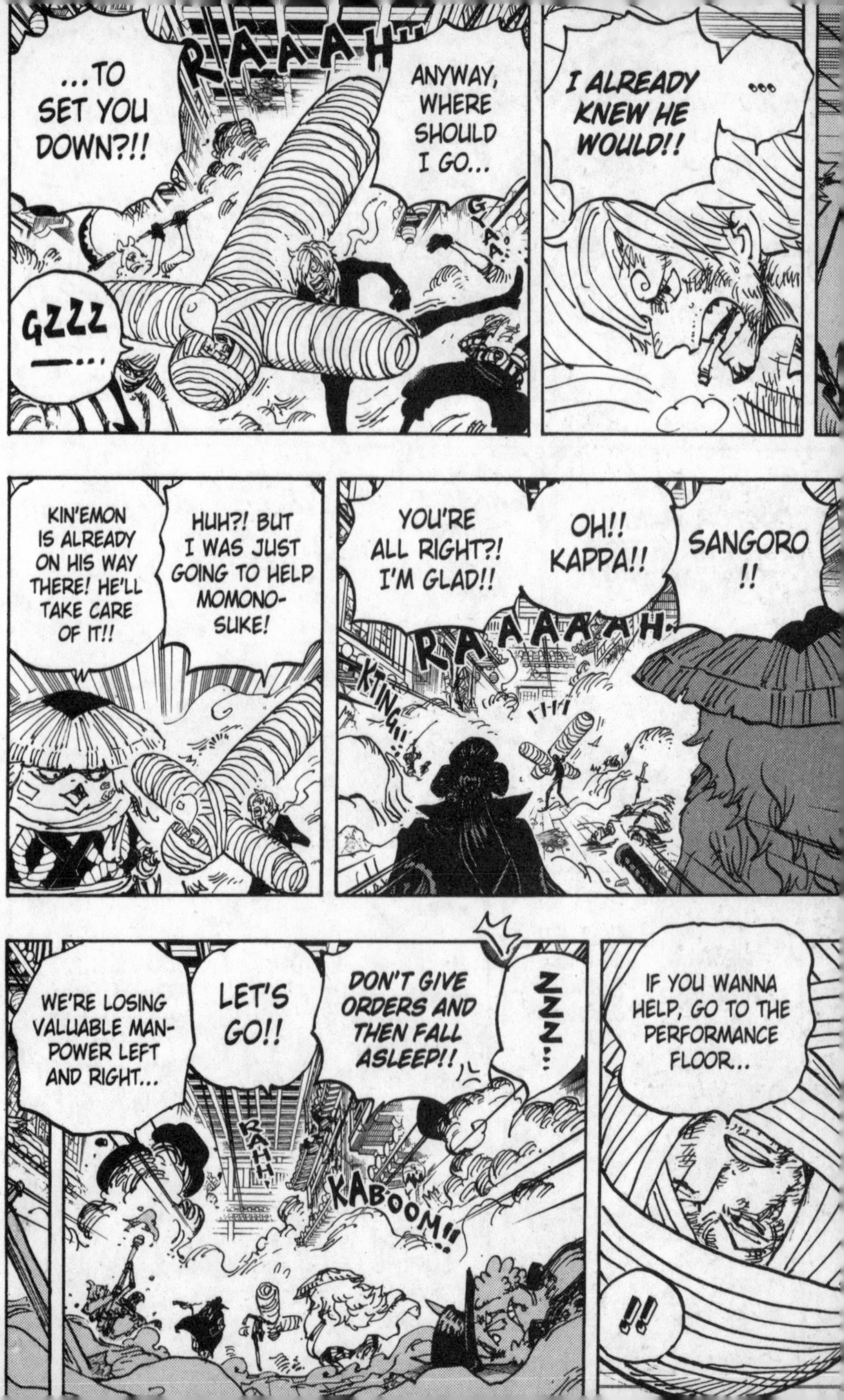
...
I ALREADY KNEW HE WOULD!!
RAAAH...
ANYWAY, WHERE SHOULD I GO...
...TO SET YOU DOWN?!!
GYAA
GZZZ—...
SANGORO!!
OH!! KAPPA!!
YOU'RE ALL RIGHT?! I'M GLAD!!
RAAAAAH
KTING!!
HUH?! BUT I WAS JUST GOING TO HELP MOMONO-SUKE!
KIN'EMON IS ALREADY ON HIS WAY THERE! HE'LL TAKE CARE OF IT!!
IF YOU WANNA HELP, GO TO THE PERFORMANCE FLOOR...
!!
ZZZ...
DON'T GIVE ORDERS AND THEN FALL ASLEEP!!
LET'S GO!!
WE'RE LOSING VALUABLE MAN-POWER LEFT AND RIGHT...
RAHH
KABOOM!!

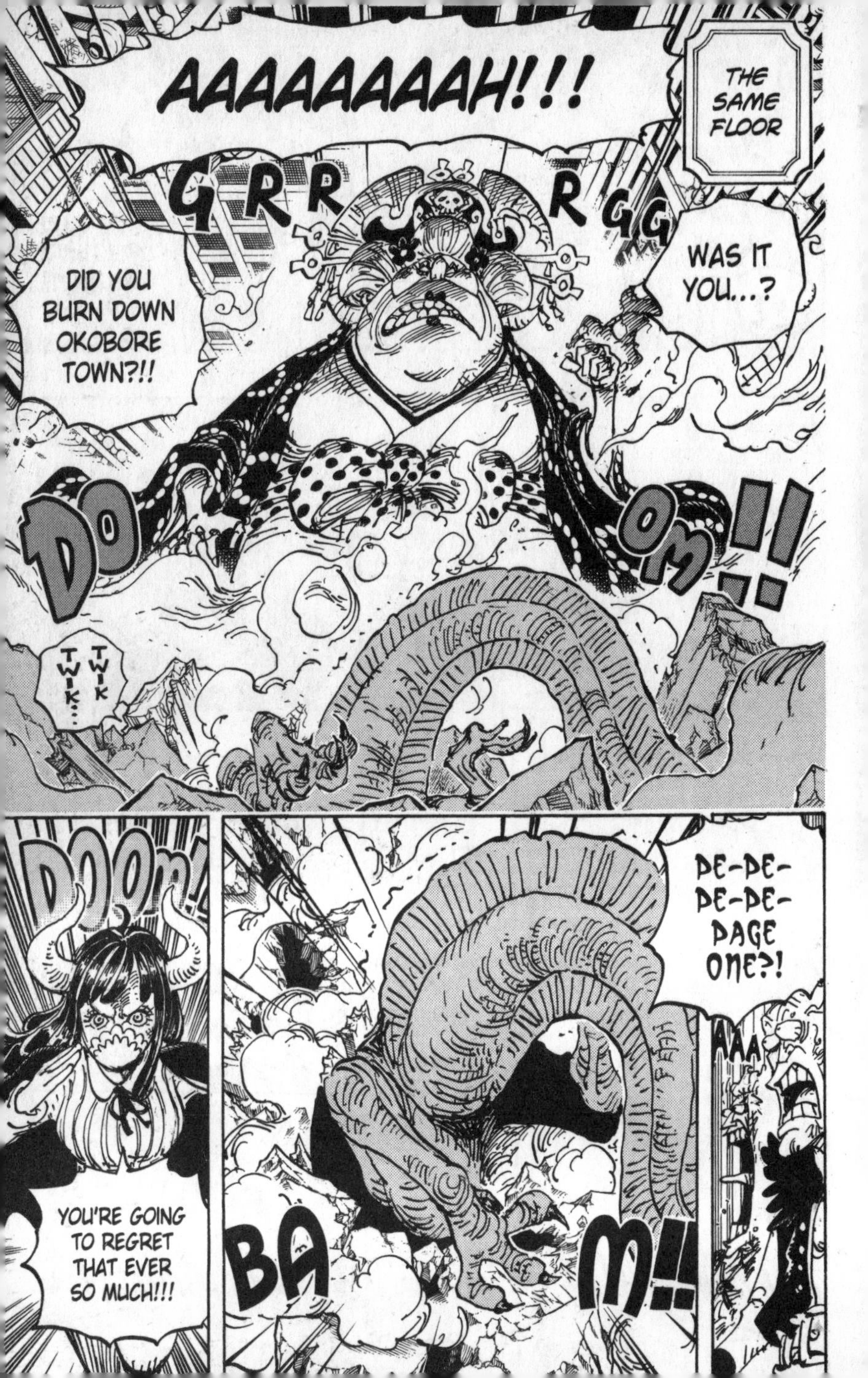
THE SAME FLOOR
AAAAAAAAH!!!
GRRRRGG
WAS IT YOU...?
DID YOU BURN DOWN OKOBORE TOWN?!!
DOOM!!
TWIK TWIK...
AAA
PE-PE-PE-PE-PAGE ONE?!
BAM!!
DOOM!
YOU'RE GOING TO REGRET THAT EVER SO MUCH!!!

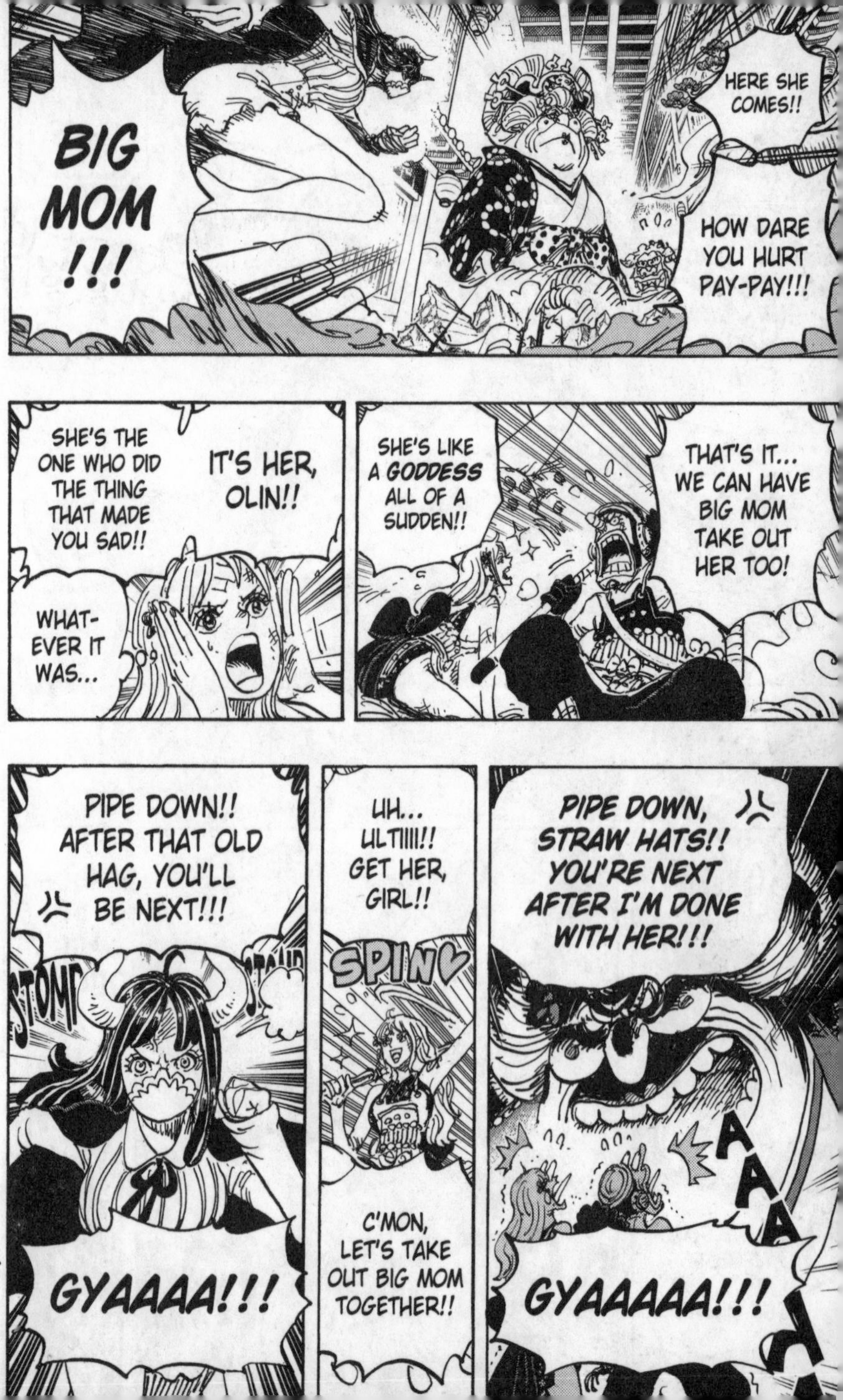
HERE SHE COMES!!
HOW DARE YOU HURT PAY-PAY!!!
BIG MOM !!!
THAT'S IT... WE CAN HAVE BIG MOM TAKE OUT HER TOO!
SHE'S LIKE A GODDESS ALL OF A SUDDEN!!
IT'S HER, OLIN!!
SHE'S THE ONE WHO DID THE THING THAT MADE YOU SAD!!
WHAT-EVER IT WAS...
PIPE DOWN, STRAW HATS!! YOU'RE NEXT AFTER I'M DONE WITH HER!!!
AAAA
GYAAAAAA!!!
UH... ULTIIII!! GET HER, GIRL!!
SPIN♥
C'MON, LET'S TAKE OUT BIG MOM TOGETHER!!
PIPE DOWN!! AFTER THAT OLD HAG, YOU'LL BE NEXT!!!
STOMP
GYAAAA!!!

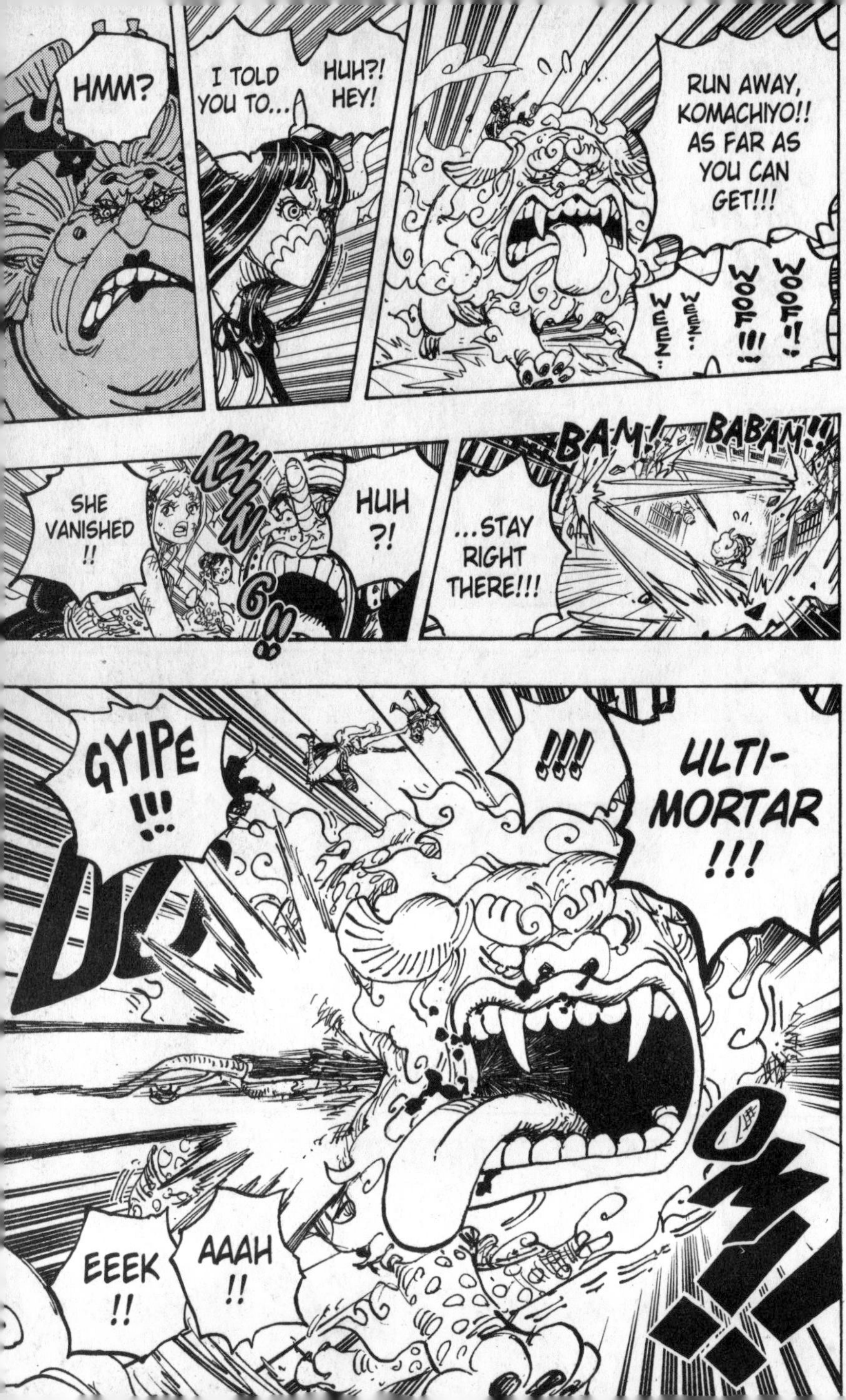
RUN AWAY, KOMACHIYO!! AS FAR AS YOU CAN GET!!!
WOOF!!
WOOF!!!
WEEZ..
WEEZ..
HUH?! HEY!
I TOLD YOU TO...
HMM?
BABAM!!
BAM!!
...STAY RIGHT THERE!!!
HUH ?!
KWING!!
SHE VANISHED !!
ULTI-MORTAR !!!
!!!
GYIPE !!!
AAAH !!
EEEK !!

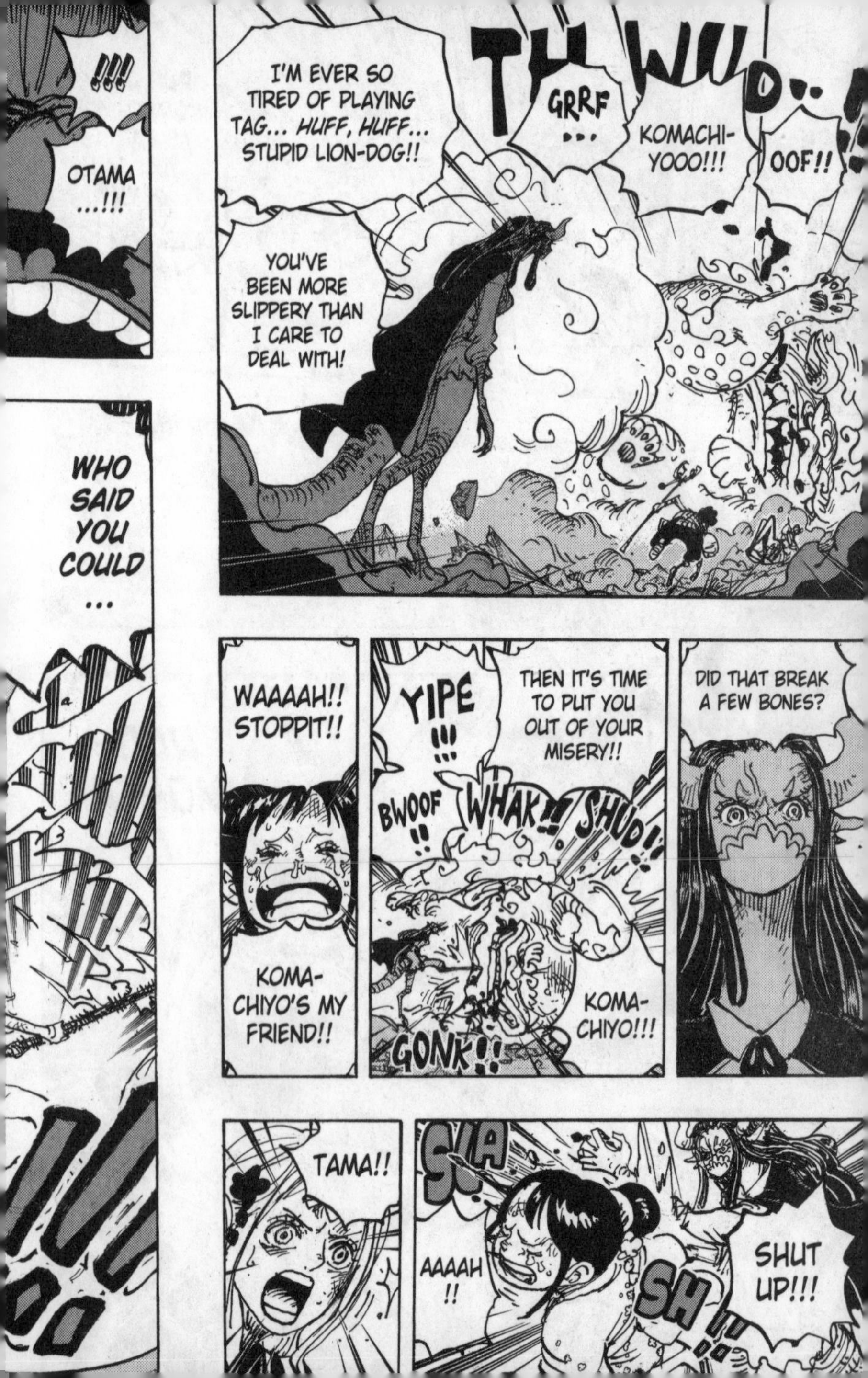
THWUD..!!
OOF!!
KOMACHI-YOOO!!!
GRRF...
I'M EVER SO TIRED OF PLAYING TAG... HUFF, HUFF... STUPID LION-DOG!!
YOU'VE BEEN MORE SLIPPERY THAN I CARE TO DEAL WITH!
DID THAT BREAK A FEW BONES?
THEN IT'S TIME TO PUT YOU OUT OF YOUR MISERY!!
YIPE!!!
SHUD!!
WHAK!!
BWOOF!!
KOMA-CHIYO!!!
GONK!!
WAAAAH!! STOPPIT!!
KOMA-CHIYO'S MY FRIEND!!
SHUT UP!!!
SH!!
AAAAH!!
TAMA!!
!!!
OTAMA...!!!
WHO SAID YOU COULD...

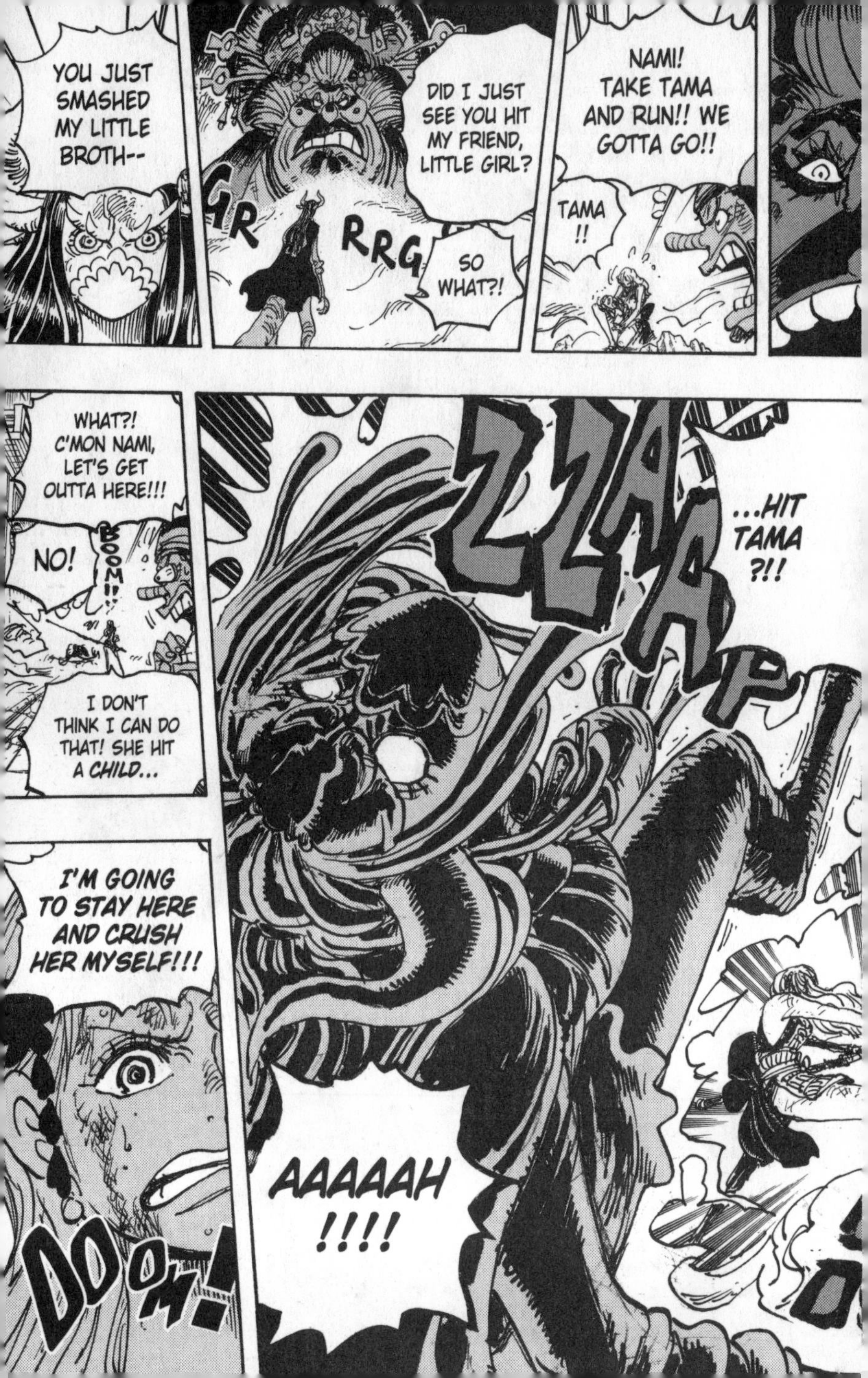
NAMI! TAKE TAMA AND RUN!! WE GOTTA GO!!
TAMA !!
DID I JUST SEE YOU HIT MY FRIEND, LITTLE GIRL?
SO WHAT?!
GRRRRG
YOU JUST SMASHED MY LITTLE BROTH--
ZZAAP
...HIT TAMA ?!!
AAAAAH !!!!
WHAT?! C'MON NAMI, LET'S GET OUTTA HERE!!!
BOOM!!
NO!
I DON'T THINK I CAN DO THAT! SHE HIT A CHILD...
I'M GOING TO STAY HERE AND CRUSH HER MYSELF!!!
DOOM!

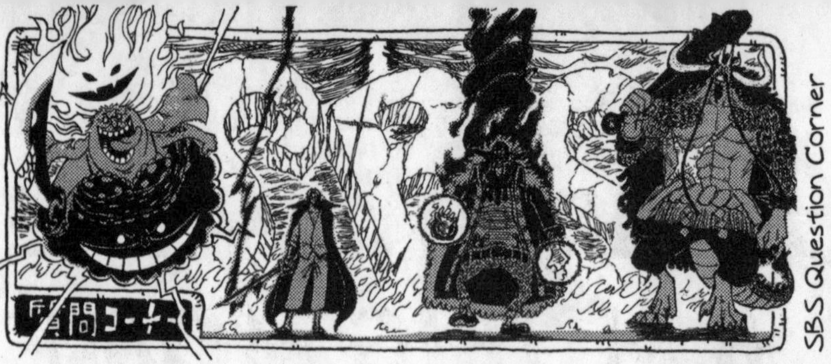

SBS Question Corner
(Nobuhiko Ohkubo, Kagoshima)

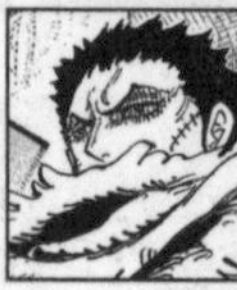

Q: Oda Sensei! I want to get married to Brother Katakuri!
--Lactobacillus Lactobacillus, Gut Function Healthy

A: That's a really long pen name!! Anyway... interesting. Are you sure, though? Have you taken into account that Katakuri is almost 17 feet tall?

Q: 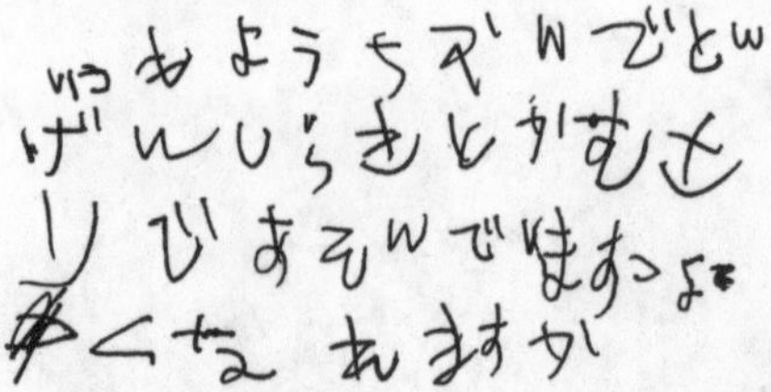

In kindergarten we like to pretend fight with Paradise Waterfall and Divine Departure. Will I get stronger this way?
--Taisei

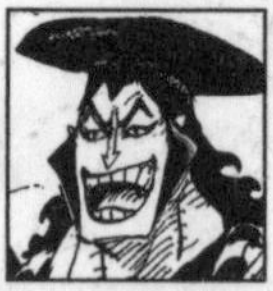

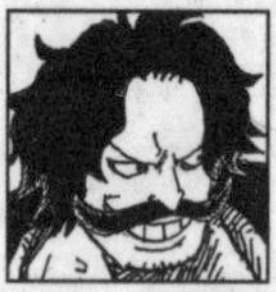

A: Aaaaah!! Thump...
.........................Ah!!
Hey! Take it easy with that Supreme King Haki!

Q: Heso, Odacchi! Here's a question! Does Kaido's club have a name?! And if it were personified in human form, how cool would it be?!
--Takase

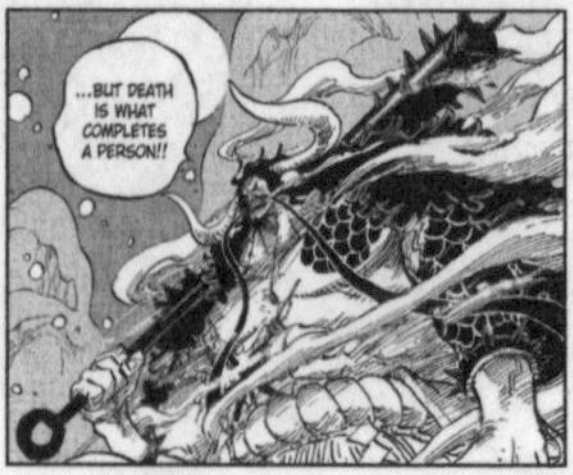
...BUT DEATH IS WHAT COMPLETES A PERSON!!

A: Here we go. It's that thing I'm really good at! You wanna see it, huh? First of all, the club's name is Hassaikai. It refers to the Eight Precepts of Buddhism. The club doesn't have any special rank as a weapon, but if it ever passes out of Kaido's hands, it'll be considered a legend, I'm sure. Now, check out its personification! It makes Kaido even scarier, doesn't it?!

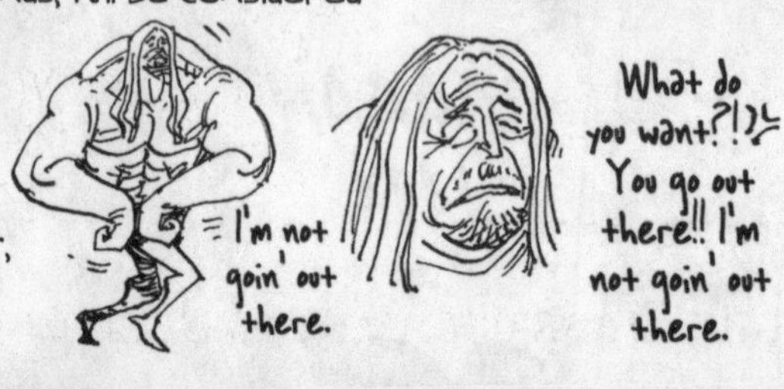
What do you want?!! You go out there!! I'm not goin' out there.
I'm not goin' out there.

Chapter 1013:

ANARCHY IN THE B.M. (BIG MOM)

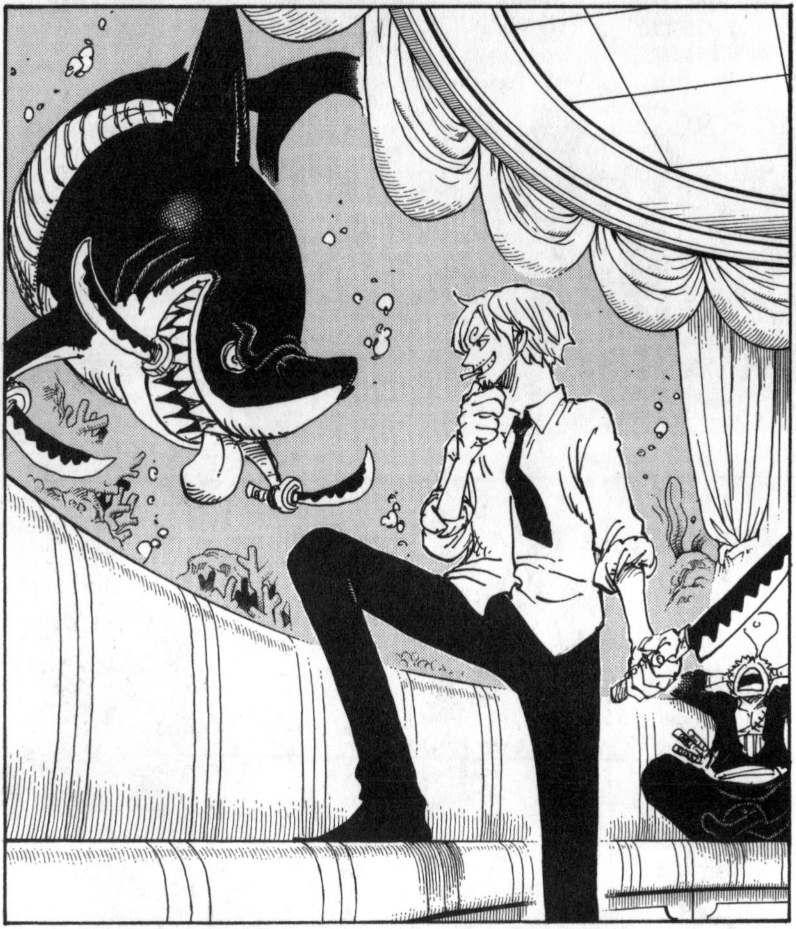

READER REQUEST: "SANJI ENVISIONING HOW HE'LL COOK UP A SHARK THAT LOOKS LIKE ZOLO" BY EBI

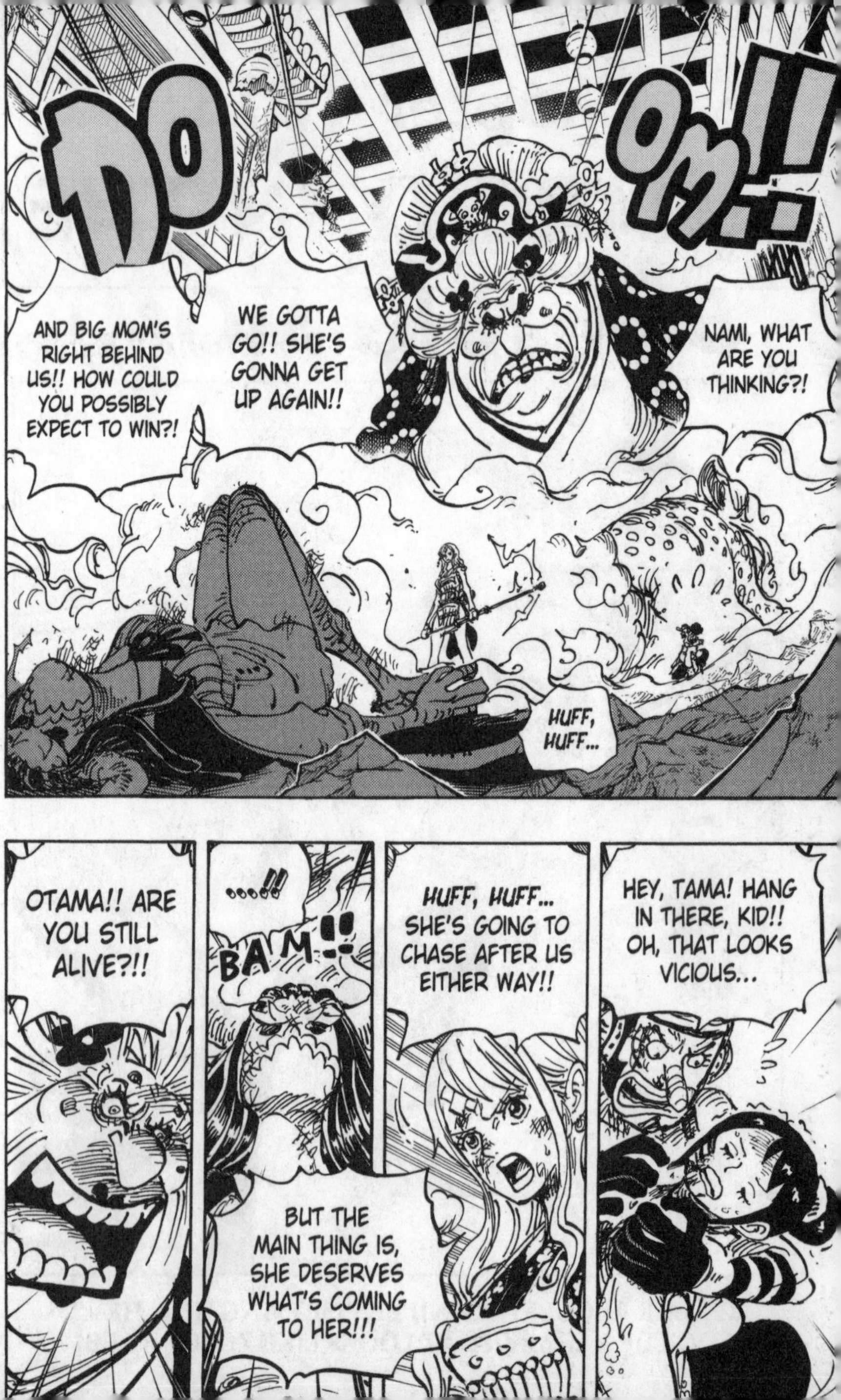
DO OM!!
NAMI, WHAT ARE YOU THINKING?!
WE GOTTA GO!! SHE'S GONNA GET UP AGAIN!!
AND BIG MOM'S RIGHT BEHIND US!! HOW COULD YOU POSSIBLY EXPECT TO WIN?!
HUFF, HUFF...
HEY, TAMA! HANG IN THERE, KID!! OH, THAT LOOKS VICIOUS...
HUFF, HUFF... SHE'S GOING TO CHASE AFTER US EITHER WAY!!
BUT THE MAIN THING IS, SHE DESERVES WHAT'S COMING TO HER!!!
....!!
BAM!!
OTAMA!! ARE YOU STILL ALIVE?!!

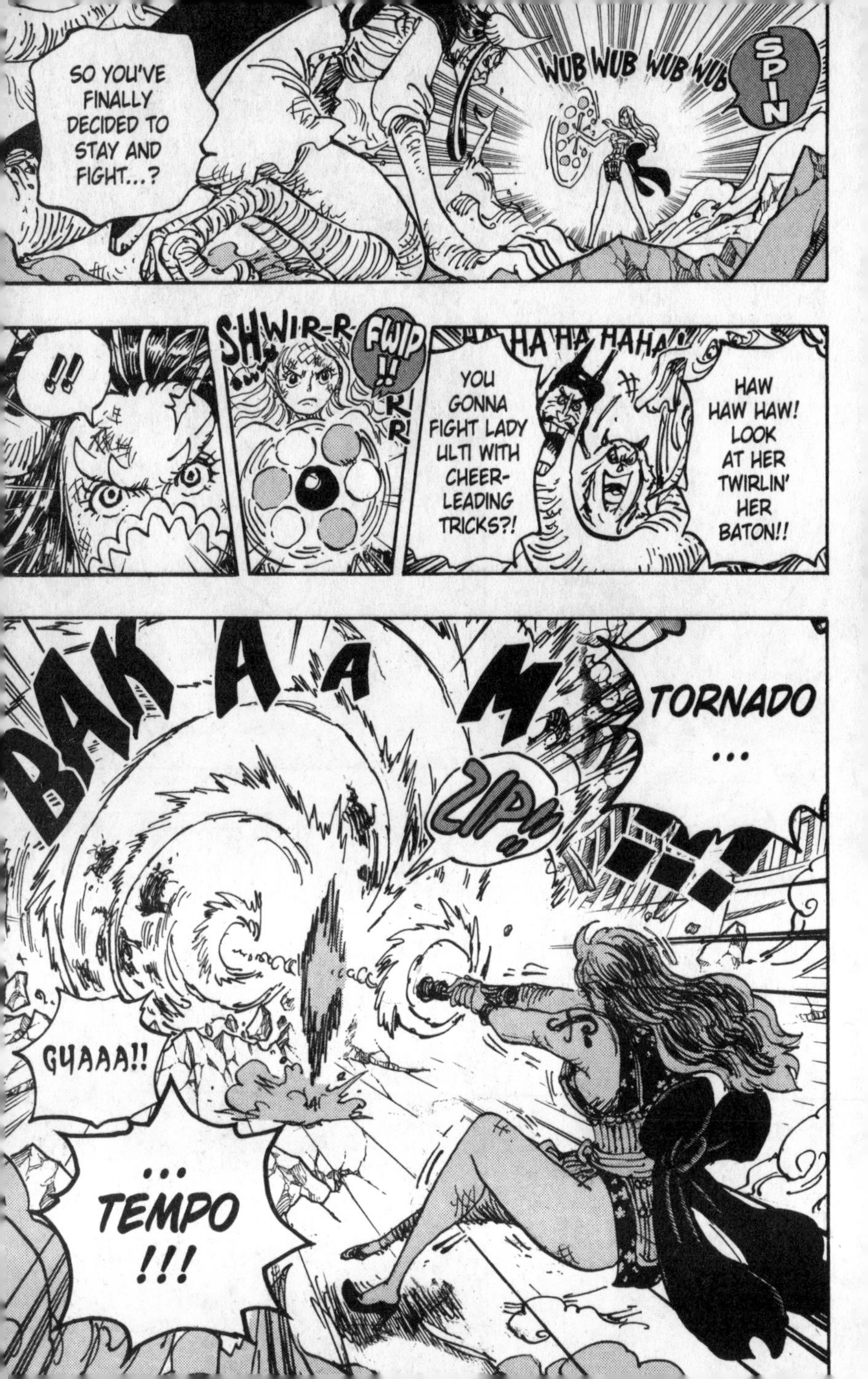
SPIN
WUB WUB WUB WUB
SO YOU'VE FINALLY DECIDED TO STAY AND FIGHT...?
HA HA HAHA
HAW HAW HAW! LOOK AT HER TWIRLIN' HER BATON!!
YOU GONNA FIGHT LADY ULTI WITH CHEER-LEADING TRICKS?!
FWIP!!
SHWIR-R-R
!!
TORNADO ...
ZIP!!
BAKAAAM
GUAAA!!
... TEMPO !!!

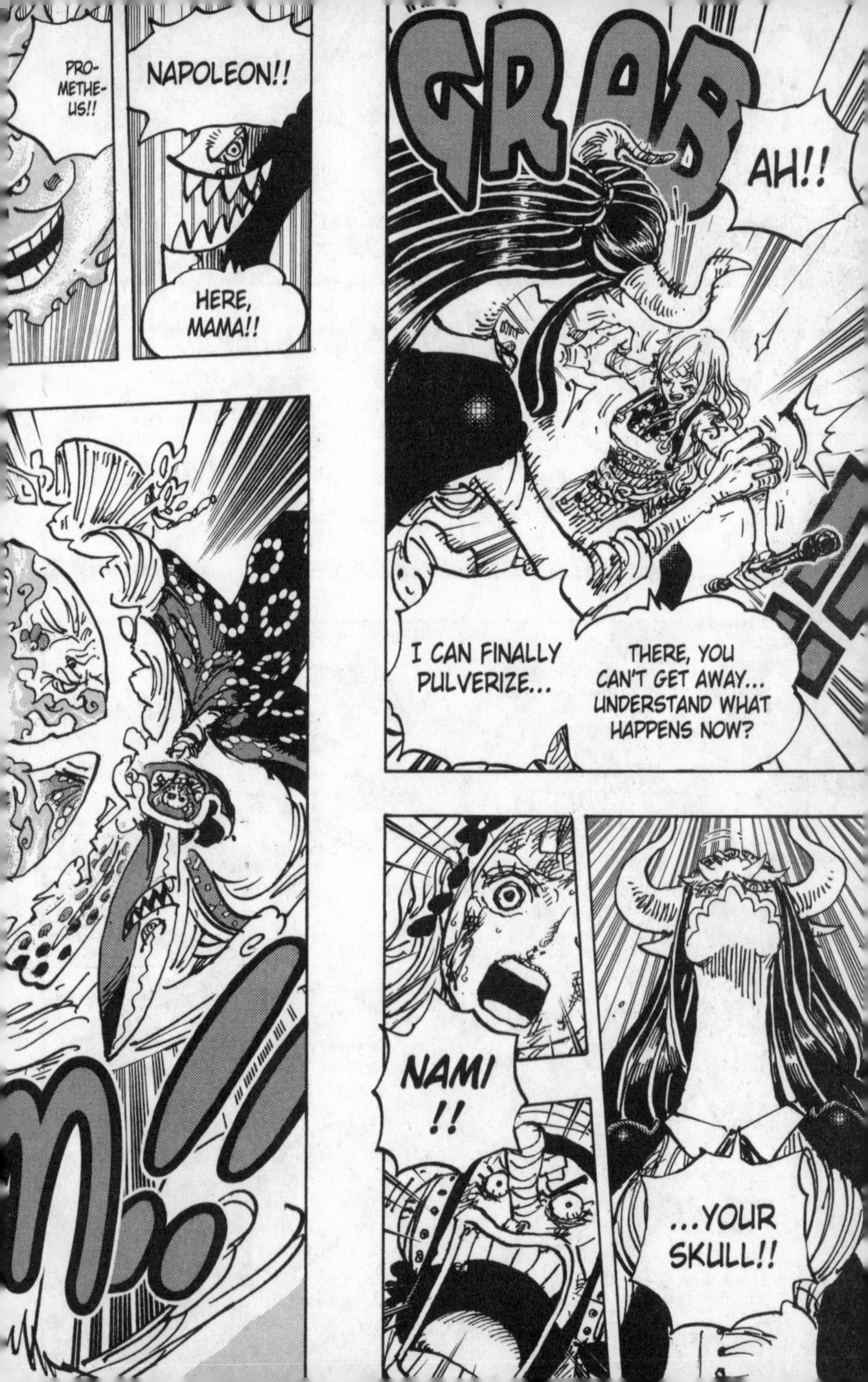
GRAB
AH!!
THERE, YOU CAN'T GET AWAY... UNDERSTAND WHAT HAPPENS NOW?
I CAN FINALLY PULVERIZE...
...YOUR SKULL!!
NAMI !!
NAPOLEON!!
HERE, MAMA!!
PRO-METHE-US!!

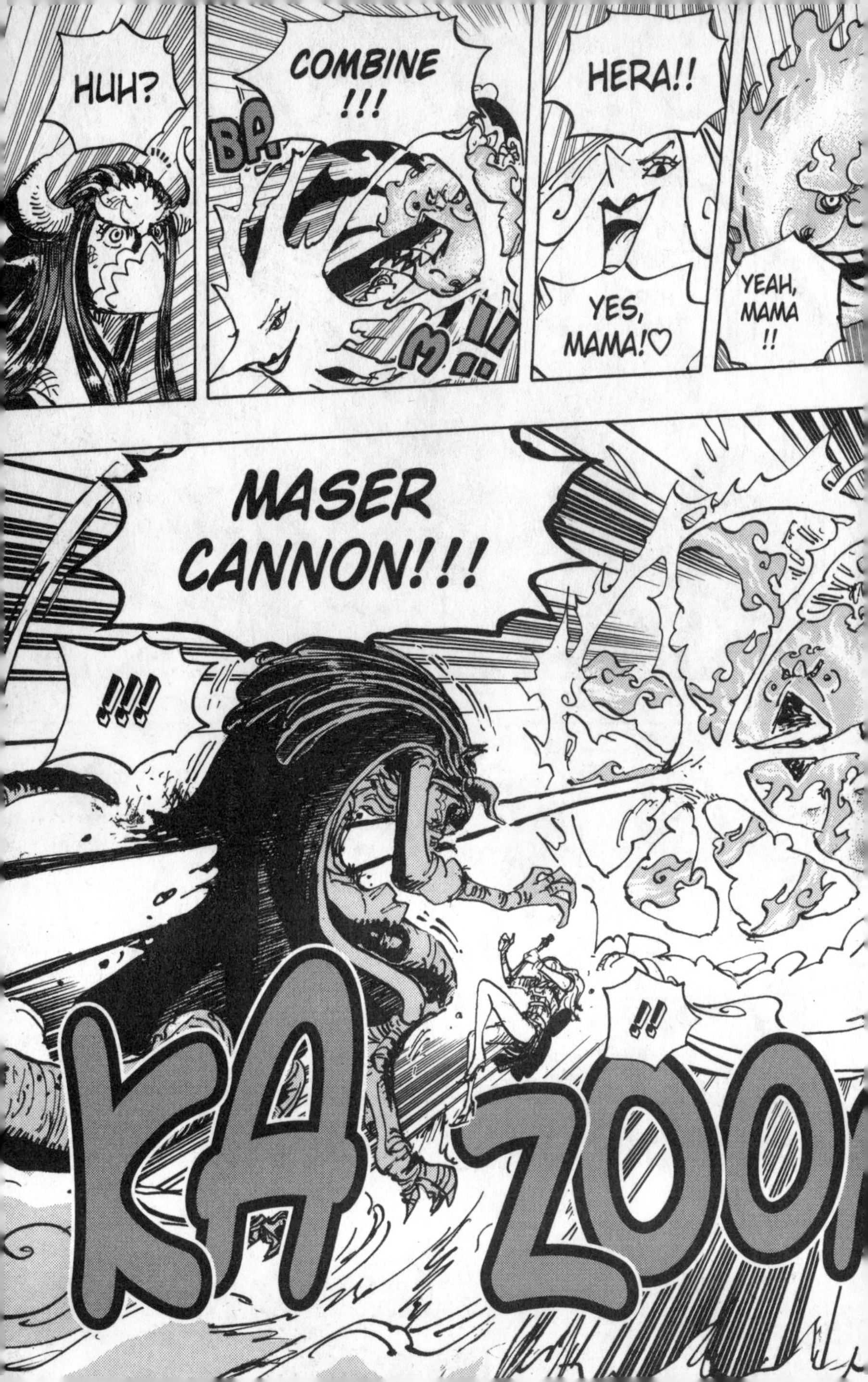

YEAH, MAMA !!
HERA!!
YES, MAMA!♡
COMBINE !!!
HUH?
MASER CANNON!!!
!!!
!!
KA ZOO

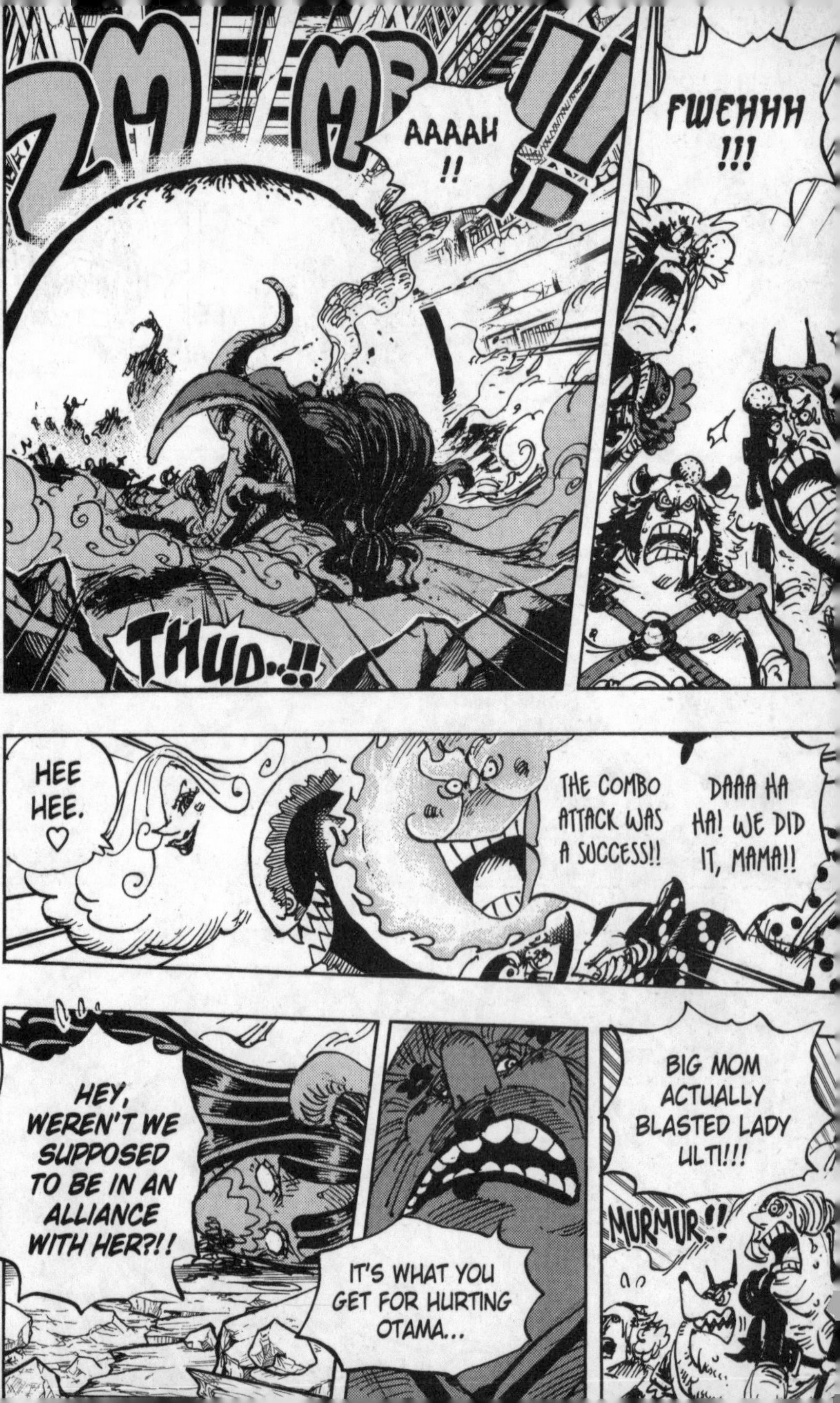
FWEHHH !!!
ZMMMP!!
AAAAH !!
THUD..!!
DAAA HA HA! WE DID IT, MAMA!!
THE COMBO ATTACK WAS A SUCCESS!!
HEE HEE. ♡
BIG MOM ACTUALLY BLASTED LADY ULTI!!!
MURMUR!!
IT'S WHAT YOU GET FOR HURTING OTAMA...
HEY, WEREN'T WE SUPPOSED TO BE IN AN ALLIANCE WITH HER?!!

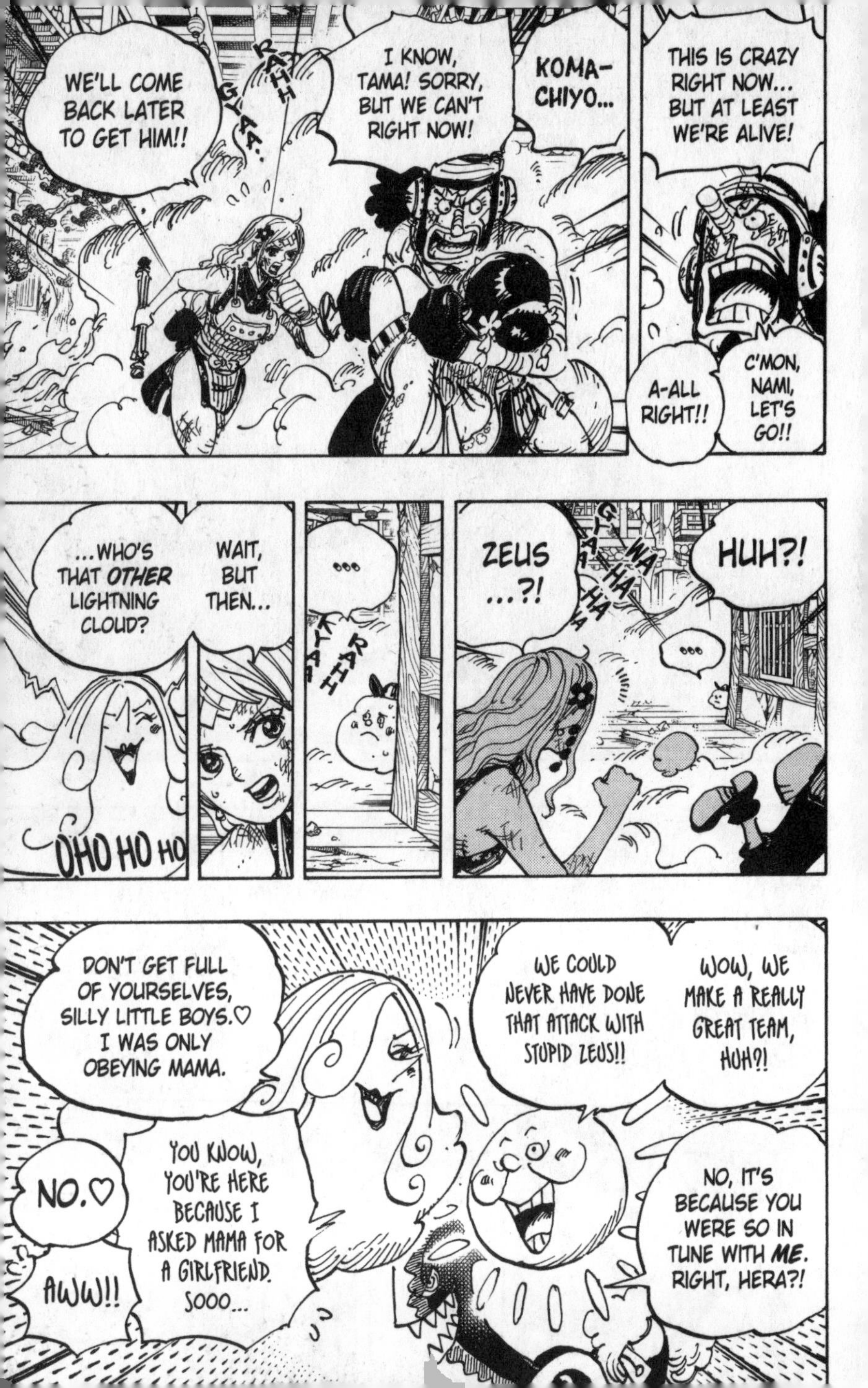
THIS IS CRAZY RIGHT NOW... BUT AT LEAST WE'RE ALIVE!
C'MON, NAMI, LET'S GO!!
A-ALL RIGHT!!
KOMA-CHIYO...
I KNOW, TAMA! SORRY, BUT WE CAN'T RIGHT NOW!
RAHH
GYAA..
WE'LL COME BACK LATER TO GET HIM!!
HUH?!
...
ZEUS ...?!
...
RAHH
KYAA
WAIT, BUT THEN...
...WHO'S THAT *OTHER* LIGHTNING CLOUD?
OHO HO HO
WOW, WE MAKE A REALLY GREAT TEAM, HUH?!
WE COULD NEVER HAVE DONE THAT ATTACK WITH STUPID ZEUS!!
DON'T GET FULL OF YOURSELVES, SILLY LITTLE BOYS.♡ I WAS ONLY OBEYING MAMA.
NO, IT'S BECAUSE YOU WERE SO IN TUNE WITH *ME*. RIGHT, HERA?!
YOU KNOW, YOU'RE HERE BECAUSE I ASKED MAMA FOR A GIRLFRIEND. SOOO...
NO.♡
AWW!!

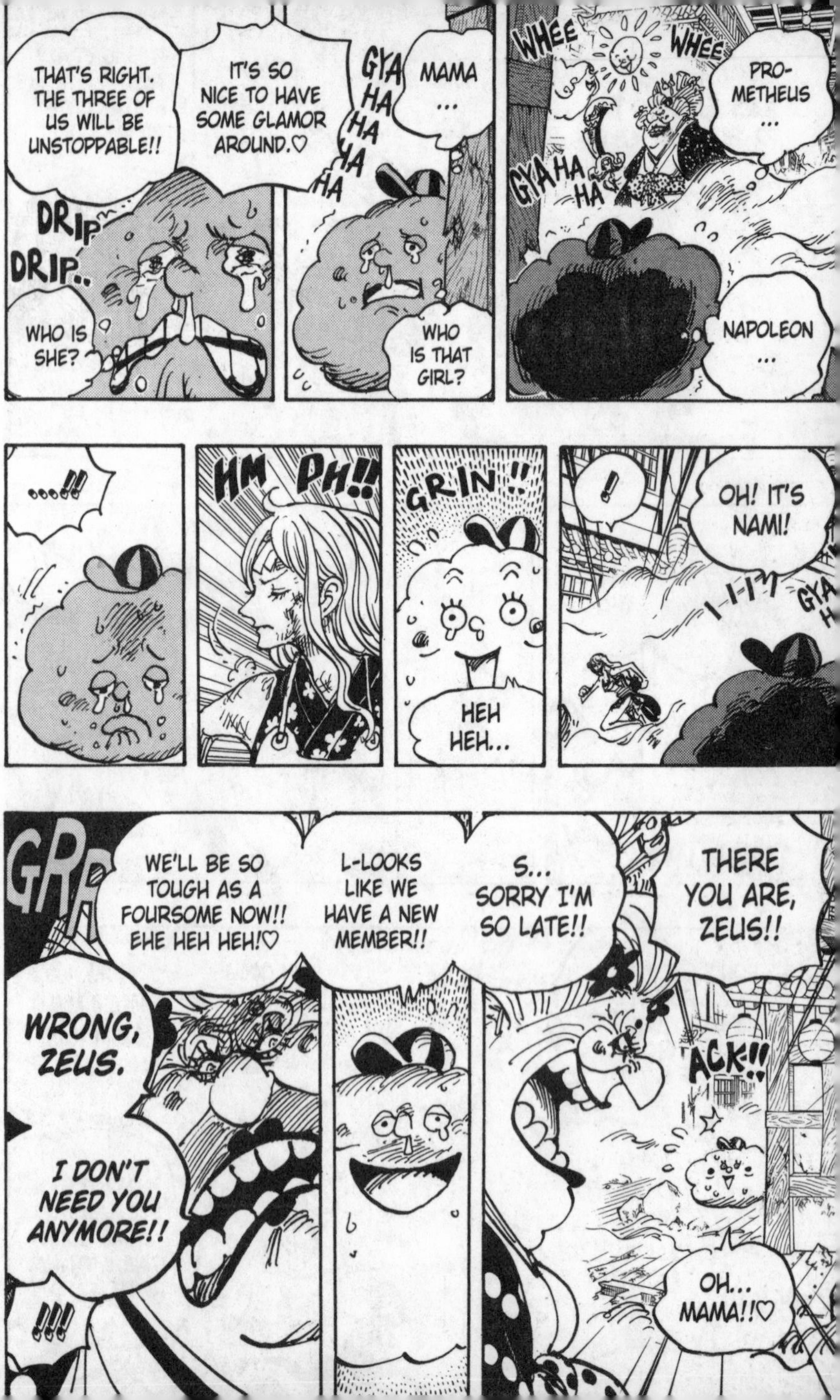
WHEE
WHEE
PRO-
METHEUS
...
GYAHAHA
HA
NAPOLEON
...
GYAHAHAHAHA
MAMA
...
WHO IS THAT GIRL?
IT'S SO NICE TO HAVE SOME GLAMOR AROUND.♡
THAT'S RIGHT. THE THREE OF US WILL BE UNSTOPPABLE!!
DRIP
DRIP..
WHO IS SHE?
OH! IT'S NAMI!
!
GRIN!!
HEH HEH...
HM PH!!
...!!
THERE YOU ARE, ZEUS!!
S... SORRY I'M SO LATE!!
L-LOOKS LIKE WE HAVE A NEW MEMBER!!
WE'LL BE SO TOUGH AS A FOURSOME NOW!! EHE HEH HEH!♡
ACK!!
OH... MAMA!!♡
WRONG, ZEUS.
I DON'T NEED YOU ANYMORE!!
!!!

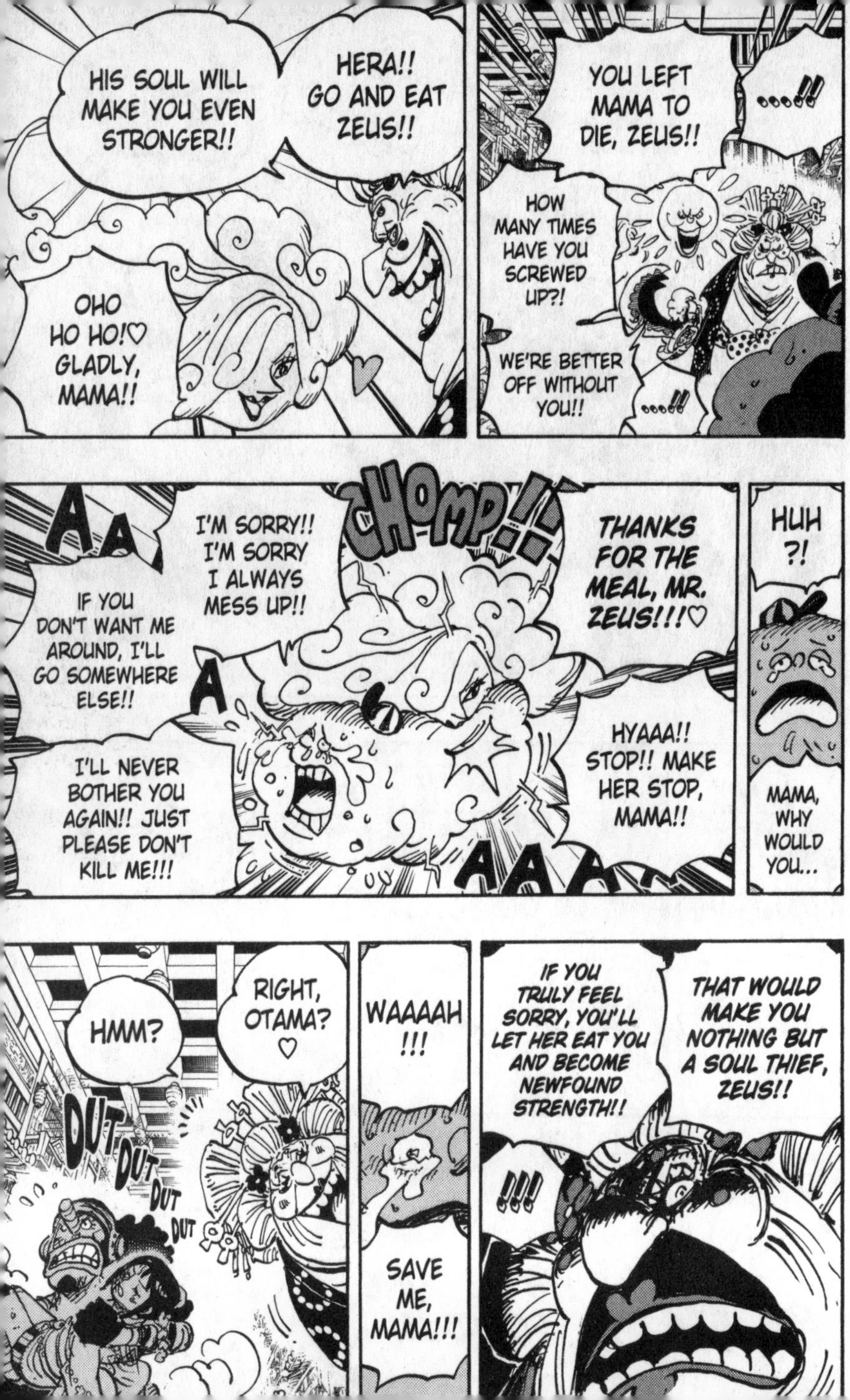
YOU LEFT MAMA TO DIE, ZEUS!!
....!!
HOW MANY TIMES HAVE YOU SCREWED UP?!
WE'RE BETTER OFF WITHOUT YOU!!
....!!
HERA!! GO AND EAT ZEUS!!
HIS SOUL WILL MAKE YOU EVEN STRONGER!!
OHO HO HO!♡ GLADLY, MAMA!!
HUH?!
MAMA, WHY WOULD YOU...
THANKS FOR THE MEAL, MR. ZEUS!!!♡
CHOMP!!
I'M SORRY!! I'M SORRY I ALWAYS MESS UP!!
AA
IF YOU DON'T WANT ME AROUND, I'LL GO SOMEWHERE ELSE!!
A
HYAAA!! STOP!! MAKE HER STOP, MAMA!!
I'LL NEVER BOTHER YOU AGAIN!! JUST PLEASE DON'T KILL ME!!!
AAA
THAT WOULD MAKE YOU NOTHING BUT A SOUL THIEF, ZEUS!!
IF YOU TRULY FEEL SORRY, YOU'LL LET HER EAT YOU AND BECOME NEWFOUND STRENGTH!!
!!!
WAAAAH!!!
SAVE ME, MAMA!!!
RIGHT, OTAMA?♡
HMM?
DUT DUT DUT DUT

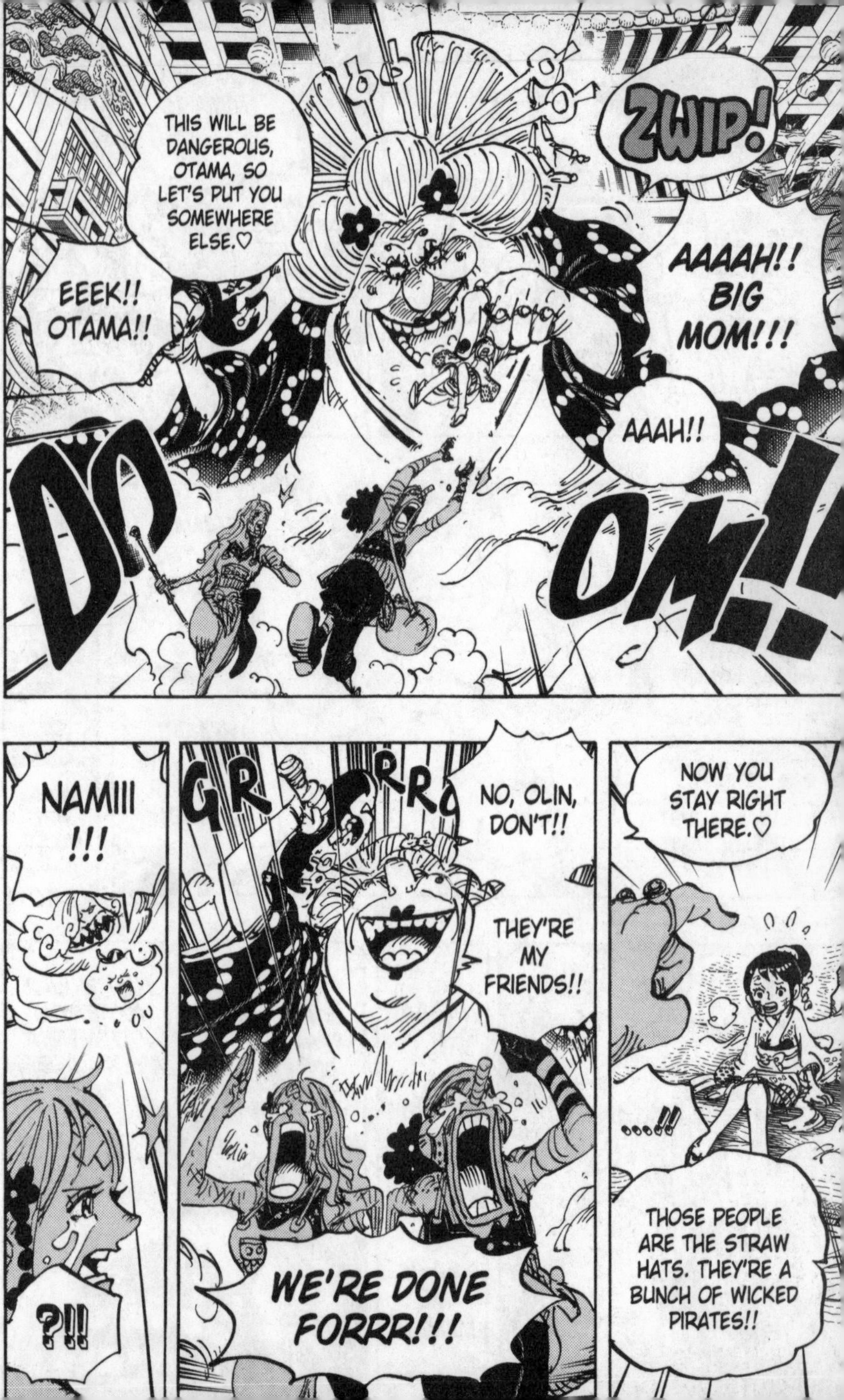
ZWIP!
AAAAH!! BIG MOM!!!
AAAH!!
THIS WILL BE DANGEROUS, OTAMA, SO LET'S PUT YOU SOMEWHERE ELSE.♡
EEEK!! OTAMA!!
DOOM!!
NOW YOU STAY RIGHT THERE.♡
...!!
THOSE PEOPLE ARE THE STRAW HATS. THEY'RE A BUNCH OF WICKED PIRATES!!
GR RR
NO, OLIN, DON'T!!
THEY'RE MY FRIENDS!!
WE'RE DONE FORRR!!!
NAMIII !!!
?!!

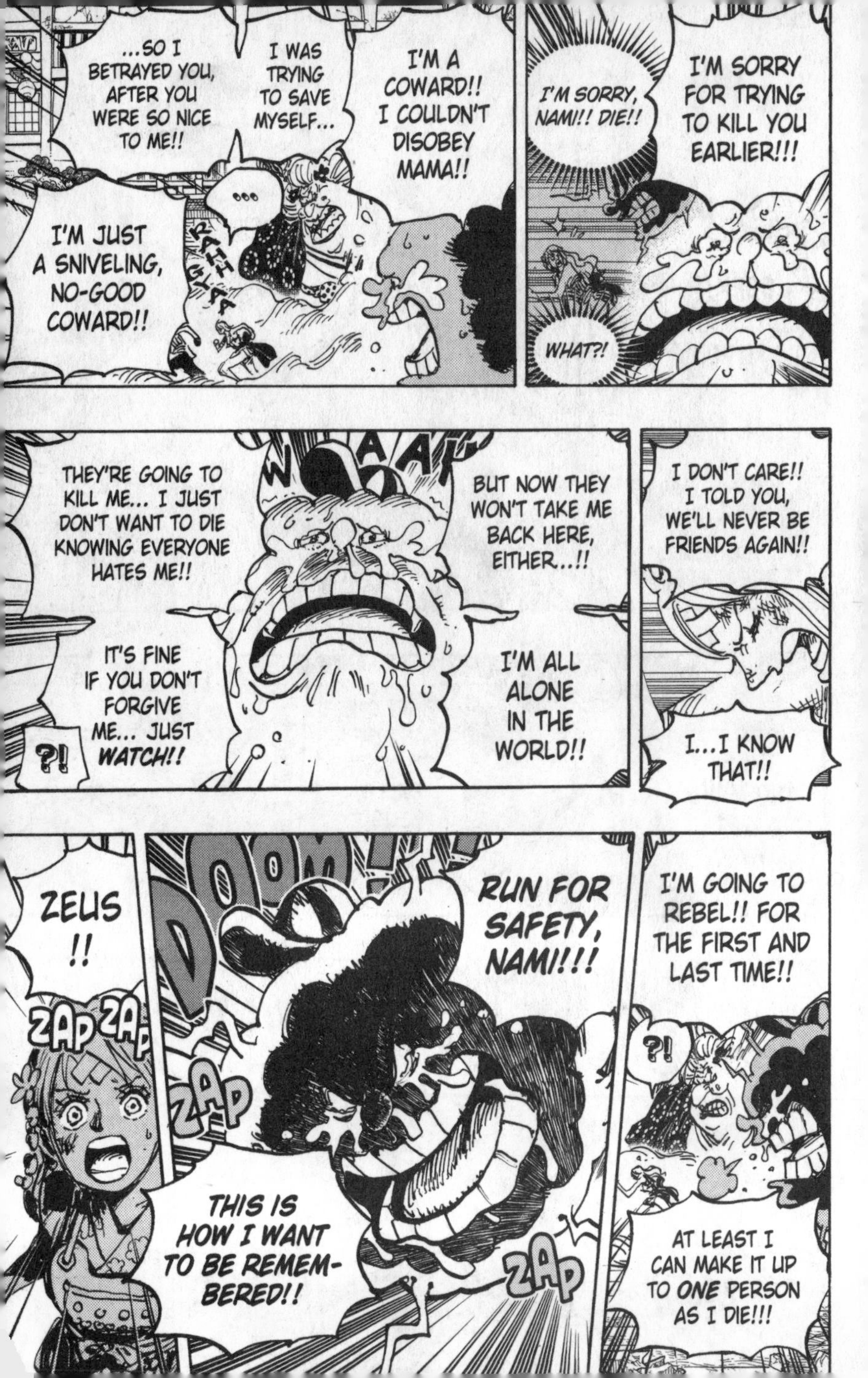
I'M SORRY FOR TRYING TO KILL YOU EARLIER!!!
I'M SORRY, NAMI!!! DIE!!
WHAT?!
I'M A COWARD!! I COULDN'T DISOBEY MAMA!!
I WAS TRYING TO SAVE MYSELF...
...SO I BETRAYED YOU, AFTER YOU WERE SO NICE TO ME!!
...
RAHH GYAA
I'M JUST A SNIVELING, NO-GOOD COWARD!!
I DON'T CARE!! I TOLD YOU, WE'LL NEVER BE FRIENDS AGAIN!!
I...I KNOW THAT!!
BUT NOW THEY WON'T TAKE ME BACK HERE, EITHER...!!
WAAAH
THEY'RE GOING TO KILL ME... I JUST DON'T WANT TO DIE KNOWING EVERYONE HATES ME!!
I'M ALL ALONE IN THE WORLD!!
IT'S FINE IF YOU DON'T FORGIVE ME... JUST WATCH!!
?!
I'M GOING TO REBEL!! FOR THE FIRST AND LAST TIME!!
?!
AT LEAST I CAN MAKE IT UP TO ONE PERSON AS I DIE!!!
DOOM
RUN FOR SAFETY, NAMI!!!
THIS IS HOW I WANT TO BE REMEMBERED!!
ZAP
ZEUS !!
ZAP ZAP
ZAP

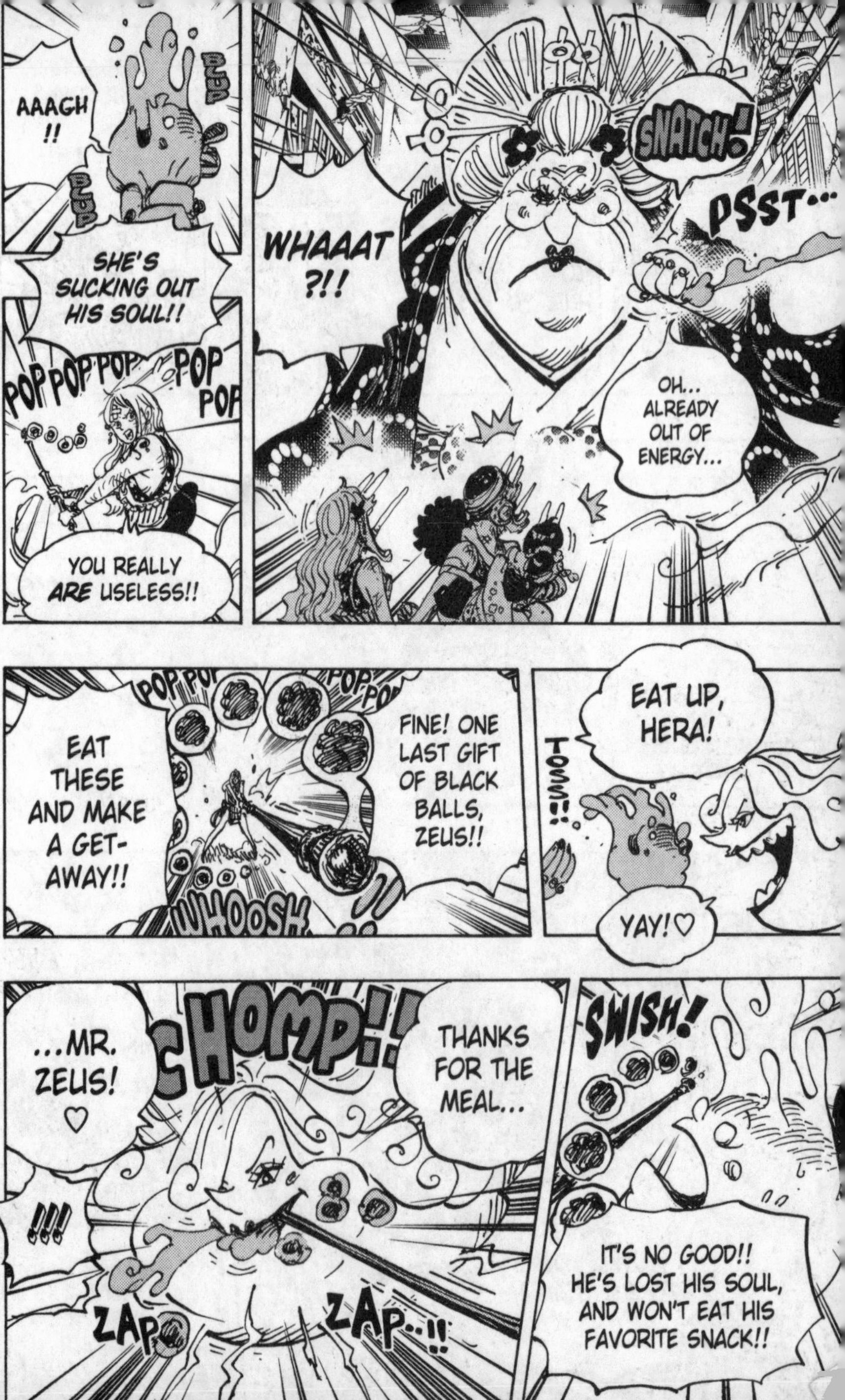
SNATCH!
PSST...
WHAAAT ?!!
OH... ALREADY OUT OF ENERGY...
BLUP
BLUP
AAAGH !!
SHE'S SUCKING OUT HIS SOUL!!
POP POP POP POP POP
YOU REALLY ARE USELESS!!
EAT UP, HERA!
TOSS!!
YAY!♡
FINE! ONE LAST GIFT OF BLACK BALLS, ZEUS!!
POP POP POP POP
EAT THESE AND MAKE A GET-AWAY!!
WHOOSH
SWISH!
IT'S NO GOOD!! HE'S LOST HIS SOUL, AND WON'T EAT HIS FAVORITE SNACK!!
THANKS FOR THE MEAL...
CHOMP!!
...MR. ZEUS! ♡
!!!
ZAP..!!
ZAP

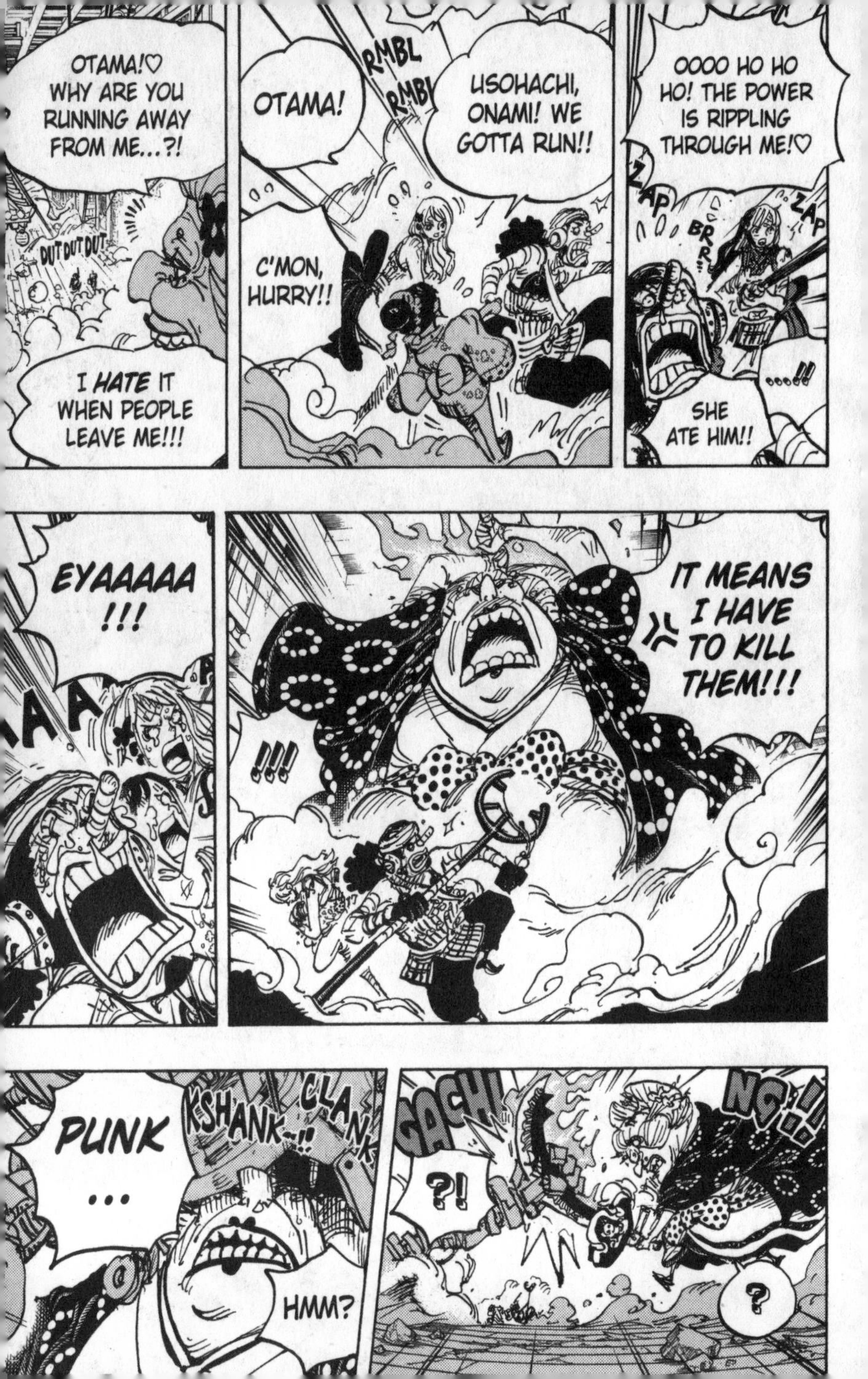
OOOO HO HO HO! THE POWER IS RIPPLING THROUGH ME!♡
ZAP
BRR
ZAP
...!!
SHE ATE HIM!!
USOHACHI, ONAMI! WE GOTTA RUN!!
RMBL
RMBL
OTAMA!
C'MON, HURRY!!
OTAMA!♡ WHY ARE YOU RUNNING AWAY FROM ME...?!
DUT DUT DUT
I HATE IT WHEN PEOPLE LEAVE ME!!!
IT MEANS I HAVE TO KILL THEM!!!
!!!
EYAAAAA !!!
NG..!!
GACH!
?!
?
KSHANK..!!
CLANK
PUNK ...
HMM?

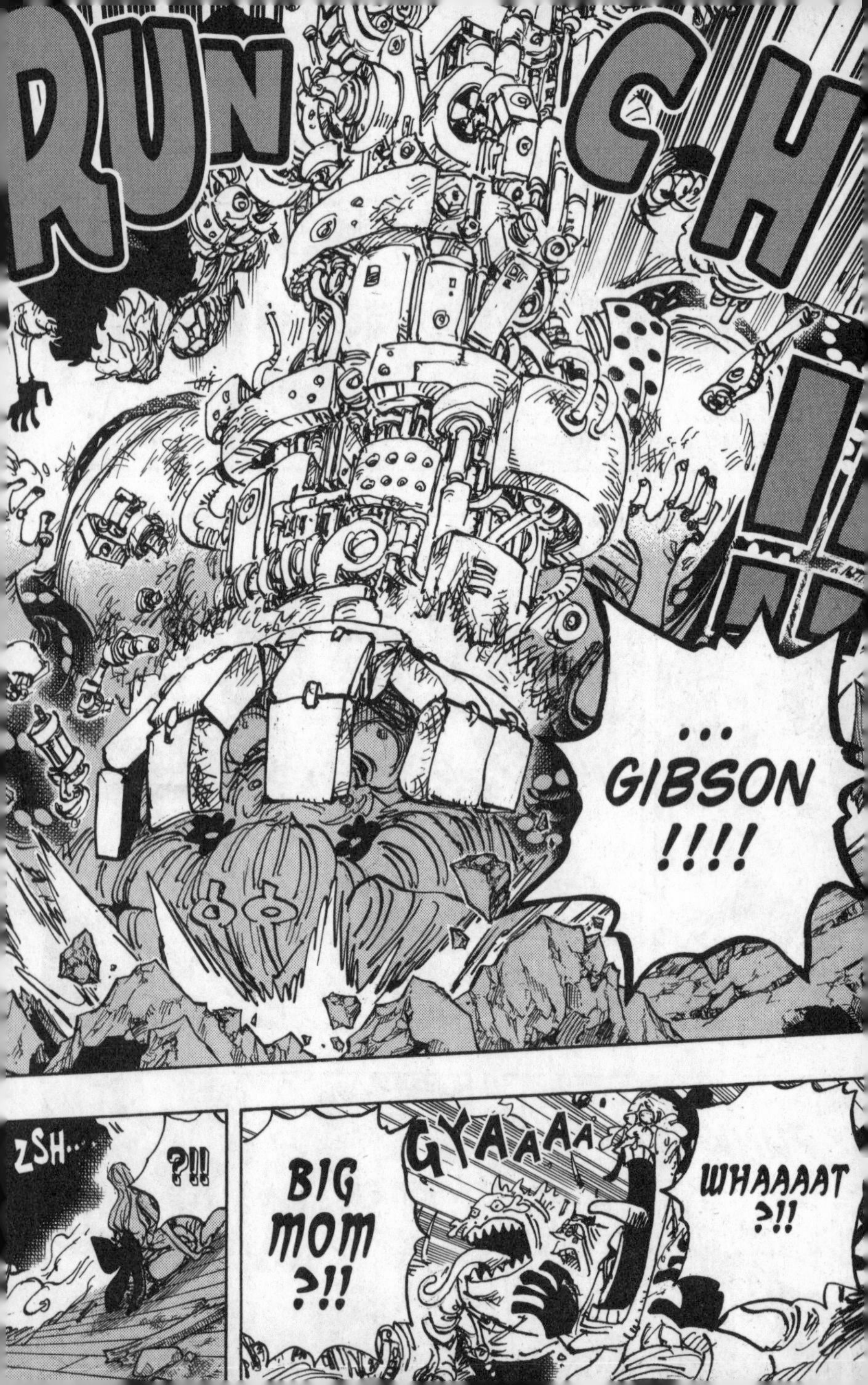
RUNCH!!
...GIBSON !!!!
WHAAAAT ?!!
GYAAAA
BIG MOM ?!!
?!!
ZSH...

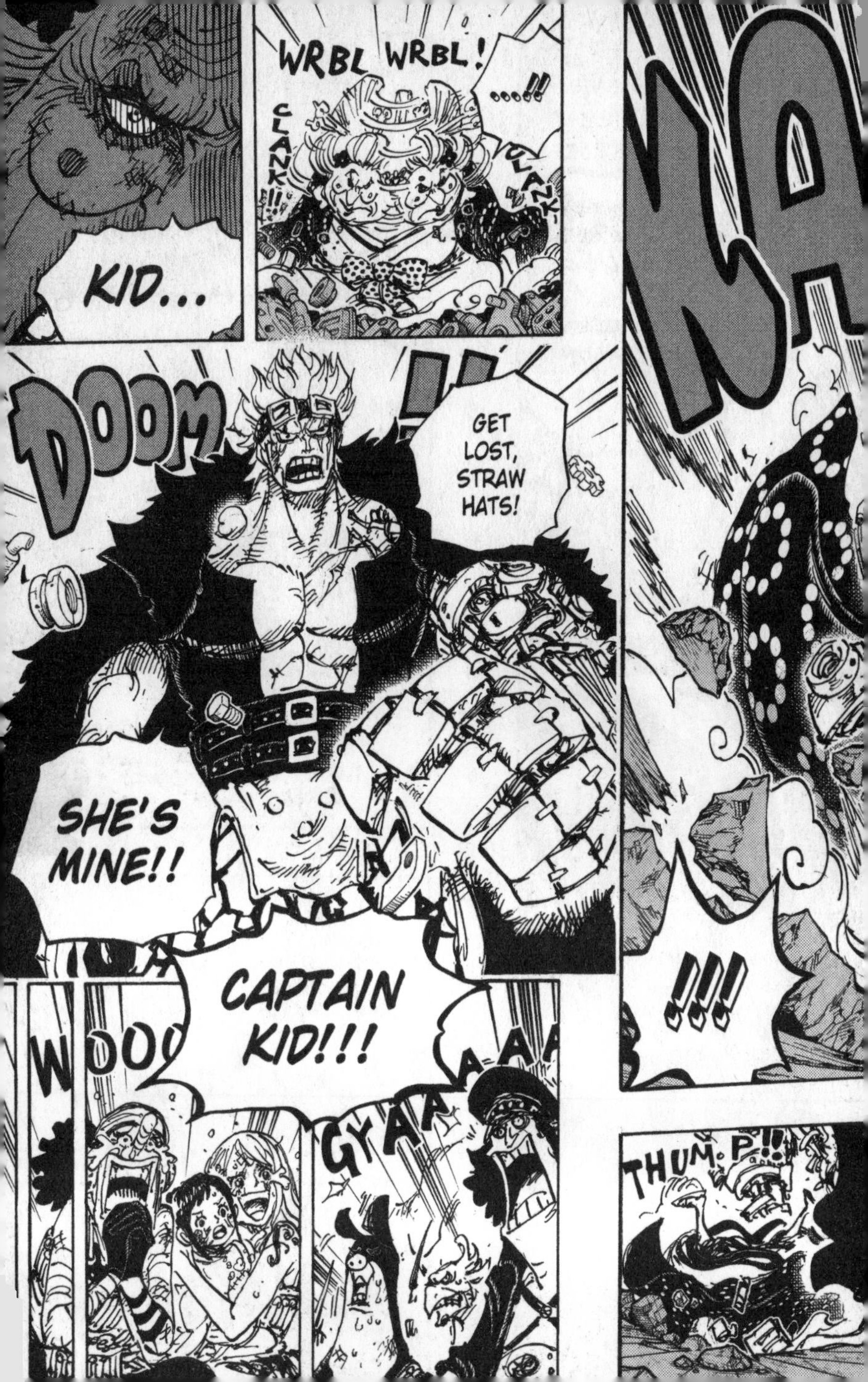
KA
!!!
WRBL WRBL!
....!!
CLANK
CLANK!!
KID...
DOOM
!!
GET LOST, STRAW HATS!
SHE'S MINE!!
THUMP!!
GYAA
AAA
WOOO
CAPTAIN KID!!!

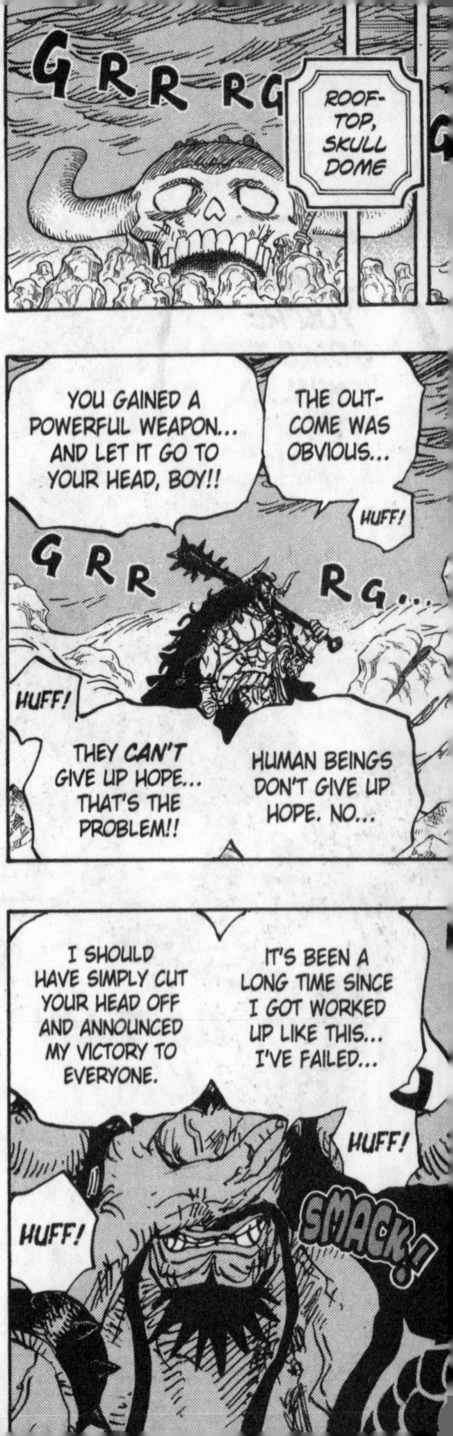
GRRRG
ROOF-TOP, SKULL DOME
THE OUT-COME WAS OBVIOUS...
YOU GAINED A POWERFUL WEAPON... AND LET IT GO TO YOUR HEAD, BOY!!
HUFF!
GRRRG...
HUFF!
HUMAN BEINGS DON'T GIVE UP HOPE. NO...
THEY *CAN'T* GIVE UP HOPE... THAT'S THE PROBLEM!!
IT'S BEEN A LONG TIME SINCE I GOT WORKED UP LIKE THIS... I'VE FAILED...
I SHOULD HAVE SIMPLY CUT YOUR HEAD OFF AND ANNOUNCED MY VICTORY TO EVERYONE.
HUFF!
SMACK!!
HUFF!
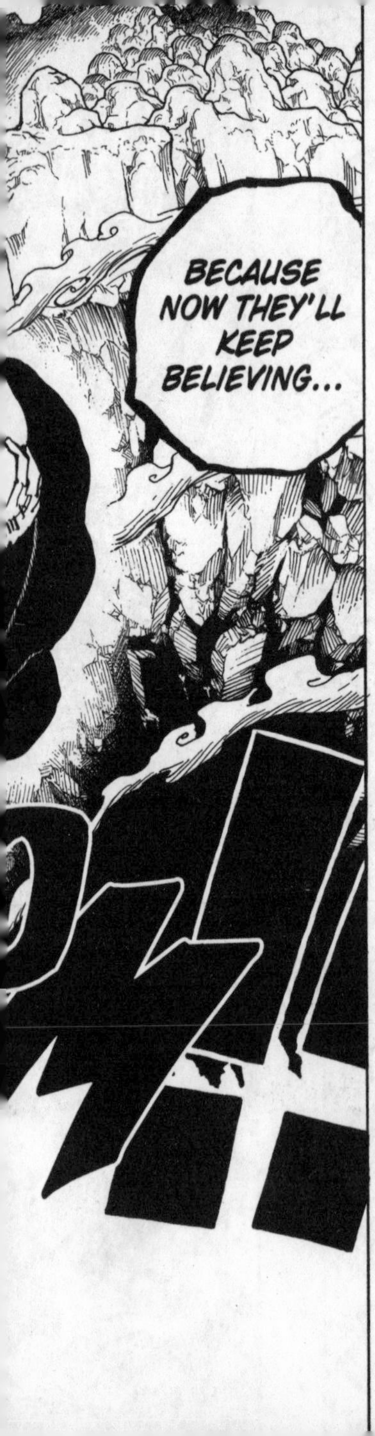
BECAUSE NOW THEY'LL KEEP BELIEVING...

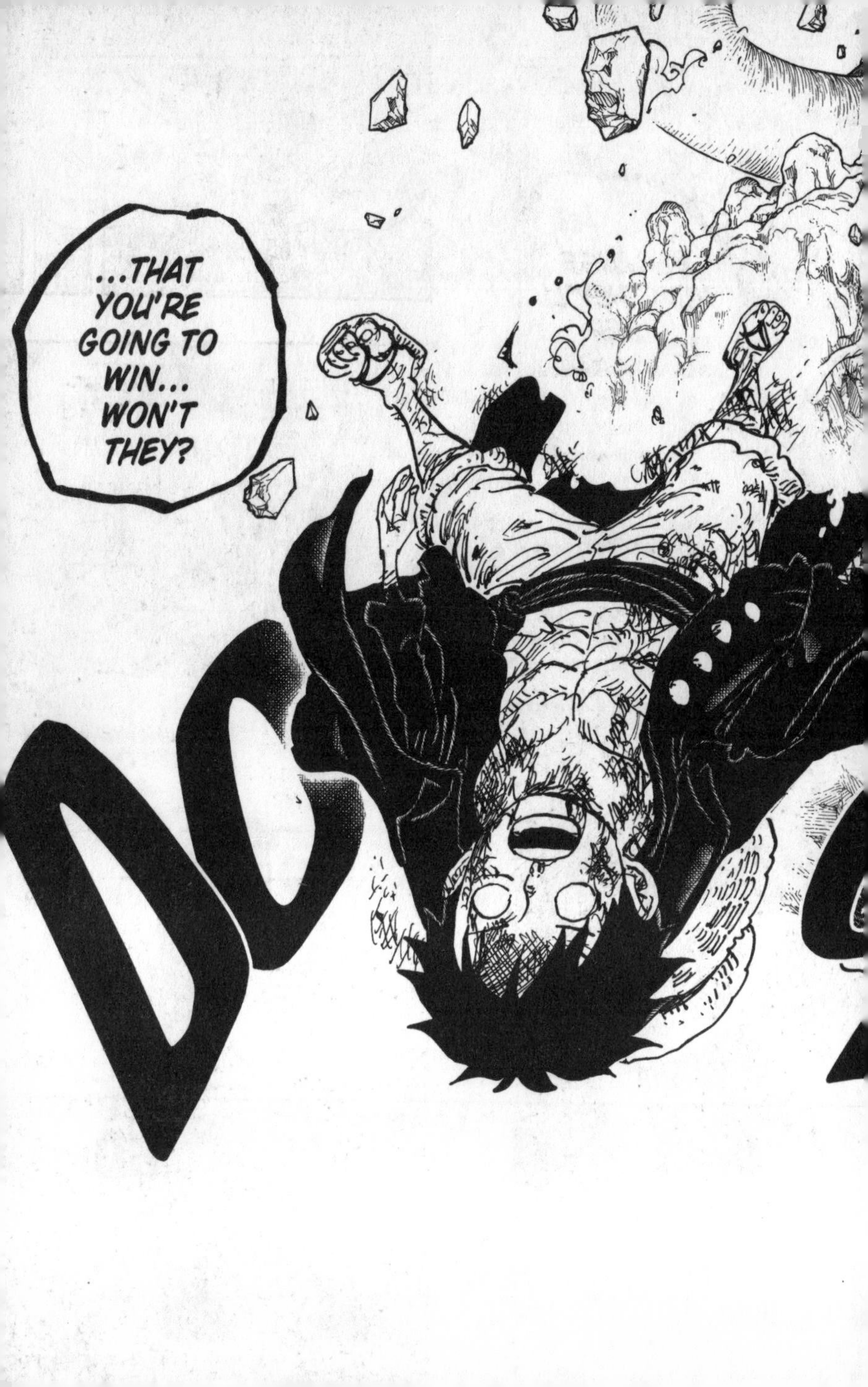
...THAT YOU'RE GOING TO WIN... WON'T THEY?
DO

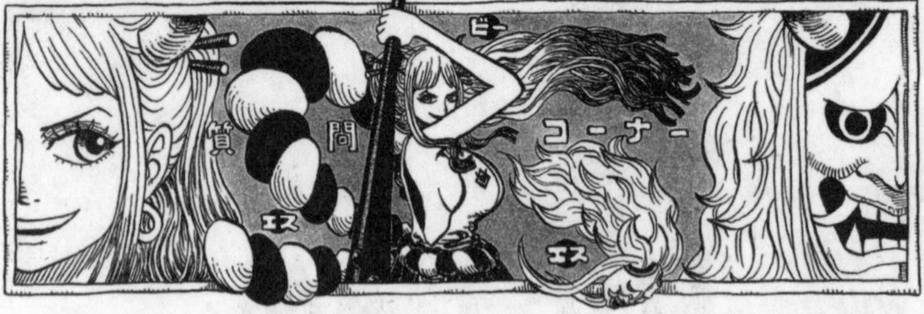
ビー
質
問
コーナー
エス
エス

(Kentaro Ito, Gifu)

Q: Hello! I love history, and I've found fascinating things to get obsessed about in not just the Edo period, but also the Heian and Taisho eras. If I could travel in time, I would love to visit those periods. What about you, Sensei? What time period would you go to?

--Momoka Amegiri

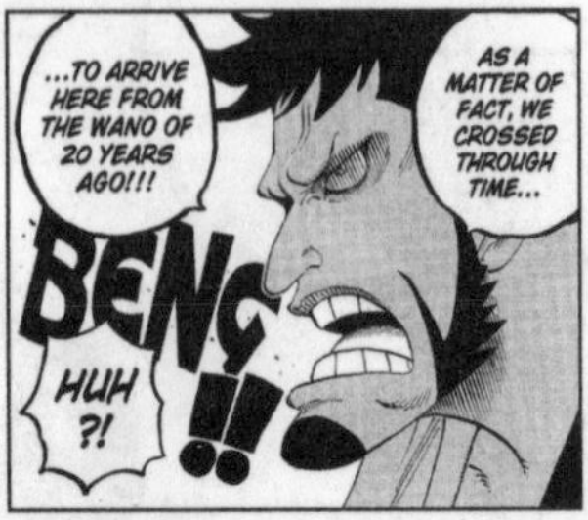
AS A MATTER OF FACT, WE CROSSED THROUGH TIME...
...TO ARRIVE HERE FROM THE WANO OF 20 YEARS AGO!!!
BENG!!
HUH ?!

A: Meaning, if I could go to the past? So like, I could see samurai? And oiran?! I love samurai stories too, of course. On the other hand, if you get a cavity, they don't have anesthetic. That trip to the dentist is gonna hurt bad. So if I could actually time travel, I would choose... the future! (LOL)

Q: Please draw Robin at age 40 and 60!!

--Issho Isho

A: Uh, you sure?

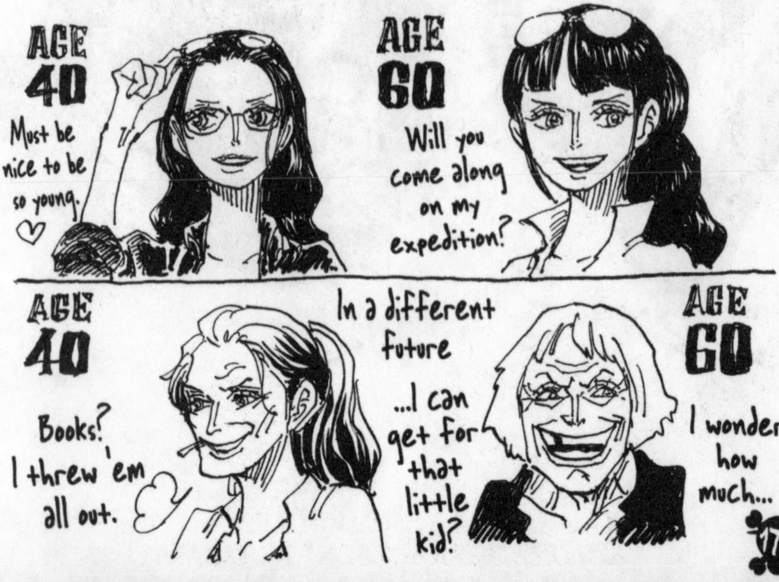
AGE 40
Must be nice to be so young. ♡
AGE 60
Will you come along on my expedition?
In a different future
AGE 40
Books? I threw 'em all out.
AGE 60
I wonder how much...
...I can get for that little kid?

Chapter 1014:
THE HAM

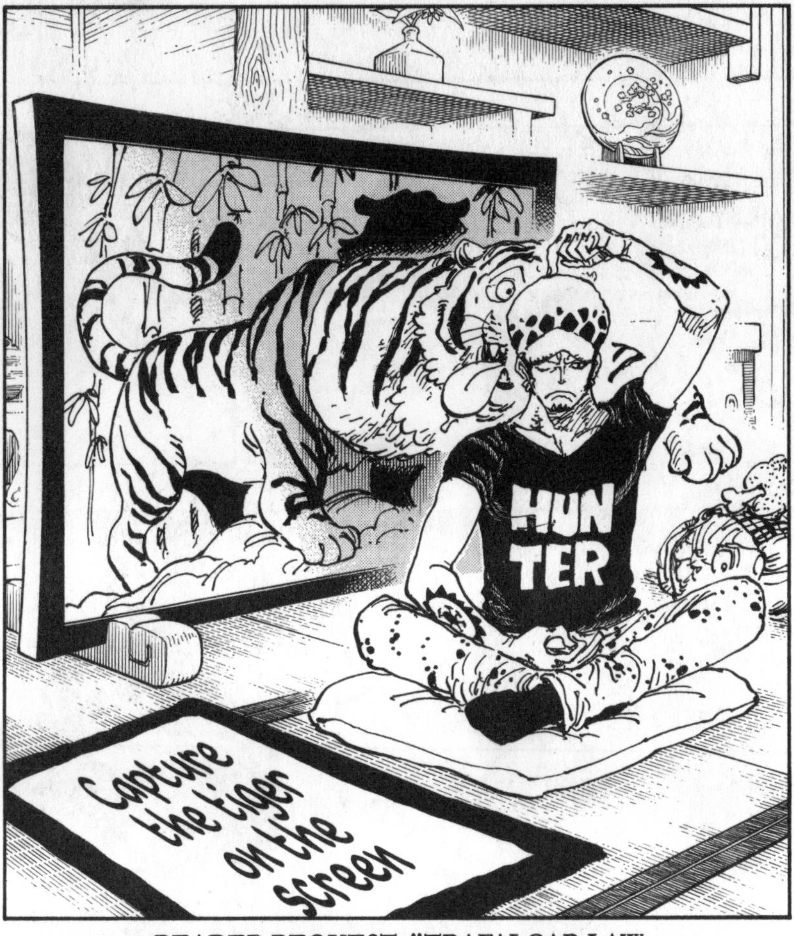
HUN TER
Capture the tiger on the screen

READER REQUEST: "TRAFALGAR LAW PUZZLING OVER A RIDDLE IN FRONT OF A PAINTED TIGER SCREEN" BY TAKASHI

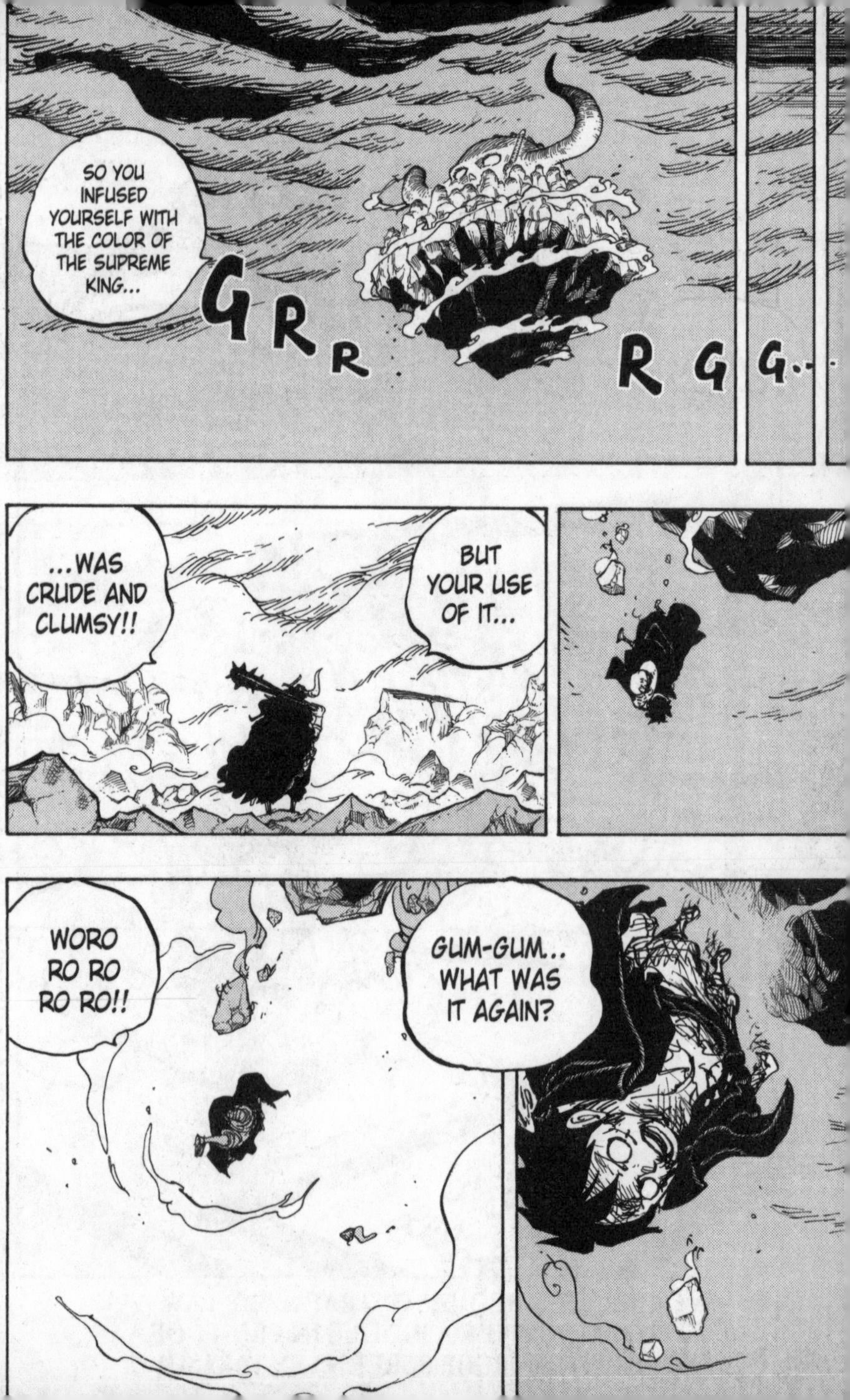
SO YOU INFUSED YOURSELF WITH THE COLOR OF THE SUPREME KING...
GRRRRGG...
BUT YOUR USE OF IT...
...WAS CRUDE AND CLUMSY!!
GUM-GUM... WHAT WAS IT AGAIN?
WORO RO RO RO RO!!

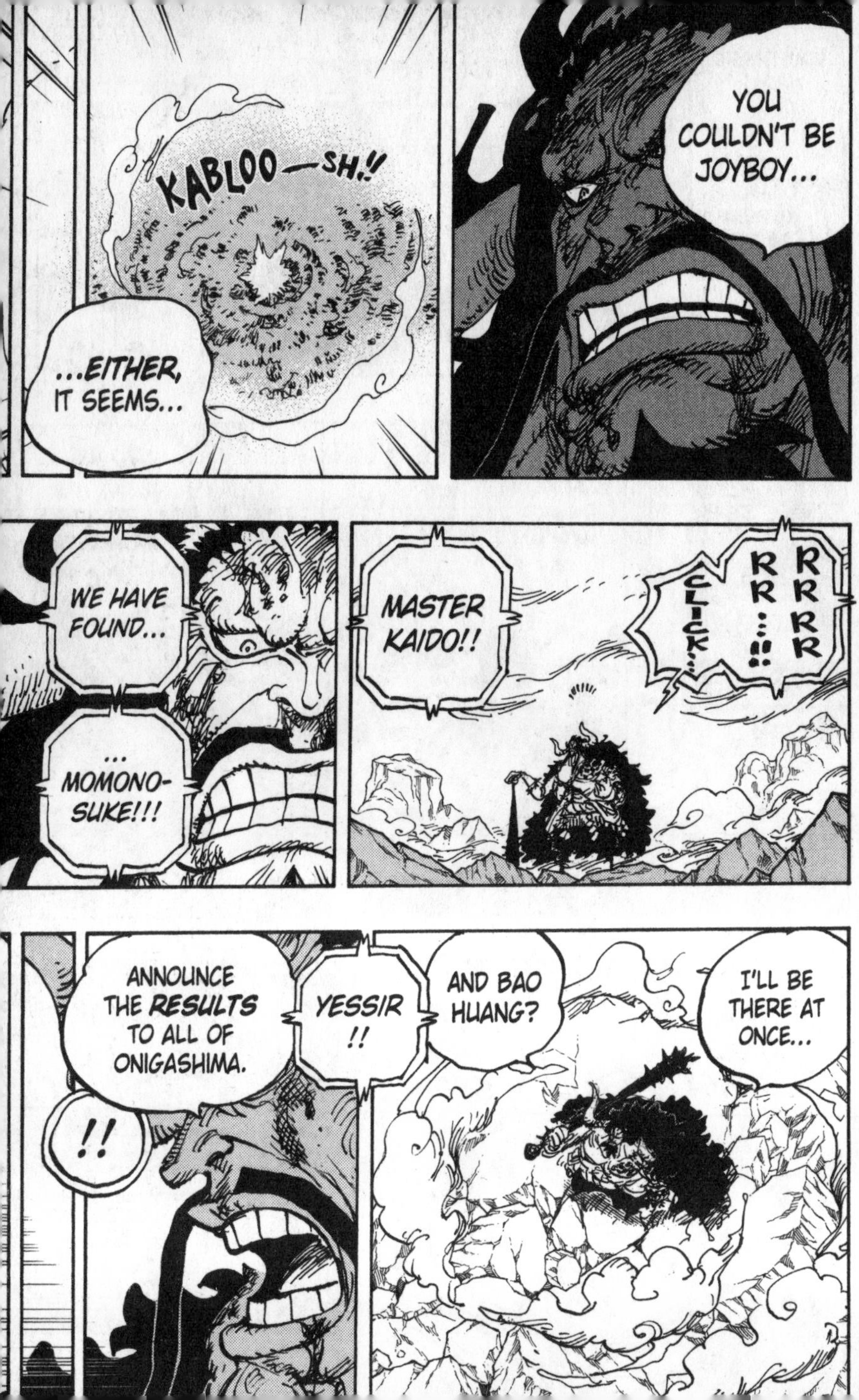
YOU COULDN'T BE JOYBOY...
KABLOO—SH!!
...EITHER, IT SEEMS...
RRRR
RR...!!
CLICK...
MASTER KAIDO!!
WE HAVE FOUND...
...MOMONO-SUKE!!!
I'LL BE THERE AT ONCE...
AND BAO HUANG?
YESSIR!!
ANNOUNCE THE RESULTS TO ALL OF ONIGASHIMA.
!!

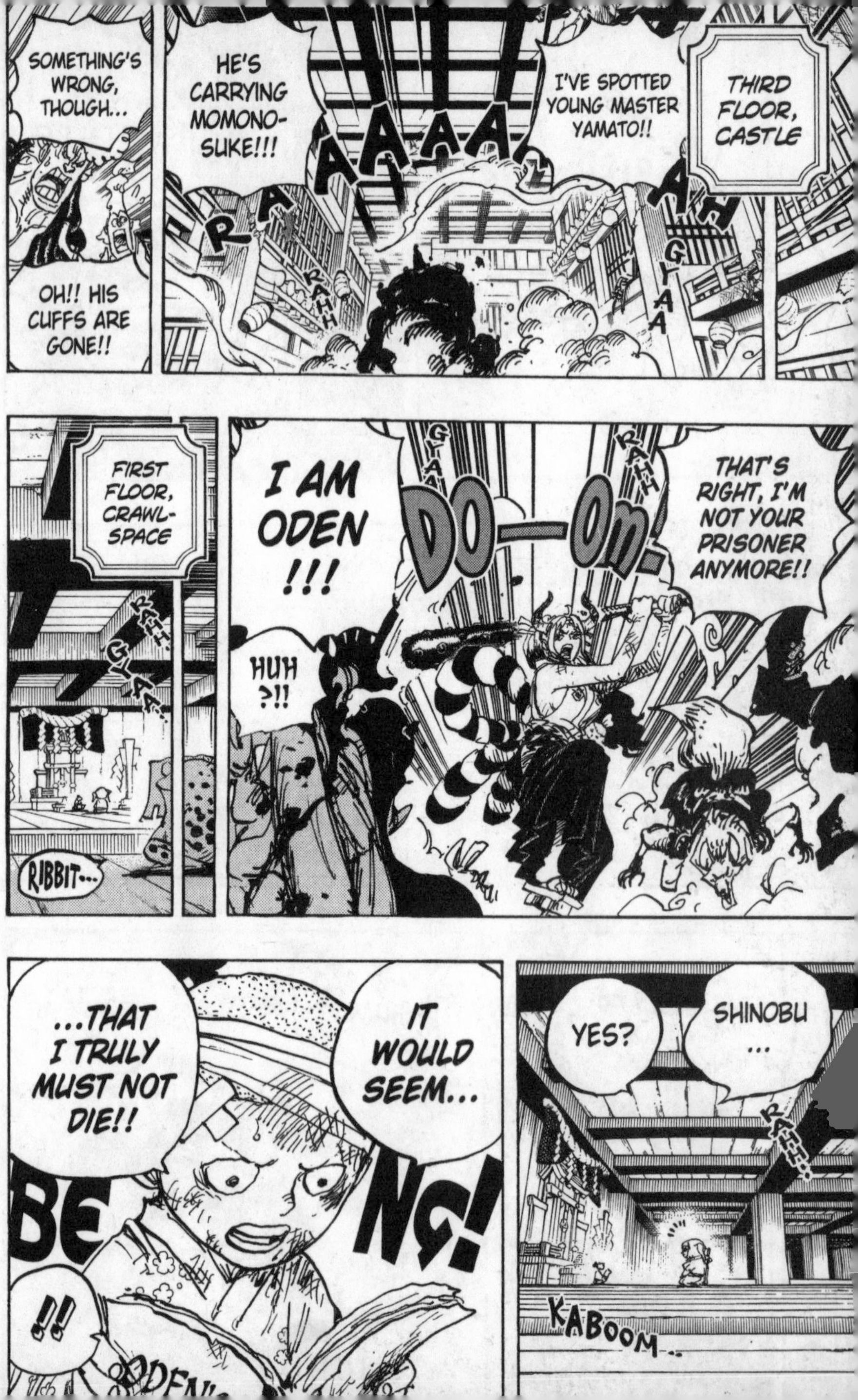
THIRD FLOOR, CASTLE
I'VE SPOTTED YOUNG MASTER YAMATO!!
AH
GYAA
AAAA
RA
RAHH
HE'S CARRYING MOMONOSUKE!!!
SOMETHING'S WRONG, THOUGH...
OH!! HIS CUFFS ARE GONE!!
THAT'S RIGHT, I'M NOT YOUR PRISONER ANYMORE!!
RAHH
DO—OM
GYAA
I AM ODEN!!!
HUH ?!!
FIRST FLOOR, CRAWL-SPACE
RAHH
GYAA...
RIBBIT...
SHINOBU ...
YES?
RAHH...
KABOOM...
IT WOULD SEEM...
...THAT I TRULY MUST NOT DIE!!
BENG!
!!

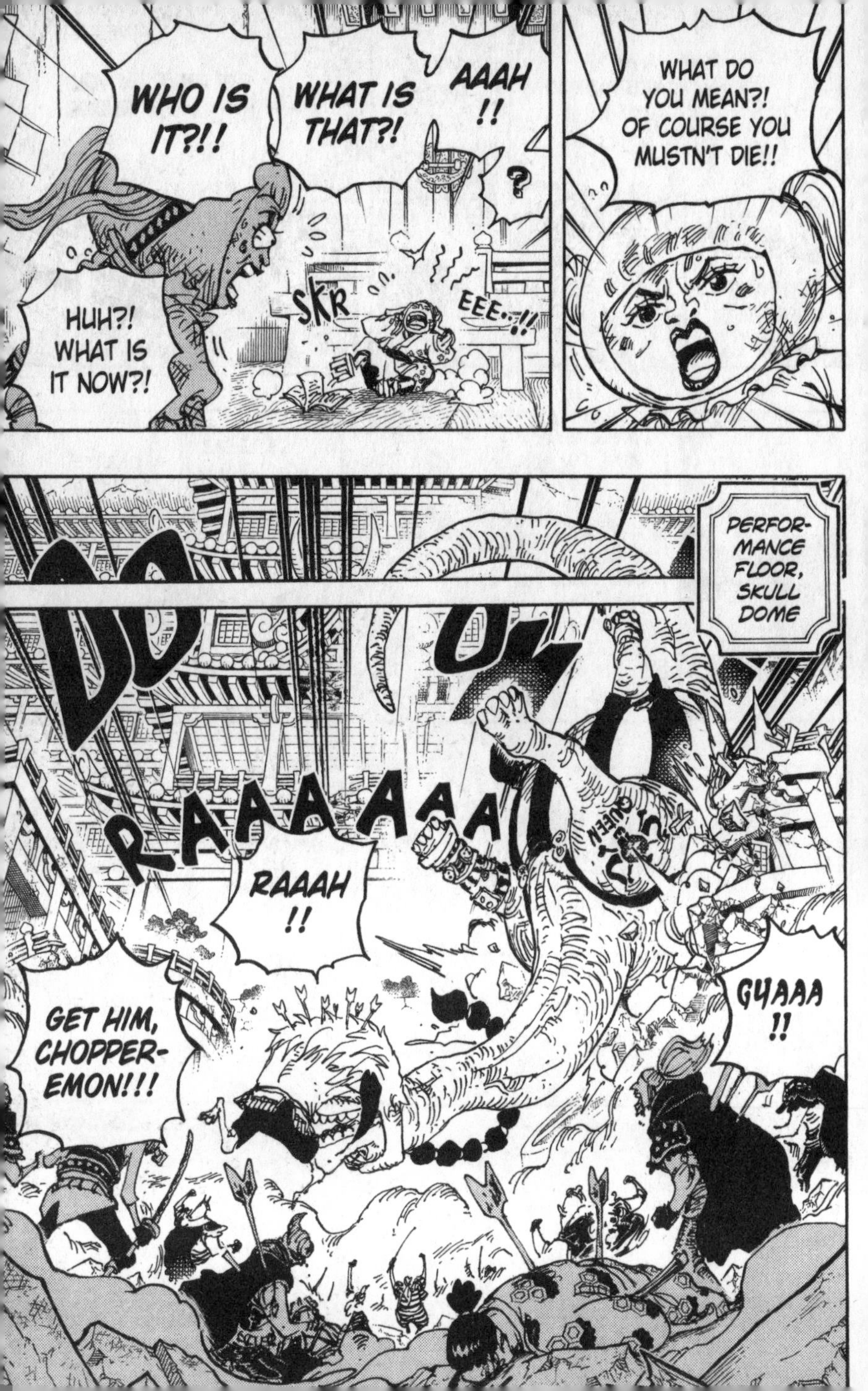
WHAT DO YOU MEAN?! OF COURSE YOU MUSTN'T DIE!!
AAAH!!
?
WHAT IS THAT?!
WHO IS IT?!!
SKR
EEE..!!
HUH?! WHAT IS IT NOW?!
PERFORMANCE FLOOR, SKULL DOME
RAAAAAAA
RAAAH!!
GUAAA!!
GET HIM, CHOPPER-EMON!!!

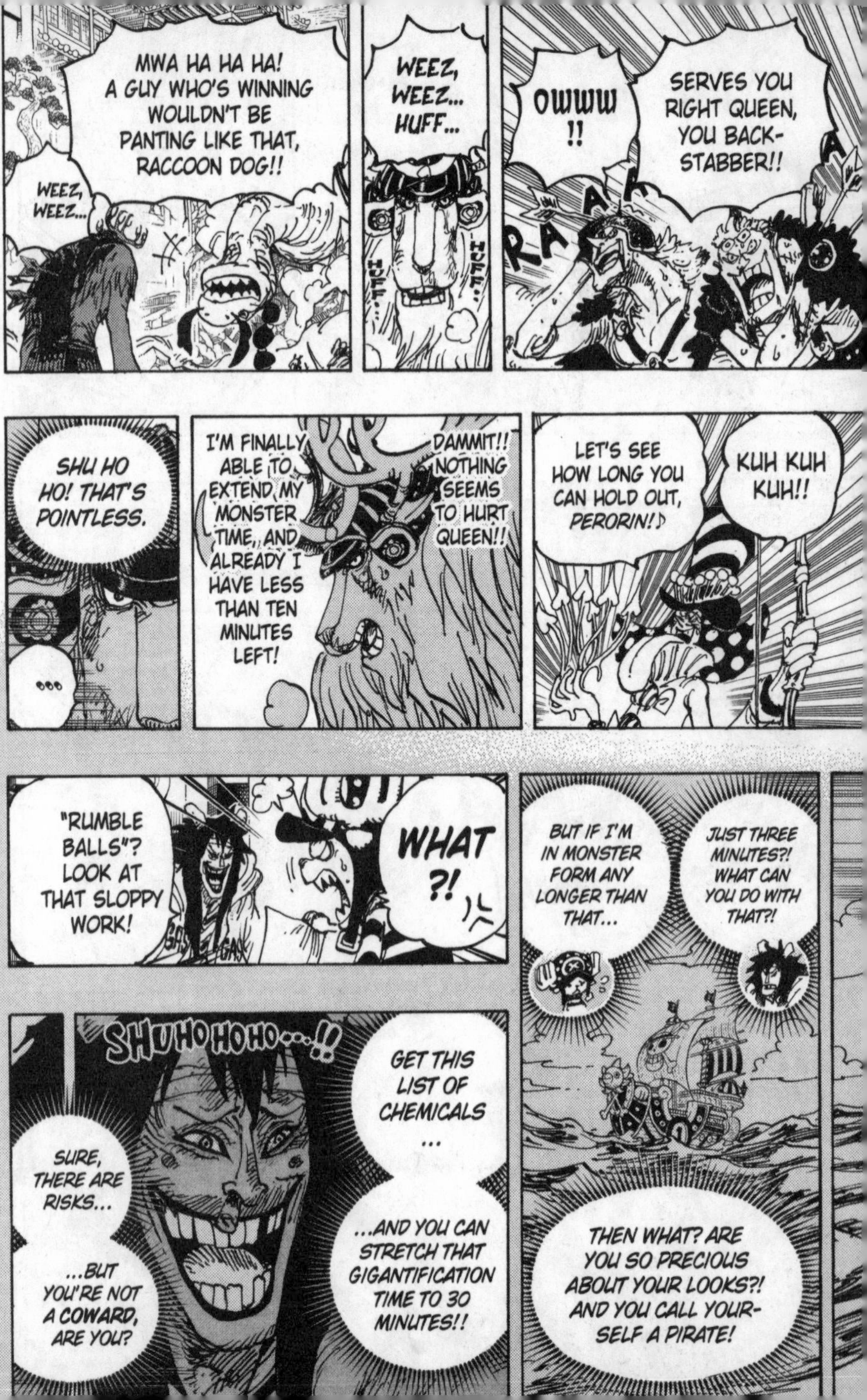
SERVES YOU RIGHT QUEEN, YOU BACK-STABBER!!
OWWW !!
WEEZ, WEEZ... HUFF...
HUFF...
HUFF...
MWA HA HA HA! A GUY WHO'S WINNING WOULDN'T BE PANTING LIKE THAT, RACCOON DOG!!
WEEZ, WEEZ...
KUH KUH KUH!!
LET'S SEE HOW LONG YOU CAN HOLD OUT, PERORIN!♪
DAMMIT!! NOTHING SEEMS TO HURT QUEEN!!
I'M FINALLY ABLE TO EXTEND MY MONSTER TIME, AND ALREADY I HAVE LESS THAN TEN MINUTES LEFT!
SHU HO HO! THAT'S POINTLESS.
...
JUST THREE MINUTES?! WHAT CAN YOU DO WITH THAT?!
BUT IF I'M IN MONSTER FORM ANY LONGER THAN THAT...
THEN WHAT? ARE YOU SO PRECIOUS ABOUT YOUR LOOKS?! AND YOU CALL YOUR-SELF A PIRATE!
WHAT ?!
"RUMBLE BALLS"? LOOK AT THAT SLOPPY WORK!
SHU HO HO HO...!!
GET THIS LIST OF CHEMICALS ...
...AND YOU CAN STRETCH THAT GIGANTIFICATION TIME TO 30 MINUTES!!
SURE, THERE ARE RISKS...
...BUT YOU'RE NOT A COWARD, ARE YOU?

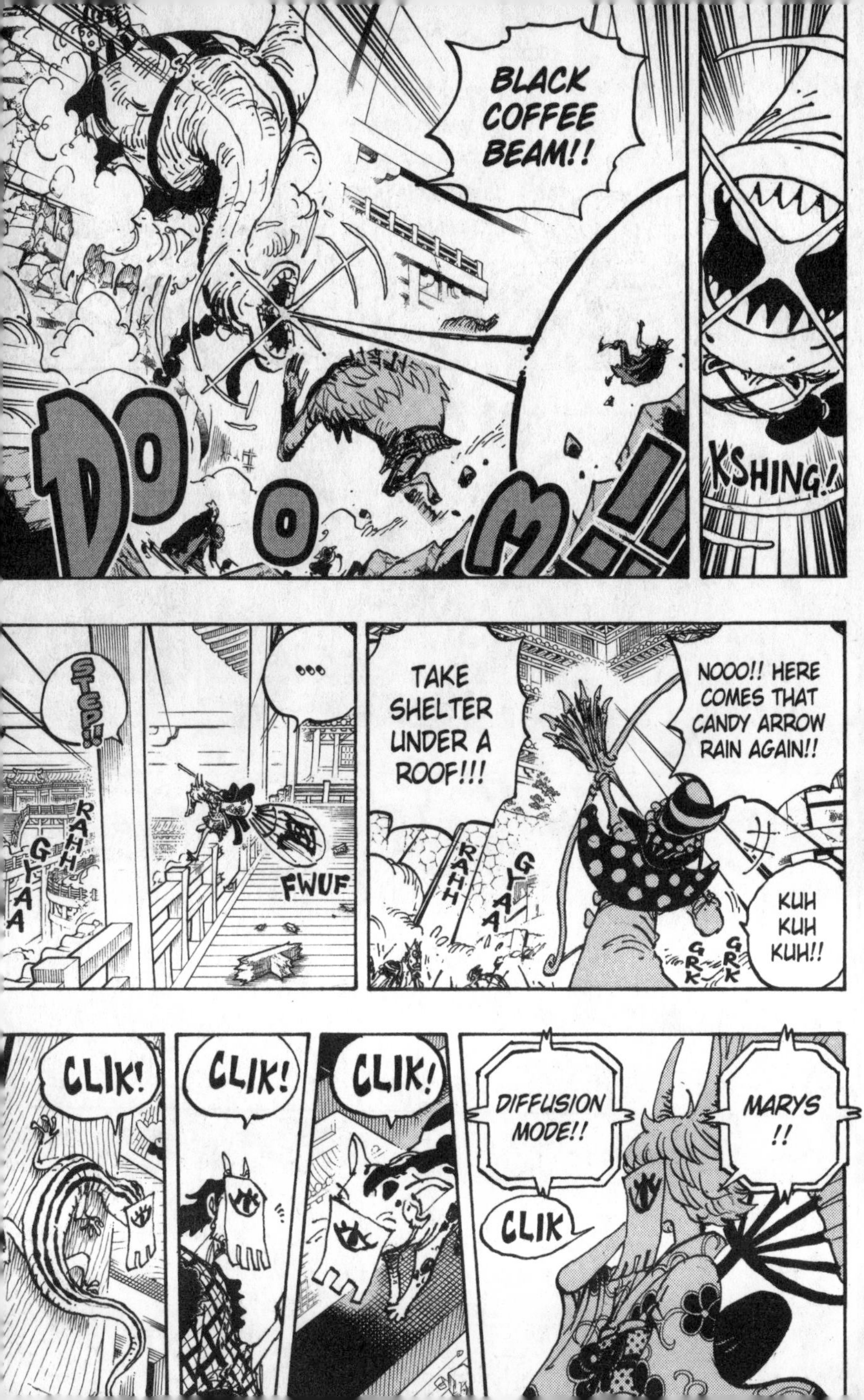
KSHING!
BLACK COFFEE BEAM!!
DOOM!!
NOOO!! HERE COMES THAT CANDY ARROW RAIN AGAIN!!
TAKE SHELTER UNDER A ROOF!!!
GYAA
RAHH
KUH KUH KUH!!
GRK
GRK
...
STEP!!
FWUF
RAHH
GYAA
MARYS !!
DIFFUSION MODE!!
CLIK
CLIK!
CLIK!
CLIK!

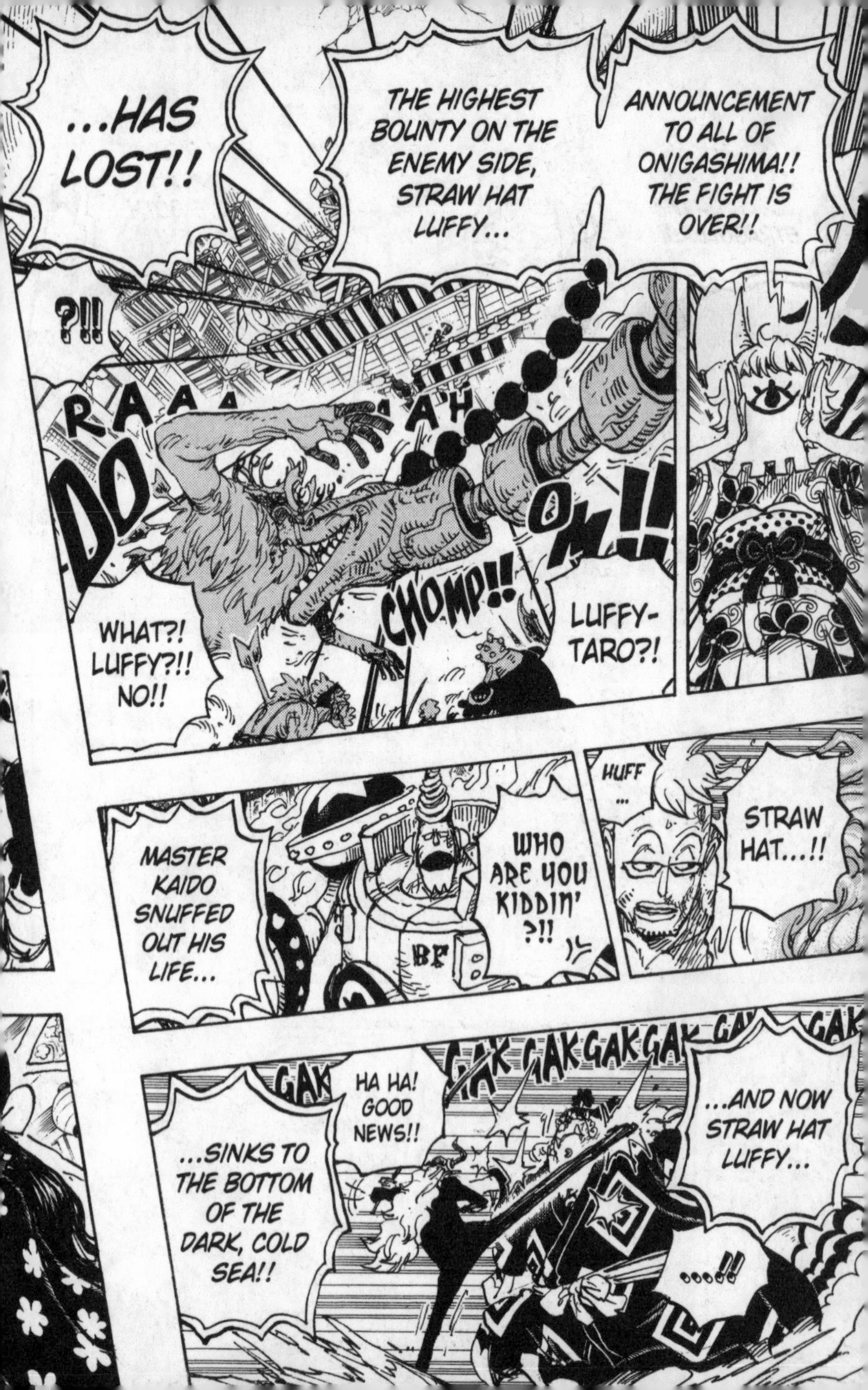
ANNOUNCEMENT TO ALL OF ONIGASHIMA!! THE FIGHT IS OVER!!
THE HIGHEST BOUNTY ON THE ENEMY SIDE, STRAW HAT LUFFY...
...HAS LOST!!
?!!
RAAAAAH
DOON!!
CHOMP!!
LUFFY-TARO?!
WHAT?! LUFFY?!! NO!!
HUFF ...
STRAW HAT...!!
WHO ARE YOU KIDDIN' ?!!
MASTER KAIDO SNUFFED OUT HIS LIFE...
...AND NOW STRAW HAT LUFFY...
GAK GAK GAK GAK GAK GAK GAK
....!!
HA HA! GOOD NEWS!!
...SINKS TO THE BOTTOM OF THE DARK, COLD SEA!!

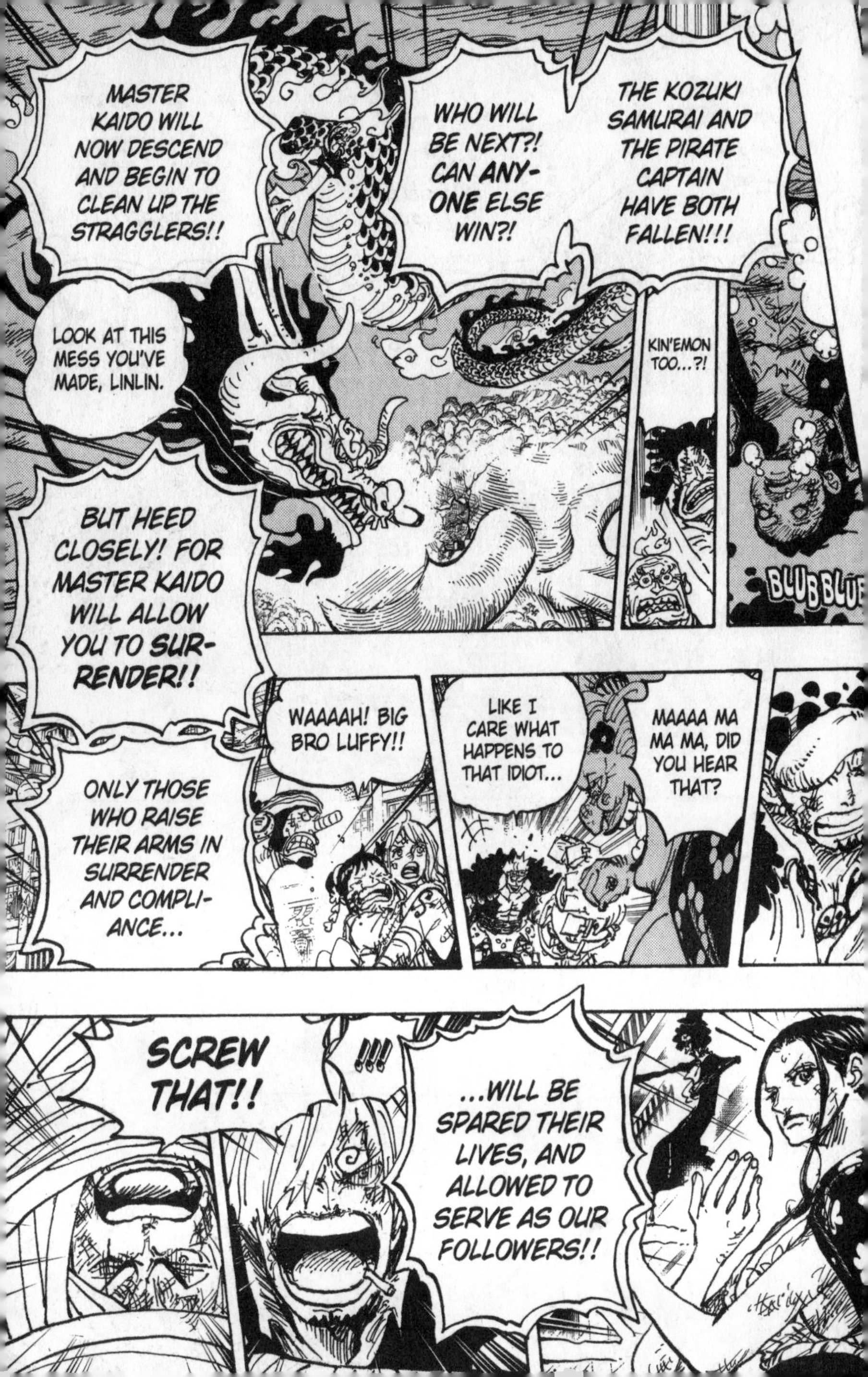
THE KOZUKI SAMURAI AND THE PIRATE CAPTAIN HAVE BOTH FALLEN!!!
WHO WILL BE NEXT?! CAN ANYONE ELSE WIN?!
MASTER KAIDO WILL NOW DESCEND AND BEGIN TO CLEAN UP THE STRAGGLERS!!
BLUB BLU
KIN'EMON TOO...?!
LOOK AT THIS MESS YOU'VE MADE, LINLIN.
BUT HEED CLOSELY! FOR MASTER KAIDO WILL ALLOW YOU TO SURRENDER!!
MAAAA MA MA MA, DID YOU HEAR THAT?
LIKE I CARE WHAT HAPPENS TO THAT IDIOT...
WAAAAH! BIG BRO LUFFY!!
ONLY THOSE WHO RAISE THEIR ARMS IN SURRENDER AND COMPLIANCE...
...WILL BE SPARED THEIR LIVES, AND ALLOWED TO SERVE AS OUR FOLLOWERS!!
!!!
SCREW THAT!!

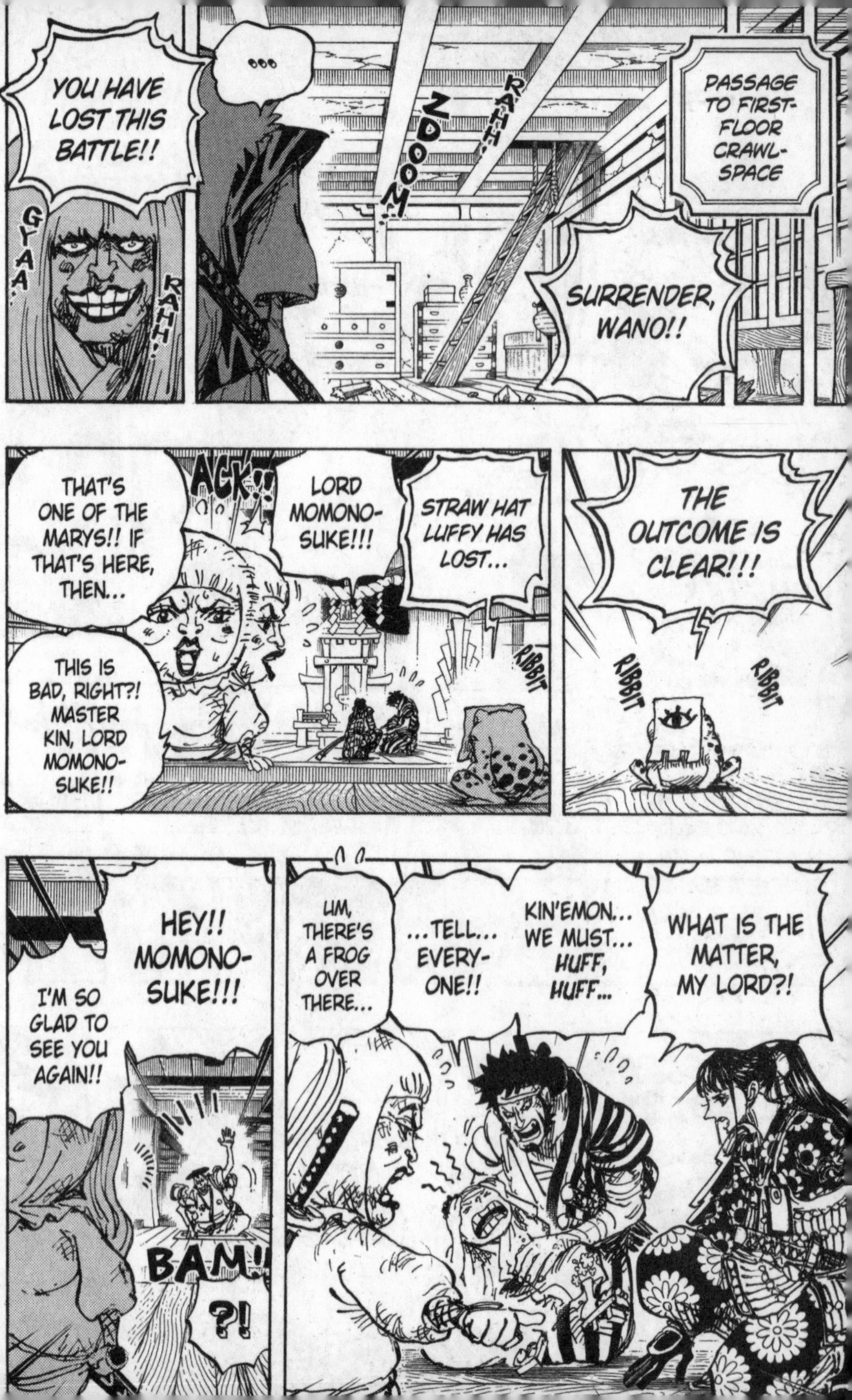
PASSAGE TO FIRST-FLOOR CRAWL-SPACE
SURRENDER, WANO!!
RAHH
ZDOOOM
...
YOU HAVE LOST THIS BATTLE!!
GYAA
RAHH
THE OUTCOME IS CLEAR!!!
RIBBIT
RIBBIT
STRAW HAT LUFFY HAS LOST...
LORD MOMONOSUKE!!!
ACK!!
THAT'S ONE OF THE MARYS!! IF THAT'S HERE, THEN...
THIS IS BAD, RIGHT?! MASTER KIN, LORD MOMONOSUKE!!
RIBBIT
WHAT IS THE MATTER, MY LORD?!
KIN'EMON... WE MUST... HUFF, HUFF...
...TELL... EVERYONE!!
UM, THERE'S A FROG OVER THERE...
HEY!! MOMONOSUKE!!!
I'M SO GLAD TO SEE YOU AGAIN!!
BAM!!
?!

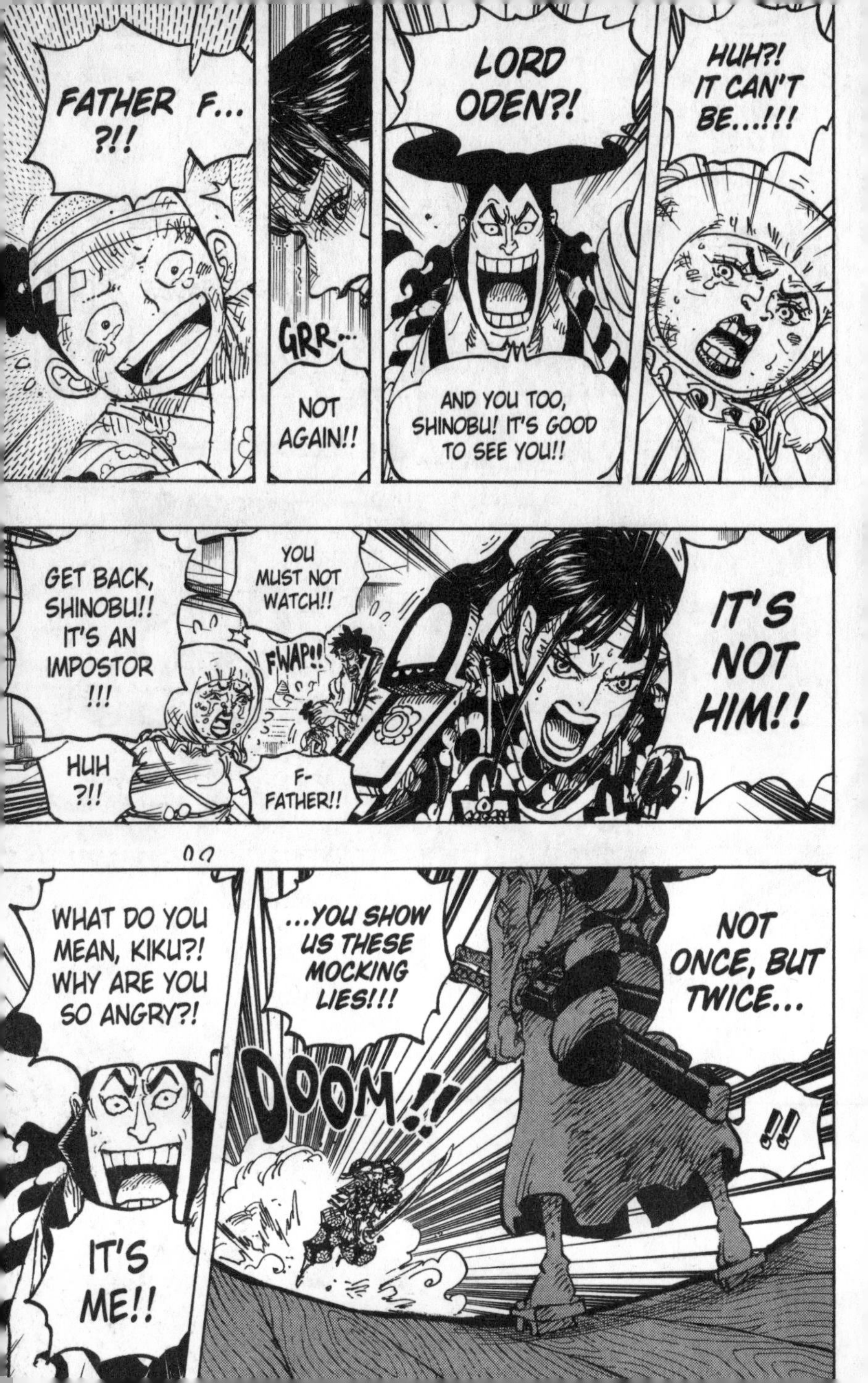
HUH?! IT CAN'T BE...!!!
LORD ODEN?!
AND YOU TOO, SHINOBU! IT'S GOOD TO SEE YOU!!
GRR...
NOT AGAIN!!
FATHER F... ?!!
IT'S NOT HIM!!
YOU MUST NOT WATCH!!
GET BACK, SHINOBU!! IT'S AN IMPOSTOR!!!
FWAP!!
F-FATHER!!
HUH ?!!
NOT ONCE, BUT TWICE...
...YOU SHOW US THESE MOCKING LIES!!!
!!
DOOM!!
WHAT DO YOU MEAN, KIKU?! WHY ARE YOU SO ANGRY?!
IT'S ME!!

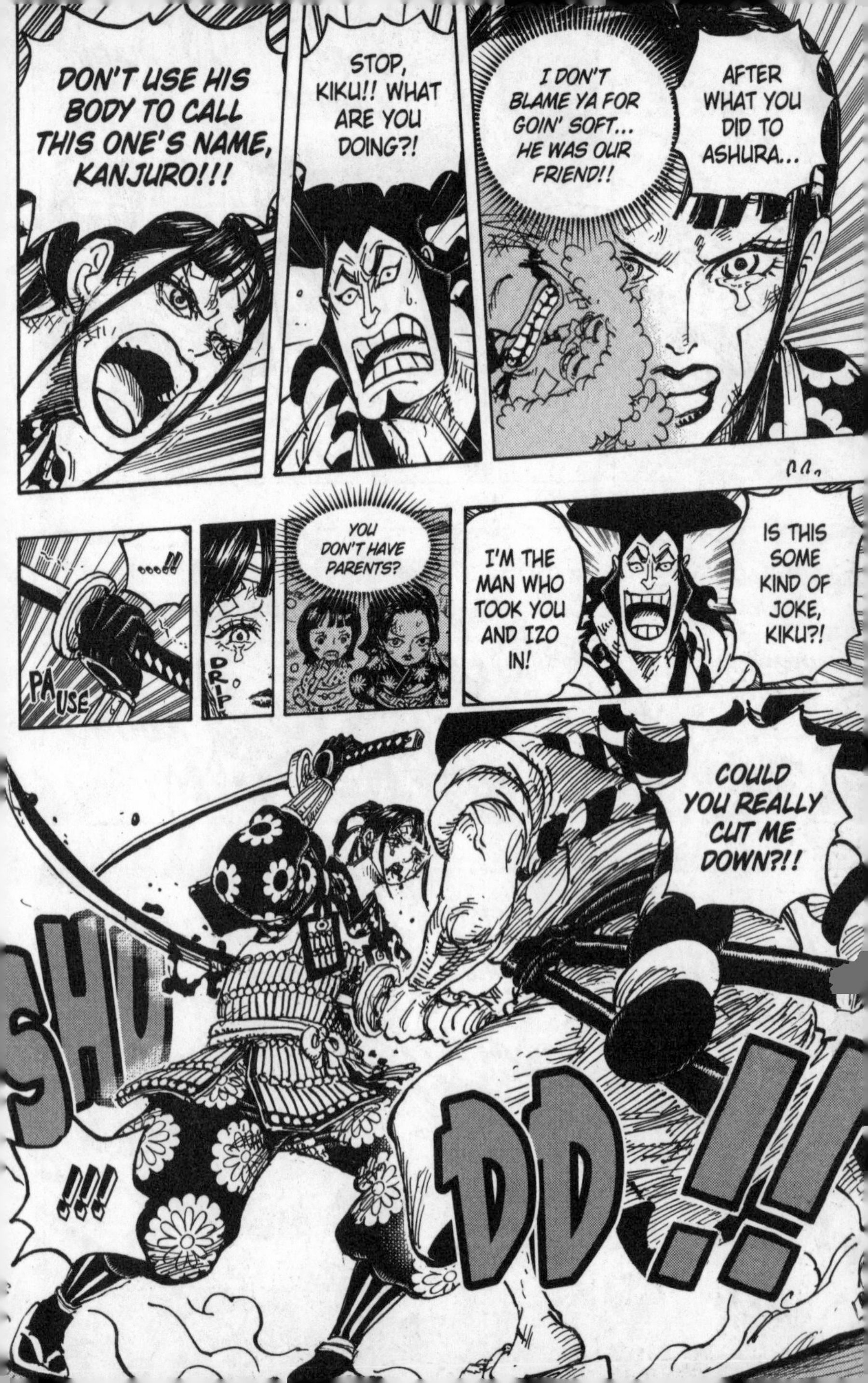

AFTER WHAT YOU DID TO ASHURA...
I DON'T BLAME YA FOR GOIN' SOFT... HE WAS OUR FRIEND!!
STOP, KIKU!! WHAT ARE YOU DOING?!
DON'T USE HIS BODY TO CALL THIS ONE'S NAME, KANJURO!!!
IS THIS SOME KIND OF JOKE, KIKU?!
I'M THE MAN WHO TOOK YOU AND IZO IN!
YOU DON'T HAVE PARENTS?
DRIP
...!!
PAUSE
COULD YOU REALLY CUT ME DOWN?!!
SHU
DD..!!
!!!

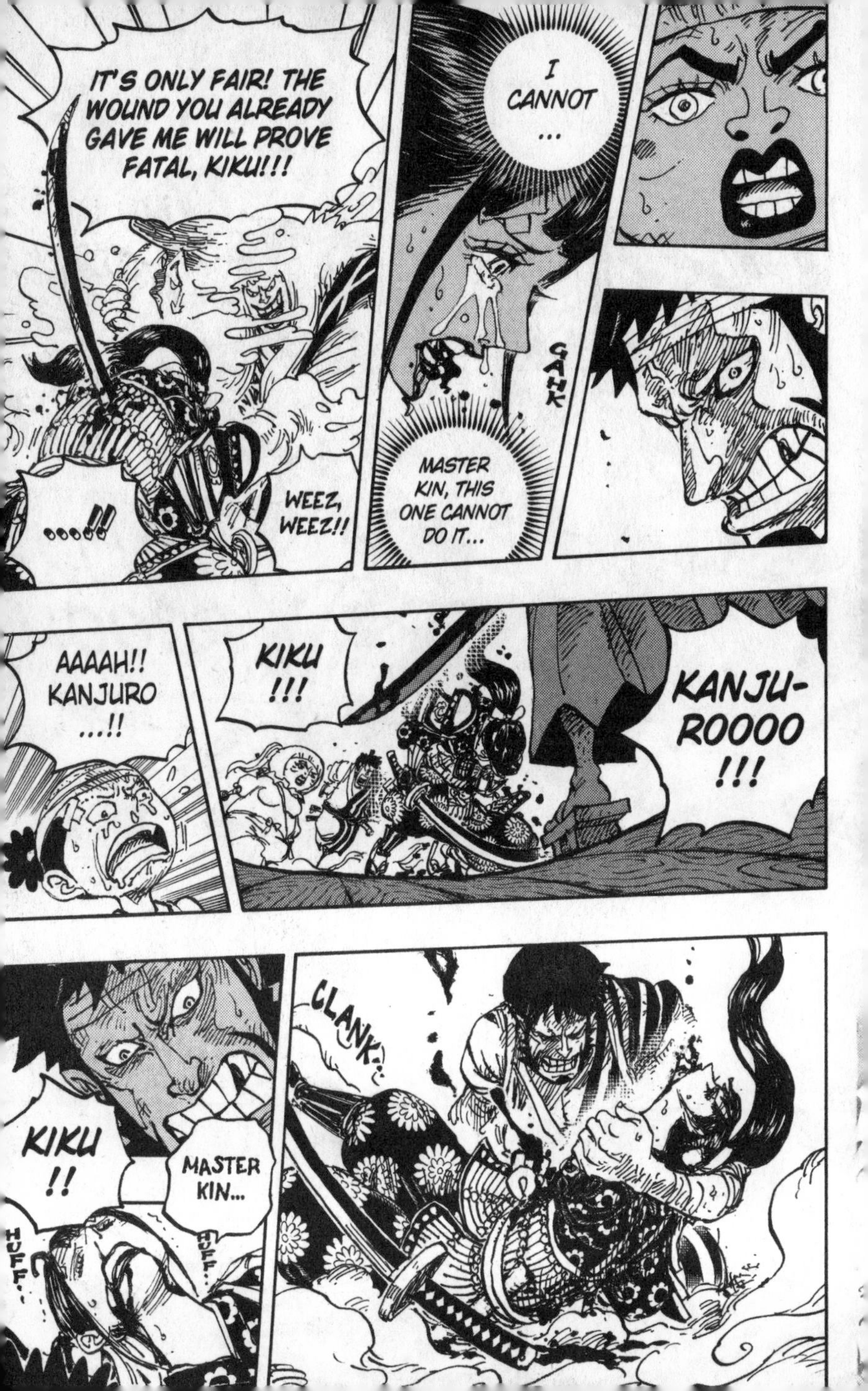
I CANNOT ...
GAHK
MASTER KIN, THIS ONE CANNOT DO IT...
IT'S ONLY FAIR! THE WOUND YOU ALREADY GAVE ME WILL PROVE FATAL, KIKU!!!
WEEZ, WEEZ!!
.....!!
KANJU-ROOOO !!!
KIKU !!!
AAAAH!! KANJURO ...!!
CLANK...
KIKU !!
MASTER KIN...
HUFF...
HUFF...

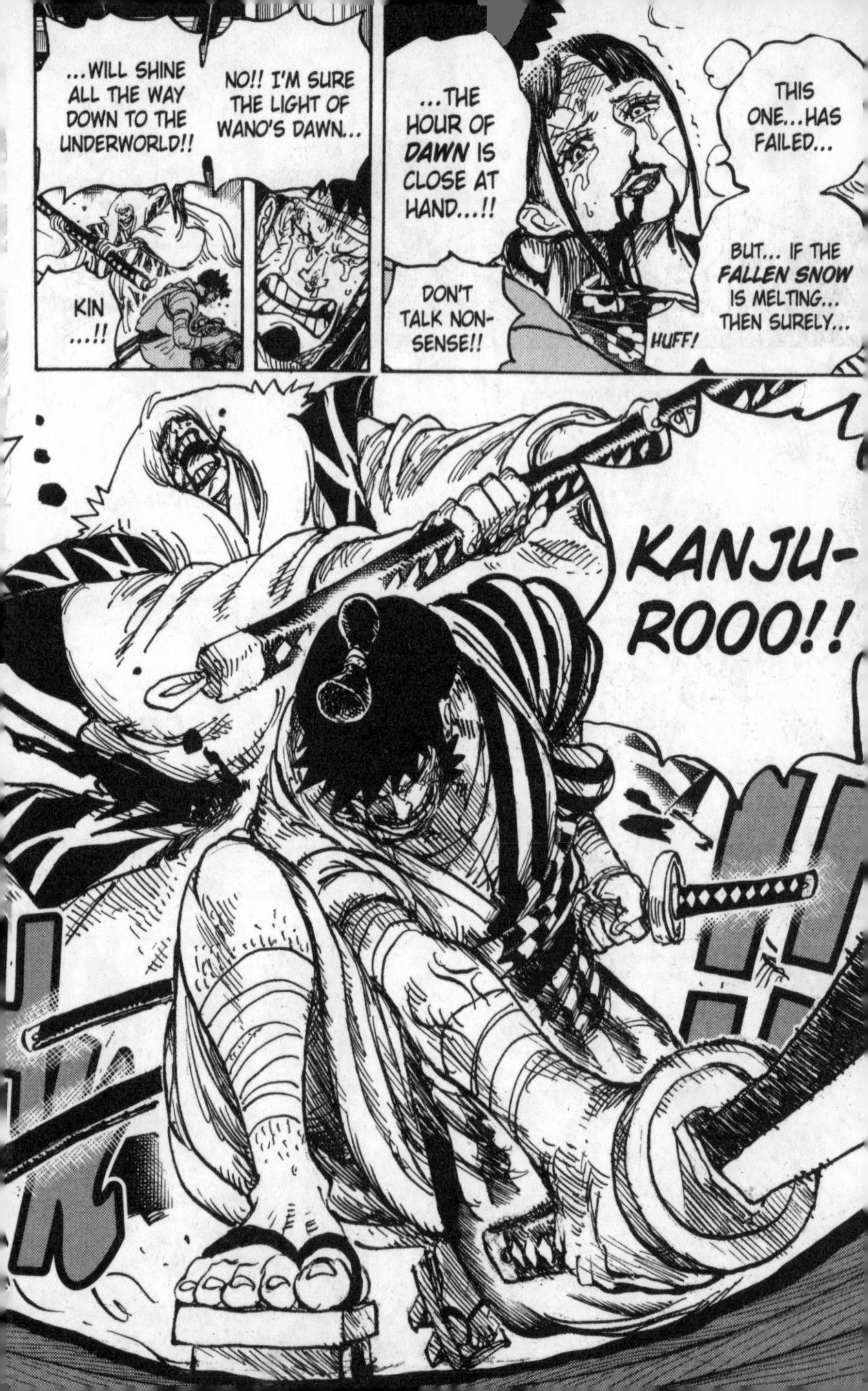
THIS ONE...HAS FAILED...
BUT... IF THE FALLEN SNOW IS MELTING... THEN SURELY...
...THE HOUR OF DAWN IS CLOSE AT HAND...!!
HUFF!
DON'T TALK NON-SENSE!!
NO!! I'M SURE THE LIGHT OF WANO'S DAWN...
...WILL SHINE ALL THE WAY DOWN TO THE UNDERWORLD!!
KIN...!!
KANJU-ROOO!!

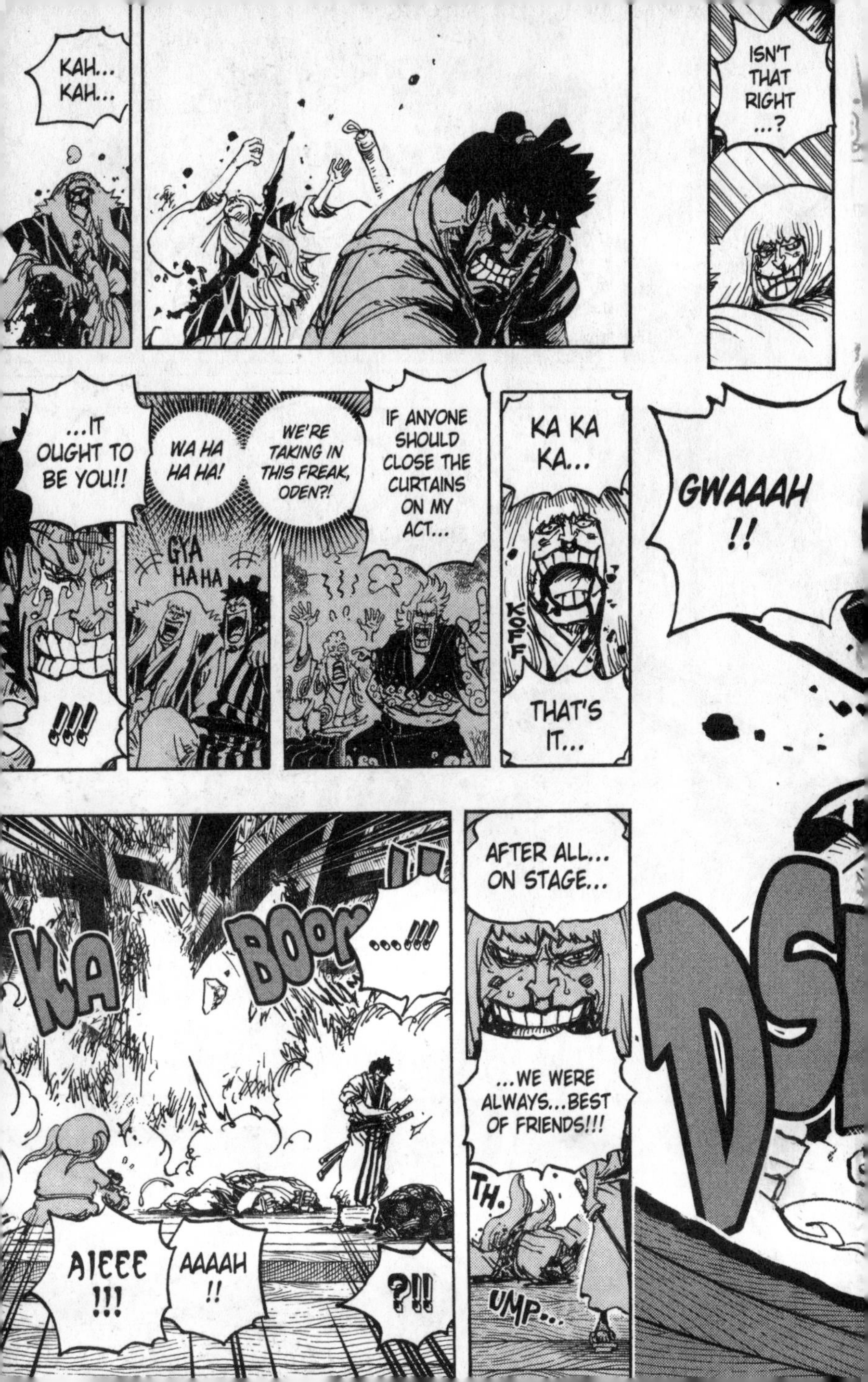
ISN'T THAT RIGHT ...?
KAH... KAH...
GWAAAH !!
KA KA KA...
KOFF
THAT'S IT...
IF ANYONE SHOULD CLOSE THE CURTAINS ON MY ACT...
WE'RE TAKING IN THIS FREAK, ODEN?!
WA HA HA HA!
GYA HAHA
...IT OUGHT TO BE YOU!!
!!!
AFTER ALL... ON STAGE...
...WE WERE ALWAYS...BEST OF FRIENDS!!!
TH.
UMP...
KA BOOM...!!!
?!!
AAAAH !!
AIEEE !!!

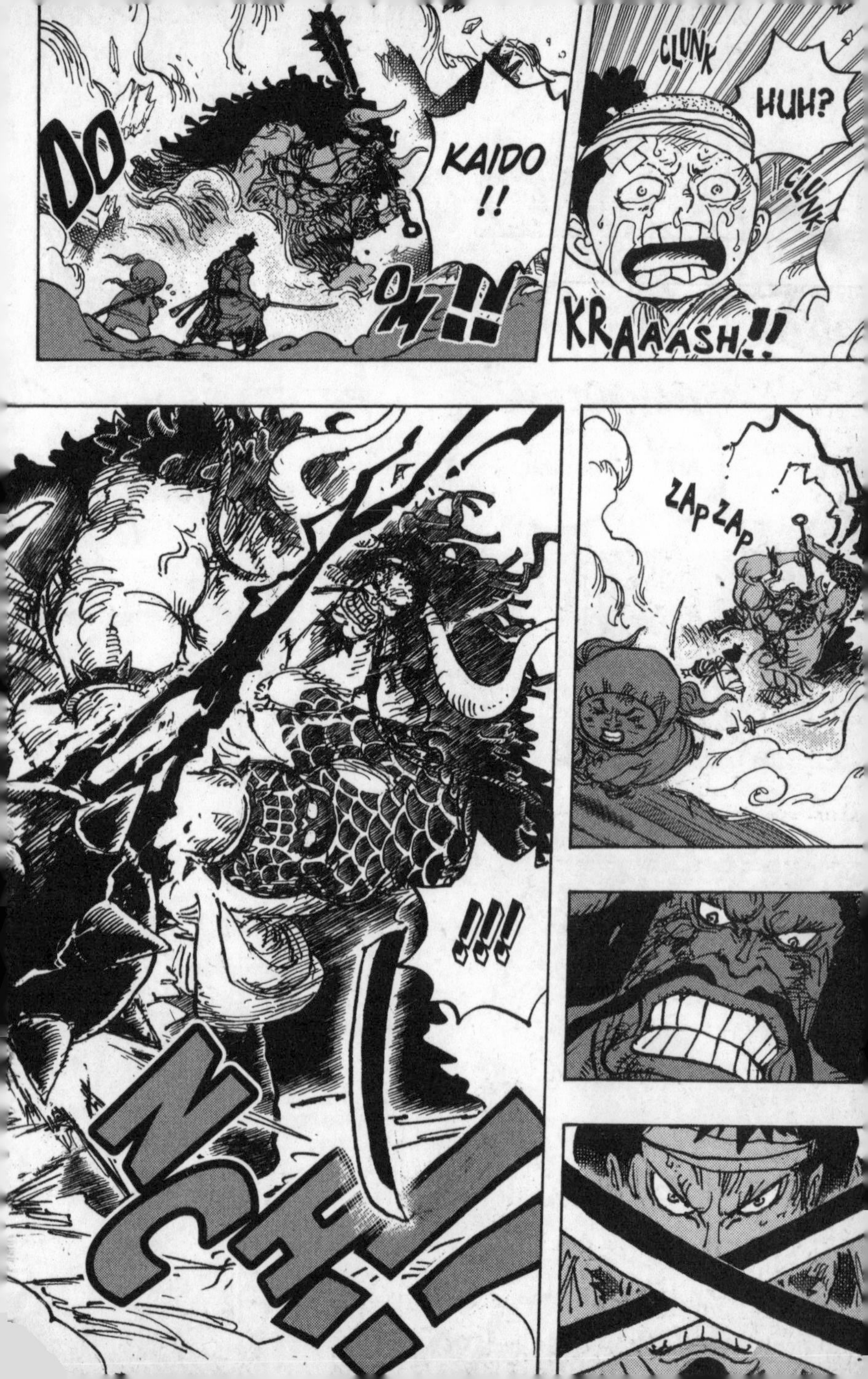
CLUNK
HUH?
CLUNK
KRAAASH!!
DO
KAIDO !!
OM!!
ZAP ZAP
!!!
NCH!!

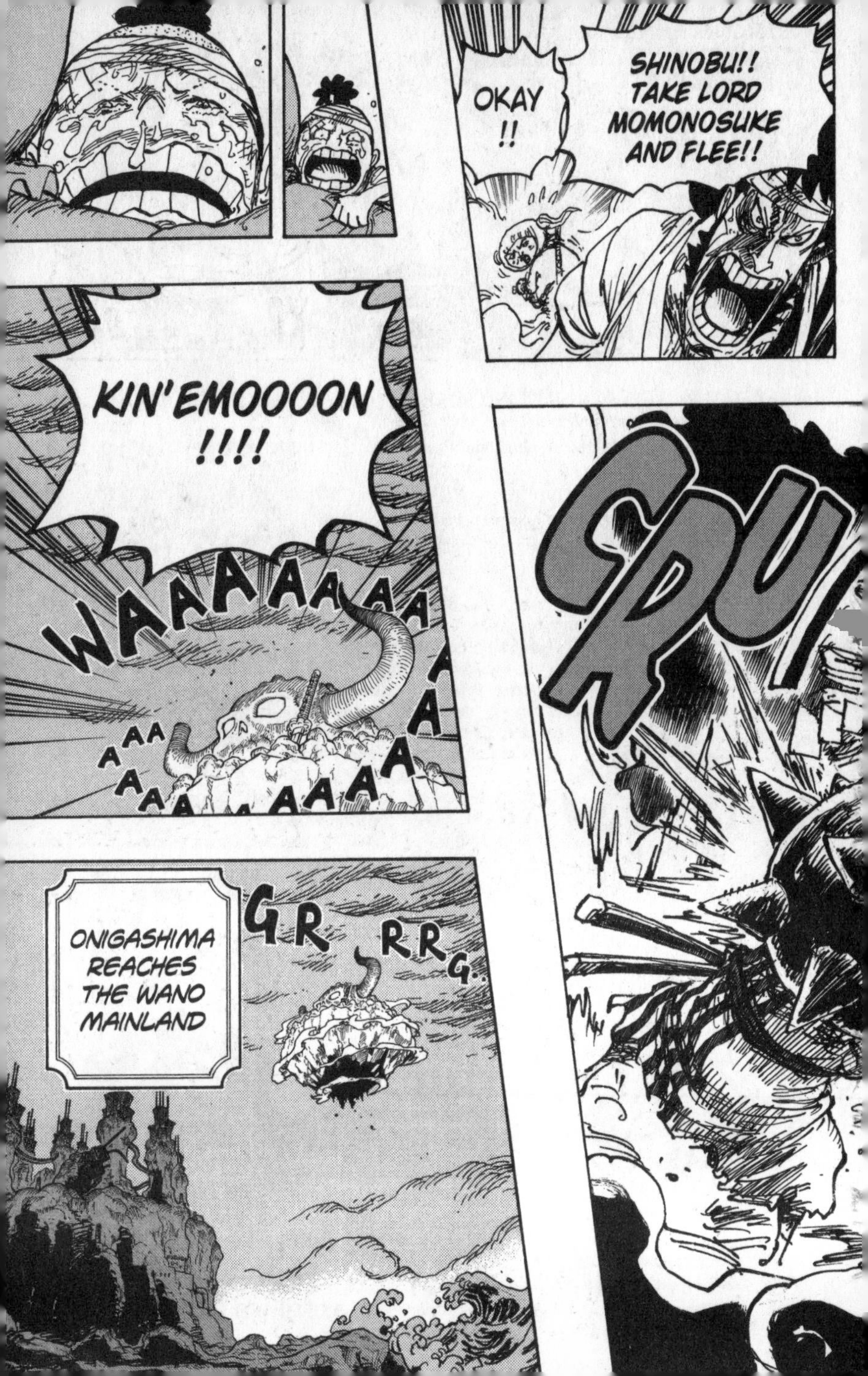

SHINOBU!! TAKE LORD MOMONOSUKE AND FLEE!!
OKAY !!
KIN'EMOOOON !!!!
WAAAAAAAAAAAAAAAAAAAAA
ONIGASHIMA REACHES THE WANO MAINLAND
GR RRG..

SBS Question Corner

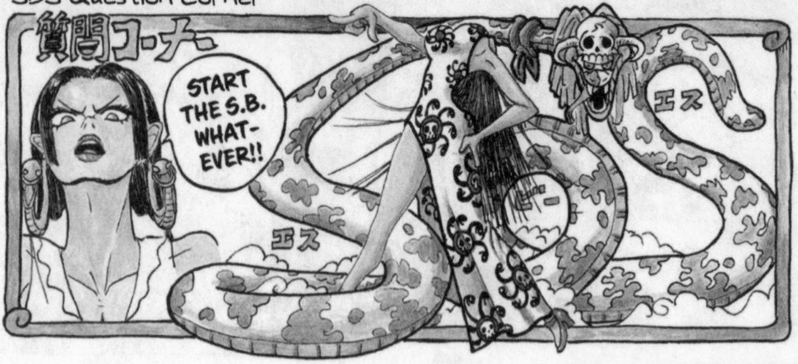

START THE S.B. WHAT-EVER!!

(Igarashi, Oita)

Q: So, I've been reading since the very first volume, and I'm just wondering, when are we going to get to the part about Odacchi's weiner?

--Interdimensional Pork Ribs

A: Never!!

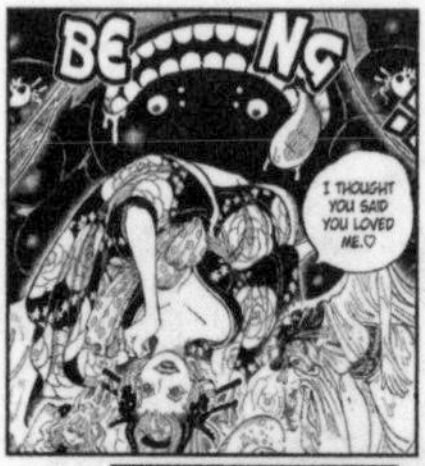

I THOUGHT YOU SAID YOU LOVED ME.♡

Q: Is it just me, or does Black Maria's transformation kind of look like Smile fruit powers?

--Ebi

A: I get what you mean! Yes, the man-beast form of previous zoans haven't had two heads, and her arms should be all spidery too. But the thing is, there's no definitive style to them. People have some level of control over their transformations, like Chopper and his many forms. I'm sure Miss Black Maria just couldn't stand the thought of looking like a freaky spider-woman like ← this and used some drugs or something to tweak her point of transformation.

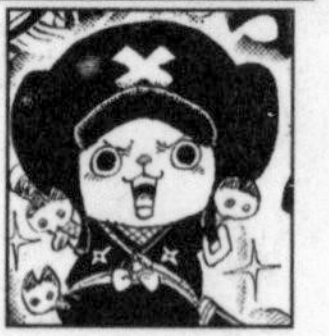

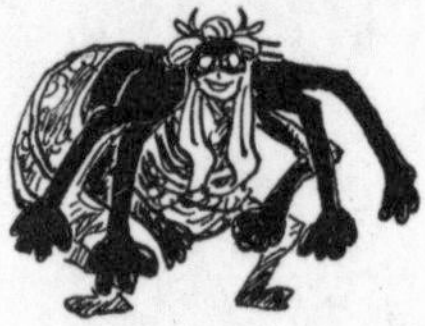

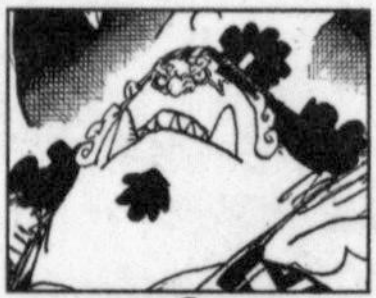

Q: I have been waiting ten years for Jimbei to join the Straw Hat Crew. I drew this mark because I have always admired him. Please make this Jimbei's mark!

--Joshua H.

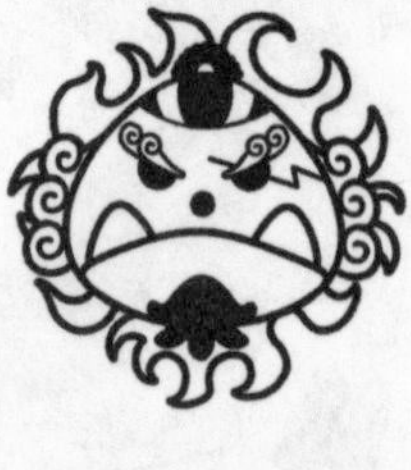

A: Oooh! That's really cool!! Man, I wish I could just use that as it is!! But there are certain rules for how the individual crewmates' Jolly Rogers look, so do you mind if I rearrange it to look like this? ↑

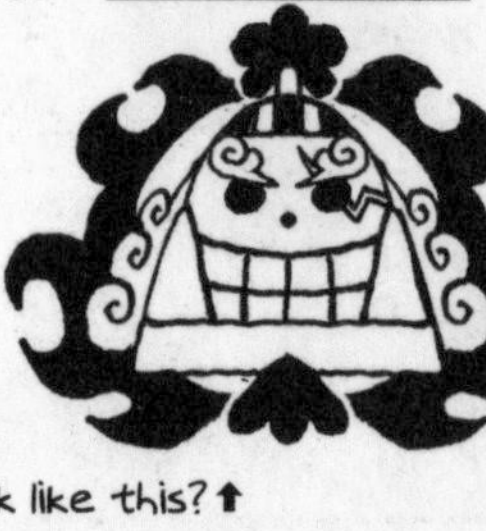

Let's make your idea official, Joshua!!
And now, that's the end of the SBS for volume 100! We're still taking questions for Jimbei's voice actor, Katsuhisa Hoki!
See you next volume!!

Chapter 1015: CHAINS

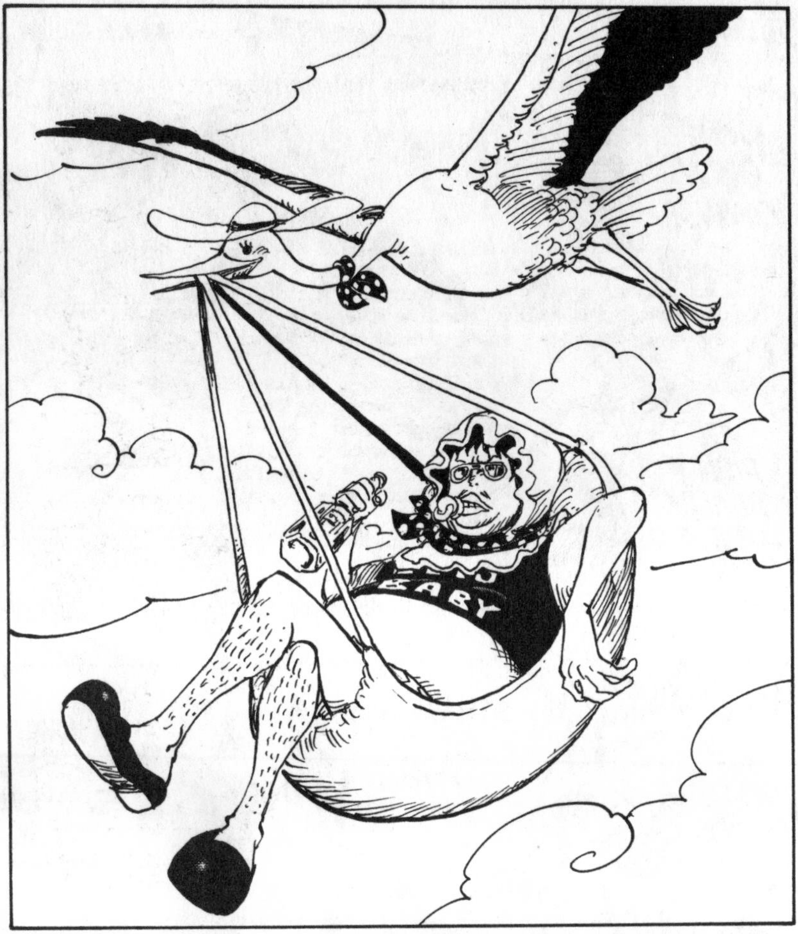
BABY

READER REQUEST: "SEÑOR PINK BEING CONFUSED FOR A BABY BY A STORK" BY TOSHIKIYA

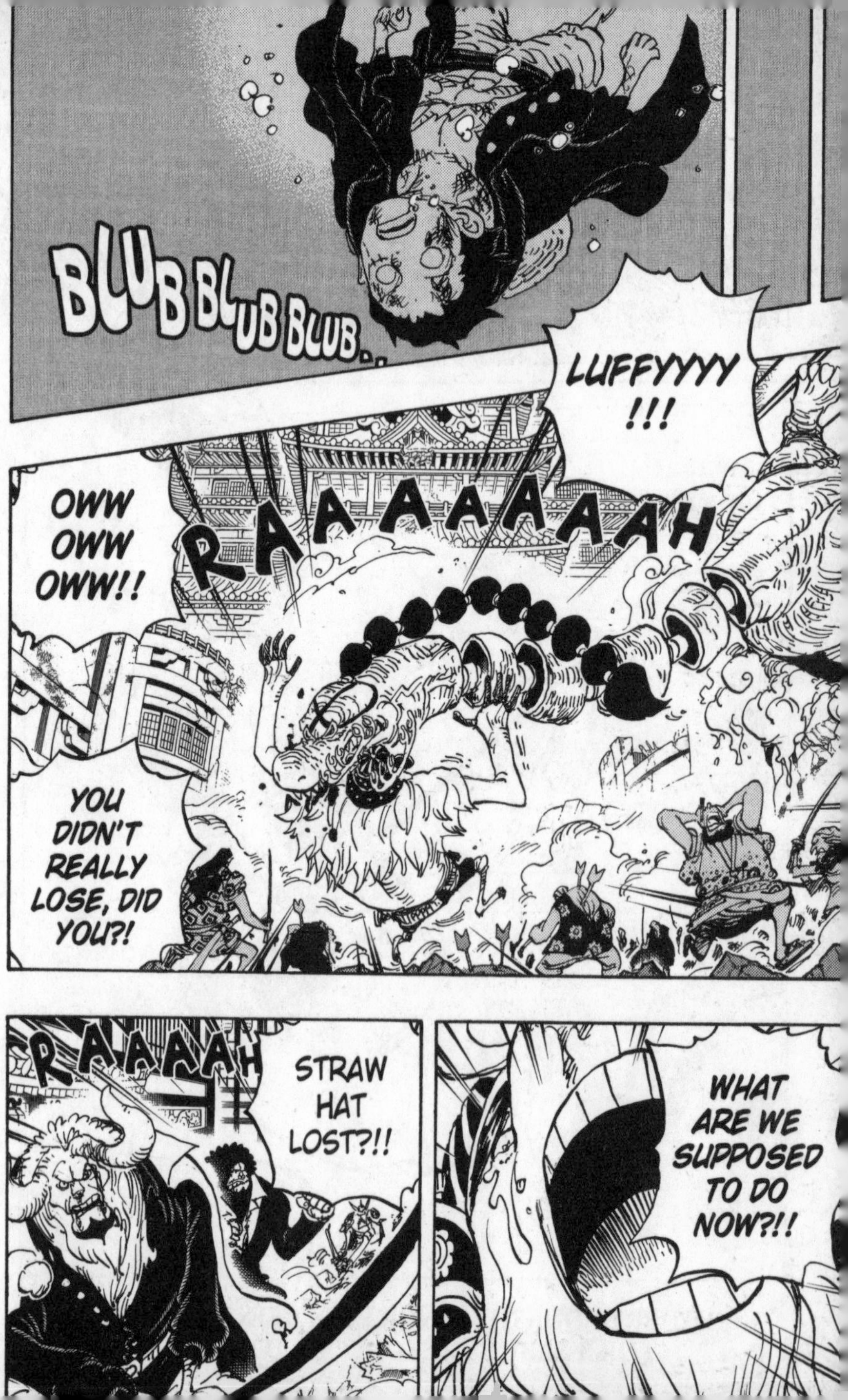
BLUB BLUB BLUB..
LUFFYYYY!!!
RAAAAAAAH
OWW OWW OWW!!
YOU DIDN'T REALLY LOSE, DID YOU?!
WHAT ARE WE SUPPOSED TO DO NOW?!!
STRAW HAT LOST?!!
RAAAAH

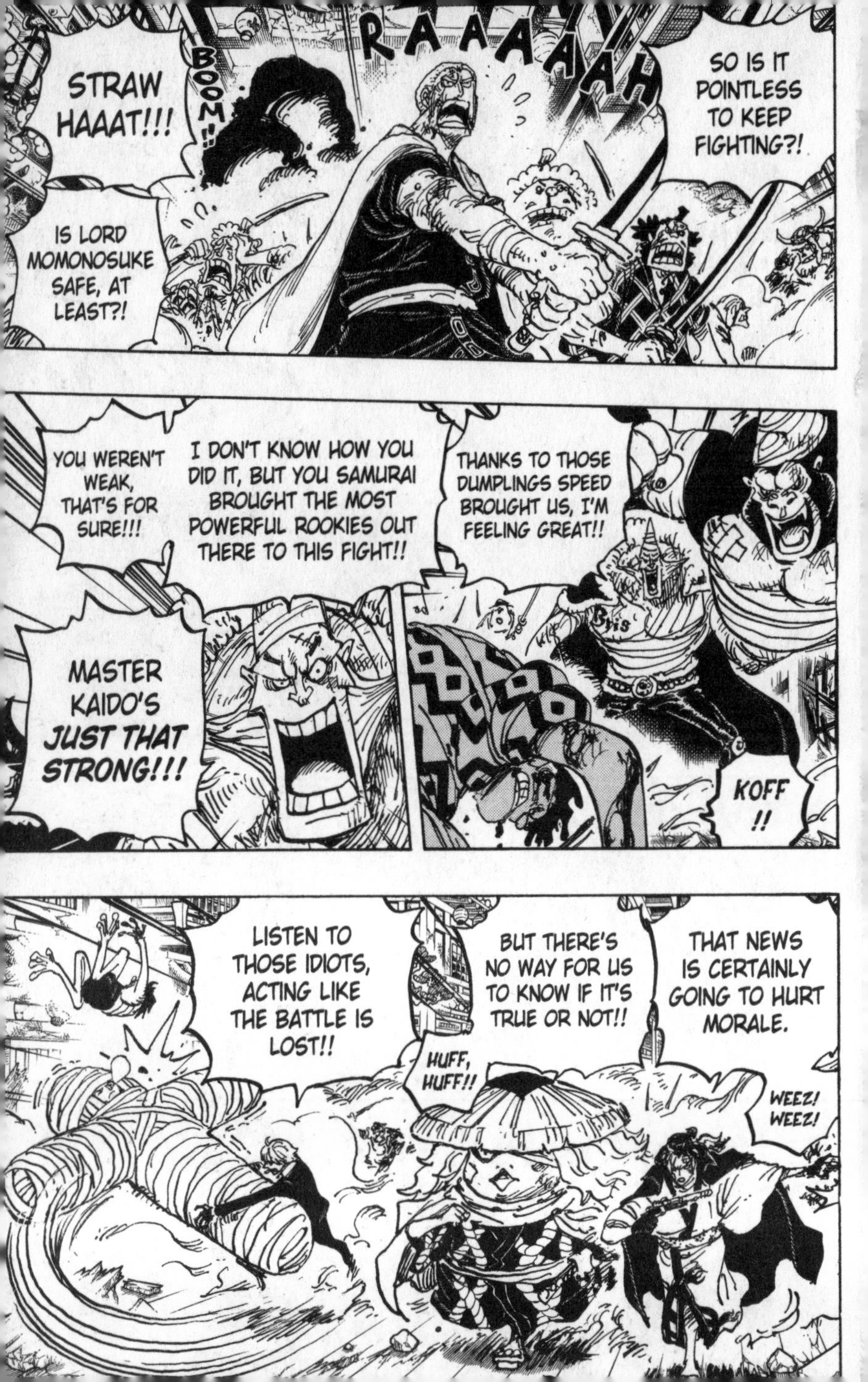
RAAAAAH
SO IS IT POINTLESS TO KEEP FIGHTING?!
BOOM!!
STRAW HAAAT!!!
IS LORD MOMONOSUKE SAFE, AT LEAST?!
THANKS TO THOSE DUMPLINGS SPEED BROUGHT US, I'M FEELING GREAT!!
KOFF!!
I DON'T KNOW HOW YOU DID IT, BUT YOU SAMURAI BROUGHT THE MOST POWERFUL ROOKIES OUT THERE TO THIS FIGHT!!
YOU WEREN'T WEAK, THAT'S FOR SURE!!!
MASTER KAIDO'S JUST THAT STRONG!!!
THAT NEWS IS CERTAINLY GOING TO HURT MORALE.
WEEZ! WEEZ!
BUT THERE'S NO WAY FOR US TO KNOW IF IT'S TRUE OR NOT!!
HUFF, HUFF!!
LISTEN TO THOSE IDIOTS, ACTING LIKE THE BATTLE IS LOST!!

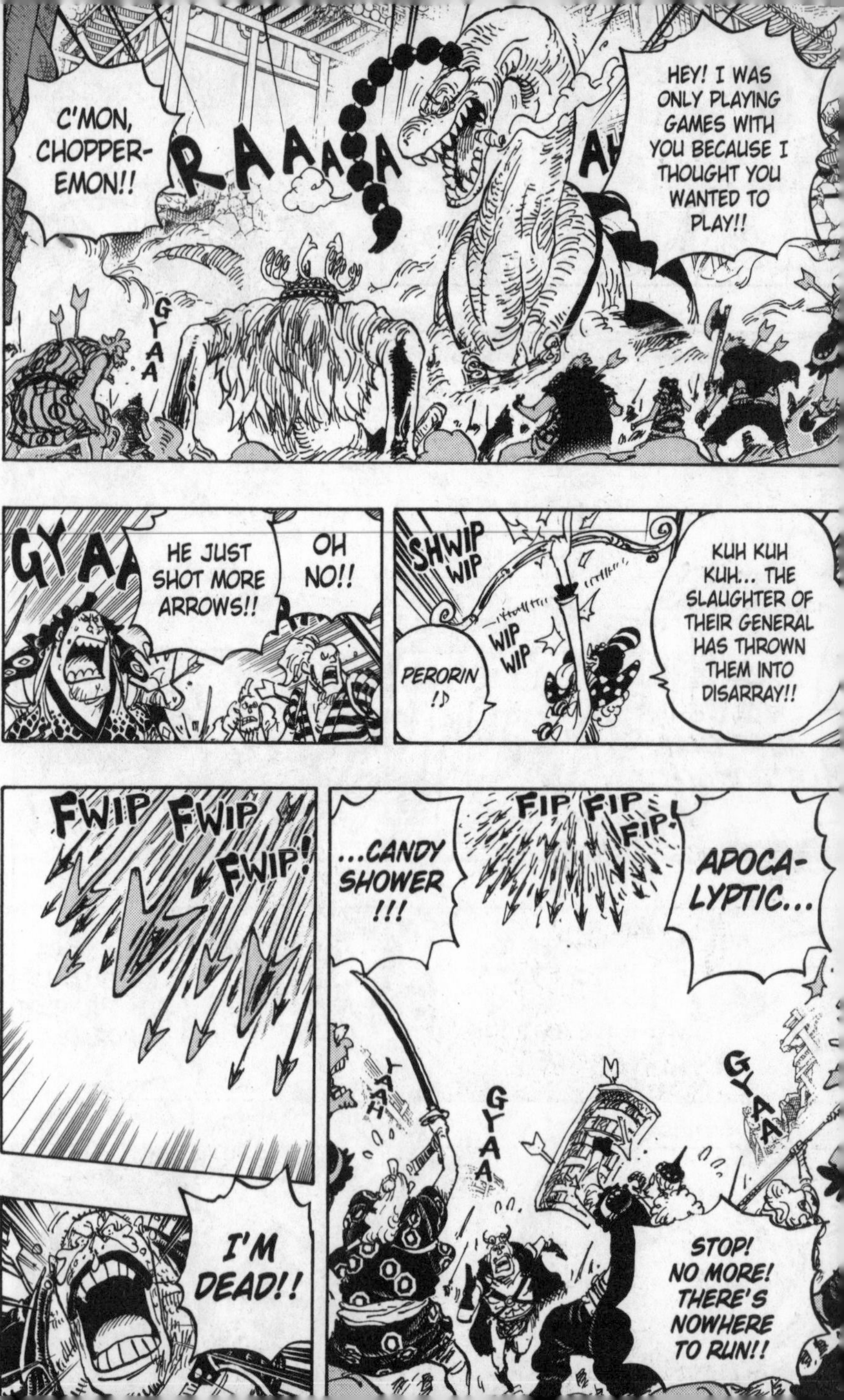
HEY! I WAS ONLY PLAYING GAMES WITH YOU BECAUSE I THOUGHT YOU WANTED TO PLAY!!
RAAAAA
C'MON, CHOPPER-EMON!!
GYAA
KUH KUH KUH... THE SLAUGHTER OF THEIR GENERAL HAS THROWN THEM INTO DISARRAY!!
SHWIP WIP
WIP WIP
PERORIN !♪
OH NO!!
HE JUST SHOT MORE ARROWS!!
GYAA
APOCA-LYPTIC...
FIP FIP FIP!
...CANDY SHOWER!!!
GYAA
GYAA
YAAH
STOP! NO MORE! THERE'S NOWHERE TO RUN!!
FWIP FWIP FWIP!
I'M DEAD!!

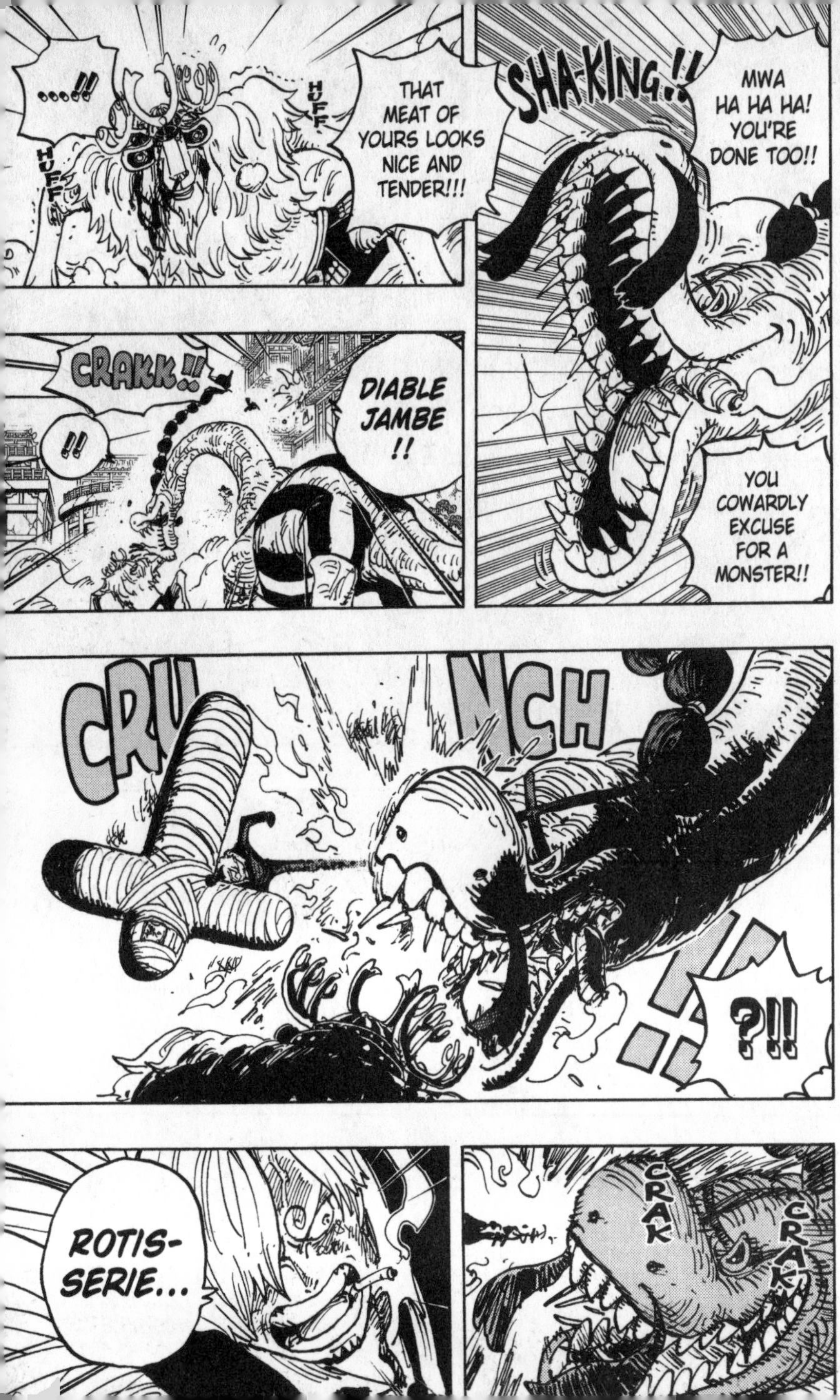
SHA-KING!!
MWA HA HA HA! YOU'RE DONE TOO!!
YOU COWARDLY EXCUSE FOR A MONSTER!!
THAT MEAT OF YOURS LOOKS NICE AND TENDER!!!
HUFF
HUFF
...!!
DIABLE JAMBE !!
CRAKK!!
!!
CRUNCH
?!!
CRAK
CRAK
ROTIS-SERIE...

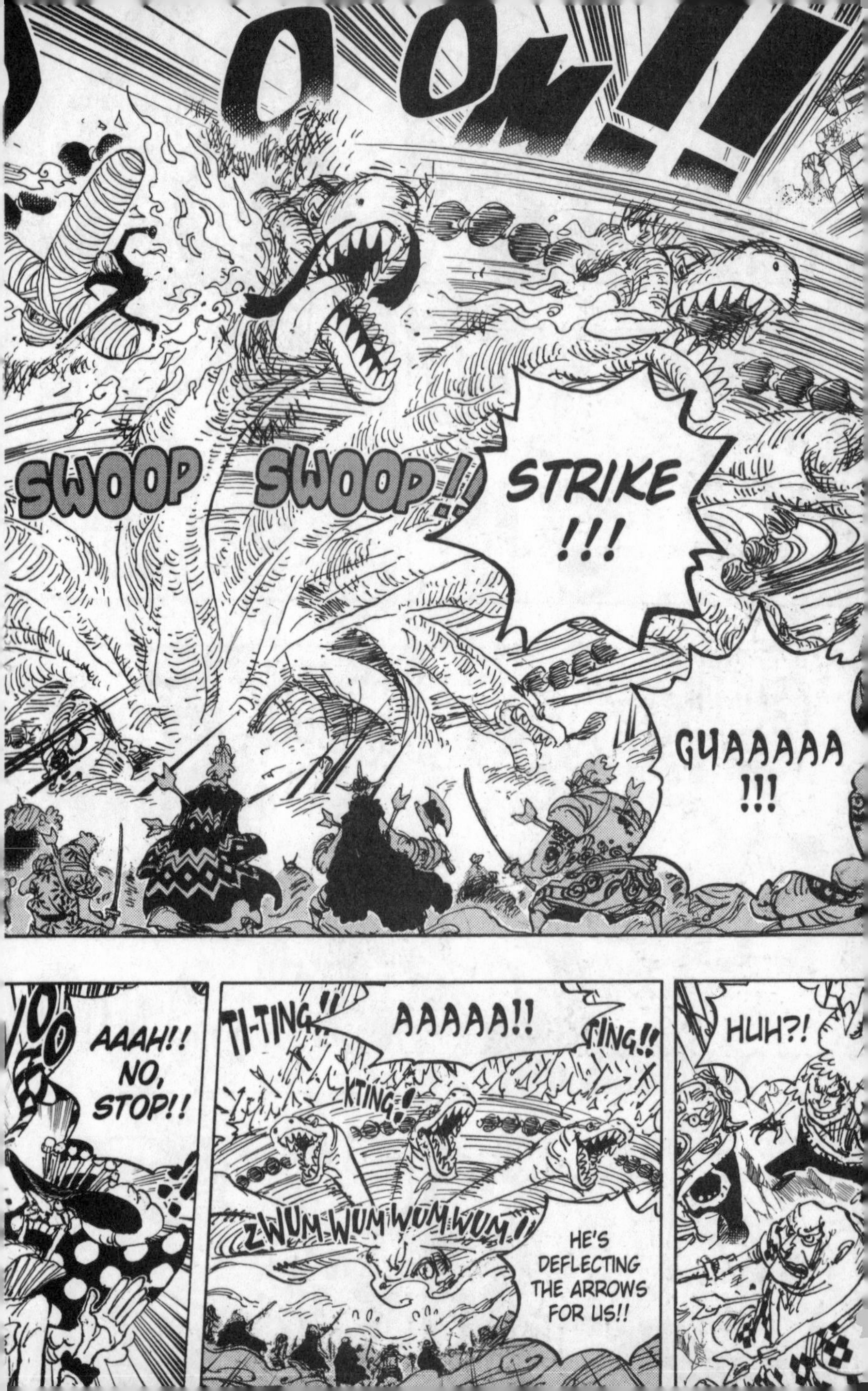
OOM!!
GUAAAAA!!!
STRIKE!!!
SWOOP SWOOP!!
HUH?!
TING!!
AAAAA!!
TI-TING!!
KTING!!
ZWUM WUM WUM WUM!!
HE'S DEFLECTING THE ARROWS FOR US!!
AAAH!! NO, STOP!!

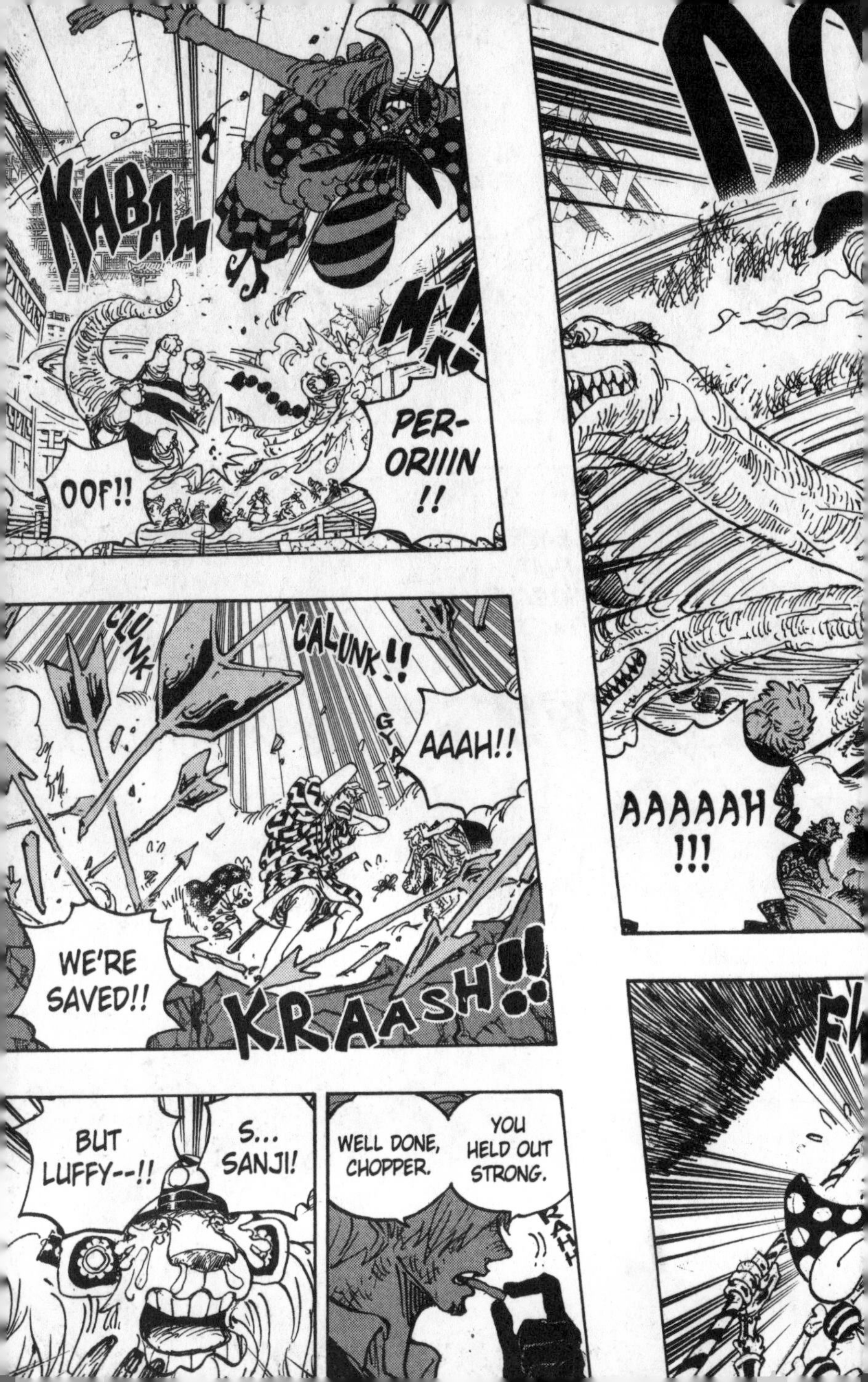
AAAAAH !!!
KABAM
PER-ORIIIN !!
OOF!!
CLUNK
CALUNK!!
GYA
AAAH!!
WE'RE SAVED!!
KRAASH!!
WELL DONE, CHOPPER.
YOU HELD OUT STRONG.
S... SANJI!
BUT LUFFY--!!

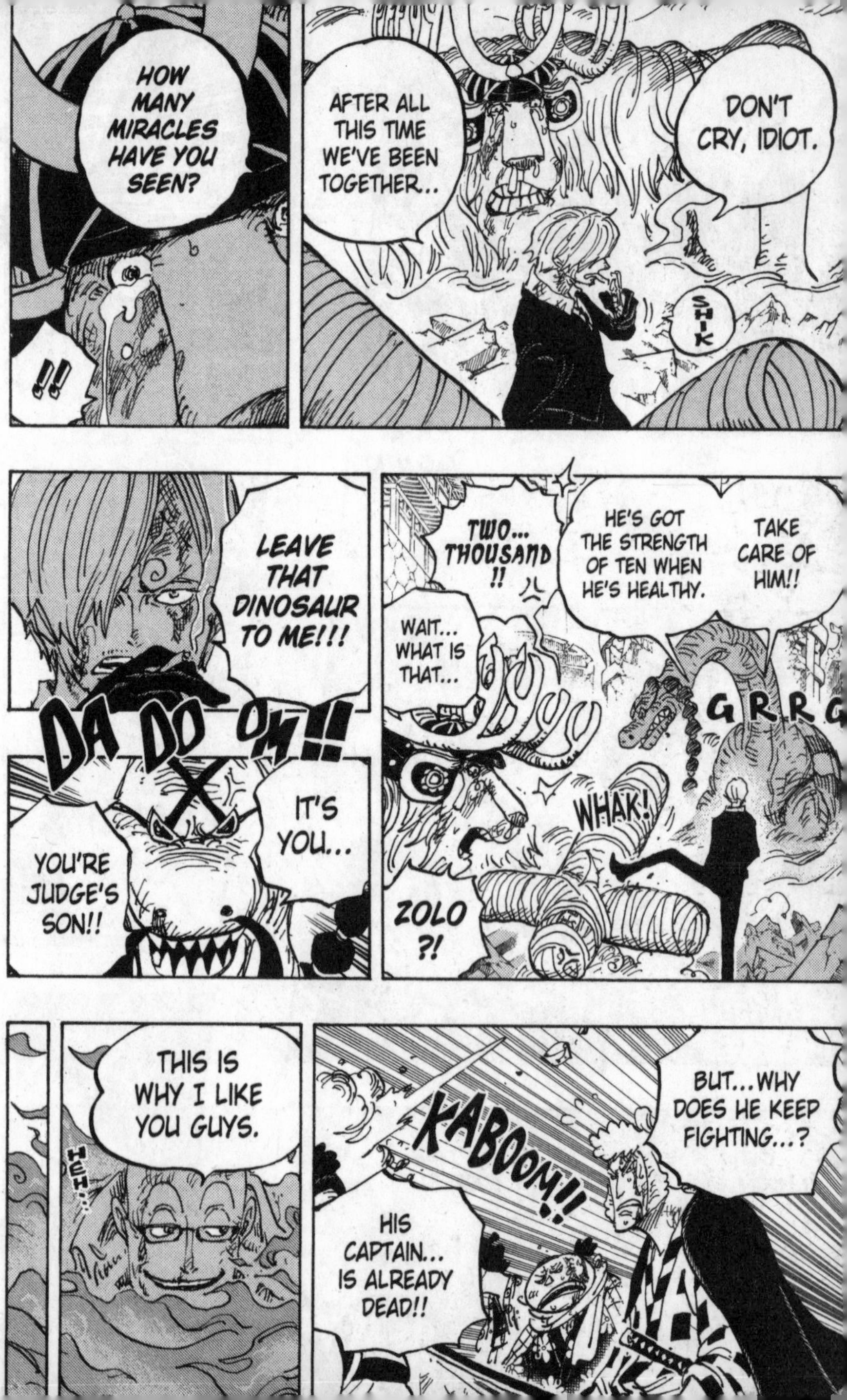

DON'T CRY, IDIOT.
AFTER ALL THIS TIME WE'VE BEEN TOGETHER...
SHIK
HOW MANY MIRACLES HAVE YOU SEEN?
!!
TAKE CARE OF HIM!!
HE'S GOT THE STRENGTH OF TEN WHEN HE'S HEALTHY.
TWO... THOUSAND !!
WAIT... WHAT IS THAT...
GRRG
WHAK!
ZOLO ?!
LEAVE THAT DINOSAUR TO ME!!!
DA DO OM!!
IT'S YOU...
YOU'RE JUDGE'S SON!!
BUT...WHY DOES HE KEEP FIGHTING...?
KABOOM!!
HIS CAPTAIN... IS ALREADY DEAD!!
THIS IS WHY I LIKE YOU GUYS.
HEH...

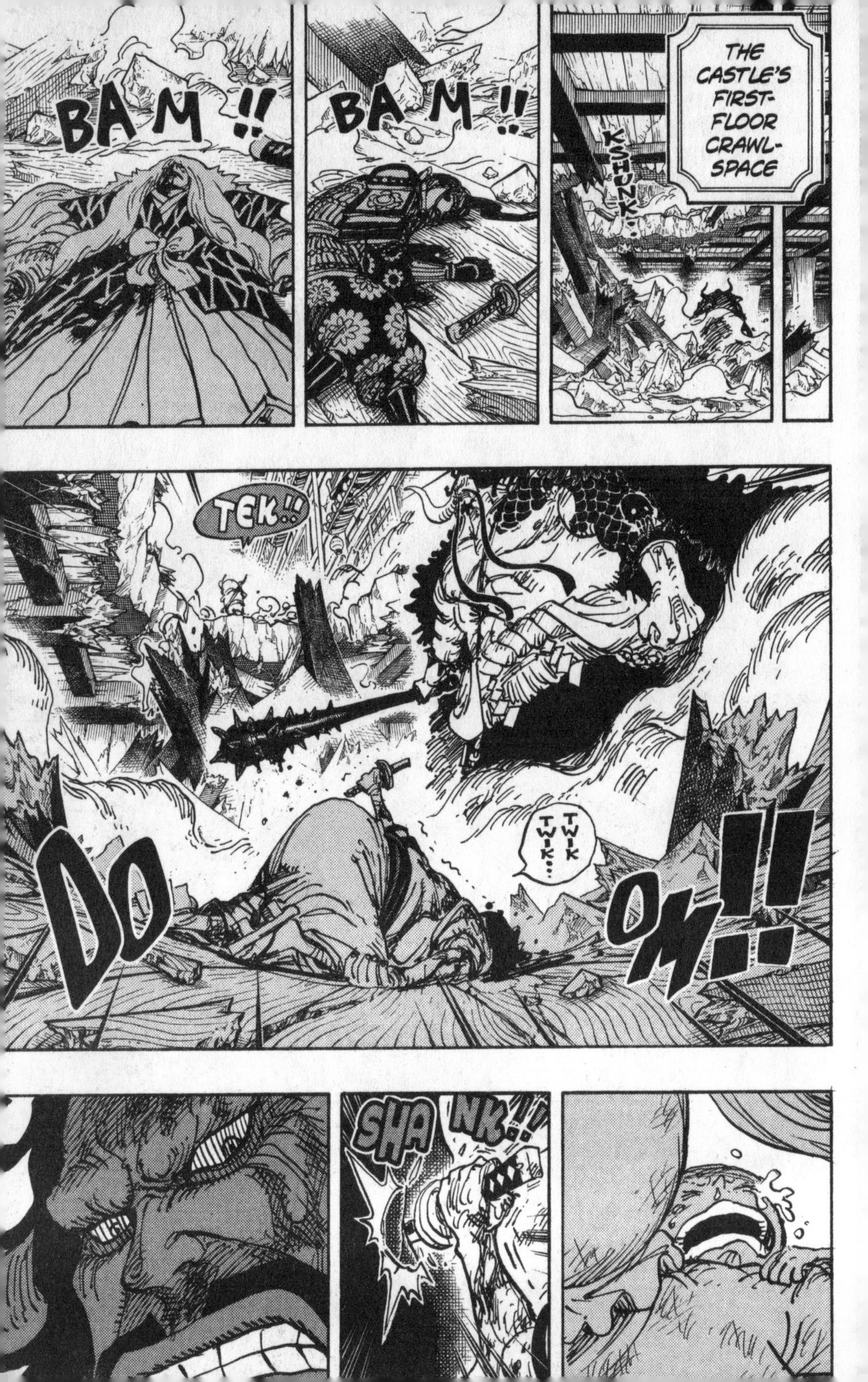
THE CASTLE'S FIRST-FLOOR CRAWL-SPACE
KSHUNK...
BAM!!
BAM!!
TEK!!
TWIK TWIK...
DOOM!!
SHANK!!

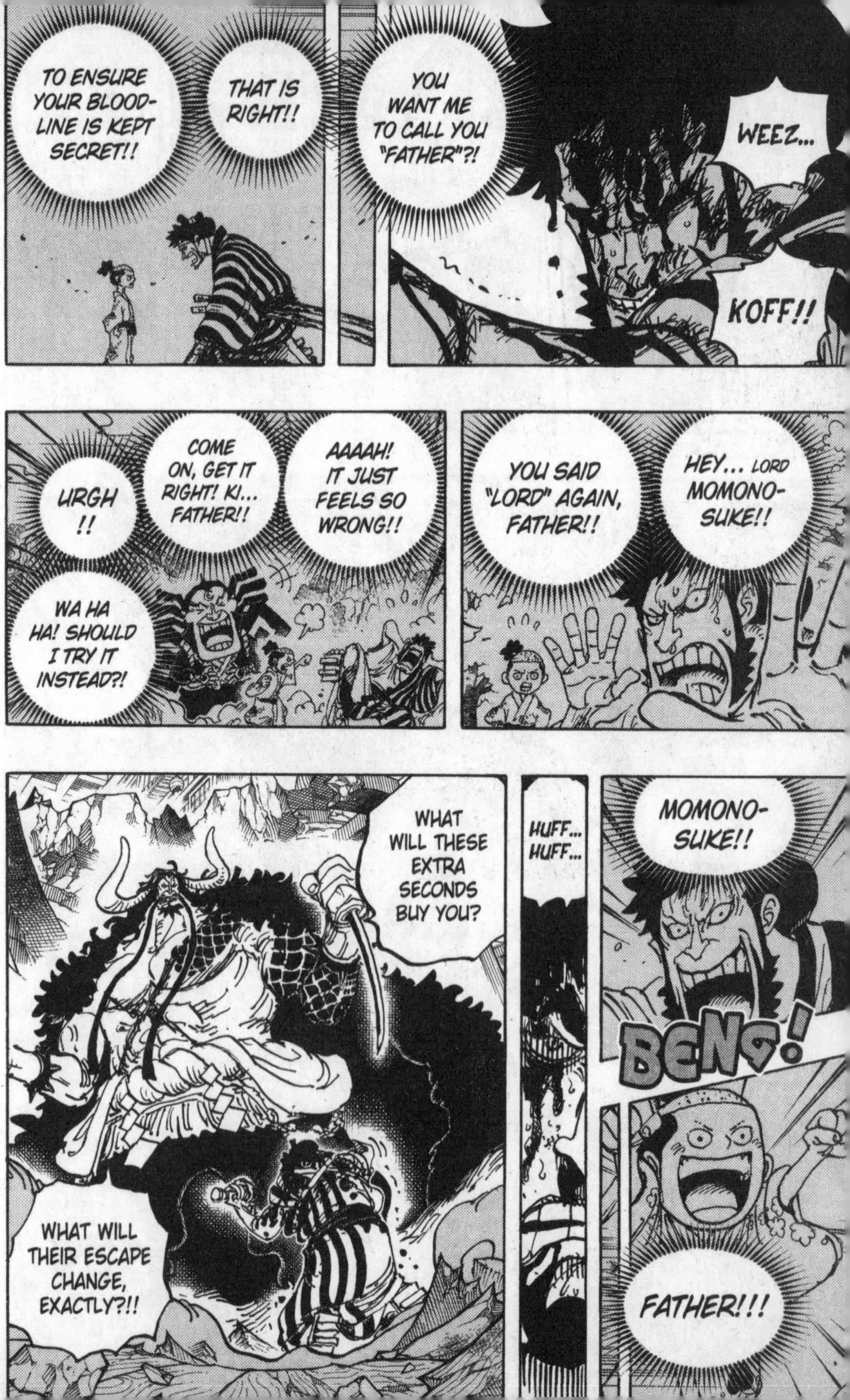
WEEZ...
KOFF!!
YOU WANT ME TO CALL YOU "FATHER"?!
THAT IS RIGHT!!
TO ENSURE YOUR BLOOD-LINE IS KEPT SECRET!!
HEY... LORD MOMONO-SUKE!!
YOU SAID "LORD" AGAIN, FATHER!!
AAAAH! IT JUST FEELS SO WRONG!!
COME ON, GET IT RIGHT! KI... FATHER!!
URGH !!
WA HA HA! SHOULD I TRY IT INSTEAD?!
MOMONO-SUKE!!
BENG!
FATHER!!!
HUFF... HUFF...
WHAT WILL THESE EXTRA SECONDS BUY YOU?
WHAT WILL THEIR ESCAPE CHANGE, EXACTLY?!!

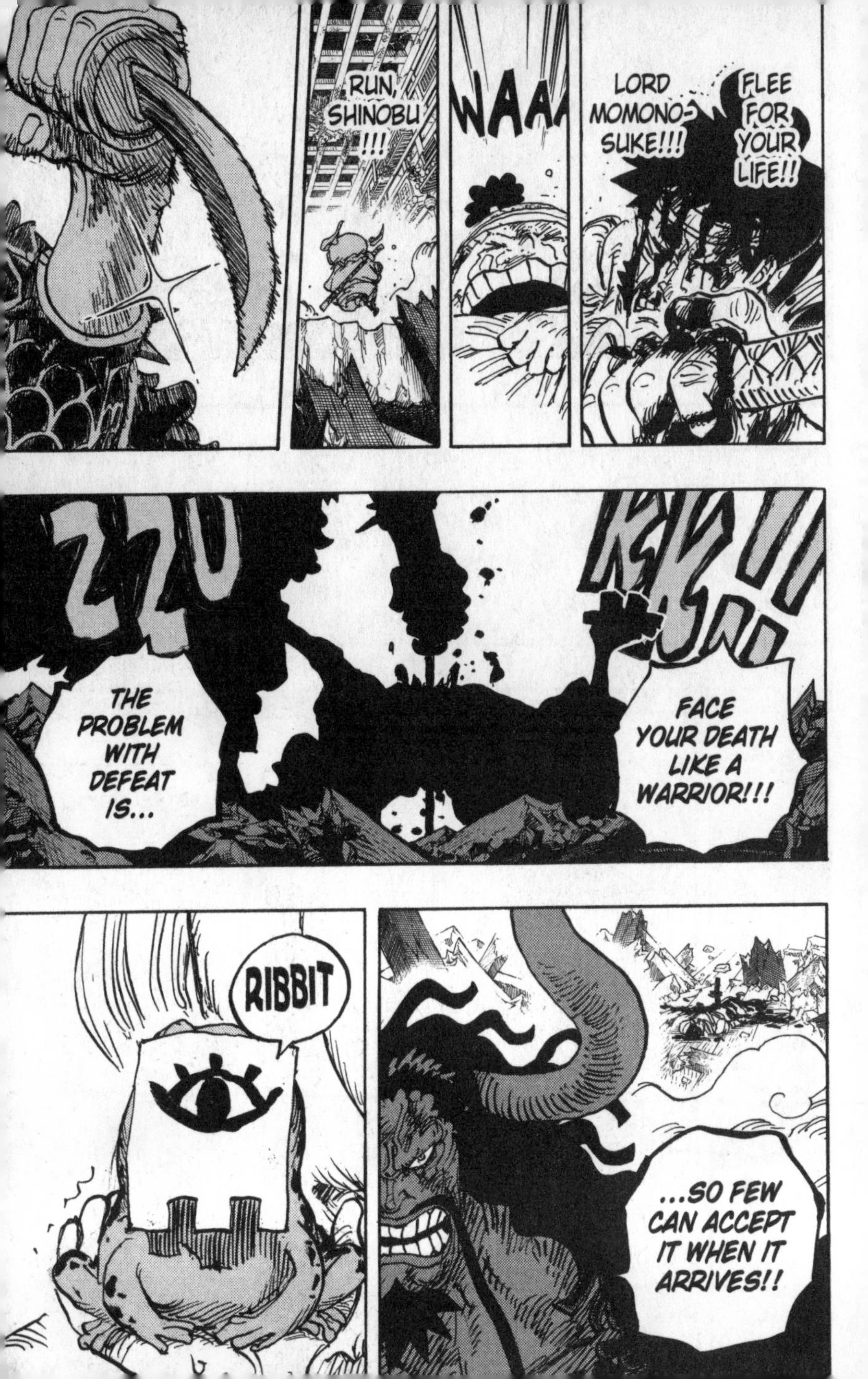
FLEE FOR YOUR LIFE!!
LORD MOMONO-SUKE!!!
WAA
RUN, SHINOBU!!!
FACE YOUR DEATH LIKE A WARRIOR!!!
THE PROBLEM WITH DEFEAT IS...
...SO FEW CAN ACCEPT IT WHEN IT ARRIVES!!
RIBBIT

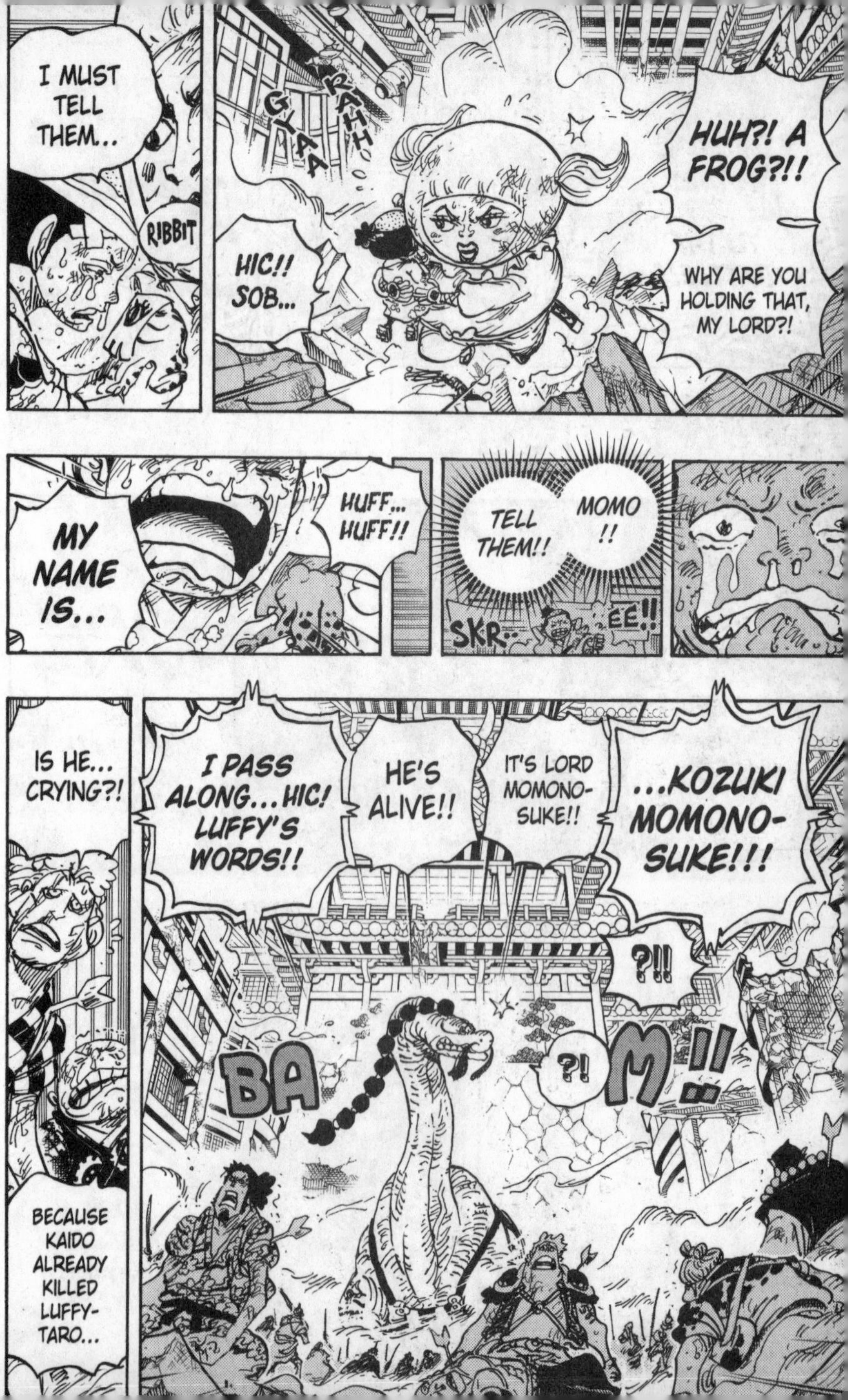
HUH?! A FROG?!!
WHY ARE YOU HOLDING THAT, MY LORD?!
RAHH
GYAA
HIC!! SOB...
I MUST TELL THEM...
RIBBIT
MOMO !!
TELL THEM!!
SKR...EE!!
HUFF... HUFF!!
MY NAME IS...
...KOZUKI MOMONO-SUKE!!!
IT'S LORD MOMONO-SUKE!!
HE'S ALIVE!!
I PASS ALONG...HIC! LUFFY'S WORDS!!
?!!
?!
BA
M!!
IS HE... CRYING?!
BECAUSE KAIDO ALREADY KILLED LUFFY-TARO...

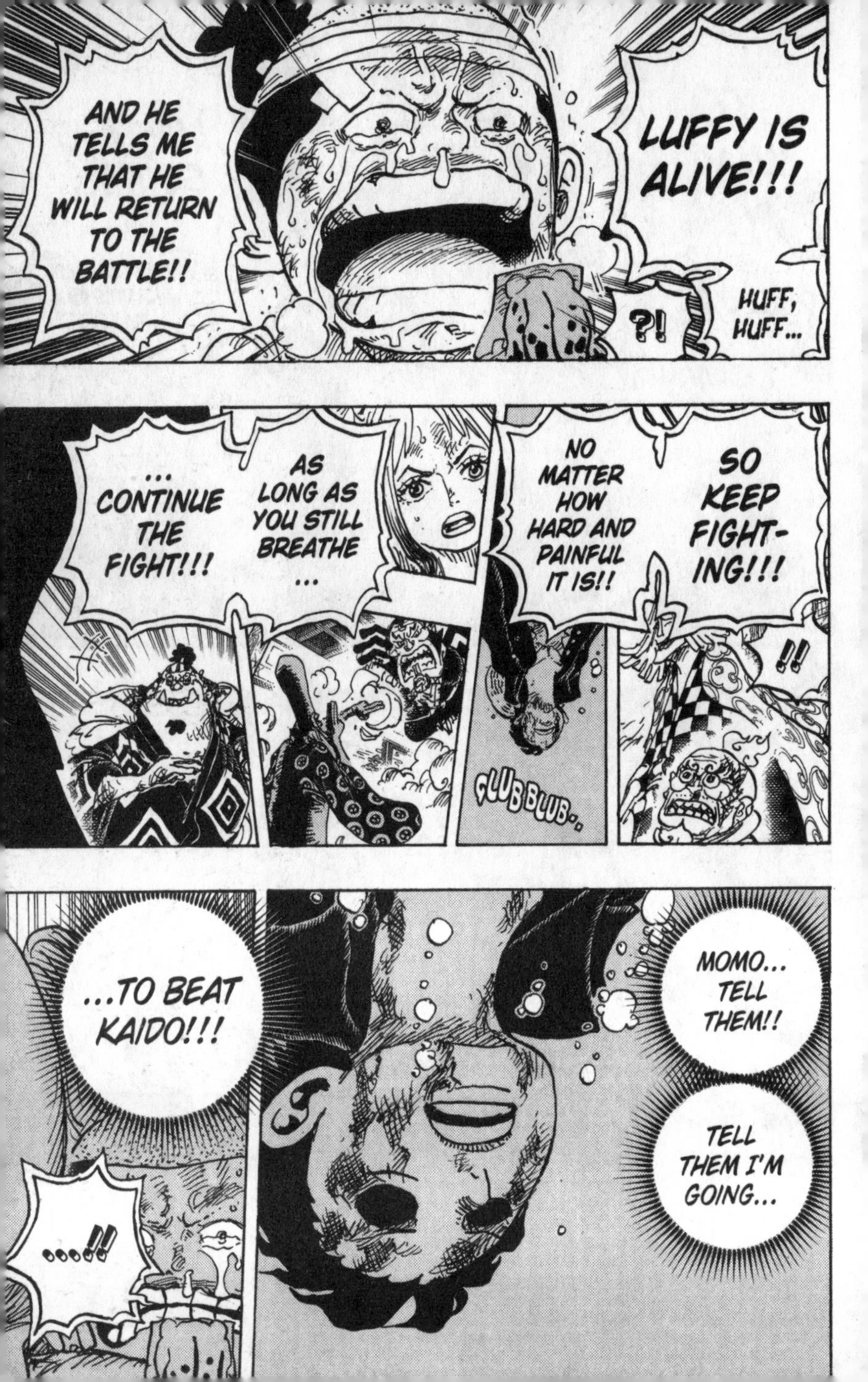

LUFFY IS ALIVE!!!
AND HE TELLS ME THAT HE WILL RETURN TO THE BATTLE!!
HUFF, HUFF...
?!
SO KEEP FIGHT-ING!!!
!!
NO MATTER HOW HARD AND PAINFUL IT IS!!
GLUB BLUB..
AS LONG AS YOU STILL BREATHE...
... CONTINUE THE FIGHT!!!
MOMO... TELL THEM!!
TELL THEM I'M GOING...
...TO BEAT KAIDO!!!
....!!

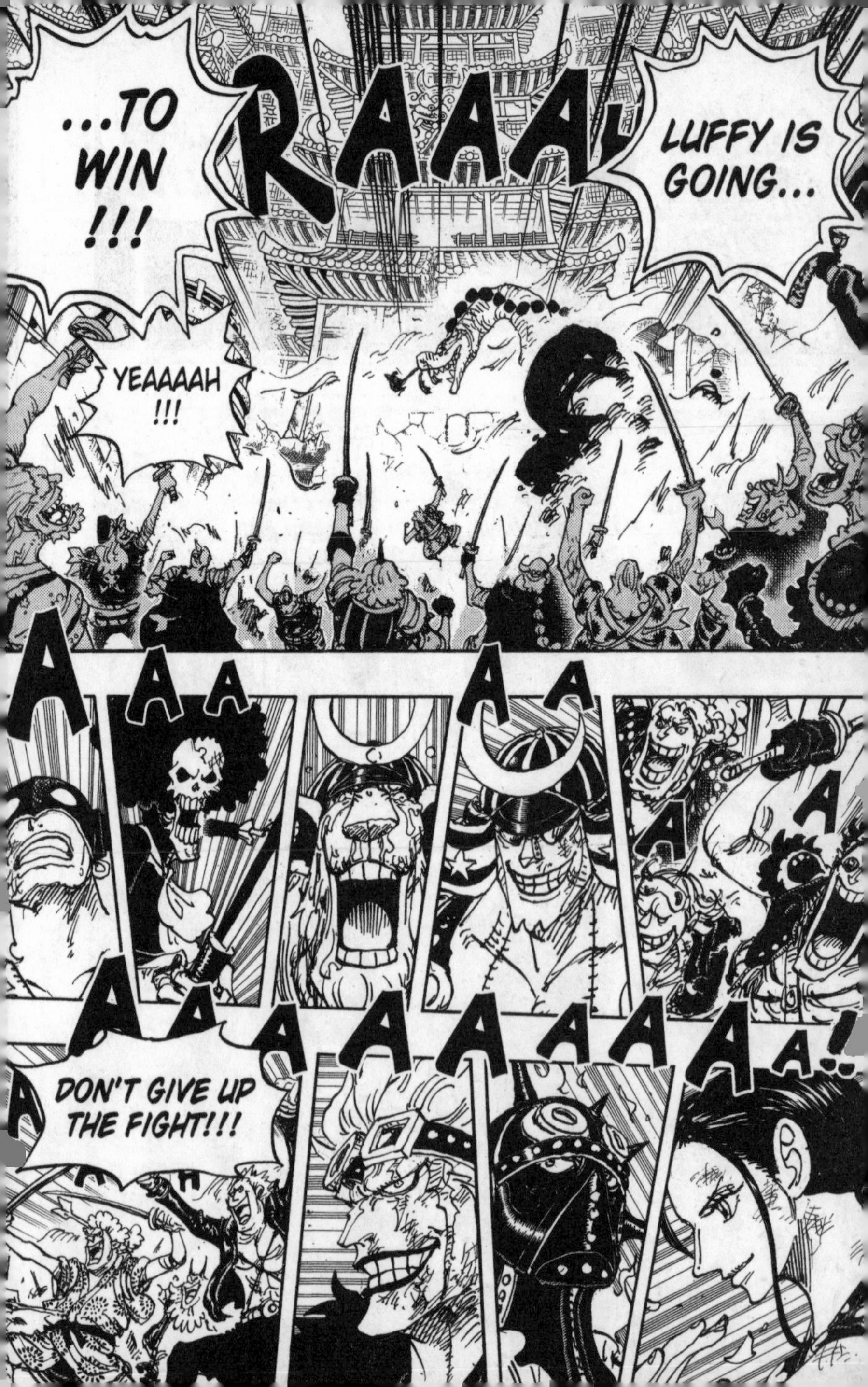
LUFFY IS GOING...
...TO WIN!!!
RAAA
YEAAAAH!!!
AAAAAAAAAAAAAAAAA!!
DON'T GIVE UP THE FIGHT!!!

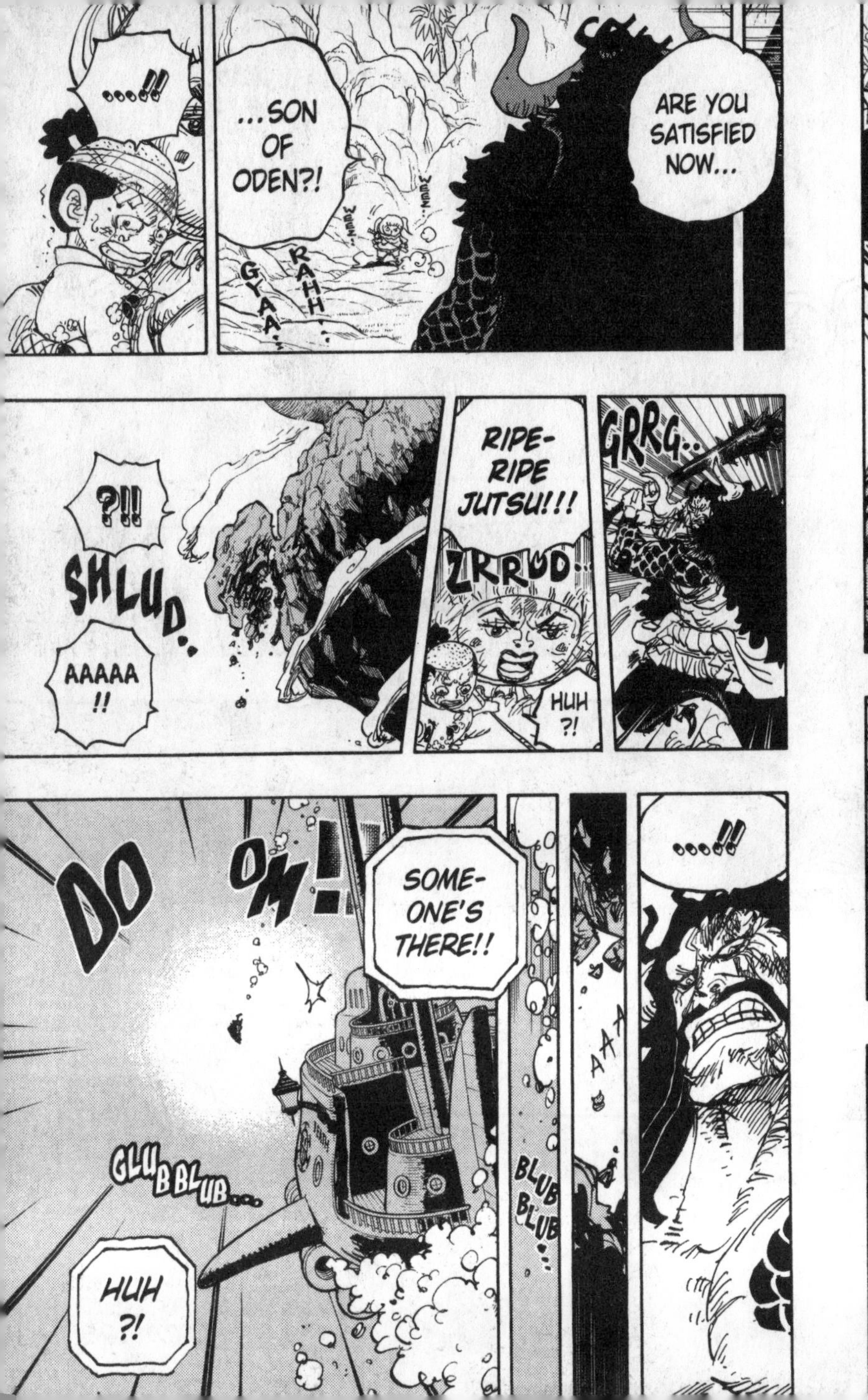
ARE YOU SATISFIED NOW...
...SON OF ODEN?!
WEEN...
WEEN...
RAHH...
GYAA...
....!!
GRRG..
RIPE-RIPE JUTSU!!!
ZRRUD..
HUH ?!
?!!
SHLUD..
AAAAA !!
....!!
AAA
BLUB BLUB..
SOME-ONE'S THERE!!
DOOM!!
GLUBBLUB...
HUH ?!

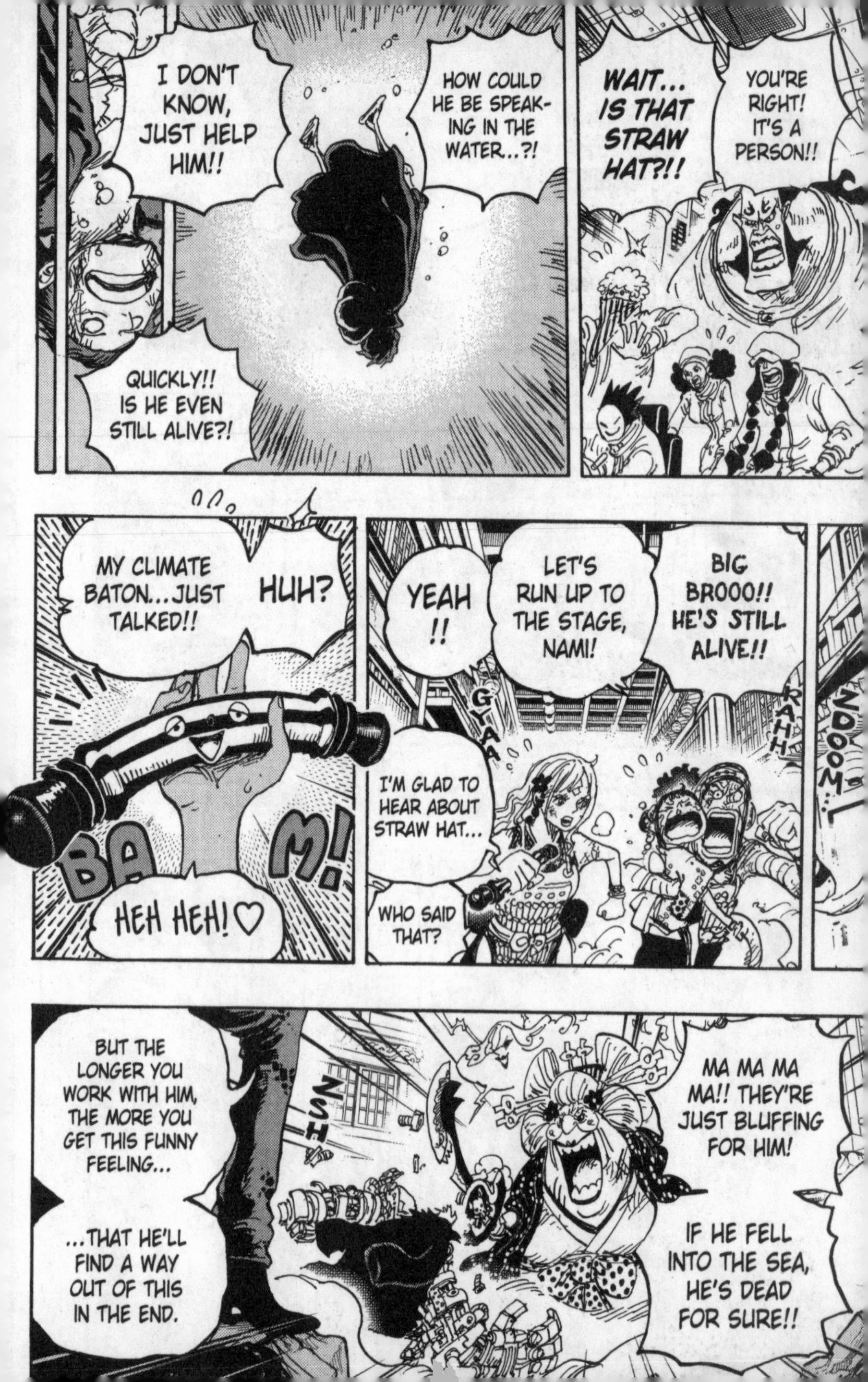
YOU'RE RIGHT! IT'S A PERSON!!
WAIT... IS THAT STRAW HAT?!!
HOW COULD HE BE SPEAK-ING IN THE WATER...?!
I DON'T KNOW, JUST HELP HIM!!
QUICKLY!! IS HE EVEN STILL ALIVE?!
ZDOOOM...!
BIG BROOO!! HE'S STILL ALIVE!!
RAHH
LET'S RUN UP TO THE STAGE, NAMI!
YEAH !!
GYAA
I'M GLAD TO HEAR ABOUT STRAW HAT...
WHO SAID THAT?
HUH?
MY CLIMATE BATON...JUST TALKED!!
BAM!
HEH HEH!♡
MA MA MA MA!! THEY'RE JUST BLUFFING FOR HIM!
IF HE FELL INTO THE SEA, HE'S DEAD FOR SURE!!
ZNSH
BUT THE LONGER YOU WORK WITH HIM, THE MORE YOU GET THIS FUNNY FEELING...
...THAT HE'LL FIND A WAY OUT OF THIS IN THE END.

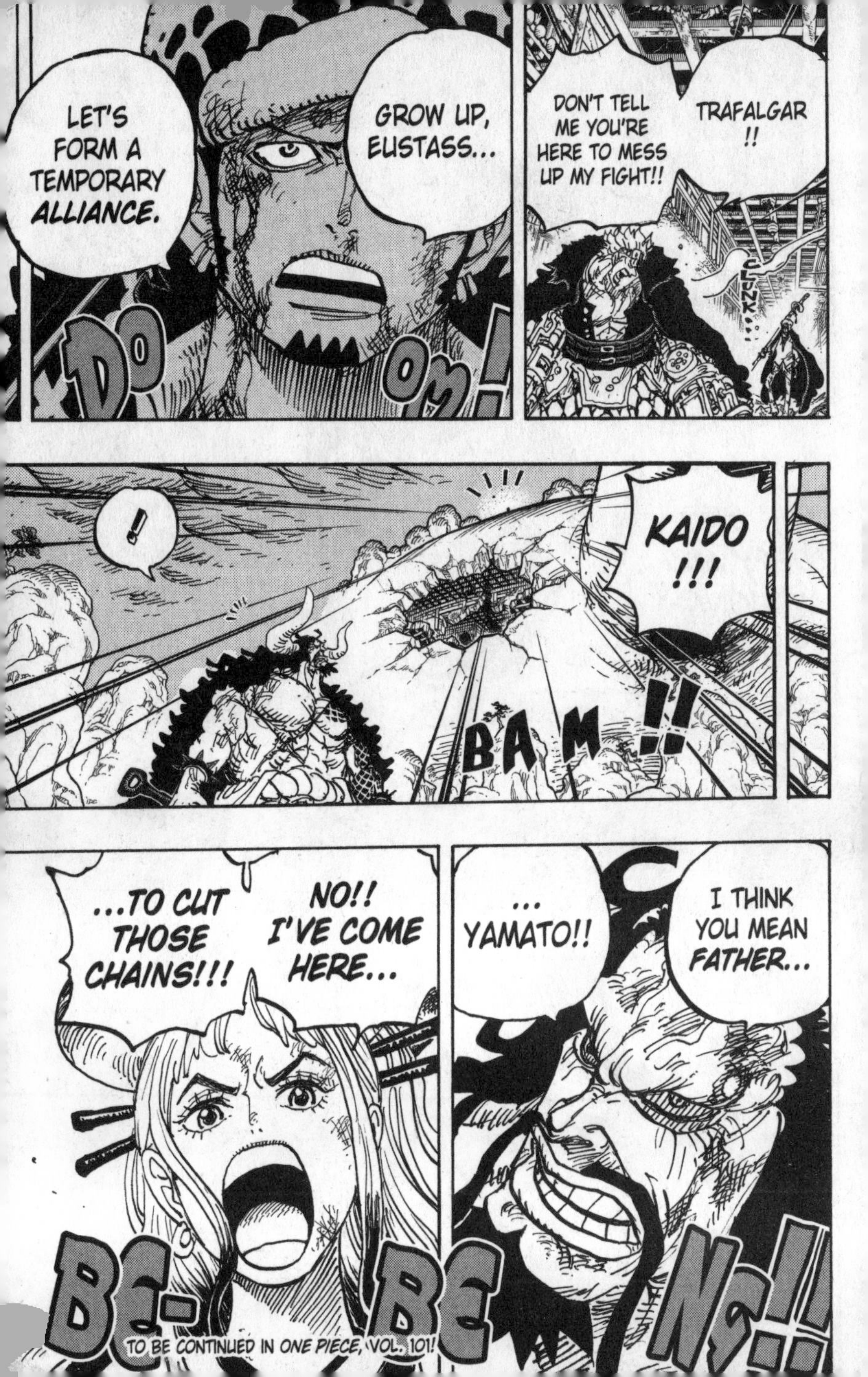
TRAFALGAR !!
DON'T TELL ME YOU'RE HERE TO MESS UP MY FIGHT!!
CLUNK...
GROW UP, EUSTASS...
LET'S FORM A TEMPORARY ALLIANCE.
DOOM!
KAIDO !!!
!
BAM!!
I THINK YOU MEAN FATHER...
...YAMATO!!
NO!! I'VE COME HERE...
...TO CUT THOSE CHAINS!!!
BE-BE-NG!!
TO BE CONTINUED IN ONE PIECE, VOL. 101!

COMING NEXT VOLUME:

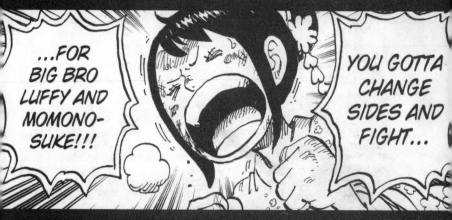

YOU GOTTA CHANGE SIDES AND FIGHT...
...FOR BIG BRO LUFFY AND MOMONO-SUKE!!!

Luffy and other members of the alliance are falling one by one to the power of Kaido and his dangerous warriors. The Straw Hats are gonna need something drastic to happen to turn the tide in this war. Could a young girl hold the keys to victory?!

ON SALE DECEMBER 2022!

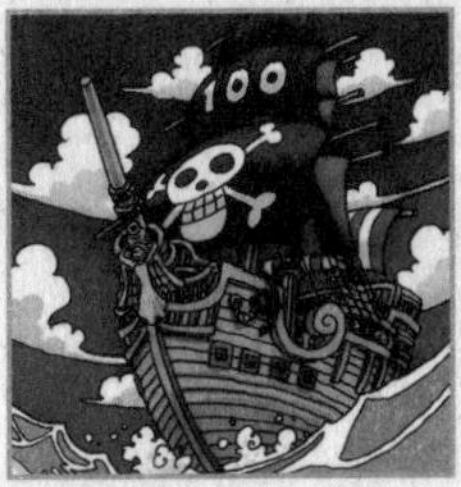

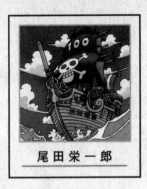

尾田栄一郎

"It sounds like there are some upset people online. I'm sorry if anyone says anything to you at school."
"I'm fine!!" says the little guardian.
Big guardian: "Cheer up!" A bunch of delicious food appears!!
"I'm so exhausted..." "Get in!!" Car drives off!! Arrive at the hot spring!!
"I caught a cold..." "Hey, that's not a cold!!" Off to check in at the hospital!!
I'm the one who gets all the glory, but when you're in the vicinity of a famous person, there are lots of bad things that happen too.
If I didn't have these bright guardian spirits around, I can tell you that I'd have collapsed long ago!!
May I use the milestone of the 100th volume to express my appreciation to them?
Thank you for everything, now and always!!
It's volume 100!! Hope you enjoy it!!!

-Eiichiro Oda, 2021

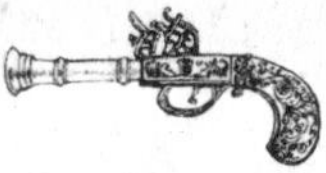

Eiichiro Oda began his manga career at the age of 17, when his one-shot cowboy manga **Wanted!** won second place in the coveted Tezuka manga awards. Oda went on to work as an assistant to some of the biggest manga artists in the industry, including Nobuhiro Watsuki, before winning the Hop Step Award for new artists. His pirate adventure **One Piece**, which debuted in **Weekly Shonen Jump** in 1997, quickly became one of the most popular manga in Japan.

Chapter 1000!!

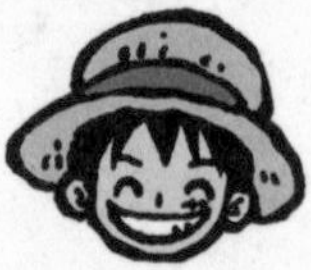

Let me tell ya, too many things have happened over the past 23 years. Half of my life spent doing a weekly series. Hah! Luffy and the crew have sailed to a number of islands and had a number of adventures. I don't even know how many people they've met by now! Behind the scenes, I've met many people too. I've been kept afloat by so many different people, but especially by my family. I'm so eternally grateful to so many. All the readers have their own busy lives, of course, and there's a theory in long-term entertainment that your audience changes out every five years. So that's why I try not to call my readers "fans." I told myself, all of these people are going to leave someday. Don't be arrogant. But you folks believe in Luffy so much, it almost makes me ashamed to have thought that way. And I've believed in you, and simply drawn the manga I want to make. At this point in the adventure, we've got one foot in the final act of the story. We've come to Chapter 1000. But there are some incredible stories that can only be told because you've been going for 1,000 chapters! It's true!! So here's a message to all of you *One Piece* fans around the world who've been with me over the years! It's been a very long story, but please stick with us just a bit longer, to see where Luffy and crew's adventure is going to take them!!

–Eiichiro Oda, 2021

ONE PIECE VOL. 100
WANO PART 11

SHONEN JUMP Edition

STORY AND ART BY EIICHIRO ODA

Translation/Stephen Paul
Touch-Up Art & Lettering/Vanessa Satone
Design/Yukiko Whitley
Editor/Alexis Kirsch

Published by VIZ Media, LLC
P.O. Box 77010
San Francisco, CA 94107

10 9 8 7 6 5 4 3 2 1
First printing, August 2022

viz.com

DEMON SLAYER

KIMETSU NO YAIBA

Story and Art by
KOYOHARU GOTOUGE

In Taisho-era Japan, kindhearted Tanjiro Kamado makes a living selling charcoal. But his peaceful life is shattered when a demon slaughters his entire family. His little sister Nezuko is the only survivor, but she has been transformed into a demon herself! Tanjiro sets out on a dangerous journey to find a way to return his sister to normal and destroy the demon who ruined his life.